■ Official Kirkwall town boundary until 1971

Official Kirkwall town boundary with the 1971 extension

■ Today's Parish Cup boundary, agreed in 2001

CW00546454

BIRTH *blood* & BOUNDARIES

A history of the Parish Cup
by Jockie Wood

To Colin and Linda

With best wishes

Jockie Wood

Illustrations by Alex Leonard

Dedication

*For my sons Alistair, Colin and Steven who all took
part to much greater effect than their father.*

Contents

Published by The Orcadian Limited (Kirkwall Press)

Hell's Half Acre, Hatston, Kirkwall, Orkney, KW15 1DW

Tel. 01856 879000 • Fax 01856 879001 • www.orcadian.co.uk

ISBN 1-902957-26-1

Printed by The Orcadian Ltd, Hatston Print Centre,

Hell's Half Acre, Kirkwall, Orkney, Scotland, KW15 1DW

Parish Map

Papa Westray

North Ronaldsay

Westray

Sanday

Faray

Eday

Rousay

Egilsay

Wyre

Stronsay

Evie

Birsay

Gairsay

Rendall

Shapinsay

Sandwick

Harray

Firth

Stromness

Stenness

Kirkwall

St Ola

St Andrews

Deerness

Orphir

Holm

Graemsay

Hoy

Cava

Fara

Burray

Flotta

Walls

Longhope

South Ronaldsay

Swona

Pentland Skerries

Birth, Blood

Introduction

The Parish Cup is something very special in Orkney's sporting history. I have been very fortunate to be involved at the final as a supporter, winning and losing player, linesman, captain of Harray, picking the man of the match, manager of Holm and now again back to being a spectator.

Let me share a few memories with you, hopefully not detracting from Jockie's stories.

The cup has always played a part in my life. As a peedie boy growing up at Nisthouse in Harray, I heard stories of previous Parish Cup games retold as neighbouring farmers helped each other with the singling of the neeps and working in the hay. At the Harray School we played on the heather between the school and Violet Isbister's shop at New Breckan. That must have been a reasonable grounding. In the class above me, Emile Flett and Alan Hutchison both went on to play for Harray. In my own class there were Alan Flett, Harvey Johnston and myself, as well as Karl Flett and Jackie Walter in the class below.

When I was old enough my uncle, Cecil Copland of Appiehouse used to take me to all the Harray and Dounby Athletic Club games. En route we always picked up Alfie Hutchison from Overhouse. He was father of Jackie, Freddie, Bobby, Ian and Eric and grandfather to Stanley, Keith and Alan who were the backbone of Harray for many years. Again memories were recalled.

I was lucky to be with Harray through the winning years. The first final I attended which Harray won was in 1964, when I crawled through the huge crowd to sit at the front. I can still sense the atmosphere.

In 1965 I was there when six Hutchisons played at the Dounby Show Park against St Andrews. Then Harray lost in the replayed final to a Russell Groundwater special which goalie Edric Clouston only heard as it whistled past him in the grimlings and fog. The next year,

Harray were again in the final. The fourth goal scored by Emile Flett – one of our seven heather playing school pals. Harry Flett picked up the cup.

I made my first appearance for Harray in 1967 at Oxtro Park in Birsay – nervous but put at ease by fellow youngsters Alan Hutchison, Alan Flett and Keith Hutchison – all much more talented than I. All three went on to represent Orkney. Harray won the final against Sandwick with Edric Clouston as skipper.

The following season, in the second leg versus Deerness, James Ward, not once but twice had a shot rebound off the back stanchion inside the net and back into play. Unlucky indeed, as neither was given! My disappointment at being substitute in the final was as bad as the deflation when John Stockan equalised in the last minute. For the replay, Harray made wholesale positional changes to counter Sandwick's danger men. Keith Hutchison received the cup after a 4-2 win.

St Andrews provided Harray with two dour struggles in 1969, followed by an easy win against Birsay in Dounby. Harray got a rude awakening in the second leg, but still made this the sixth final in a row, plus two replays. Before we left the pavilion in the Bignold for the final, Harry Flett said:

"Well boys we have no Bobby Hutch! no Ian Hutch! no Keith Hutch! no Frankie Johnston! no Peter Aim and no Robbie Scott!

So it's up to you young lads to bring the cup back to Harray"

That we did, with probably one of the youngest teams ever to appear in the final, because six of the twelve in the squad were 19 years or younger. Harry Flett settled us with an early goal and Alan Hutchison collected the cup.

In 1972 Harray played their first game on the new pitch at the Harray Hall. It was a real community effort, with many locals helping and we

youth club members gathering stones twice a week. The first goal scored there, though, was not scored by a Harrayman but by Alan Flett of Gelderhouse playing for Birsay. We still won and then played Sandwick and Firth to get to the final, where we met South Ronaldsay. We won 3-1 and I was lucky enough to be captain and collect the hallowed trophy.

At last in 1973 Sandwick, after a considerable number of finals, got their hands on the cup. Their success rate since then has been absolutely outstanding. I played in two more finals for Harray in 1974 and 1976 but we lost to an ever improving Sandwick. Both years we had two matches in the North Isles, four tremendous trips!

I played my last game for Harray in the Parish Cup in 1985 and the following season I played for my new parish – Holm. The outer North Isles showed their passion for the cup with a big crowd supporting Sanday in the final that year and again three years later when Westray went one better by winning.

The years 2003 and 2004 were special ones for Holm. We won in 2003 with Robbie Stanger becoming the first player to win with three different parishes. The next year we lost the final after extra time – the first year ever with no West Mainland team in the semi-finals.

When Firth won in 1992 I was a peedie bit down the line from Jockie Wood, whose jumping up and down resembled a Masai Warrior! He has brought that same enthusiasm for the game and the cup by gathering the history and results into book form. The quantity of information and the amount of time spent gathering this has given Jockie a great deal of pleasure. I would like to pay tribute to his meticulous efforts. He shows the same commitment and ability as a writer that he showed as a very fine player.

John G Copland.

Harray and Holm

Birth, Blood

Today's Orkney Saga

Some of the most colourful events in Orkney's history are told through the medium of the Sagas, in particular the *Orkneyinga Saga* which records the story of the Earls of Orkney over a period of some 300 years. Contained therein are tales of long-running feuds, spectacular battles, vicious murders, cunningly executed revenge, glorious victories, humiliating defeats. As the years unfold, out of these many conflicts emerge great warriors whose deeds ensure everlasting fame. Each generation produces its own heroes - or villains - and often they appear from the same genetic line.

And amidst all this drama, what is at stake? As with all major conflicts, gaining or securing of territory is at the root of things and in this case the major prize is the Earldom of Orkney itself. But there are spin off benefits. For those who help to make victory possible there is the feeling of power that goes with being in control: for other supporters of the cause, there is simply the honour of being associated with the winners and a share in the spoils of victory, whatever they may be.

Now if you thought that the nature of the events described in the Sagas was firmly consigned to ancient Orkney history, then think again! I wish to offer a modern Saga for comparison.

It too is a tale which has spanned several generations and continues with unrelenting vigour to the present day. Setting aside 'vicious murders' it contains all the hallmarks of the original Saga – feuds, 'pitched' battles, revenge, victories, defeats, the lot! Indeed, if the law of the land were to turn a blind eye to the occasional killing, then we would almost certainly be treated to the sight of the winners driving off with the heads of the vanquished dangling, not from the horse's saddle as in days of yore, but from the bumper of a car.

Great 'warriors' also grace this story, local heroes whose deeds are marvelled at whenever people of a like mind meet. Admittedly they may no longer bear terror inducing names such as Dave Skullsplitter, Jim Bloodaxe, or Bob the Mighty (more than one *have* been known to answer to 'Killer' or 'Hacker'), but they are spoken of with reverence in their home patch nevertheless.

Once again the conflict is territorial in nature and the warring factions emerge from their own strongholds within clearly defined boundaries.

And what is at stake for today's fighters? This time the prize comes in the form of a magnificent silver cup to symbolise supremacy over all the other parishes and islands of Orkney. For the winners, there are the age old bonuses of power, status and honour that go with being 'top dogs' in your own land.

For an up-to-date story that will uncover little known or mostly forgotten details of our recent past, that will feed the appetite for intrigue, quench the thirst for scandal, and even satisfy the bloodlust, I give you a Saga of our times, Orkney's very own Parish Cup!

Jockie.

Birth, Blood

Acknowledgements

Researching this project has been a source of great pleasure from beginning to end and for that I have many people to thank. At Kirkwall Library I received excellent advice and first class service from Sarah Jane Gibbon, Lucy Gibbon, Annie Manson, David Mackie and Colin Rendall. It was there I met Leslie Foubister from Toab who offered me the use of his substantial file of newspaper extracts which has been of great value. A very useful parish map was supplied by George Gray from the Family History Society while boundary maps were provided by Denis Stevenson from Orkney Islands Council. Mike Berston, secretary of the O.A.F.A., was kind enough to give me copies of the association constitution and minutes

Next I wish to highlight the contribution of several people whose work appears within these covers and which greatly enhances the final product: Rae Slater, who has made freely available his vast collection of photographs covering the 'Sandwick years' and the modern era; Ken Amer of Orkney Photographic for permission to use his archive from the 80's and 90's and Britt Harcus and Sarah Lynch who kindly collated these on disc; John Copland of Harray and Holm, a Parish Cup devotee like myself, who, in addition to granting access to his great storehouse of knowledge, did some vital proof reading and readily agreed to write an introduction to the book.

Then came the 'fieldwork', speaking to players and former players about their experiences, digging up the old stories, borrowing photographs, checking details. As I expected this was an absolute delight. Of course many a time we spoke about everything but football but that was part of the enjoyment.

In thanking everyone individually, I run the great risk of missing someone out but since I strongly wish to acknowledge personal contributions, I will take a chance and do so according to parish affiliations: From *Birsay*, Robbie Norquoy Snr., Jim Sabiston, Sandy Brown, Raymond Stanger, Alfie Stanger, Jimmy Ritch, Edwin Harvey, Harold Esson, Billy Wylie, Eddie Spence. *Sandwick*, Brian Leonard, Geordie Leonard, Bob Slater and his father the late Jimmo Slater, Calvin Poke, Harvey Spence, Colin Davidson, Stevie Linklater, Rae Slater, Jackie Nicolson, Jimmy Walls, Charlie Merriman. *Harray*, Jackie, Freddie, Bobby and Eric Hutchison, Harry Flett (with special mention for his informative tour of the boundaries near Dounby), Leslie Flett and Elsie Flett of Nistaben. *Stenness*, Fraser Anderson. *Stromness*, Charlie Clouston, Ian Taylor, Norris Chalmers, James Kirkpatrick. *Orphir*, Eoin Clouston, Kenny Firth, the late John Lennie, Sheila Sclater, Billy Brown, Alan Clouston. *Firth*, Bertie Robertson, Alistair Shearer, Graham Shearer, Phillip Stout, John Heddle, Peggy Gray of Wasdale, Molly Cooper, Mona Clouston. *St Ola*, Russell Groundwater, Brian Kemp, John Moodie, Cyril Parkes, Eric Kemp, Kevin Groundwater, Fraser Byers (with special mention for his tour of the complex St Ola boundaries), Eoin Learmonth, Bobby Leslie, John Foulis. *St Andrews*, Dave Pottinger, Eddie Craigie, Sidney Garrioch, Stewart Dennison. *Holm*, Davie Moss, Robbie Stanger, Marty Flett, Robbie Thomson. *Burray*, Douglas Montgomery. *South Ronaldsay*, Alex Rosie, Calvin Slater, Billy Taylor. *Deerness*, Jimmy Foubister, Colin Allan, Mabel Eunson, Meg Harrold, Leslie Foubister, Margaret Irvine. *Shapinsay*, Jim Sinclair, Jim Hepburn, Johnny Bews, Kenny Meason. *Sanday*, George Brown, Andrew Skea, Alistair Muir, Jimmy Lennie, Eric Walls. *Stronsay*, Norrie Firth, Paul Miller, Don Peace, John Eccles (*Eday*). *Westray*, Jim Rendall, Marty Tulloch, Steven Tulloch, Raymond Rendall. *North Ronaldsay*, Beatrice Thomson.

Finally, I am most indebted to my wife Fiona who has converted every scrawled word and figure into readable type script, a task which has consumed many hours. As well as her prowess on the keyboard she has had to show as much patience and tolerance as at any stage during 37 years of marriage. I think we have come through unscathed!

Finally, finally, I am most grateful to James Miller of The Orcadian who agreed to publish the manuscript and who has been most supportive and helpful all along the road to publication. In thanking him I must also express my admiration for his highly skilled staff who have worked so hard to achieve such a polished and professional finish.

But for all the expert assistance I have received, this story would have remained no more than an assortment of scribbles kept for my own amusement in a desk drawer.

Birth, Blood

& Boundaries

*The original Parish Cup, showing the scars
of many past triumphs and celebrations*

Birth, Blood

Maradonna and the Parish Cup

Certain "where were you?" moments are etched on the memory forever. First, there is probably the most famous one, "Where were you when you heard that President Kennedy had been assassinated?" (At the Firth Harvest Home on Friday evening of November 22, 1963, actually!)"

Then there are some of these other defining moments in history. "Where were you when you heard the Berlin Wall had fallen? … when Neil Armstrong walked on the moon? … when Princess Diana was killed in a car crash? … when Cassius Clay defeated Sonny Liston?

Now, while you ponder your answers, here is another example to consider.

For years, I had been hoping that my home parish, Firth, would draw one of the North Isles teams in the Parish Cup. I had grown increasingly envious hearing tales of hilarious boat trips, island hospitality, pub sessions after the game. I always felt a lingering sense of deprivation, as if I had missed out on something … until, finally, in June, 1986, Firth drew Sanday in round one.

After a 1-1 draw in the home leg, the return in Sanday was eagerly anticipated by the Firth 'Faithful'. In a football sense, a result was just possible against the strong Sanday side, but the spin-offs from the trip would be ample compensation in the event of a defeat.

Sunday, June 22, was a day of clear skies and stiff breeze as the Firth team and supporters were packed aboard the m.v. *Guide* at Kirkwall pier for the two and a half hour journey to Sanday. It had all the trappings of a 'Sanday Trip Day'; families laden with picnic baskets, young kids chatting excitedly, already on their fourth packet of crisps, some senior citizens comparing notes on former island outings, and young lads impatient to broach their bags of beer but so

far showing remarkable restraint. As for the footballers themselves, they sat subdued and, for the time being, totally focussed on the task ahead.

The beautiful weather continued on Sanday and most of the spectators got sunburnt. The game was a dour, nervy affair from which Firth emerged 1-0 winners. There followed the usual splendid hospitality in the community centre laid on by the Sanday committee and then it was on to the Kettletoft Hotel where celebrations got properly into gear.

Eventually, several hours later, after much patient cajoling by Captain Willie Pottinger and his crew, the party were persuaded to leave the pub to embark on the journey back to Kirkwall. It seemed that most of the island turned out on the pier to see us off.

Now by coincidence, another football match (although one of slightly less importance) was taking place that day, England v Argentina during the World Cup in Mexico. One or two well prepared travellers had transistor radios stashed in their picnic hampers so these were switched on for the benefit of the many Argentina supporters on board.

The wind had now gone down and the listeners sat outside, mellow with beer, admiring the still views of the islands they passed in the late evening sun. Then suddenly, just off the northernmost tip of Shapinsay, Argentina scored! The serene atmosphere was shattered, half empty cans were hurled into the air! It was a header, where Maradonna had jumped with England goalkeeper Peter Shilton but had got there before him and steered the ball into the net.

But what controversy was to follow! Televised replays showed it had not been the great man's head at all; he had handled it, and England had been cheated. Later, he would claim there had been divine intervention!

But all this had no effect on the

rejoicing mob on board m.v. *Guide* and before we reached Kirkwall pier, Maradonna had done it again, dribbling through the entire England defence before side footing the ball into the net.

It was a blissfully happy Firth party which disembarked, reflecting on two famous victories; Firth defeating Sanday in the Parish Cup, Argentina defeating England in the World Cup. And to the timeless question, "Where were you when Maradonna scored his 'Hand of God' goal?", the answer, in well-honed North Isles speak, "Cheust North o' the Galt, buey!"

* * *

It should be clear that this small slice of reminiscence is inseparable from the event which spawned it, Orkney football's inter-Parish Cup competition. From the many years of its existence, everyone involved will have plenty of stories to tell, ranging from the happy and humorous right through to those with a bitter edge … and when they are recounted, it is usually with a relish and a passion which you rarely encounter elsewhere.

With the possible exception of Kirkwall's Ba' game, there is no sporting contest in these islands which captures the imagination, kindles the spirits or raises the hackles quite like the Parish Cup. Matches in any round of the competition are better attended than any other sports event and crowds watching the final easily surpass those at inter county games, including the oldest fixture of them all, Orkney versus Shetland.

Many of those who go to the Parish Cup games go to no other football and if you intend to go yourself, you have to be quick off the mark. If you leave it too late, you will arrive at a country ground well before kick-off, to find the pitch surrounded by cars, often two or three deep all the way round. All vantage points may be taken and, no matter how inclement the weather, you will be forced to join ranks of diehards braving the elements on the touchline.

To attempt an explanation as to why this competition has such a hold on the Orkney public will be one of the purposes of the ensuing pages. But before venturing down that road or attempting to trace the history of this unique institution, I will try to explain just what the Parish Cup is, so that all readers can begin, to use a modern sporting cliché, on a level playing field.

First of all, what actually constitutes a *Parish*?

For those less well acquainted with local geography, Orkney is divided up into a number of different 'Parishes' as shown on the accompanying map. From this it can be seen that the Mainland consists of 13 different parishes while the bigger islands are recognised as parishes in their own right.

Each *Parish*, which is made up of various districts and 'tounships', is a product of land division which has been in existence for centuries. As an illustration of their antiquity, many of the parish names in use today can be found in the Orkneyinga Saga, with some slight variations in spelling: Stenniss or Steinsnes (now Stenness); Sandvik (now Sandwick); Orfjarao (Orphir); Dyrnes (Deerness); Rognvaldsey (South Ronaldsay) and so on. We are therefore looking at identifiable land areas which go back over 1,000 years.

From the map, we can also see that some parishes are much bigger than others but we would be wrong to assume that size alone confers advantage when it comes to finding players for a football team. A few contain large uninhabited areas of hill or moor land so the population may not be any greater than that of a smaller parish.

A much better indicator is the number of inhabitants of an area at any one time and to give some idea of that, the table below shows the distribution of population throughout the parishes at three points during the past 70 years, the time span within which the Parish Cup competition has been played.

While the first two figures are accurate according to the Census returns, the most recent is more a 'guesstimate' using Electoral Rolls, school rolls etc. since the Census no longer presents figures according to individual parishes. However, it shouldn't be too far off the mark.

Mainland Parishes

	1931	1961	2001
Birsay	1024	839	770
Harray	584	560	465
Evie		430	309
Rendall	751	301	342
Firth	605	513	797
Stenness	469	392	472
Holm	710	578	655
St Ola	880	1379	1212
St Andrews	612	464	491
Deerness	543	395	314
Sandwick	901	832	814
Stromness	518	516	515
Orphir	670	507	416

Islands

	1931	1961	2001
Sanday	1130	670	478
Westray	1243	872	563
Stronsay	943	504	358
Shapinsay	576	416	300
South Ron	1303	980	854
Burray	379	262	357

The Mainland parishes retaining the highest populations have consistently been St Ola, Birsay and Sandwick whilst Evie, Rendall, Stenness and Deerness have generally had fewest inhabitants. In several parishes, which hit a trough in the middle part of the century, such as Firth, Holm and Stenness, an increase in house building has seen the numbers creep back up.

In 1931 the figure for Evie and Rendall is combined in the Census. This is rather ironic given that these parishes have applied to become a united force in the Parish Cup but have been turned down on the grounds that according to all reliable records, they are most definitely separate parishes. Taken together, their numbers would be no more than a good average of the others.

In the North Isles, the story has been one of steady depopulation with numbers decreasing by more than half over 70 years. However, various initiatives designed to halt the exodus, are showing signs of bearing fruit and the next Census return may well produce heartening results.

The South Isles, with their fixed links to the Mainland, have bucked the trend in recent years with Burray almost back up to its high figure of 1931.

Of course, as far as football is concerned, we cannot read everything into raw statistics. It is perfectly possible that football will not be a popular sport among youth in a well populated parish whereas a few families in a small community may well produce several top class footballing offspring.

But as a general guide, the numbers are worth noting and at some stage, readers may feel like comparing them against the tournament's successful teams.

In the beginning . . . the Rules

An appropriate point at which to begin the story of the Parish Cup is to consider the current rules for the competition laid down by Orkney Amateur Football Association. I use the term 'current' deliberately as, over the course of several decades, these rules have undergone much change and modification. The most significant of these alterations will be alluded to from time to time in this chapter

To begin with, the rules state:

"The Parish Cup shall be played on a knock-out basis by teams representing a Parish in the County of Orkney subject to the following rules:

Two games shall be played for each tie on a home and away basis. The team with the highest aggregate of goals shall pass on to the next round. If both teams have an equal number of goals after two games the away rule will apply. If they are still tied, extra time and penalties will apply."

So far, very straightforward. An annual football tournament played in accordance with conventional rules. The 'home and away' format has been in place ever since the very first year of the competition, when only a single game was played. Club officials very quickly recognised the popularity of the game and, noting the opportunity for picking up valuable income, promptly introduced a contest in each parish. The end result, they also felt, would be a fairer one.

The final however has always been a single match played on neutral ground and since the very beginning this was the Bignold Park in Kirkwall. For many years a tied match used to lead to a replay but nowadays, in accord with football everywhere, extra time and penalties are used to settle the issue.

If there was nothing more to it than that, the Parish Cup would scarcely merit particular attention. Just another football tournament. But there is more to it than that! Much more! The fact that it is played by 'parishes' rather than clubs, requires a set of specially customised rules. The first of these address the key question 'Who is eligible to play?'

"Either a player must have been born in . . .

or his mother's usual address, as recorded by the register of births, must have been in . . .

or he must qualify for residence in . . .

the Parish for which he plays."

Quite a lot to take in on a first reading but what it boils down to is that there are three criteria determining a player's right to represent a parish. Very rarely nowadays is anyone literally born at home, although in rare instances it may happen; most people are born in hospital so that is why the point relating to the mother's home address is included.

For many years, until modern maternity arrangements came into being, the 'mother's usual address' clause was not included. The rule simply stated:

"A player must either be born in or resident in the parish that he plays for."

However, the extra wording was inserted after numerous controversies arose.

For example, an expectant mother would often return to her parents' home to prepare for giving birth. Once the child had been born she would return to her marital home and the child, should he grow up to be a footballer, would be entitled to represent either his 'birth parish' **or** 'residential parish'. This was fine until he grew up and moved away from home to live in a different place - he could no longer play football for the parish where he had grown up and where his natural allegiance lay.

Hence the pressure built up for the modification of the 'birth' rule but it should be noted that, no matter whether a player is born at home or born in hospital, he will still claim the right to state "I was *born in* Harray or Deerness or Westray" or wherever.

When it comes to the 'residency' clause the local football association are quite specific and apply a minimum qualification period:

"To qualify by residence a player must have been resident in the Parish for three consecutive months immediately prior to and at the time of playing."

No flitting in and out of the parish is allowed. No going to stay with Auntie a day or two before a game and returning home immediately after. A player must prove he is an established presence in a community before he can represent it.

Many players are able to play for two different parishes so come Parish Cup time, they will have a choice to make. It is technically possible that someone could enjoy the luxury of choosing between three parishes - for example, *born in* Sandwick at grandparents' home; *mother's usual address* in Birsay; now *resident* in

South Ronaldsay. What a position of bargaining power!

Given the privilege of choice, what decision would a player be most likely to make? There is no doubt that the short statement " I was *born in* such and such a parish" carries with it a great deal of emotional weight. It encapsulates a sense of belonging, identifies where the heart lies and when these five words are uttered, it is usually with some degree of pride. It may well be that the family history in the parish goes back for generations and in such a case, the feelings of patriotism will run deep.

While someone qualifying on minimum residential grounds may not feel the same attachment as those 'born and bred,' many who have made a parish their home and lived there for a long time, can feel just as passionate for the cause.

There may, therefore, be some real soul searching to be done before a choice is made. It may lead to friction within families if, for example, the son chooses to go with his adopted parish rather than the place of his birth where, perhaps, parents or other relatives still reside. On the other hand, a long term resident of a parish may incur the wrath of his neighbours if he elects to represent the land of his birth. Quite a dilemma!

However, the decision may not be difficult at all. One of the parish teams might have better players and a far better chance of winning! The prospect of securing a prestigious cup winner's medal soon puts an end to any possible loss of sleep.

The 'Eligibility' rules themselves lie at the very heart of the Parish Cup's appeal. The restrictions that they impose mean that a team cannot augment their resources by signing or poaching good players from other teams. At any given time, they are stuck with who is available to them

through birth or residence.

This contrasts with most forms of football or team sports in general, where the successful teams inevitably get better by attracting the best players to them, while poorer teams simply get poorer. The result? A far less interesting competition. We need look no further than the Scottish Premier League or, more recently, the English Premiership, to see the consequences of this practice.

Similarly, restrictions are imposed upon the individual. He cannot move freely from team to team to please himself, although, as already mentioned, a limited choice is sometimes possible. Generally speaking, if he wants to take part, he has to play for the team for which he qualifies, irrespective of their prospects!

With these limiting factors in place, what should arise is, in theory, a much fairer competition where success will be shared around. It should be a case of 'swings and roundabouts.' A parish which does well for a time may start to decline as the better players grow older or key individuals leave the area. Meanwhile, in another part of the county, a new wave of young talent emerging or a player of high quality moving into the district, could improve dramatically, the fortunes of that parish.

For Parish Cup enthusiasts, the sight of new houses going up in the local area inevitably sets the pulses racing. The number one question is unlikely to be "Will the newcomers be good neighbours?" or "Will they be valuable members of the community?" Much more likely it will be "Can any of them play football?" Occasionally their prayers are answered.

On one final point regarding eligibility to play, or, in this case 'ineligibility', the Orkney Football Association are quite clear:

*"Residents in the Burghs of Kirkwall and Stromness shall **not** be eligible to play in the competition."*

To the people from the country districts of Orkney, this is a hugely important factor. It is their tournament and nothing to do with the towns!

The source of this unwavering stance is probably the age old rivalry between town and country but from the beginning, it was seen as a competition among equals from a common background. Those taking part would have been farm workers or tradesmen and as such, their numbers would have been fairly evenly distributed throughout the parishes,

To allow entry to the Burghs, where the population was significantly greater and the life experience different, would have been wholly out of keeping with the spirit of the tournament.

This leads us on now to the thorny issue of parish boundaries. Here the rules state:

"Parishes shall be determined by reference to the Parish Boundary Map 1971 but

excluding the Papdale Housing Scheme."

and

"Parish representatives will decide on Parish boundaries."

The 1971 map is a specific point of reference and all parishes must adhere to it. However, in marginal cases, where there may be some doubt as to which side of the boundary someone's house is situated, final agreement should be arrived at by parish representatives themselves, since they live in the area and will possess local knowledge.

We might expect this devolving of power to create rather than solve problems but it is remarkable how well the system works. Those most closely involved with parish football are experts in local geography and, in an instant, will trace boundaries along fences, down farm tracks, over burns, along hill dykes, under bridges, across 'Rights of Way', before uncovering under a layer of decaying vegetation, an ancient boundary stone. I know, I have seen it done … well, most of it! When you see such expertise in action, it is hard to escape the conclusion that the Parish Cup is to geography what darts playing is to mental arithmetic.

While most boundary issues are settled amicably, there are a few 'hotspots' where disputes can arise. The most contentious of these is, as we would expect, the line which separates the Burgh of Kirkwall from the parish of St Ola.

Over the years it has given rise to countless complaints as new housing developments have sprung up in all directions on what used to be empty farmland outwith the town boundary. This has caused the population of the parish to rise significantly and other parishes have argued, at times with some justification, that unfair advantage has been given to St Ola in terms of numbers of players to choose from.

Although the boundary was extended on the eastern side of the town in 1971, it has not kept pace with the house building. Every few years, therefore, the O.F.A. have been forced to hold meeting upon meeting in attempts to resolve the situation to everyone's satisfaction.

As a result, 'local agreements' have come into force. For a time, everyone was content with the actual

boundary as long as the Papdale East housing scheme, part of which is in the parish, was ruled 'Out of Bounds' to parish selectors. This would filter out footballers residing there. But that did not suffice for long as new chunks of housing continued to appear on parish land.

In the Spring of 2001, parish representatives sat down to try and reach a compromise once and for all. After much wrangling, the outcome was a line of demarcation created solely for the purposes of the Parish Cup, one which bore little resemblance to the official Burgh boundary.

The map located inside the cover shows the various stages along the way to the current position:

i. The blue line indicates the official town boundary until 1971.

ii. The yellow line indicates the official boundary with the 1971 extension.

iii. The red line indicates the boundary agreed in 2001 for the purposes of the Parish Cup.

To follow the Parish Cup boundary (red line) readers should start at the bottom of the Craigiefield Road and, walking in a clockwise direction, follow the road round past Weyland Farm, turn left into Annfield Crescent, turn left and proceed along the length of Berstane Road ….

If you actually walk the boundary enjoy the exercise and the scenery but also take time to reflect on what is 'parish' and what is 'town'. Here, there is a simple and clearly understood 'rule of thumb'; everything to the left is St Ola, everything to the right is Kirkwall ….

Turn right along Berstane Loan, turn right on to Inganess Road … etc. The wide circuit of the town finally ends down at the Ayre Mills, leaving Hatston firmly in the parish.

Readers will be happy to know

that the placing of this boundary is due to be reviewed again any time soon when, no doubt, more heated debate will ensue … and, who knows, further adjustments may be recommended.

Just for the record, it is worth noting that, despite the perceived advantages to St Ola, they have won the trophy only twice in the past fifteen years.

Sparking fewer arguments is the situation in Stromness (see boundary map inside cover) where, with the exception of the top edge of the Grieveship housing estate, all new building developments are still well within the town boundary. But just wait, in years to come ….

The village of Dounby, where new houses frequently appear, is another place ripe for controversy. Here, the three major parishes of Harray, Sandwick and Birsay converge and before a new footballer living in the vicinity of the border dares to turn out for one of these 'giants', very careful checks have to be made.

A good illustration of the high stakes involved concerns the case of brothers Brian and Harvey Spence, both highly coveted players during the 60s and 70s. They were born in Sandwick but while still very young the family moved to a house just over the boundary into Birsay, thereby giving the boys, should they become footballers, dual 'nationality'. Well, both developed into excellent players, representing Orkney at both junior and senior inter county level, and when it came to the Parish Cup, they chose Birsay, following in the footsteps of their father, Archie, and his three brothers.

The complication occurred when Harvey got married and moved to a new house on the Market Green in Dounby, less than a stone's throw from his parents' home. This caused much debate among the footballing fraternity. Rumours abounded that

Birth, Blood

he was now living in Sandwick, so anxious Birsay officials armed themselves with a tape measure and descended on the new premises to check for themselves. Alas! Their worst fears were realised! By taking a straight line from the nearest marker stone, they had to concede that the house was indeed in Sandwick … although only by a few metres!

But all hope was not lost! The garden shed was still in Birsay. However, despite his allegiance to that parish and impassioned pleas from the Birsay management, Harvey was not prepared to spend six months of the year living in his shed. So he gave in and opted instead to play for Sandwick.

The story does have a happy ending

though. Harvey did not remain grief stricken forever and went on to win a handful of cup winners medals with Sandwick in the early 1970s.

These then are the Parish Cup rules. They have been specially formulated by the O.F.A. to cope with the nature of the competition and deal with any difficulties which may crop up. But it must be emphasised that the rules tend to be self enforcing, rather like the game of golf, where the true spirit of the game is maintained through honesty, where there is honour in upholding the rules and ever lasting disgrace for breaching them. And, let's not forget, in a small community like Orkney, if you cheat, somebody is bound to find out the truth anyway.

Disputes, therefore, are compara-

tively rare, but when they happen, and there have been a few high profile cases over the years which will be referred later in the book, they are liable to shake the ethos of the competition to its very core!

Just one final point regarding disputes. All differences, no matter how intractable, must be sorted out at local level. The Scottish Amateur Football Association, the final arbiter in all aspects of the amateur game in the country, *do not recognise* the Parish Cup. As far as they are concerned, since players are not registered and parish clubs are not properly affiliated, they will have nothing to do with it.

So, we are on our own! It is all ours, our own creation, a completely unique Orkney institution!

Old Style Football

The Parish Cup was first contested in 1929 but football in the country districts, including some inter-parish matches, was played much earlier than that. In order to appreciate just how the competition originated, it is worthwhile looking at some evidence of the early development of the game in Orkney.

John Robertson, in his book *Uppies and Doonies* and later updated edition, *The Kirkwall Ba*, gives a great deal of information about 'old style football' as distinct from the Ba' itself, and describes how it was played in virtually every Orkney parish and island during the nineteenth century.

'Old style football' generally took place on Christmas or New Year's Day at the appointed field in the parish: 'Palace Green' in Birsay; a field known as 'Jobel' opposite the Post Office in Harray, Gorseness Ba' Green at Hogarth in Rendall, and so on.

The game was very rough and ready as you can imagine. Whoever turned up got to play and there were no limits on numbers. Occasionally there might have been teams representing parish districts, such as Clouston and Isbister in Stenness, but that was not necessarily always the case. It was more than likely a free-for-all with rules kept to a minimum. The only rule which seems to have been generally agreed upon was that there should be no lifting of the ball.

No doubt these occasions could be very enjoyable and great fun, especially if everyone in the parish appeared to be on good terms at the time. This seems to have been the situation in Rendall in 1864 when a wholehearted but good natured game lasted from 1 o'clock until dark.

The Orcadian of January 12 reports:

"The very best of good humour prevails first to last; not a shade of ill feeling; not a 'cross word' or ugly look can be discerned. Although a fellow gets a tumble, he falls on the green sward and feels nothing, but a slight regret that he can't kick away on his beam ends without losing time by getting on his pins again. What a hearty, genial affair the Yule day 'game at the Ba' is in the country, the occasion is a great jubilee when all

OLD-STYLE FOOTBALL IN FINSTOWN

previous injuries are forgiven and all former animosities forgotten"

Sounds like a very pleasant afternoon was had by all but this was not always the case, and sometimes, with the absence of rules or referees, games could descend into a state of chaos.

The Orkney Herald of January 23, 1878, describes a game played on the main road in Finstown which got completely out of control:

"On Monday 14, about eleven o'clock in accordance with the old custom, numbers of men, lads and boys assembled in Finstown and began to kick at football on the road or street leading up through the village. Play was kept up in the usual rough style for some time till all were mud be - spattered from head to foot, the heated and thirsty frequently resorting to the 'Pomona Pump' to damp their ardour. Quarrelling began with two or three parties and soon - Drink in the man, Sense in the can - there was a general melee in which blows and kicks fell like winter shower and, blood flowed freely. Some were carried bleeding and senseless into the neighbouring houses where their wounds were sewed and bandaged. The contingent of fighting men was augmented by reinforcements from Kirkwall and Harray: traffic was stopped for a time and the screaming of women and swearing of men rose above the general uproar … "

Ah! To have been alive in those good old days!

Old style football, then, seems to have been a primitive form of its modern day equivalent. It is not clear what was used as goalposts but there is some evidence of their existence, the name used in Harray being identical to the Shetland term, 'hails'. The ball in its most basic form was simply an animal's scrotum or bladder stuffed with grass, cork or horse hair. Where a willing cobbler existed, the skin would be covered in leather or indeed, the entire ball made purely from leather and filled with similar, natural materials.

This early version of football was conducted with great enthusiasm for many years but as the nineteenth century drew to a close, there were signs of declining interest. In some parishes it seemed to have ceased altogether while in others, the game only reappeared intermittently. It appears to have taken place in Holm in 1910, for example, as *The Orcadian* of January 8 reported, "football was engaged in the Ayre Park during part of New Year's Day and as the day advanced, they came to the village and the East and West Gates of the village had a contest."

This seems to indicate a merging of old style football with traditional Ba' playing.

There are further examples of occasional informal gatherings in parishes around the turn of the century for the purpose of playing football but these became increasingly rare with the gradual introduction of the game in its more organised form which we would recognise today.

Admittedly, 'new style' football was only played in the towns to begin with but perhaps news of this new fangled sophistication was filtering through to the country and casting a shadow over their rudimentary game. On the other hand, fashions change, and the young lads were maybe finding something different to do on their few precious 'days off.'

Play takes on New Style

In the early days of 11 a side Association Football in Kirkwall, 'sophistication' was perhaps the wrong term to use. *The Orkney Herald* of April 3, 1907, describes a match between Rangers and Rovers where matters got out of hand and shows that the transition from 'old style' to 'new style' was far from complete.

The report begins:

"On Saturday last the second replay in the final for the shield was played at Warrenfield. The result of the two former matches had been draws of 3-3 and 1-1 and much interest was taken in the competition which was the first of its kind in Orkney."

As this game proceeded the crowd enjoyed an exciting spectacle and with time running out, Rangers led 3-2. Then shades of old style football began to creep back:

"There being still about fifteen minutes to go, the 'Rovers' began to press, but the tactics of the 'Rangers' gave them no chance to get on equal terms. The 'Rangers' commenced to kick the ball into touch whenever they got the chance, and several of them made no attempt to play the game in a sportsmanlike way. The climax was reached when, from a place kick, the ball was deliberately kicked over the wall into an adjoining field. The referee protested, and took time off till the ball was brought back, but the 'Rangers' appeared to have completely lost their wits, one player going the length of lifting the ball from in front of the goal posts, after the referee had blown his whistle for the kick, and setting it down as far as possible to the side of the goal, whence it could be more easily kicked into touch. The referee ordered the ball to be replaced, and, after some unseemly scenes among the players and spectators, the ball was again kicked over the wall by one of the 'Rangers' backs. The

'Rovers', protesting, left the field amid much excitement, the game now being finished. The matter is to be fully laid before the committee, when it is hoped a decision will be obtained that will put a stop to unsportsmanlike-like tactics in connection with any future matches. If football is to be encouraged in Kirkwall, exhibitions of the kind seen on Saturday will have to be put a stop to. It is more to be regretted, seeing that a good percentage of both teams were juniors and this tournament was got up to give a stimulus to football in Kirkwall."

So, there was some way to go yet in terms of playing to the spirit of the game. Still hankering for the freedom of the old days maybe?

Although this appears to be the first competition with a trophy at stake, these were certainly not the first official football clubs in Orkney. In fact, both these sides were 'Selects', from other clubs already in existence in Kirkwall, 'Rangers' being composed of players from 'Thorfinn' and 'Britannia' while 'Rovers' were formed from representatives of 'Norsemen' and 'St Magnus'.

That same year, 1907, there were further signs that the game was moving forward. A team representing Lerwick in Shetland visited Orkney and played two matches, against Thorfinn at Warrenfield and Stromness at the Market Green. Such was the success of the visit that, according to *The Orcadian* of May 28, "participants hoped a shield would be presented for competition between teams in both Counties. It would remain in the County of the team who won the final match for a year."

This wish was duly answered the following year when a cup was presented, supposedly, by Bailie Alec Milne, the first chairman of Aberdeen F.C., who might also have been a representative of the North British Mercantile Assurance Company of Aberdeen. (Some doubt still exists as to the true identity of Mr Milne). In May 1908, a team representing Kirkwall travelled to Shetland aboard the s.s. *Queen*, where they faced a team from Lerwick at the Gilbertson Park. Although the 'Lerwegians' triumphed 5-1, the Milne Cup fixture was born and has continued,

Kirkwall F.C. after they retained the Milne Cup in 1909, beating Lerwick 3-2. Back row, left to right, (players only) D. Thomson, J. Heddle, D. Gordon. Middle, H. R. Morrison, A. J. Grant, J. M. Work. Front, P. Thomson, J. Croy, R. Forbes, W. Sinclair, K. McKay.

(Picture: Orkney Library)

Birth, Blood

interrupted only by the war years, ever since.

Football now continued to grow in popularity in both Kirkwall and Stromness but in the main, matches tended to be of the 'friendly' variety, arranged on an ad hoc basis. In 1910 however, a general meeting was held in Stromness Town Hall where it was resolved that there would be a local league of three teams named 'The Wanderers', 'The Rose' and '1st Stromness' the last named being composed of members of the Boys' Brigade. Team captains were appointed at the meeting and furthermore, it was decided that teams would play for 'badges.'

This tournament may be seen as the Stromness equivalent of the already well established Kirkwall Challenge Shield which, in the same year, was won by a team known as 'Ramblers' after a 3-2 victory over Kirkwall City.

Occasional inter town contests also took place around this period and, again in 1910, Kirkwall Thistle, probably a select side, overcame their counterparts Stromness Vikings, 3-0.

But rivalry was not confined to the men and the following year, 1911, saw the start of what was to become a regular feature, football matches between Orkney's two main schools. *The Orcadian* of May 13 notes that, "the game throughout was of pleasant character and we think such contests among scholars should be encouraged." The final result was a 4-0 win for Kirkwall Burgh School but by1913, Stromness Academy had caught up and achieved a 2-2 draw at the Bignold Park. This encounter had been watched by a large number of spectators, including most of the Burgh School who had been given a half day holiday in order to spectate.

Organised football had now developed its own momentum and it would have been merely a matter of time before the game took root in the country districts. However, not only sport but most other aspects of life had to be put on hold over the next four years as the cream of Orkney's youth was skimmed away to fight for their country in the First World War.

Every parish and island in the county was to lose many of their young men who had their whole lives in front of them. For instance, Sanday alone lost 46, Westray, 38.

It would, therefore, take some considerable time for families to come to terms with their loss and for communities to once again engage in any sort of meaningful social activity.

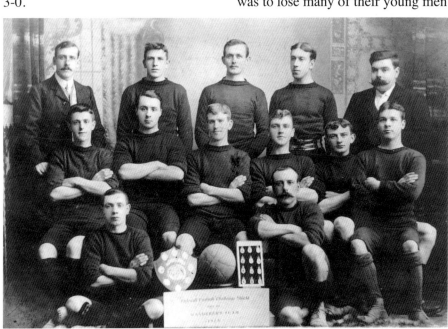

Wanderers, Kirkwall Shield winners of 1908. Back row, left to right, T. Fyffe, Jack Work, W. Hume, W. Grant, T. Drever. Middle. J. Omand, A. Walls, K. Mackay, W. Costie, R. Spence, J. Work. Front. W. Sinclair and Jas. Dearness.   *(Picture: Orkney Library)*

A League game takes root

It was 1920 before very much happened by way of competitive football but when conditions were right for the sport to resume, it was at a level of organisation much advanced on previous efforts.

An Orkney League was established and no fewer than seven teams entered. These included Stromness United, three Kirkwall teams, Rovers, Kirkwall City and Britannia, plus teams representing military personnel still in Orkney, R.A.F. Houton, Lyness United and Red Triangle Northern. The trophy at stake was to be the Orkney Challenge Shield.

There was no doubt that after the grim years of war, folk now had an appetite for the game. More than 500 spectators turned out to see Stromness United versus Kirkwall City at the Market Green and it seemed that wherever they went, the Stromness side took with them a vigorous and lusty support.

During one league game at the Bignold Park where Rovers were the opponents, spectators allowed their high spirits to spill over.

The Orkney Herald reports:

"At this juncture, to add to the excitement, certain of the spectators, not finding enough in the play, set up a sideshow for themselves and what is generally termed "a scrap" took place between a Stromnessian and a Kirkwallian. The game for a moment was forgotten and all eyes turned to the pugilists. As play was being interfered with, the referee stopped the game until matters were adjusted. Such incidents are regrettable as up until then, the competition had been carried through in a sportsmanlike manner."

After things calmed down again, the game eventually restarted and the teams fought out a 2-2 draw. But at the completion of the tournament, the first winners of the Orkney Challenge Shield were Stromness United.

As football continued to develop in the towns, inevitably the time would come when young men out in the country districts would graduate from 'kick abouts' to something more organised. Some of the first evidence is to be found in 1924.

Down in St Margaret's Hope, excitement was mounting. Burray were visitors and 'a park at the East Side of the village with a considerable fall', was the venue for the contest between the two islands.

According to *The Orkney Herald* of June 18:

" … Football is a new thing in South Ronaldsay but has taken on very strongly …. About 7p.m. the village band, always conspicuous at great events, came out and met the Burray team and conveyed them to the Temperance Hall. From then, to the kick off at 8p.m. quite a gathering of people were about the village front and it was only when they were gathered in the park, that one saw how many people had an interest in

Stromness United, first winners of the Orkney League 1919/20. Back row, left to right, Bill Spence, Dougie Johnston, Buck Spence, Binnie Harvey, Tom Mowat, Jim Wilson, Duncan Watt, John D. Johnston, R.W.Clouston. Middle, John Smith, "Bulltie" Campbell, Willie Wood. Front, Norman Flett, "Yoka" Johnston, Herbert Spence, Mike Mathieson, Jackie Leask. (Picture: Orkney Library)

Birth, Blood

the game. They were there from far and near, great and sma', all keen on the leather. A surprisingly good gate was made at the rate of 3d each.

"Let us hope that this is the first of many such events and the fact that so much interest is taken in the game, should encourage the youths to do their utmost so that at the return match on Links, Burray, the 'Hope boys may get their own back."

South Ronaldsay lost that game 2-1 but, just to complete the picture, they won the return game 1-0. Again, it was a memorable occasion with two boats, m.v. *Ibis* and the *Hoxa Head*, laden with players, committee and spectators arriving in Burray for the match. After a sporting contest, the locals and visitors made their way to the Temperance Hall where a convivial evening of song and dance was spent … but, given the venue, without the benefits of alcohol, I would imagine!

Well, to what extent were events in the South Isles being mirrored elsewhere in Orkney? Make no mistake about it, major advances were afoot.

The Orkney Herald of the following week, June 25, reported the formation of the Orkney Football League as a properly constituted body. The first match was scheduled to take place at Orphir between the home team and Stromness Athletic and the following week, Thornley Binders were to face Dounby. Other fixtures would be announced in due course.

Initially this new body did not find favour with everybody. *The Orkney Herald* report continued: "The Orkney Football League rules have been duly approved by the Scottish Junior Football Association, the supreme body for football matters, even for this county. The formation of the League was well

advertised in the local newspapers and a hearty invitation extended to all football clubs in the county. It is a matter of regret that Kirkwall footballers prefer to remain part of a body which calls itself the Orkney Football Association but does not even advertise the date of its annual meeting and whose members are unknown outside their own little circle."

Some hints of a clique or a 'closed shop' among the Kirkwall teams there, as they declined to join the new organisation.

The five teams who entered this first open Orkney League championship were Stromness Athletic; Orphir Wanderers; Dounby Celtic; Firth Rangers; and Thornley Binders. The first league champions were Stromness Athletic, but a fine show had been put up by the other teams, including the three representing country districts.

But the season was not yet over. Buoyed by the success of the first tournament, one of the teams was about to present a trophy for a knockout competition, a cup which would one day, achieve special fame in the history of Orkney football.

Stromness F.C., the Orkney League winners in 1923. Back row, left to right, J.D. Johnston, "Bull-tie" Campbell, Johnny Gowans, William Cutt, Taff Fraser. Middle, Binnie Harvey, Maynard Young, Tommy White. Front, Edwin Findlay, "Yoka" Johnston, Lammie Campbell, Attie Campbell and Sydney Findlay. (Picture: Orkney Library).

Thornley Binders and County glory

A company named Thornley Binders had first set up in Stromness in 1923 under the guidance of managing director, Mr F. C. Thornley. The plan was to extract chemicals such as potash and iodine from local seaweed and produce a residue which could be mixed with coal dust to form coal briquettes. This venture had created great anticipation in Stromness. Thornley forecast that his production could reach 2,000 tons a week so a new 200 foot pier and factory had been built with huge sums of money invested. High employment seemed assured for years to come.

The firm was very keen to get involved in community life and part of its commitment was realised in the magnificent football trophy, bearing the company's name, which was presented for knockout competition among the Orkney Football League teams during the 1924 season.

The same teams entered and the final, which took place on the neutral ground at Bea, near Dounby, was won by Stromness Athletic who defeated Thornley Binders' own team 2-0.

This brought to an end a very successful footballing year and it was clear that the Kirkwall players, who had earlier shown lack of interest, were now keen to get a slice of the action. Firth Rangers, in their semi-final against Stromness, had fielded no fewer than seven Kirkwall players in their team, among them a few regular county 'caps'. Stromness won the game 9-0!

Of the country teams taking part in the league and cup competitions, making the strongest impression had been Orphir Wanderers. They had fielded a side composed of local men and had come close to winning the league, finishing just behind Stromness.

Their usual team in 1924 read as follows:

Omand Muir: Billy Tait and Collie Brass: Tommy Lennie, John Lennie and Robert Flett: John Roy Omand, Sidney Findlay, William Cutt, Charlie Findlay and John Cutt.

Of these, the most well-known player was schoolteacher William Cutt, who had played centre forward for Orkney v Shetland for the past three years, scoring on each occasion.

The promise shown by this group of Orphir players was now to be fully realised in 1925. This year five teams again entered for the Orkney Football League - Stromness Athletic; Orphir Wanderers; Thornley Binders; Kirkwall United (a team composed of the best players taking part in Kirkwall's internal league); and Cox and Danks, a team representing the firm who were undertaking the salvage of the German Fleet in Scapa Flow.

The might of Kirkwall United. was to emerge victorious in the league but the Thornley Cup was won by Orphir. In the final played on the Firth pitch at Savil, they defeated Kirkwall United 3-2. Orphir scorers in this famous win, the most significant by a country team to date, were Charlie Findlay, William Cutt and o.g. from a Kirkwall defender.

A report of this match appeared in *The Orkney Herald* and I am sure readers would find it interesting to see how formal the proceedings were at the end of the game.

PRESENTATION OF CUP

"On the conclusion of play both teams lined up for the presentation of the cup, which was performed by Mrs Mathieson, from Stromness. In a few appropriate words Mr Welsby, Stromness, secretary of the football association, congratulated the Orphir team on their victory, and called on Mrs Mathieson to present the cup to the captain of the winning team.

"Mrs Mathieson then handed over the cup to Mr Cutt in a pleasing manner, and congratulated the winners on their fine achievement. Mr Cutt, on behalf of the Orphir team, thanked Mrs Mathieson and Mr Welsby for their kind remarks, and in a few words thereafter, said he thought the better team had lost, although, at the same time, the most enthusiastic one had won.

"The Orphir team, although they came there that night to do their best, never once dreamt of taking the cup back with them. He thought it might do good for football in the country districts, for there was nothing to prevent other districts from doing what Orphir had done.

"In conclusion, Mr Cutt stated that every member of the team belonged to Orphir, with the exception of himself, which, he was sure, was all the greater honour to them (applause and cheers). Mr Cutt then called for three cheers for Mrs Mathieson for presenting the cup, which was very heartily responded to."

This remarkable Orphir team, now minus William Cutt who had departed to take up a new job, went on to retain the Thornley Cup the following year, 1926, when the final was once again played at Bea, in Dounby. On this occasion the spectators witnessed a "splendid game, very fast and end to end on the pitch."

The final score was Orphir four Stromness Athletic nil, but Orphir did come in for a little criticism for their win. Since there were no rules to prevent it, Orphir had succumbed to the temptation often afflicting winning sides and that is to try to make the team even stronger by bringing in players from outwith the club. For the final they had fielded county players, goalkeeper Tommy Thomson, fullback 'Nuckie' Norquoy, and left winger Teddy Corsie. As the reporter said, "It would have been better if they had restricted their team to local lads."

However, for the team photograph that year, it was indeed "all local lads" who were asked to be present.

While Orphir's success still marked the summit of achievement for country football teams, in other parts of Orkney the noble game continued to prosper. In South Ronaldsay a district league was established with teams from Grimness, Widewall and St Margaret's Hope. The Garden Trades Cup was begun in Kirkwall, and friendly matches between teams from different parishes began to appear fairly regularly.

In 1927, Harray mustered a team and went "on tour", first of all drawing 1-1 with Evie at Aikerness in a game where " … at times play was good and fairly fast but the lack of sufficient practice and combination was manifest among the Evie players."

Harray then moved on to meet Rendall's finest, but this turned out to be " a rather one sided game of football. Play resulted in some fast work at times but, from the start, Harray proved the better team." The final score was 3-0 to Harray.

While these games were great social events and sources of entertainment in local communities, there was no doubting now the status enjoyed by the game of football at its top level in Orkney. The inter county match for the Milne Cup was accorded the kind of ceremony reserved for a State occasion such as a Royal visit.

For the 1927 game, played on a Friday afternoon in the Bignold Park *The Orcadian* stated: " …on the recommendation of Kirkwall Town Council, all places of business were closed for three hours to allow townspeople to attend the match. A large number of Stromnessians were present, Stromness Town Council having fixed the town's Spring holiday to coincide with the date of the match. Comparatively few, however, were present from the

Orphir, the Thornley Cup winners in 1926. Back row, left to right, Billy Findlay, William Tait, Omand Muir, Collie Brass, James Flett. Middle, John Lennie, George Findlay, Cecil Yorston. Front, Tommy Lennie, John Roy Omand, Charlie Findlay, Johnny Liddle, Willie Inkster.
(Picture: Orkney Library)

country districts as farmers, long handicapped in their ploughing and sowing operations by wet weather, were busy in their fields.

"In honour of the occasion, flags were flown from the flag staffs of the Town Hall and Burgh School and the Kirkwall Town Band paraded at the pitch where they played selections before the commencement of the match, during the interval and at close of play."

Orkney five Shetland one was the final score, Orkney's first win over the 'Auld Enemy' for six years. The end of the game was marked by scenes of jubilation: "When the final whistle blew, the Brass Band struck up *See The Conquering Hero Comes* and as the Orkney team went off the pitch, a crowd surged round Norquoy, their captain, and he was carried shoulder high for some distance towards the pavilion" according to the newspaper report.

Ah yes, football was definitely on the way up, enjoying an ever increasing popularity. On the way down, alas,

was the Thornley Binders company. The anticipated success of the venture had just not happened and by 1927, financial disaster threatened. A buyer could not be found and by mid summer the factory closed with the resulting loss of jobs and heavy blow to the local economy.

As for the Thornley Binders Cup, it was contested once more, the following year, when Thorfinn F.C. were the winners, before being withdrawn for the time being as if in sympathy with its donors.

Football fever takes hold

Although relatively few country players had been able to attend the 1927 inter county match, news of this famous triumph would circulate throughout the parishes and provide an inspiration for even more boys to start playing the game. And that year's post match celebration was not a 'one-off'! When the cup was retained in Shetland the following year, the Orkney public went to extraordinary lengths to join in the victory parade.

The Orkney Herald describes the events: "After the 1928 Milne Cup victory in Shetland, the football and hockey teams (3-2 and 6-0 winners respectively) were given a heroes welcome by a huge crowd at 2.30 a.m. The pipe band played as the steamer sailed into the bay. The crowd surged around the gangway. President William Scott carried the cup ashore and was showered with confetti while streamers were thrown from pier to ship. When the teams disembarked the band reformed and played them up the pier followed by a great cheering procession up through the streets.

"The referee, Peter Craigmyle, was totally bemused by this reception. He commented 'You would think that it was the winning of the Scottish Cup itself'."

Just imagine! All that in the hours of the morning! sporting success was now at an all time high and the spin offs, in terms of developing interest in football, were massive. As the summer went on, it appeared that the game was being played throughout the length and breadth of Orkney.

Deerness now had a team and on their pitch at Langskaill, defeated their neighbours, StAndrews by 2-1. They followed this win with a 6-2 victory over Holm, *The Orkney Herald* noting that "a large number of spectators were attracted to the Deerness pitch where the spectacle of a properly organised game has

Orkney, winners of the Milne Cup, 1928. Back row, left to right, J. "Nuckie" Norquoy, Tommy Thomson, David Wooldrage. Middle, George Clouston, Hugo Munro, John "Yoka" Johnston, Dugald Stout. Teddy Corsie. Front, James "Mosh" Marwick, Bob Johnstone, Bob Findlay.
(Picture: Orkney Library)

only lately become familiar."

Having acquired the taste for conquering opponents, Deerness continued to overpower all comers. A 6-3 win over Kirkwall Bankers was followed by a visit to Harray where the hosts were defeated by five goals to one.

Their triumphant season concluded with another victory down in Burray but they had to come from behind to eventually win 6-2. *The Orcadian* of September 6 gave some indication of the reasons behind Deerness' great run:

"Much local interest in the game has been created by their successful contests and many well wishers journeyed to Burray to witness the game between the mainlanders and the islanders. Lady friends turned out in goodly numbers and their presence, may have helped the local footballers considerably!"

The age-old secret revealed! Behind every good man ... etc. But make no

mistake about it, the Deerness boys were dropping big hints of great days ahead.

While Deerness was a 'hot-bed' of activity, in other parts of Orkney, scores of young men were taking to the field. In Longhope, North Walls played against South Walls for the first time. In Sanday, an internal league was started where district teams of Burness, Cross and Lady contested the Sanday Challenge Cup. In South Ronaldsay, their inter district league continued while over in Rousay the football club, apparently a body of some standing in the community, presented the local doctor, Dr Thomson, with an inscribed cigarette case 'to show their gratitude.'

For what, I have absolutely no idea!

All parish football, and there was a lot of it about, still went under the tag 'Friendly' and for the early part of summer, 1929, teams were content to arrange games on that basis. The only football trophies on offer that year were the Orkney Challenge Shield, which was regarded as the preserve of the 'good' players from Kirkwall and Stromness; the Kirkwall Junior Cup; and the Garden Trades Cup.

The demise of the Thornley Cup had happened just at a time when more parish teams might have been tempted to enter and now there was nothing else for them. But they soldiered on quite contentedly … for now.

Sandwick was the latest parish to form a team, obviously quite a good one too as they drew 0-0 with Stromness and went on to crush Stenness 6-1. The Sandwick correspondent of *The Orkney Herald* had some encouraging words for the vanquished: "This is certainly the season for football and what can be more beneficial to the youth of the parish than a game after a hard day's work. Do not be down hearted, Stenness! Try again!"

But soon all local football was forgotten as the build up commenced for another inter county with Shetland to be played in Kirkwall.

Once more in charge was to be the highly respected international referee, Mr Peter Craigmyle from Aberdeen. (Generations of Orkney footballers will be familiar with the Craigmyle Cup, which he presented for competition among local teams.) In those days top referees did not merely officiate at the game itself but, wherever they went, they endeavoured to spread the gospel of football.

On the evening prior to the match, accompanied by Mr James Phillip, an international selector and director of Aberdeen F.C., Mr Craigmyle gave a lecture " illustrated by lantern slides and a diagram board." The very latest pictures of the Scotland v England match had been recently secured by these gentlemen and were shown to the public for the first time in Kirkwall. This lecture, which lasted almost three hours, proved a great attraction among the football fraternity and the Town Hall was well filled with an enthusiastic audience.

The day of the inter county match was every bit as special as the previous two occasions. Businesses were shut from 1.30 until 5 p.m.;

excursions were made by boat from the South Isles to Scapa Pier; fleets of buses arrived in Kirkwall from many country districts bearing crowds of eager supporters.

Orkney lost the match and the Milne Cup by 3-1 but that did not deter post match rejoicing, and the visitors, complete with trophy, were piped all the way from the Bignold Park to the Queens Hotel in Harbour Street where the reception was to take place.

Who could not fail but be swept along by the euphoria and grandeur of the whole occasion? There were precious few opportunities to create or acclaim local heroes … but these footballers … they were treated as heroes all right!

Many young men would get back on their buses and return to their homes in the country, dazzled by the scenes they had witnessed and craving the opportunity to have their own chance in the limelight … or maybe even the prospect of holding aloft a piece of glittering silverware before their own adoring supporters.

But how could this come about? There was simply nothing to play for.

Huge enthusiastic crowds attended inter county matches during the late 1920s. Here is a section of the 1927 crowd making their way to the Bignold Park balcony after Orkney's 5 – 1 victory over Shetland.

(Picture: Orkney Library)

The Parish Cup is born

It just so happened that out east, in the parish of Holm, local youths had caught the football 'bug' to the extent that, during the summer, a Holm league had been formed. Three teams competed: Holm East, St Mary's and Holm West. The firm James Flett and Sons Ltd. of Bridge Street, Kirkwall had donated a 'handsome cup' for the competition. For the record, Holm East ran out winners of the trophy after home and away fixtures against the other two teams.

Most Holm residents would have been contented no matter who had won because their overwhelming feeling would have been one of relief at seeing the men of the districts engaged in relatively harmless rivalry on the football pitch.

Only nine years previously, in 1920, the Holm East United Free Presbyterian Church (the 'U.P.Kirk') had been gutted by fire started allegedly by supporters of a campaign to restore services at the West Kirk, which had been closed by the Presbytery in an attempt to unify the congregation. Unity was not the outcome!

This act, which was said to have been the culmination of a feud between the East and West kirks going back several generations, caused a sensation throughout Orkney. No one was ever convicted of the crime although it was rumoured that the culprits were known to the authorities.

By 1924 the East Kirk had been rebuilt and remains in use to the present day but, at the time, resentment continued to fester.

A story which I picked up from the parish illustrates this well. It tells of a beast from the east side of the parish being driven along the road to be sold at the mart in Kirkwall, some time during the 1920's. On the way, animal and owner had to pass through the west portion of Holm but somewhere in this district, it broke

free and stampeded into a woman's garden, possibly even her house.

In the commotion that ensued, the excited animal 'skittered' all over her property. As she viewed the scene of devastation, the householder declared bitterly, "I widna' minded sae much, but hid wis a U.P. baest!"

How remarkable then to see, so soon after events almost verging on civil war, the men of the parish playing football together. And it went further.

Inspired by the success of their tournament, the Holm footballers began to look for a wider scale of competition in which they could compete as a united team.

The Orkney Herald of June 26 reported: "The general feeling in Holm is that a league or cup for the mainland, excluding the Burgh of Kirkwall or Stromness, should be organised as it would create interest especially among the supporters of various teams. If such a feeling exists in other parishes, it is not yet too late in the season to organise a competition on either of these lines. The travelling expenses would be a considerable drain but with the increased attendances which, it is felt, attend these matches, that difficulty would soon be got over"

Given the amount of parish football now taking place, I suspect that the visionary men of Holm knew that they were pushing at an open door. When the idea was floated, there was immediate interest and seven teams came forward to compete for an inter Parish Cup with the format of one game, straight knock out. I would imagine that the lateness of the season would have influenced the decision not to play it as a league or even consider home and away fixtures.

The seven pioneering teams were: Deerness: Orphir: Firth: Tankerness: Sandwick: Harray: Holm.

In the opening round, Firth defeated

Tankerness 4-1; Orphir had a 6-2 win over Sandwick while Deerness demolished Harray 5-0. Holm received a bye into the semi final where they eventually overcame Firth after a replay. The first game ended 1-1 but the result of the replay was not reported.

Holm's opponents in the first ever Parish Cup final were Deerness, who defeated Orphir in their semi final, although again, we have no idea of the score.

So the stage was now set for the final itself which was to be played at the Bignold Park on Friday evening, August 16. It was clear that the competition had captured the imagination of the Orkney public because large numbers flocked to the town from not only the competing parishes but from Kirkwall, Stromness and many parts of the mainland.

The teams which lined up on what was to prove a historic occasion were as follows:

Holm: Benny Norquoy; Austen Brown; and Bob Wylie; Bill Pratt, Jim Laughton and William John Hepburn; Archie Voy, Davie Drever, Geordie Budge; Bertie Bews and Sam Aim.

Deerness: Artie Skea; Ronald Aitken and Jock Mowat; Peter Johnstone, Billy Ritch and Jock Clouston; Davie Scott, David Ritch, Robbie Skea, Andrew James (Peem) Skea and Jock Aitken.

Referee: Mr D. Linklater, Kirkwall.

The only downside to the occasion was the heavy rain which fell before and during the game, making the playing surface very difficult and the wet, greasy ball bad to control.

But despite the weather, the game itself proved to be a closely contested affair. Holm. took an early lead with a low shot from Drever and doubled their advantage shortly afterwards when Bews capitalised on a poor Deerness clearance. Just before half time, Robbie Skea reduced the deficit when he got possession and beat the Holm keeper with a fast rising shot. Half-time, 2-1.

Midway through the second half, the same player equalised with a shot which Norquoy in the Holm goal "saved" but carried over his own line. It was now anybody's game but, despite Deerness carrying the greater threat, it was Holm who were to score the winner after Budge got possession and ran through to slip it past Artie Skea, in the Deerness goal. Although Deerness kept up steady pressure, they were unable to save the game which ended in a 3-2 victory for Holm.

In summing up the match, *The Orcadian* reporter stated that, "considering the state of the weather which was of the flood type, the attendance of spectators was remarkable and showed how great a

grip the competition had taken in the parishes." Although Holm had won the trophy, Deerness were deemed to be, "superior in passing and tackling but lacked finishing power."

The Orkney Herald also concluded that Holm were somewhat fortunate to win but reserved its most considered match comments for the display of sportsmanship: " … it is to the credit of the players that they never questioned the referee's decisions from start to finish, a lesson which some of our more experienced players in the towns would do well to copy … "

In fact, the reporter was so moved by the noble behaviour on view that he continued: " … if the weather had been more favourable, this most sportsmanlike contest would have appealed to the heart of any football follower."

Bring back the good old days!

It was clear from this first staging

of the tournament that the Parish Cup was here to stay. The initial instincts of the organisers had been vindicated in the level of interest shown and it was thought that more parishes would wish to take part next year.

The importance attached to the event was demonstrated in the cup presentation ceremony. No handing over on the field of play or even on the balcony of the Bignold Park: a dance was held that evening in the Town Hall where Bailie Grant handed over the trophy to the victorious Holm team. In his speech he praised the success of the competition and urged the Orkney Football Association to set up a league next year to stimulate football in the county.

As the evening came to a close it was an integrated and well bonded team from all corners of the parish that made its way back to Holm, proud possessors of the Parish Cup. There was no sign of any friction among this bunch and who knows, on the bus home, one player might have leaned towards another, patted him warmly on the shoulder and murmured, "Buey, we've come a right piece in the last ten year. This fairly baets burnin' doon kirks, eh?"

First ever winners of the Parish Cup, Holm in 1929. Back row, left to right, Bill Manson, Austen Brown, Benny Norquoy, Bob Wylie, William John Hepburn. Middle, Archie Voy, Davie Drew, Geordie Budge, Bertie Bews, Sam Aim. Front, Bill Pratt, Jim Laughton.

(Picture: Orkney Library)

The 30s

1930:
'Peem' Skea is
Deerness' hero

An early response to the first successful running of the competition was to change the format to the 'home and away' system which has remained unaltered ever since. If public interest had been aroused by one game, surely it would be heightened by two and after all, it was only fair that if you had played your opponents in your own backyard, you should have to visit theirs. Only then would the true winner emerge!

Although it was hoped that more teams would enter in 1930, it was the same 'Magnificent Seven' who put their names forward again.

This year, many of the parish players would enter the tournament well warmed up by other football because the O.F.A. had indeed heeded Bailie Grant's advice and established a county league championship. Although no parish team felt confident enough as yet to compete on their own against the formidable Kirkwall and Stromness sides, two composite teams from the East and West Mainland were entered. The East team was made up of the best from Holm and Deerness whereas Firth, Harray and, to a lesser extent, Orphir supplied the West line up.

Despite putting up brave resistance, the country teams proved no match for the likes of Stromness Athletic and Hotspur. But when it came to the eagerly anticipated East v West fixture, in the Bignold Park, it was the West who, surprisingly, emerged victorious winning by 5-1. Clearly, when it came to this year's Parish Cup, Deerness and Holm would not have it all their own way.

When the first round got underway, the results were as follows:

Deerness clinched the trophy in 1930. Back row, left to right, Frankie Allan, Ronald Aitken, Artie Skea, Jock Mowat, Bobby Mowat. Middle, Peter Johnstone, Billy Ritch, Jock Clouston. Front, Davie Scott, David Ritch, Robbie Skea, Peem Skea, Jock Aitken.

(Picture: Orkney Library)

Holm	10	Orphir	2
Orphir	5	Holm	1
Sandwick	2	Deerness	2
Deerness	8	Sandwick	0
Tankerness	0	Harray	1
Harray	0	Tankerness	0

Firth - bye.

It was now on to the semi finals where Deerness and Holm were again kept apart, so a repeat final was a distinct possibility.

In the first match, Deerness again demonstrated their all round strength and scoring ability by crushing Harray 7-1 on their home pitch at Newark. The goal scorers on this occasion were David Ritch (3), A.J. (Peem) Skea (3) and Robbie Skea. Unfortunately the second leg (if indeed, Harray were up for it!) was not reported.

Deerness were through to the final but it was not to be a repeat of last year. Again, only the first leg of the other semi final was reported, but in

it, Firth had clearly established an unassailable 3-1 lead over Holm. The keen interest in this game was shown by the crowd of about 300 who turned out at Firth's home pitch at Savil to enjoy a good old fashioned cup tie. According to *The Orkney Herald*, " ... play was of a robust nature and players on both sides trusted more to weight than to skill."

Goal scorers for Firth were George Craigie (2) and Hughie Craigie while Geordie Budge scored for Holm.

So the scene was set for an exciting final between Deerness and Firth at the Bignold Park on Thursday August 7. East v West was expected to give an added edge to the game and the large crowd of supporters who travelled with both teams was not to be disappointed.

The teams who would serve up 90 minutes of thrilling entertainment were as follows:

Deerness: Artie Skea; Ronald Aitken

and Jock Mowat; Peter Johnstone, Billy Ritch and Jock Clouston; Davie Scott, David Ritch, Robbie Skea, A.J. (Peem) Skea and Jock Aitken.

Firth: George Lamont; George Heddle and James Clouston; Jock Lamont, Charlie Craigie and Jim Lamont; Hughie Craigie, Mackie Heddle, Harold Wood, Tom Davie and George Craigie.

Referee: George Newlands, Kirkwall.

The effect that certain families were to have in the destiny of the competition was illustrated by the fact that three sets of three brothers took the field; the Lamonts and Craigies for Firth, the Skeas of Aikerskaill for Deerness.

Deerness played downhill and after ten minutes had taken the lead through 'Peem' Skea but before half time Firth had scored twice with goals by Harold Wood and George Craigie.

It had been a thoroughly exciting half with a lot of fast end to end football and after half time both teams continued to attack. 'Peem' Skea equalised for Deerness with a shot into the roof of the net which their fans clearly enjoyed as according to *The Orcadian*, they responded with "hilarious delight."

Both teams were now committed to all out attack and soon the irrepressible Peem Skea completed his hat-trick with a hard drive low into the corner of the net. But this lead was not to last long as George Craigic headed the ball over the keeper's head into the Deerness net. 3-3.

A dramatic finale was assured and we can imagine the tension of the supporters as both teams went all out for the winner. A 'goal' for Firth was disallowed while at the other end, the Deerness forwards 'literally bombarded Lamont.'

A goal had to come and when it did

it was from a penalty awarded to Deerness for hand ball in the Firth area. Who should step up but Peem Skea and his shot found its way into the net after being partially saved by Lamont.

This proved to be the winner and the outstanding Deerness forward had scored all four of his side's goals to clinch the trophy in a pulsating match. Final score: Deerness 4 Firth 3. In his presentation speech, Bailie Grant said it was the best game he had seen in the Bignold Park for a long time and *The Orcadian* reporter was equally impressed. He commented: "There is supposed to be very little talent in the County but I am afraid opinions have to change now. In both teams there were individual stars but to mention them would only jeopardize other players who showed up magnificently in a stern and thrilling tussle."

Despite the reporter's reticence, there would be little doubt in peoples minds who was man of the match.'

After the game, both winners and losers made their way to the Town Hall, "where a large company spent the remainder of the evening and part of the morning dancing to music rendered by the 'Cheerful Chums Jazz Band' accompanied by Messrs. Keldie and R.O. Watson."

To those taking part it was plain to see that the competition was beginning to enjoy considerable status within Orkney and, having witnessed a final such as this, the football public would have plenty of talking points in the weeks ahead.

The future of the Parish Cup looked even more secure.

1931:
Firth take the cup west

If the organisers had expected more parishes to enter the 1931 competition they were again to be disappointed. Once more the entry consisted of seven teams but there was one notable difference; Sandwick had not entered but their place had been taken by Shapinsay, the first island outwith the Mainland to submit a team. As events were to prove, they were not there simply to make up numbers.

The early fixtures were largely unreported in the Press but what can be deduced is that last year's beaten finalists, Firth, accounted for Tankerness while the strong Holm side eliminated Harray.

Great interest then centred on newcomers, Shapinsay, who were drawn against the holders, Deerness. For the away tie played at Newark Links (no report was available for the home leg), the island team and supporters had to travel to Kirkwall by the m.v. *Iona* and then on to Deerness by bus, which would have been a fairly time consuming trip more than 70 years ago. However, this proved to be no disadvantage as Shapinsay defeated Deerness 1-0 to send the holders out of the competition.

That would have set football tongues rolling!

The semi final again presented Shapinsay with a tough draw as they were to face Holm while Firth would play Orphir, who had the good fortune to earn this year's 'bye.'

For their tie Shapinsay and Holm reached agreement to play both legs in the Bignold Park. This would save Holm having to travel across the water and Shapinsay would not have to endure the bus trip to St Mary's.

1931 Parish Cup winners, Firth. Back row, left to right, George Lamont, James Clouston, Tom Davie, Dugald Stout, Tom Anderson. Middle, Hughie Craigie, Harry Craigie, John Lamont, Harold Wood, George Craigie. Front, Eddie Laughton, Charlie Craigie, James Lamont.
(Picture: Orkney Library)

Stout, a Hotspur and inter county player who qualified for Firth by virtue of having been born at Lettally on the Lyde Road.

The full teams were:

Firth: Tom Davie; James Clouston and Jock Lamont; Eddie Laughton, Charlie Craigie and Jim Lamont; Hughie Craigie, Harry Craigie, Harold Wood. Dugald Stout and George Craigie.

Shapinsay: Jim Rendall; Bill Budge and Jim Sinclair; Billy Bews, Bill Learmonth and Eddie Sinclair; Jim Groat, Jim Kirkness, Joe ('Bunny') Bruce, Mackie Kirkness and Bill Heddle.

Referee: Mr D. Linklater, Kirkwall.

As a spectacle. the game failed to reach the heights of the previous year's encounter but was nevertheless, very hard fought. Shapinsay demonstrated the same determination that had marked their semi final win and went in at half time a goal ahead through Mackie Kirkness, who struck a low shot into the net after it had rebounded off goalkeeper Davie's legs.

In the second half, however, Firth took control and scored three times, first with a Harry Craigie header, followed by a hard low shot from his brother George and finally to seal Shapinsay's fate, their half back Eddie Sinclair sliced the ball past his own keeper.

Final score. Firth 3 Shapinsay 1.

It was generally agreed that Firth had been the better team overall and had played with a lot of confidence, especially in the second half. Charlie Craigie was singled out for praise, performing well as both attacker and defender while Dugald Stout used his skill and experience to open up play.

Shapinsay had done remarkably well in their first year to reach the final and all agreed that more would be seen of this team in the future, once they "improved in tackling and

Fair enough, I suppose!

In the first leg, on the Tuesday evening, Shapinsay won a close game 3-2, which meant that, with the outcome wide open, the Saturday evening return would be keenly contested. A large crowd from all over Orkney saw Holm take a 1-0 half time lead through centre forward Geordie Budge and they doubled their advantage early in the second half with an Austen Brown header.

Holm were playing the better football and should have had the game sewn up but the longer it went on the more Shapinsay's strength, fitness and determination swung the game their way.

In the space of 20 minutes they scored four times through Jim Groat, Joe (Bunny) Bruce (2) with an own goal by the Holm keeper finally

sealing his team's fate. Shapinsay had reached the final in the first year they had entered! Who would they face?

Firth looked strong last year and they were to make no mistake, defeating Orphir handsomely both times, 3-6 and 6-1.

To give an idea of the potential danger men for Firth the goal scorers in the second leg were Harold Wood (3), Dugald Stout (2) and Hughie Craigie.

So, on Friday evening, August 7, Firth met Shapinsay in the third Parish Cup final at the Bignold Park before almost 2,000 spectators.

Firth's team showed a few changes from last year, Tom Davie moving from the forward line to goalkeeper, a fourth Craigie brother, Harry, joining the forwards, as did Dugald

passing" and learned to curb "over keeness".

Mentioned in dispatches for their generally good standard of play, were keeper Rendall, full back Jim Sinclair and winger Jim Groat.

In presenting the trophy at the Bignold Park pavilion to Firth Captain Jock Lamont (note the downgrading of ceremony but maybe Shapinsay had their boat to catch?), Provost Slater reiterated that "the best team, just, had won." This view was echoed by Shapinsay Captain Jim Kirkness who felt, however, that his team had been affected by the loss of two regular men through injury.

In his interview, Jock Lamont had high praise for the Shapinsay goal keeper but also made a plea for an end to a practice he deplored on the football field, "deliberately kicking the ball into touch." Surely this was still the tactics of choice to frustrate opposing attackers.

So, for the first time the Parish Cup had gone west and this would have been a source of great satisfaction to the Firth men after last year's final defeat. In fact, there were now three different winners in three years.

Next year? Well, Holm, Deerness and Firth all had strong teams while Shapinsay looked very promising. It should be another fascinating competition in prospect.

1932:
Deerness regain their crown

A sure sign that the competition had taken root was revealed in the number of entrants in 1932 … ten in all! This included first appearances for Birsay and Stenness and the return of Sandwick after a year's absence. Not satisfied with this response, *The Orcadian* correspondent was critical of other sides who, he believed, could easily have entered: "There are several notable absentees. South Ronaldsay has not entered and neither has Rousay, both within easy reach of the Mainland."

His rebuke would have been based on the fact that both islands had been playing against some of the strong teams from Kirkwall and Stromness.

Early in the season Rousay had put up stout resistance to the touring Kirkwall Rovers team before going down 6-2. Far from being downhearted, the home team had later entertained their visitors in Trumland where the meal "was purveyed by the footballers themselves."

With such hospitality beckoning, surely Mainland teams could persuade Rousay to enter next year. South Ronaldsay, or 'St Margaret's Hope' as they were still called, were likewise very active in pursuing friendly games and entertained both a Kirkwall select and Stromness going down by 8-1 and 6-1 respectively.

It is not clear whether they provided any tea!

Maybe after these setbacks, the 'Hope still lacked confidence to 'have a go' in the Parish Cup.

Once again, results and reports of early games in this year's cup competition are fairly 'thin on the ground' and this is a pity because

the fate of newcomers Birsay and Stenness is unknown. The only first round result recorded is Orphir's 5-3 home win over Tankerness.

But one game which the Press were not going to ignore was the semi final between two of the strong teams of the era, Deerness and Shapinsay.

This year Deerness had spared little in their preparations for the tournament.

Friendlies against the likes of Kirkwall Hotspur showed how committed they were. Although going down 4-1, the experience would have stood them in good stead. They were described on this occasion as being "full of fight but not full enough of football", and as having "plenty of dash but lack of subtlety ." However, they were forecast to do well in the Parish Cup.

Shapinsay, last year's beaten finalists, had now found a 'secret weapon', a new light keeper at Helliar Holm by the name of Crowe. It was felt that his influence would be crucial especially as Deerness would not have their playmaker 'Peem' Skea for the first leg, as he had not yet returned from his veterinary studies at Aberdeen University.

"A crowd of considerable dimensions" turned out to witness this first meeting in the Bignold Park and the outcome was a 2-0 win for Shapinsay. Crowe appeared to be a player of craft and intelligence and his promptings led to both goals being scored by 'Bunny' Bruce,

The return game, also in Kirkwall, produced a 2-0 win for Deerness so the tie had to be settled by a third game at the same venue. Now fortune was reversed! Star inside right Crowe was not available, presumably due to work commitments, while Skea, the Deerness 'star' was back home from Aberdeen.

His inclusion made all the difference. He generally dictated play, scoring twice, once from a free kick and once from the penalty spot, in a 3-0 victory. Under strength Shapinsay had no answer and were eliminated.

Deerness now progressed to the final where they would meet the cup holders, Firth, whose progress to the final is unrecorded.

This fixture between two of the foremost teams of the time was sure to be an attractive one and sure enough, as *The Orkney Herald* records, " … a huge crowd of fans from all over the Mainland turned up in ideal weather to witness what promised to be a thrilling encounter."

Both teams were along familiar lines and read as follows:

Deerness: Benny Norquoy; Ronald Aitken and Jock Mowat; Billy Ritch, Jackie Laughton and David Ritch; Jim Foubister, Davie Scott, Robbie Skea, 'Peem' Skea and Jock Aitken

Firth: George Lamont; James Clouston and Jock Lamont; Edwin Laughton, Charlie Craigie and Jim Lamont; Hughie Craigie, Tom Anderson, John Sinclair; Dugald Stout and George Craigie.

It is worth singling out a player from each team for special reference. Firstly, Deerness had a notable addition in goalkeeper Benny Norquoy. He had previously appeared in goal for the winning Holm team three years previously. Like many young men of the time he was a farm servant who moved frequently between farms and now he was working at North Keigar in Deerness.

Firth's 15 year old centre forward, John Sinclair, of Maitland Place, Finstown, was a footballer of immense promise. He played left half for Rovers and with his all round athleticism and skill, was being talked about as a certainty to represent Orkney before much longer.

The stage was set for a great match. After their previous cup final encounter where they saw seven, the crowd was expecting goals.

How many did they get?

Correct, seven again, although not distributed identically.

Firth opened the scoring when Norquoy drove the ball at Sinclair and it rebounded off him into the net:

"First blood to Firth and their supporters let the world know it," declared *The Orkney Herald*.

Shortly afterwards, Jock Lamont handled in the penalty area and 'Peem' Skea equalised for Deerness from the spot. End to end play then saw Robbie Skea give Deerness the lead before George Craigie again put Firth level from close in. Half time 2-2.

In some games you know instinctively that there will be more goals to come, and so it proved. Surviving an early Firth onslaught, Deerness gradually took control and added three further scores through Scott and Robbie Skea (2), the latter completing his hat trick This made the final score: Deerness 5, Firth 2.

Various players earned special commendation. For Firth, Laughton at half back was outstanding, breaking up many dangerous Deerness raids while Charlie Craigie played "a rare bustling game" at centre half.

Deerness were well served by their full backs and of course, their three goal centre forward, but the left wing trio of David Ritch, Jock Aitken, and 'Peem' Skea were especially praised as they "combined beautifully, at times completely baffling their opponents with the perfect understanding between them."

Skea was considered the outstanding player on view. He seemed to be everywhere on the field, "working like a Trojan" and played with great vision. Inspired by him, Deerness played better as a team whereas, according to the newspaper headline,

Deerness became the first side to win the Parish Cup for a second time in 1932. Back row, left to right, Davie Eunson, Ronald Aitken, Benny Norquoy, Jock Mowat, Jock Clouston. Middle, Jim Foubister, Davie Scott, Robbie Skea, Peem Skea, Jock Aitken. Front, Billy Ritch, Jackie Laughton, David Ritch. (Picture: Orkney Library)

"FIRTH LACKED CO-OPERATION."

From my experience that was never a quality lacking in Firth folk … more especially after the game was finished!

So, four finals played, 23 goals scored, crowds averaging well over 1,000, Deerness back on top. Plenty to look forward to in 1933.

Footnote:

While still only 17 and a pupil at Kirkwall Grammar School, John Sinclair did indeed go on to play for Orkney v Shetland in 1934, and acquitted himself well. He was beginning to realise his potential but later that same year, tragedy was to strike.

As he was cycling to school one morning in October into the teeth of an easterly gale, he decided to "hitch a ride" by catching hold of a ladder on the side of a passing van. He was towed along quite happily for a while, the driver unaware of his extra "passenger", until, near Quanterness, a particularly strong gust caught him and he was thrown from his bike and killed.

John Sinclair's death cast a shadow over his community, school and Orkney football circles for a long time to come.

1933: Shapinsay 'corner' cup for isles

The tournament of 1933 was to be a memorable one for several reasons: the early exit of the powerful cup holders, the emergence of a new force from the West Mainland and yet another first time winner of the prized trophy. In addition, the cup was won by what would nowadays be regarded as very unconventional means.

Deerness might have been expected to repeat last year's success but their progress was halted at the first hurdle by a resurgent Holm team. Deerness did win their home leg 3-2 but in the return leg at St Mary's, Holm scored a comprehensive 4-1 victory.

This fine Holm side, which had been partially rebuilt since their cup win in 1929, now went on to defeat Sandwick in the semi finals, on both occasions by a 4-1 score line. In the second leg, centre forward, Austen Brown had scored all four of his side's goals.

So Holm were in the final for the second time. But who would they face?

Possibly new opponents altogether. With no more early round games reported, we go straight to the second semi final where Stenness had emerged to be a team to be reckoned with. After two very keenly fought games against Shapinsay, both of which ended in draws, a replay in the Bignold Park was necessary to separate the teams.

The eagerly awaited third game attracted, according to *The Orkney Herald*, "one of the biggest crowds ever seen at a football match in Orkney outside the inter county game … and there were scenes of extraordinary excitement throughout the match."

The teams served up a memorable game which ended in a 2-1 win for Shapinsay, their goal scorers being Jackie Bews and 'Bunny' Bruce, while Sammy Firth hit the Stenness counter.

Again *The Orkney Herald* was at pains to describe the lively atmosphere: "When Bruce scored the islanders' winning goal, there were amazing scenes of enthusiasm. At points, the crowd surged over the touchline and dozens of spectators, ladies as well as men, flung their hats into, the air!"

Mercifully, they stopped at hats!

So Stenness were out but they had certainly made their mark. John Anderson's play in all three games had been outstanding." "The player's work was well up to County standard. An attractive style and accurate timing made his play a delight to watch." Also singled out were Willie Muir at centre half, and William Anderson, "a keen forager with a grand shot." Many spectators felt that it was only a matter of time before this Stenness team reached the final.

This year, however, the final was between Shapinsay and Holm and after the drama of the semis, many wondered if this match could possibly attain the same heights.

Conditions on the night were not favourable for good football, or the comfort of another large crowd. A cold cross wind blew across the Bignold and the heavy rain which greeted the teams, was to fall for much of the game.

The teams were as follows:

Shapinsay: Jim Rendall, Bill Budge and Jim Sinclair; Billy Bews, Eddie Sinclair and Davie Bews; Jim Groat, Hughie Craigie, 'Bunny' Bruce, Jackie Bews and George Craigie.

Holm: Benny Norquoy; Bill Pratt and Bob Wylie; Hugh Budge, Willie Gorn and Kennedy; Archie Voy, Jim

Foubister, Austen Brown, Chris Muir and Bertie Bews.

Referee: David Linklater.

A brief comment on the different line-ups. As well as fielding three Bews brothers of 'Strathore', Shapinsay were able to call on two of the Craigies who had been previous winners with Firth. Surprisingly there was no Firth entry this year so, having been born at 'Westhill' in Shapinsay, Hughie and George decided to 'exercise their birthright'.

Holm showed no fewer than five changes from the previous cup final team but sharp eyed readers will have noted that Benny Norquoy was back working in the parish and back in his rightful place 'between the sticks'. He certainly had a knack of picking a cup final team.

Despite the weather conditions, the teams provided the crowd with an outstanding first half but it ended goalless.

Immediately after interval, Shapinsay showed signs of making better use of the wind and within two minutes, Hughie Craigie netted from close range. Play continued in true cup final fashion and with ten minutes remaining, Muir equalised for Holm in a goalmouth scramble. The deadlock now remained until full time which meant extra time of half an hour would have to be played.

According to the competition rules operating at the time, if the sides were still level after extra time, the team ahead on corners, gained within that extra time period, would win. No replay or that 'modern' innovation, penalty kicks!

No further goals were scored so, by forcing three corners to their opponents one, Shapinsay were declared the winners.

For the first time, an island team had won the Parish Cup and no one could grudge them their success. Beaten finalists two years ago, they had shown great determination, travelled many times across the 'String' for both home and away matches, and now had earned their reward. Although cold and wet, it was a very vocal and enthusiastic crowd who greeted Mr Gilbert Archer, a director of R. Garden Ltd., to make the presentation.

In his speech, Mr Archer seemed to capture the true spirit of the Parish Cup. He thought the inter parish competition was a splendid idea:

"It engenders an interest that the local teams in Kirkwall and Stromness could not arouse, and a spirit of loyalty that was very desirable in the football world. (Hear! Hear!) After all, however much pleasure one gained by winning individual prizes, the greatest pleasure was obtained when one wins a prize for one's parish, county or country. That is Shapinsay's reward!" (Applause) reported *The Orkney Herald*.

Amid prolonged cheering - cries of "Good old Sheep!" could be heard above the general crowd noise - the cup was presented to Jim Rendall, the Shapinsay goalkeeper and captain.

Driving by bus through your home parish bearing the spoils of battle is one thing; to travel by boat amidst a packed, jubilant throng of supporters and arrive at your home harbour to be met by more cheering hordes, desperate to slap you on the back and sing your praises, is quite another.

Such a reception now awaited the new cup winners. News of the victory spread rapidly and sure enough, the steamer sailed into Shapinsay with virtually the entire population on the pier to greet them.

Yes, they would be dancing in the streets of Balfour, all night and probably every night for weeks to come!

The cup winners in 1933, Shapinsay. Back row, left to right, Bill Budge, Jim Rendall, Jim Sinclair. Middle, Hughie Craigie, Jim Groat, Joe "Bunny" Bruce, Jackie Bews, George Craigie. Front, Billy Bews, Eddie Sinclair, Davie Bews. (Picture: Orkney Library)

1934: Deerness in 'sensation' final

The question now being asked was, 'Will any of the other island teams be inspired by Shapinsay's example and decide to enter the competition?' After the experience of Kirkwall Hotspur last year, Mainland teams would be hoping that Stronsay stayed out of it. *The Orkney Herald* of July 12 printed the following salutary tale:

S T R A N D E D!

——

Footballers in a Fix at Stronsay

——

STEAMER SAILS AWAY WITH EQUIPMENT

——

"Eleven Kirkwall footballers who travelled to Stronsay on Saturday to engage in a football match with the local eleven found themselves in something of a fix shortly after they arrived there.

"They travelled by the s.s. *Earl Sigurd* taking advantage of the excursion trip run by Kirkwall Pipe Band.

"Arriving at Whitehall Pier, they went gaily ashore, leaving their boots, shorts, jerseys, in fact all their gear, aboard the steamer with the intention of returning to collect it just before they were due to begin their game.

"A shock awaited them, however, when an hour later they returned to the pier to find that the bird had flown. The steamer, in other words had gone.

"For a little while the footballers remained petrified with amazement, consternation, and dawning horror.

"Feverish inquiries were instituted, and it was discovered that the steamer had gone to Sanday. 'At least,' a grinning fisherman added, 'she went in that direction.'

"Disconsolate, the stranded footballers stood around the corner of a curing shed, wondering whether they should play in mufti or not play at all.

"'Nice fools we'll look if we don't play,' muttered somebody.

"'Nicer fools if we do,' retorted someone else.

"Half an hour passed. At the end of that time somebody looked out to sea and observed a ship approaching.

"It was the truant steamer herself.

"No prodigal son was ever welcomed so cordially as was the *Sigurd*, and it was a relieved, though belated, team that scrambled into their soccer gear and trotted out to the 'field of battle.'"

——

Yes, travelling teams would have more than the opposition to worry about on a trip to Stronsay. As a matter of interest, the game eventually took place and a high quality contest it was, ending in a 2-2 draw. The herring fishing was still a major industry in the island at the time and the home team were able to field players from places such as Portgordon, Macduff, Banff and Aberdeen, some of them very accomplished indeed.

Now, if the herring had only stayed in the same place long enough, these lads could have gained the residential qualification for the Parish Cup … and then … who knows? But, the shoals moved on and so did the fishermen.

Reports and results of Parish Cup games once again received only patchy coverage in the Press during 1934 but what was described was the fate of the holders, Shapinsay.

Harray was a parish which had consistently entered the competition but had, as yet, failed to gain any notable success. However, their side was steadily improving and, this year, they claimed their biggest 'scalp' to date!

The Bignold Park was once more the venue for both legs of the quarter final tie between Harray and the holders, Shapinsay. The first game played before the usual 'large and enthusiastic' crowd resulted in a 3-2 win for Harray, whose goals were scored by Jim Flett of Nistaben (2) and Billy Jolly. This was a particularly robust encounter with frequent tough challenges going in, and towards the end Jim Flett (Garth) received 'a nasty kick on the mouth.' We were not told whether he was standing up or lying down at the time.

A player whose overall performance earned special praise was Agmond Flett. *The Orkney Herald* described his judgement and positional play as "remarkably good" and "he kicked the ball cleanly and powerfully throughout. He was the outstanding player afield."

Readers will have noted a similarity in the surnames mentioned. In fact, the Harray team contained no less than *five* Fletts that day - fortunately the game was not being broadcast on radio.

Despite being a goal in arrears, it was expected that Shapinsay would come through in the second leg, but it was not to be. A 1-1 draw ensured that there would be different winners again this year and extended the pattern of no side yet retaining the cup.

The final did not, however, feature Harray. The question remains, 'Who eliminated them?' and 'what progress did Stromness make?' or 'what happened to Holm?' It appears that if no reporter was assigned to cover the game, the clubs themselves did not bother submitting the result to the Press.

What was clear was that the final was to be between Deerness once again, and newcomers to this stage, Sandwick.

Deerness, with most of their winning side of two years earlier still around, looked very strong on paper. 'Peem' Skea, home and available once more, was still reckoned to be their top player, but he now had serious competition for that accolade since David Ritch had represented Orkney against Shetland at inside right in last years' inter county match, a rare honour for a player from the country. Ronald Aitken, the full back had

been one of the reserves.

For Sandwick, the only player of comparable status was school teacher Frank Kent who had played in the Orkney side of 1931 but as you read the team names, you will now come across a very familiar name indeed. No, your eyes are not deceiving you! Sandwick's goal keeper? Yes, that's correct! Benny Norquoy! He was on his travels again and now his work had taken him to Vola in Sandwick. In a short space of time he had become the driving force behind football in the parish and had helped guide them to their first final. From a personal point of view he was now poised to achieve a unique hat trick: three cup winner's medals with three different teams.

The full teams were as follows:

Deerness: Jim Foubister; Ronald Aitken and Colin Allan; Davie Eunson, David Ritch and Artie Skea; Davie Scott, 'Peem' Skea, Jackie Laughton, Jock Aitken and Robbie Skea.

Sandwick: Benny Norquoy; Arthur Stanger and Ronald Keldie; Edwin Ritch, Peter Elphinstone and Ronald Park; Jimmo Stockan, James Linklater, Frank Kent, Andrew Eunson and Jim Sinclair.

Referee: Mr A. Stephen, Kirkwall.

The match, watched by a crowd well in excess of 1,000, was characterised by plenty of excitement, eight goals and one 'sensation'!

Deerness took the lead with a 'Peem'

Deerness' successful squad in 1934. Back row, left to right, Ernie Park, John Budge, Ronald Aitken, Jim Foubister, Colin Allan, Frankie Allan. Sidney Omand. Middle, Davie Scott, Peem Skea, Jackie Laughton, Jock Aitken, Robbie Skea. Front, Davie Eunson, David Ritch, Artie Skea.
(Picture: Orkney Library)

Birth, Blood

Skea header after twelve minutes and soon afterwards, the same player made it two with another header from a cross by Scott. There was no holding Skea, and when Deerness won a penalty for Norquoy elbowing an opponent, up he stepped to score his and Deerness' third.

Now came the 'sensation'. Ronald Aitken the Deerness full back got into an altercation with Sinclair, the Sandwick the left winger. He lashed out with his boot, catching his victim full on the 'rear end' and the referee had no hesitation in sending him off. From the resultant penalty, Kent scored for Sandwick. 3-1.

However the 'sensation' was not yet at an end. At half time, Aitken along with his captain Jim Foubister and a deputation of team mates, approached the referee, apologised for his action and *asked that he be taken back on the field*. The official was, naturally, unmoved.

If he had let him back on, now that would have been a sensation … possibly a first in world football!

Negotiations having failed, Deerness resumed with ten men but they need not have worried. Within a minute Laughton had scored a fourth, and although Kent pulled another one back with a shot from a Stockan corner, two late goals by Laughton made the final score, Deerness 6 Sandwick 2.

The result was a " fitting triumph for the superior brand of football served up by Deerness," according to *The Orkney Herald*. " Sandwick fell far short of the standard of their opponents."

A new sports columnist in the newspaper, "Mercury" went further. He said, "Deerness and Holm are a class above the western country teams as far as football skill is concerned. Personally I would like to see the honours going west for a change, but that will never happen until such teams as Sandwick,

Birsay, Harray and to a lesser extent Stenness, make a real effort to improve their play individually and as teams. I imagined that contact with Stromness in the Thornley Cup league would help the country teams, but an official of Stromness Athletic told me that instead, the Stromness team was developing the kick and rush tactics of the country teams. It sounded funny to me but my informant was far from amused!"

Not very complimentary about parish football in one part of the county, and after these comments, I suspect that this correspondent did not often venture west of Kirkwall. But he did contribute one useful piece of information: the Thornley Cup was out of hibernation and being played for on a league basis by West Mainland parish teams and Stromness 'B'. Maybe the benefit of all these extra games would be seen in future years. Incidentally, the winners in this first year of competition were Stenness. Worth bearing that in mind!

But the champion parish yet again was Deerness, who this year had two hat-trick heroes in their ranks.

Benny Norquoy, captain of Sandwick, congratulated his opposite number Jim Foubister who then received the cup from Mr John Learmonth, president of the O.F.A. amidst prolonged cheering from the assembled crowd.

Deerness fans really let their hair down this time and shouted 'Good old Deerness!' at the tops of their voices. Steady on folks! Unlike their winning counterparts last year, Shapinsay, there was no sign of the parish nickname being roared with patriotic fervour. I wonder why?

"Good old SkateRumples!" That has a certain ring to it, don't you think?

1935: 'Hope enter the fray

The growing popularity of this tournament was reflected in an entry of 13 teams in 1935, a record number to date. All Mainland parishes were represented with the exception of Stromness and Rendall, while St Margaret's Hope, not yet connected to the Mainland by the Churchill Barriers, became the second island entry, along with Shapinsay.

Considerable interest centred on how this team would fare. For years, the 'Hope had performed well in friendly games and the structure of football on the island was now geared to producing a strong parish side. At the beginning of each summer, four evenly balanced teams were selected to compete in a league with a fine challenge cup the prize for the winners. The best players were then chosen by committee to represent the parish and this year's team featured such highly regarded players as Benny Doull (goalkeeper) full back Bill Omand and inside forwards Harry Forbes and Bertie Robertson, were expected to progress far in the Parish Cup, provided they could overcome first round opponents St Ola, who could call on the services of players from the top Kirkwall teams.

The tie was never in any doubt after the first leg in the Bignold Park. The St Ola team, containing the three Hutchison brothers of Glen Orkney in the forward line, were defeated 3-0. The 'Hope goal scorers were Forbes and centre forward Dougall (2).

The football played in this match was described as being "considerably higher than the average parish standard and not so very far below the quality of play in Kirkwall and Stromness." St Ola were unable to make any impression in the return leg so St Margaret's Hope progressed to the next round with the "highly fancied" tag firmly in place.

This year, teams appear to have been very diligent in submitting their scores to *The Orcadian* so the full first round results read as follows:

Tankerness	1	Shapinsay	5
Shapinsay	4	Tankerness	1
Stenness	8	Firth	0
Firth	2	Stenness	1
Sandwick	3	Birsay	0
Birsay	2	Sandwick	4
Evie	1	Holm	5
Holm	8	Evie	0
St Ola	0	St Mgts Hope	3
St Mgts Hope	4	St Ola	0

The quarter finals now saw Harray, Orphir and Deerness enter the competition but the tie which seized the public interest was the meeting between St Margaret's Hope and Stenness, who had demolished Firth in the last round.

The Bignold Park was selected as the venue to save both parties hiring two modes of transport and the first game, watched by Aberdeen F.C. Manager Paddy Travers who was in Orkney looking at local talent, was one to whet the appetite. The 'Dons boss witnessed a thrilling game which the 'Hope won by five goals to four, with hat tricks being scored by Dougall and the Stenness centre forward William Anderson. Mr Travers was said to be "impressed."

After the appetizer, 1,500 spectators turned up for the 'main course' also in the Bignold Park and, remember, this was only the quarter final! On a windless evening, the crowd saw another exciting encounter in which Stenness reversed the situation winning 3-2. In fact Stenness should have finished the tie but two late goals by that man Dougall again, meant that a third game was required.

The replay watched by another 'bumper' crowd failed for once, to live up to expectations. It turned out to be very one sided with Stenness emerging as runaway, 7-0 winners. Another three goals by William Anderson underlined the value of the Stenness centre.

Various reasons were offered for the unexpected score line. 'Mercury', *The Orkney Herald*, columnist blamed a very stormy crossing

Football was actively played in South Ronaldsay and pictured are St Margaret's Hope (Swifts) in 1935/36. Back row, left to right, Billy Taylor, Jock Mathieson, David Simison, Norman King. Middle, William Tomison, Bill Omand. Bertie Robertson, Harry Forbes, Bob Sinclair. Front, Davy Cursiter, Danny Sutherland.

(Picture: Orkney Library)

of Scapa Flow for upsetting the constitution of the 'Hope players but the real reason probably lay in the unavailability of key performers through injury. Their regular inside forwards Forbes and Bertie Robertson were both missing, the latter with broken ribs, and their absence rendered the high scoring Dougall much less effective. To add to the St Margaret's Hope gloom, the news broke that Dougall, (although unconfirmed, probably a bank employee in the village) was to leave the island, so a major vacancy would be created in the goal scoring department.

But this was to take nothing away from this excellent Stenness team. Once again at the head of the West Mainland Thornley League, they were installed as one of the firm favourites for the Parish Cup.

Quarter final Results

Deerness	2	Orphir	1
Orphir	2	Deerness	6
Holm	5	Harray	2
Harray	0	Holm	6
Shapinsay	1	Sandwick	0
Sandwick	0	Shapinsay	2
St Mgts Hope	5	Stenness	4
Stenness	3	St Mgts Hope	2
Replay			
Stenness	7	St Mgts Hope	0

The semi finals now pitched Stenness against Shapinsay while Deerness would face close neighbours, Holm.

Shapinsay were too experienced in Parish Cup campaigns to be over concerned with reputations and in the first game, they set about their opponents in no uncertain manner. Playing with a gale force wind in their favour in the first half, they were four goals up by the interval. Demoralised by this onslaught, Stenness were unable to make the wind count in their favour in the second half and ended the game 4-0 down. Shapinsay goalscorers were

Bunny Bruce (2), Jim Groat and Sandy Drever.

Apparently the main contribution of the wind in the latter stages was to send "ladies' headgear careering across the field of play." A poor night then for Stenness; the men had lost their reputation, the women had lost their hats!

In the return leg Stenness could not recover and went down again 3-2. So for the third time in six years Shapinsay would contest the cup final.

In the other semi final, attracting a little less countywide attention, Holm and Deerness also required a third game to separate them. After a 3-1 victory for each side, Deerness eventually got on top in the replay at Bignold Park and ran out 3-0 winners with goals by Robbie Skea, David Scott and Jackie Laughton.

The final, between two sides who had now accumulated seven cup final appearances between them, was scheduled for Friday evening, August 2. The Deerness team showed three changes from that which had beaten Sandwick last year but Shapinsay had undergone a bigger transformation, replacing five of their 1933 cup winning side.

The full teams were as follows:

Deerness: Jim Foubister (Barns); Ronald Aitken and Jock Mowat; Jimmy Foubister (Skaill); Davie Eunson and Artie Skea; David Scott, A.J. (Peem) Skea, Jackie Laughton, Sydney Omand and Jock Aitken

Shapinsay: Davie Scott; Bill Budge and Jim Sinclair; Davie Bews, Eddie Sinclair and Willie Muir; Jim Groat, Ernie Park, 'Bunny' Bruce, Andrew Eunson and Sandy Drever.

Referee: Mr J.A. Norquoy, Kirkwall.

Deerness, playing with a slight breeze in their favour took the leads after ten minutes with a header by Laughton but looked to have thrown away their lead a few minutes later

when they conceded a penalty for hand ball by Ronald Aitken. However, Foubister saved Bruce's shot.

Deerness continued to dominate after half time and soon 'Peem' Skea scored a fine goal with a header from a Jock Aitken corner. When Laughton forced the ball over the Shapinsay line after a goalmouth scramble to make it 3-0, the game was effectively over.

The final whistle signalled a fourth cup victory in seven years, a remarkable achievement by one of the smallest parishes in Orkney. Although it had been a scrappy game which had never reached the heights of some of their earlier triumphs, Deerness had been the better team and deserved their win. Shapinsay, on the other hand, had lacked much of their usual fire.

Mr J. Christie, Manager of R. Garden Ltd., presented the cup this year to 'Peem' Skea, the Deerness captain, and he was full of praise for the concept of the Parish Cup: "I think this competition, of all competitions, is probably one of the best I have ever known. It gets to the foundation of football in the more remote parts of Orkney Islands and their Mainland."

He went on to proclaim the game of football as an important way of instilling discipline into your life: "There is no doubt about it, that the man who can play the game in the field of sport can be calculated upon at all times to play the game in the business of life!"

This noble philosophy might well have been true in the 1930's but had he foreseen the arrival of such luminaries as George Best, Jim Baxter, Diego Maradonna, Paul Gascoigne, Wayne Rooney et al, Mr Christie might have made some small modifications to his speech.

1936: Winners have divine quality!

It is always easy after the event, to look back and declare that it was bound to happen sooner or later anyway. Such claims are made all the time by people, referring to issues of a totally trivial nature to those of national importance. At what point on that scale the winning of the Parish Cup is placed, depends entirely on your point of view, but after its destiny was decided in August 1936, you can rest assured that many would swear they 'saw it coming all the time!'

To be fair, the evidence was there and their assertion would have been based on results over quite a long period of time, quality of individual players and the general team work of a side representing another of Orkney's smallest parishes.

This year's entry saw the numbers fall back to ten, with Orphir, Tankerness and Evie all dropping out. However with a number of strong teams in contention, plenty of hard competitive games were anticipated.

While the results service is generally good this year, only the outcome of the first leg matches in round one were published. After their great showing last year, St Margaret's Hope's trip to Deerness proved to be a real anti climax as they found themselves on the receiving end of a 6-0 drubbing. This effectively ended their hopes of further progress this time.

The first leg between St Ola and Holm produced a 2-2 draw in Kirkwall but the return match went unreported. However, it was Holm who took the quarter final place where their opponents in another clash of 'Eastern Giants' would be Deerness.

Stenness were the team of the year in 1936, winning both the Parish Cup and Thornley Cup. Back row, left to right, Tommy Cursiter, Willie Scott, Nicol Firth, Jim Spence, John Anderson, John Isbister, Cecil Yorston. Middle, Sammy Firth, Jackie Thomson, Willie Muir, Fraser Anderson, Jim Seatter. Front, James "Winky" Harrold, Jim Kemp, William Anderson, Mansie Spence, Ned Spence. *(Picture: Orkney Library)*

Meanwhile, up West, the 'big two' from that region, Stenness and Harray, were also drawn to face each other.

Quarter final Results

Firth	3	Shapinsay	2
Shapinsay	5	Firth	0
Holm	1	Deerness	2
Deerness	4	Holm	0
Harray	2	Stenness	2
Stenness	3	Harray	2
Birsay	2	Sandwick	1
Sandwick	4	Birsay	2

The semi final draw now saw last year's finalists Deerness and Shapinsay meet again while the second match would be an all West Mainland affair between Stenness and Sandwick, both of whom squeezed past their opponents by the narrowest of margins. Both ties resulted in clear cut victories. Not even Benny Norquoy's presence in the Birsay goal was sufficient to deny one of his many former clubs!

Semi final Results

Shapinsay	0	Deerness	3
Deerness	2	Shapinsay	0
Stenness	3	Sandwick	2
Sandwick	1	Stenness	6

Whenever a new team appears at the final stage, it captures the public imagination. They are immediately given the label 'underdogs' and everyone, bar the opposition that is, likes an underdog.

But how slender were the chances of this Stenness team winning the cup? Let's look at the facts.

They were sitting proudly at the top of the Thornley West Mainland League with six teams trailing in their wake; they could field three Anderson brothers, John, William and Fraser, plus Willie Muir, who all represented Stromness Athletic in the Orkney County League - John was actually on the point of being selected by Orkney; Mansie Spence, now resident in the East Mainland, was a highly rated player who turned out regularly in East Mainland

Selects; Their team was relatively unchanged over the past three years, with the only newcomer, Jim Kemp, manager of the Aberdeen Savings Bank in Kirkwall, who was born at Quoynamoan in Stenness, a player who could add craft and guile to their forward line.

Deerness, favourites by virtue of their experience and success at this level, had eight of last year's winners on view, but significantly, not a Skea in sight, missing presumably due to a combination of work commitments in the south and injury. At least two of the three brothers had appeared in all of Deerness' previous final teams. Would this be an omen? They would certainly be missed but this was still a strong experienced side with current 'star', centre half Davie Eunson, being spoken of as a possible county 'cap'

Teams were as follows:

Stenness: Jim Spence; Nicol Firth and John Anderson; Jackie Thomson, Willie Muir and Fraser Anderson; James (Winkie) Harrold, Jim Kemp, William Anderson, Mansie Spence and Ned Spence.

Deerness: Jim Foubister; Ronald Aitken and Jock Mowat; Jimmy Foubister, Davie Eunson and Jock Clouston; Tommy Bichan, Edwin Stove, Jackie Laughton, Sydney Omand and Jock Aitken.

Referee: Mr Alexander Stephen, Kirkwall.

A crowd of 1,200 saw the final assume a familiar pattern when, after 15 minutes, Jock Aitken scored for Deerness, direct from a corner. However Stenness were not showing signs of being overcome by the occasion and before half time, William Anderson equalised with a volley from a Kemp cross. Half-time, 1-1.

After the break, Stenness took complete control. Kemp scored a brilliant solo goal before Anderson latched on to a loose ball and ran through the defence to score his second and Stenness' third.

Stenness now looked winners all the way and shortly before the end, Harrold sealed victory with a rising shot to make the final score, Stenness 4 Deerness 1. The 'underdogs' from the West had done it!

The Press were loud in their praise of Stenness: "I don't expect we shall see for a number of years, a final which will enthral the spectators as this one did … Deerness were well beaten by one of the finest combining teams yet seen in the Bignold Park, Stenness." stated *The Orkney Herald*.

According to *The Orcadian*: "The Stenness keeper (J. Spence) was safe and daring, the backs steady, the middle men fast in covering up and following through. Laughton, the Deerness leader, was blotted out by Muir while the Deerness wings were well policed by Thomson and Fraser Anderson. Star man was Kemp, brains of the attack."

Mr John Learmonth, O.F.A. president, was full of praise for the winners and the quality of the match, before handing the cup to Willie Muir, captain of Stenness. This was a famous victory for the West Mainland side who had achieved their win, to be followed by the Thornley Cup, with only twelve players.

But finally, it is worth mentioning one other factor vital to the team's success. The regular trainer was Cecil Yorston, but this year he had an assistant who worked very hard with the team, a divinity student at the Stenness Church of Scotland, Mr Andrew Alexander M.A. Stenness were a fine team and may well have won without his assistance but let's face it, when push comes to shove, it's no bad thing to have God on your side!

1937:
Pitch invasion halts final

Having now reached the pinnacle, it would have been assumed in Orkney footballing circles that Stenness could stay there for some time. The same players were still available and just to add to their strength, a fourth Anderson brother from Moa, Kenneth, was set to make his debut this year. As an indication of the team's all round capability, both Fraser Anderson and Willie Muir got as far as the county trials while John Anderson actually played in the side which beat Shetland 4-1.

So it looked as if Stenness would be hard to dislodge … as long as they kept clear of injuries.

Despite the obvious popularity of the competition, only eight teams entered in 1937. There was no sign this year of Firth, St Margaret's Hope or St Ola, all teams of some repute, although Tankerness did make a reappearance.

Again there are some gaps in the results but the first round went roughly as follows:

Holm eliminated Tankerness (no scores available); Deerness defeated Orphir after establishing a 6-1 lead at home; Stenness beat Sandwick 2-1 (away) and 3-0 (home). The tie which captivated the Press was the almighty struggle between Harray and Shapinsay which required a third game to separate the teams.

The contest began quietly enough with Shapinsay winning the first leg in the Bignold Park, 1-0. The pace then stepped up in the second game at the same venue where Harray reversed the situation winning, 3-2. A crowd of more than 500 now turned up to see the replay and they witnessed a match to remember. Goals were plentiful and the game see-sawed back and fore: Sandy Drever scored for Shapinsay, Jim Flett (Nistaben) for Harray, Hughie Craigie for Shapinsay, Jackie Hutchison for Harray, Bunny Bruce for Shapinsay, Jim Flett again for Harray. With the score 3-3 Hughie Craigie broke clear to give Shapinsay the lead for the fourth time and that was enough to see his side go through to a semi final meeting with Holm.

There was no doubting Shapinsay's resilience and with new blood continuing to be introduced, they were again a force to be reckoned with. But readers will now be noting Harray's progress. They were improving every year and had gone on to displace Stenness as this year's winners of the Thornley League. Also observed will have been the surname 'Hutchison' among the Harray goal scorers. It won't be the last time you see that name mentioned in a Harray context!

After such heroics in the last round, it is frustrating that the Press chose to ignore Shapinsay's semi final efforts but the end result was that they eliminated Holm to claim a place in the final for the fourth time. Attention instead focussed on the tie between Deerness and Stenness, and it was expected to be close … but not for very long!

With all four Andersons on the park, Stenness destroyed Deerness down at Newark by five goals to one. Although Deerness made a fight of it on the Stenness ground at Cuminess, and actually won the game 3-2, the home side had done enough to reach the final again and this time they would most definitely not be as 'underdogs'

This was another final to stir the public interest and 1,800 people made their way to the Bignold Park on Saturday evening, July 31. The Stenness team showed two changes from last year, Kenny Anderson replacing Jackie Thomson and Jim Seatter taking the place of last years 'man of the match', Jim Kemp. Shapinsay still had a nucleus of seven of the 1935 finalists but were slowly evolving as a team, and two new forwards, Bob Mathieson, a lighthouse keeper, and Jim Meason, were worthy of particular note.

Teams were as follows:

Shapinsay: Jimmy Bews; Bill Budge and George Lamont; Eddie Sinclair, Davie Bews and Tommy Groat; Hughie Craigie, Bob Mathieson, Bunny Bruce, Jim Meason and Sandy Drever.

Stenness: Jim Spence; Nicol Firth and John Anderson; Fraser Anderson, Willie Muir and Kenny Anderson; 'Winky' Harrold, Mansie Spence, William Anderson, Ned Spence and Jim Seatter.

Referee: Mr David Walker, Kirkwall.

Under the influence of Mathieson, Shapinsay dominated early on and after a long period of pressure, they achieved the break through when Meason scored with a hard drive from 20 yards. Stenness fought back and had numerous attempts on goal but could not score. Half time, Shapinsay 1 Stenness 0

The second half had only just began when an astonishing incident took place. A number of Stenness supporters broke through the ropes surrounding the pitch (eye witnesses said the rope had been cut) and refused to leave the field of play.

Referee Walker threatened to abandon the game and, with no police present, had to call on the Stenness players to try to persuade their fans to get back behind the

The Shapinsay team of 1937. Back row, left to right, Bill Budge, Jimmy Bews, George Lamont. Middle, Hughie Craigie, Bob Mathieson, Jim Meason, Joe "Bunny" Bruce, Sandy Drever. Front, Tommy Groat, Eddie Sinclair, Davie Bews. (Picture: Orkney Library)

ropes. The players then demonstrated their skill as negotiators by quelling the disturbance thereby enabling the game to continue. So ended the first 'riot' at a Parish Cup final.

What had been the cause? Perhaps the supporters had seen the 'writing on the wall', sensed it was not their night and had tried to get the game abandoned. On the other hand, they had maybe indulged in too big a 'carry-out' from that fine hostelry in Stenness ….

Whatever their intentions, the incident did nothing to help their team. With only two minutes of the second half gone, a long looping shot by Bruce hit a rough piece of ground and bounced over the keeper into the net. Shapinsay continued to lay siege to the Stenness goal and soon Meason scored his second and Shapinsay's third. It looked like the game was over.

But there was still plenty of fight in the cup holders and Muir pulled a goal back with a "powerful drive which stretched the roof of the net". It was all Stenness now and after Mansie Spence had added a second goal, it seemed as if they might force a replay.

However, it was not to be. Time ran out, with Shapinsay holding on to win 3-2.

Mr A.J. Grant, O.F.A. president, remarked that both teams had fought well and hard and were very equally matched but "it was a case of the lucky team winning; on this occasion Shapinsay had been the lucky team." (Loud applause).

For the second time the cup would go home on the m.v. *Iona* to a rejoicing island and no doubt many expected this to happen again in years to come. But just as likely, Stenness could come back stronger than ever next year, Deerness should never be discounted, while Harray appeared to be a team on the way up. Perhaps some new unheralded force

would emerge and catch everyone by surprise!

Next season's Parish Cup was a fascinating prospect.

One thing is certain, if Stenness reached the final, the O.F.A. officials would have to look at measures of crowd control. Police ringing the ground? Mounted police outside the Bignold? A 'stop and search' policy and confiscation of screw-tops? They might even go the whole way and alter kick off time from seven o'clock on a Saturday evening to noon on Sunday! Is that not the fate which awaits unruly football supporters everywhere?

1938:
Final sees seven goal thriller

A letter to *The Orkney Herald* in July, 1938, from "A Football Fan" contained a plea - nay, *a demand* - for Orkney Football Association to stage a series of showcase matches in the Bignold Park on Saturday evenings. Part of his submission went as follows: " … one wants to see the following matches. We MUST get the opportunity to see them.

Saturday July 23: Shapinsay v Winners of Garden Trades Cup

Saturday July 30: Shapinsay v Winners of Craigmyle Cup

Saturday August 6: Shapinsay v County Team

Given decent weather, these matches would pack the Bignold Park. Come on O.F.A., get going!"

No prizes for guessing which team this fan supported. But what justification did he have for believing his team could take on the world? Events of this season may supply the answer.

The Parish Cup competition began again with a very much diminished entry of seven teams and the cup holders wasted no time in restating their right to be known as the champions. Their opening fixture produced the following outcome:

Shapinsay	6	Sandwick	2
Sandwick	2	Shapinsay	7

They were on the march again and this result would have sent a shiver through the other teams still remaining. But, when closely examined, this level of performance was not totally unexpected. Three of their players, all of whom played for Hotspur on a regular basis, had been involved in the county trials this year. Bunny Bruce and Bob

Mathieson did not make the final eleven but Bill Foubister, formerly of Tankerness but now living in Shapinsay, played outside left in the side that was beaten 7-4 by Shetland. Solid and dependable in all positions, the team needed a 'finisher' and right now, Jim Meason the centre forward was certainly capable of doing just that.

In the other first round games Deerness squeezed past Harray by 1-0 and 2-2 while Stenness' victory over Orphir went unreported. I wonder if they were being punished for their fans' indiscretions last year?

The semi final story is now very quickly told. First of all, Shapinsay's path to the final was unopposed. Holm, "owing to various reasons" (unspecified), "have been obliged to withdraw from the competition". Such a shame to witness the decline of a once very fine team.

The news embargo on Stenness continued in the other semi final and that is frustrating because their match with Deerness must have been a clash to savour. What we do know is that Deerness emerged winners as it was they who lined up in the final against Shapinsay before a crowd of 2,000 on Saturday evening, July 16.

Shapinsay's only change from last year was the inclusion of Bill Foubister but significantly for Deerness, two of the Skea brothers, Artie and Robbie, were available and it is worth noting that the Aitken brothers, Ronald at right back and Jock at outside left, were in the same positions they had occupied in every Deerness cup final team in the past ten years.

Shapinsay might be favourites but they would not have it all their own way. Deerness had recently played Rovers, one of Kirkwall's top teams, in the Craigmyle Cup, and defeated them 4-0.

Full teams were as follows:

Shapinsay: Jimmy Bews; Bill Budge and Jim Sinclair; Eddie Sinclair, Bill Foubister and Davie Bews; Hughie Craigie, Bob Mathieson, Jim Meason, Bunny Bruce and Sandy Drever.

Deerness: Jim Foubister; Ronald Aitken and Jock Mowat; Jimmy Foubister, Davie Eunson and Colin Allan; David Scott, Sydney Omand, Artie Skea, Robbie Skea and Jock Aitken.

Referee: Mr R. Linklater, Kirkwall

The game itself turned out to be another Parish Cup final classic, producing seven goals, no end of thrills and a very close result.

Shapinsay had a 2-0 lead by half time with goals by Bruce and Meason and as a further indication of their dominance, Bruce had missed a penalty when he struck his shot against the post.

Drever made it three for Shapinsay shortly after half time when he shot home from close range, before Deerness got going with a fine goal by Robbie Skea. The Deerness fight back appeared to be short lived, however, when Meason made it 4-1 to Shapinsay with a fierce drive into the corner of the net. It seemed like too high a mountain for Deerness to climb now.

But to their credit, they did not lie down and after Artie Skea had dribbled right through the defence to tap into an empty net, the crowd were set for an exhilarating finish. Deerness were awarded a penalty for hand ball and Davie Eunson converted: 4-3. They now pressed frantically for an equaliser but the Shapinsay defence held firm to ensure that they retained the trophy in what had been a highly entertaining match.

Shapinsay retained the cup in 1938. Back row, left to right, Billy Budge, Jimmy Bews, Jim Sinclair. Middle, Hughie Craigie, Bob Groat, Jim Meason, Joe "Bunny" Bruce, Sandy Drever. Front, Eddie Sinclair, Bill Foubister, Davie Bews. (Picture: Orkney Library)

Observers concluded that, over 90 minutes there was little between the teams but Shapinsay had been the better balanced overall and had taken their chances well. Special mention was made of Eddie Sinclair and Budge in defence and Mathieson and Bruce among the forwards.

The pick of the Deerness side had been Foubister in goal, Ronald Aitken at back, Eunson, outstanding at centre half, and Robbie Skea up front.

The cup final record of these sides, undoubtedly the best parish teams of their era, now made very impressive reading: Deerness, seven finals, four wins; Shapinsay, five finals, three wins.

We will leave the final comment this year to our letter writer who, based on all evidence to hand, might not have been far off the mark when he thought his team was ready for all comers: " … Shapinsay playing as well as they did on Saturday night will take some beating.

Yours etc.

Football Fan."

1939: Orkney prepares for war outbreak

The year 1939 is likely to be remembered by most people who lived at that time for reasons other than football. In a year which saw war being declared, the sinking of the HMS *Royal Oak* and the first air raids on Orkney, it is not easy to recall who won the Parish Cup. Yet, despite the almost total transformation in Orkney's way of life, football was played and the Parish Cup did take place.

It was inevitable that preparations for war would impinge on the daily lives of people in Orkney in fairly significant ways. Compulsory conscription was announced at the end of April for all men aged 20 - 21 in order to undergo six months intensive army training. This being a prime age for a footballer, most clubs and parishes would have been depleted as a result.

Yet it was not all doom and gloom. The inter county match against Shetland was played on June 7, 1939, in Kirkwall before a crowd of 4,200 and life still felt normal as the Press afforded extensive coverage to Orkney's 2-0 victory.

A most interesting encounter then followed a week later when Rovers played a 'friendly' game against a team from the German navy fishery protection vessel, *Weser*. The game ended 2-2 and a very cordial occasion concluded with a dance in the drill hall in the company of members of the Orkney Territorial Army. No sign of the menace of war here!

But, despite such overt signs of friendliness between the nations, the clouds of war were gathering and news reporters turned their attention to local preparations. 21,000 respirators were assembled

for distribution; Prime Minister Chamberlain visited Orkney to inspect defence measures; restricted lighting on motor vehicles was enforced, contributing to a spate of road accidents. On the sporting front, the Archer Shield football match with Caithness was postponed on account of the international situation.

Amidst such tension and focussed activity, what had happened to the Parish Cup? Well, it was ticking over, albeit in a very low key fashion and with scant coverage in the newspapers.

What can be deduced is that Orphir had defeated Tankerness and cup holders Shapinsay had succumbed to old rivals, Deerness, but the scores for these matches were not recorded. What we can say, however, is that Shapinsay's hopes of three wins in a row had disappeared.

Only six teams had entered this year so now Orphir played Deerness for a place in the final and most people would have assumed the outcome to be a formality. But this match was to produce a major upset. Deerness duly won the first leg 3-2 in Orphir but, in what must have been a thrilling battle, Orphir overturned this deficit on Deerness soil, winning 5-3, to force their way into their first ever final.

Harray and Sandwick contested the other semi final but no information was available on this match. However, Harray were the winners because the final between Orphir and Harray was advertised to take place on Saturday July 23, " *but only after the Heavy Brigade return from camp*." This Unit would comprise the young men of the parishes who were off at camp training to use the heavy artillery anti aircraft guns located throughout Orkney. Here was further evidence that football was becoming a secondary concern.

In fact there must have been a delay in the homecoming of some

Due to the outbreak of war, no picture was taken of the winning Harray team. This photo shows mostly the same players with the Thornley Challenge Cup 1937. Back row, left to right, Bertie Flett (Woodwyn), Davie Flett (Furso), James Johnston, Alfie Flett (Furso), Henry Stevenson. Middle, Danny Gray, Bob Flett (Netherhouse), Peter Elphinstone, Norman Flett (Woodwyn), Maurice Johnston. Front, Jackie Hutchison, Jim Flett (Garth), Agmond Flett (Furso).
(Picture: Orkney Library)

Orphir or Harray men because the final was not played until Saturday, August 5. But even then, despite the lengthening shadow looming over people's lives, large enthusiastic contingents of supporters descended upon the Bignold Park to see which of the two first time finalists would have their name inscribed on the Parish Cup.

Although only briefly commented upon in the Press, it would appear that another 'cliff hanger' was witnessed. The sides were level, 1-1, at half time. Then Orphir 'resumed as if they were going to carry all before them' and with a few minutes to go, led 3-2. The closing stages however, saw a "sensational recovery by Harray who rattled in two quick goals to win a thrilling game and the trophy for the first time."

Harray's winning goal had *allegedly* been of a controversial nature, when Orphir's 14 year old goalkeeper, Alan Anderson, was bundled into the net by a Harray forward. But sadly, that information is only hearsay.

Both teams had been well served in defence but Orphir forwards did not take all their opportunities. "All things considered it was a fair result with Harray's directness and fighting qualities deserving the reward."

Because of the brevity of the report, players' names were not included, but drawing on evidence of other Harray and Orphir line ups of the time, it is likely that the teams would have contained most of the following individuals:

Orphir: Alan Anderson; Jim Hay, Jim Sinclair, Jock Cursiter, John Marwick, Jim Findlay, Willie Muir, Bobby Mowat, Robert Clouston, Charlie Kemp, Peter Elphinstone, Geordie Flett.

Harray: Jim Johnston; Bertie Flett (Woodwyn), Davie Flett (Furso), Alfie Flett (Furso), Tom Aitken, Jim Flett (Nistaben), Jackie Hutchison, Jim Flett (Garth), Agmond Flett (Furso), Danny Gray, Bob Flett (Netherhouse), Norman Flett (Woodwyn), Maurice Johnston.

Did Harray field *eight* Fletts? It's perfectly possible!

It should be said that Peter Elphinstone appears in Sandwick's 1934 parish team and Harray's 1937 Thornley Cup winning picture, but by 1938 he was named in an Orphir team. They are therefore "getting him" on this occasion.

So Harray had won but Orphir fans please note for future reference, your team came within a few minutes of lifting the Parish Cup. No consolation I suppose, but surely there would be more opportunities. Now that they had tasted success there was every possibility that Harray would go on and repeat the feat in years to come … if given the chance.

As it happened, the announcement made by Neville Chamberlain on Sunday, September 3, 1939, would drive thoughts of the Parish Cup far from Orcadian minds for the next six years.

Birth, Blood

While parish football came on leaps and bounds during the 1930s with the introduction of the Parish Cup, the inter counties with Shetland continued to be well supported by the Orkney public. Here is a selection of Orkney teams and occasionally, just occasionally, a parish player can be spotted.

This Orkney team won 3 – 1 in Shetland in 1930. Back row, left to right, "Mosh" Marwick, Dave Walker, Tommy Thomson, Bob Findlay, Dave Wooldrage, J. Findlay. Kneeling, J. "Nuckie" Norquoy, Hugo Munro, J. "Yoka" Johnston, A. Campbell and Teddy Corsie.
(Picture: Orkney Library)

The 1931 Orkney side that defeated Shetland 5 – 2. Back row, left to right, R.O. Watston (secretary), G. Flett (president), J. "Nuckie" Norquoy, Tommy Thomson, Dave Wooldrage, "Mosh" Marwick, Sandy Tait (OFA). Middle J.M. Campbell, "Yoka" Johnston, Hugo Munro, Frank Kent, Jim Findlay. Front. J. Bews, J.S. Findlay and R. Findlay.
(Picture: Orkney Library)

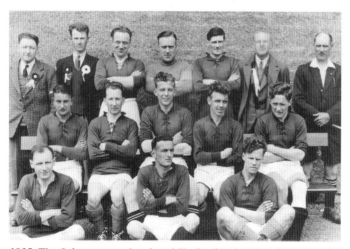

1935. The Orkney team who played Shetland in the Bignold Park and won 3 – 1. Back row, left to right (players only) G. Sinclair, Tommy Thomson, W. Marwick. Middle. J. Brown, W. Collier, T. Cooper, Teddy Corsie, Angus Buchanan. Front. "Mosh" Marwick, J.S. Findlay and Bill Groundwater.
(Picture: Orkney Library)

Finally, let us remember Deerness F.C., Parish Cup team of the decade with four cup wins. Here is the 1935 team with cup No. 4. Back row, left to right, Colin Allan, Tommy Bichan, Ronald Aitken, Jim Foubister, Jack Mowat, Robbie Skea. Middle. Davie Scott, "Peem" Skea, Jackie Laughton, Sidney Omand, Jock Aitken. Front. Jimmy Foubister, Davie Eunson and Artie Skea.
(Picture: Orkney Library)

The 40s - Wartime

Pause for Reflection

Six years would now pass before football could resume in an organised form in Orkney. Rather than jump straight ahead to 1946, it is worthwhile just to pause and reflect a little on the decade during which the Parish Cup football tournament became established as the principal sporting event in rural communities.

Speaking to those who played during the 1930's, and there are very few surviving who did, it is clear that football was, apart from the occasional dance, the main social activity for young folk. In most parishes, crowds of local youth would gather at a designated spot, not necessarily the official parish pitch, and play football till dark.

Fraser Anderson of Voan, Stenness, a member of the 1936 winning Parish Cup team, remembers the venue being a field in the village opposite where the Post Office is situated. Most evenings the youth of the parish would make their way to this spot, and indulge in a few hours vigorous activity, before cycling home again.

In Harray, recalls Jackie Hutchison, several times a Parish Cup winner, the gathering place was a field in the centre of the parish, also opposite the Post Office, where between 40 and 50 young folk would regularly congregate and games of 20 plus a side were common. This ground had one disadvantage in that the ball would frequently land in the adjacent burn, but in its favour, its proximity to the Post Office meant it was possible to get refreshed with lemonade when the game was finished.

These scenes would be typical of what was happening in every parish or island and the simple conclusion to be drawn? … nobody went short

This disconsolate goalkeeper reflects the sad condition of the Bignold Park. The 'Ducky Pond' can be seen in the Papdale Valley behind.   *(Picture: Orkney Library)*

of exercise. Team pictures of the time consist almost exclusively of lean, well honed young men with virtually no evidence of anyone being overweight.

The lifestyle did not lend itself to obesity. After leaving school, most folk undertook hard manual work, cycled or walked everywhere and for recreation, ran about some more. A day in the life of the great Shapinsay forward, Bunny Bruce illustrates perfectly how physical exertion and fitness was simply a matter of course.

Bunny was sometimes invited to attend county trials in Kirkwall and on such a day his routine would have gone something like this: up early in the morning to start work about 7am; tramp the fields behind a pair of horse all day; break off in the late afternoon to get ready for the trial; cycle three miles to the pier to catch Nicolson's boat to Carness; walk two miles to the Bignold Park; play the match; repeat the journey home again; and get some rest ready for resuming work at 'crack of dawn' the next day.

Although the notion of 'training' was an alien concept to young men of the period, strength and stamina were certainly qualities needed to overcome the demands made by the football pitches themselves. The local pitch was usually a field not required by the farmer for cultivation that year and the football team were granted permission to share the space with the animals which would be driven off to the side while the game was on. The grass was rarely, if ever, cut and often it could grow up to a foot in length.

Some details on the various parish pitches coming up, but what of the principal football ground of the time, the Bignold Park … supposedly the Hampden or the Wembley of Orkney?

Readers will have noted in the account of the 1937 final that Shapinsay scored a somewhat fortunate goal when, according to *The Orcadian* reporter, "a long drooping shot hit a rough piece of the field and bounced over the keeper's head into the net." Apparently

Birth, Blood

the Bignold was regarded by all sports people - footballers, hockey players, cricketers - as "a disgrace." Correspondents were urging the town council to "awaken from the lethargy into which they have fallen", and do something to improve matters. Much of the field was let for grazings and the person who held the let did not cut any grass till August by which time it was "knee high with weeds etc. almost topping the dykes."

The council was urged to turf the goal mouths and centre circle, and acquire a motor mower to keep the grass under control, *after it had first been cut with a machine suitable for longer grass!*

If this was the 'best' pitch what were the rest like? Another item in *The Orcadian* made it clear that the problem of long grass was not uncommon and could pose problems for both player and referee: "Grass, or should it be hay, has been allowed to grow so long, there is a real danger of footballs being lost during a game. In one match recently, the referee could only make out 10 players in one team but eventually discovered a diminutive outside left in the grass near the corner post!"

Not all pitches were that bad but some set different challenges.

The Harray field at Garth on the Lyde Road and Sandwick's at both Garson and Housenea, were of the 'heather and tussock' variety, rough moorland ground which was never cultivated and where, since there was little prospect of it rolling any distance, the ball had to be kicked constantly to keep it moving. Given that the leather ball in use at the time became progressively heavier in wet conditions, this could sometimes be a demanding task. "Hid wis like keeckan a stone!" was one expression I noted down.

Deerness fared better on their Links ground at Newark where the grass stayed short but here the main

problem was rabbit holes. They were so widespread that, according to one local exponent, 'anybody disappearing doon wan hid tae try and mak' sure he cam' up the sam' hole.' A touch of exaggeration maybe and to be fair, the caverns were filled in now and again.

Challenging pitch conditions then, but it was not all bad news: sometimes its features could be used to advantage.

When the kye were ushered off before a game, maybe a shovel was used to remove the worst of the freshly laid cow-pats … maybe not! Such a site would be the very place to settle an old score, get your own back for some injustice earlier in the game or on a previous occasion. Just wait for your 'victim' to encroach on the appointed area and SMACK! land him in it! It was not uncommon to see players soldiering on , "skitter fae head tae feet."

Picture also, dips or undulations on the pitch or just to the side, which might have gathered water after heavy rain … and I don't think I need say any more.

How widespread was the practice of settling 'old scores' I am not sure. Most games reported in the Press praise the sportsmanship on view and sendings off were extremely rare. But, reporters could not have been present at a game in Firth when the visitors, Shapinsay, appear to have been lucky to have escaped with their lives!

At the end of the match, which must have contained a 'degree of niggle', the Firth players sought revenge by trying to tip the Shapinsay bus with their team and supporters inside.

When they didn't succeed, they resorted to bombarding the vehicle with stones and the driver had his work cut out to depart with his cargo intact. Now, an eye witness account of that would have made a good story!

Not only would the modern player,

accustomed to flat manicured surfaces, have found playing conditions of the 1930's difficult to master, but similarly used to custom built changing rooms, he would have shuddered (literally) at some of the facilities on offer at this time.

Most would have counted themselves lucky if, as was the case at Hilton on Shapinsay, the pitch had a stone dyke round it. Here, at least, the players could usually find a lee side to get changed.

But for others more fortunate, accommodation was positively 3 Star. The Stenness pavilion at their Cuminess ground consisted of a tattie shed conveniently situated in the actual field, while the Holm players, whose pre-war pitch was at 'Greaves' at the back of St Mary's village, changed in a barn.

But no matter how primitive, these places were not lacking in atmosphere and young boys, were often allowed in to get a 'feel' for the game and get close to their idols. One of Holm's post-war stalwarts, a hero worshipping schoolboy at the time, recalls the scene vividly, in particular the intoxicating smell of embrocation.

"When you were that age," Davie Moss reminisces, "that was as good as it got!"

Well ahead of their time appear to have been Deerness F.C. Leslie Foubister, Inverairn, Toab, notes that the club paid for a pavilion to be built at Newark by 'Bob o' the Storehouse' and 'Alfie o' Peedie Grindigar', out of heavy corrugated iron. Both home and away teams could take advantage of this facility. So well constructed was it that it was used in the war years as accommodation for personnel manning the searchlight but, like many other small buildings in Orkney, it finally surrendered in the face of one of the hurricanes of the 1950's.

But, if basic accommodation usually sufficed for the home team, for the visitors things could be surprisingly sophisticated. They were able to change in the bus! Very few players had cars and with bus hire being relatively cheap, this was the mode of transport favoured by most teams.

There were a good number of bus hire firms from which to choose.

West Mainland teams tended to favour buses from 'Bank's','Wishart' of Stromness, or from 'Flett and Hay', one of whose drivers, Tom Cursiter, also had a large Hudson car which on one occasion, managed to transport the entire Stenness team to their game. 'Laughton's' bus from Deerness was usually chosen by teams from the East Mainland.

I was fortunate to receive from John Heddle, 19 Glaitness Park, Kirkwall, a copy of Firth FC's accounts for 1932, meticulously recorded by his father, George Heddle, club treasurer. These details give an excellent idea of the bus hires and general costs involved in running a football club for a season, in this case, a year during which the team reached the Parish Cup final for the third year in a row. For interest, the information is printed here but be prepared for some bad news … at the end of the season the club were 5 $\frac{1}{2}$d in debt.

From these accounts it is clear that with bus trips, games to go to, dances etc., the local football team was the hub round which much of the social activity of the parish revolved. In Stenness, however, the footballers appear to have been the instigators in the creation of a very special 'hub' which was to go on to become one of the most famous social venues in Orkney.

On their way to or from their Cuminess pitch, some of the boys would stop by a house at the end of the Ireland Road to visit the householder, who was skilled in the art of repairing boots. The resident,

a certain William Farquhar, would replace studs or restitch loose parts of a boot, and being a kind hearted soul, would get in tea and lemonade for the lads coming. Eventually, as the visits grew more frequent, he spotted a business opportunity and began to get supplies in from passing shop vans. The customers were quite happy to pay.

So 'Willies' became a regular venue. It would be used as a gathering place, especially at weekends. One Sunday evening, Willie's mother had a big pot of tatties boiling on the stove for the hens. The hungers could not have been satisfied that night because first one youth, and then another, began helping himself to the contents. Before long the tatties were

1932 EXPENDITURE				1932 Receipts			
June 6th HIRE OF KELDIE'S CAR to Stenness	–	8	–	16 May Balance from 1931 £1	6	4	
Entry fee for Parish Cup. Postal	5	6½		" Subscriptions		8	
Postage		1½		30 " "		1	
		1½		June 1 Collection on field			
July 1st "		1½		Firth v Stenns	2	5½	
" 11 HIRE of Couper's Bus to Sandwick		16		" 11 Subscripts		4	
June 16 HIRE of Keldie's Car to ORPHIR		9		" 4 Collect on field Stromness v Firth	5	6	
July 11 TUBE for Ball	1	6		July 11 Bus fares to Sandwick	4	6	
14 Refreshments		6		14 Collect on field F v Sandwick	13	5½	
July 22nd "		7		Collect " "			
" " FEE for HALL		12		F v Holm	1	1	11½
" 14th HIRE OF CAR for Referee.		8		Drawings at dance		12	
				Don. Mr Tait Dentist		1	6
Entry for Five-a-side Tourney	2	6		Don. on field		2	
Ref's fare on Holm Bus		2		Fares to Holm collected	2	5	
Hire of Couper's Bus to Holm	1	10		Fares to CupFinal		1	
" " Sutherland's Holm	1	10			9	4	8½
Hire of M'Kay's Car to S-aside		7					
Aug 10 Hire of Couper's Bus to Stromness	1	1		Total Receipts £	9	4	8½
Postage		1		Expenditure -	9	8	1
July 4 Secretary's fare to meeting in Kirkwall		2		Deficit —	—	—	5½
Aug. Hire of Sutherland's Bus to Final	1						
	9	8	1				

finished. Now Willie deduced that, with appetites like these, he could sell even more food, so he began to buy in large quantities of 'Bully Beef' in order to make sandwiches to sell with the tea.

Willie Farquhar's became known as the 'Golden Slipper' and it eventually grew into Orkney's most famous unofficial night club. But at this time, it was just a haunt for local boys and there was no question of alcohol being available.

Incidentally, it is worth pointing out that alcohol did not seem to play too significant a part in the social life of this period. It was certainly less readily available and more expensive. Even at dances, having a good time did not appear to be dependent on 'having partaken.' In Deerness for example, according to Jimmy Foubister of Skaill, cup winner in 1935, the perspiring dancers were quite happy to refresh themselves from a 'jeck' dipped into a bucket of water set at the side of the stage.

But I digress. Before moving on with the story of the Parish Cup, I should reflect for a moment on the teams and individual players who excelled in the early years of the competition. If an awards ceremony had been held, the title 'Team of the Decade' would have been won by Deerness whose four cup wins was one more than achieved by Shapinsay.

The 'Most Promising Team' prize would have gone to Harray, winners in 1939 and who, but for the intervention of war, might have gone on to record a string of victories.

As for individuals, the choice of 'Player of the Decade' is more problematic. One way to look at it is to consider which players from the country got picked to play for Orkney v Shetland … but this does not provide a wholly satisfactory answer since very few were selected ahead of players from the town.

However, the short list of the favoured few does identify some of the best players of their era:

Frank Kent (Sandwick) 1931
- Inside left

David Ritch (Deerness) 1933
- Inside right

Jim Findlay (Orphir) 1933
- Outside left

Benny Norquoy (Birsay)1936, 37, 38
- Goalkeeper

John Anderson (Stenness) 1937
- Outside left

Bill Foubister (Shapinsay) 1938
- Outside left

Bill Foubister (Shapinsay) 1939
- Right back

Frank Kent, inter county "cap" and Sandwick parish player.
(Picture: Orkney Library)

Of course, it should be noted that most of these players played for a town team in addition to their parish. One name barely mentioned up to this point is Jim Findlay, whose Orphir team did not enjoy much success during the 1930s. When Jim was chosen for the 1933 inter county, he became the *fifth* Findlay brother to represent Orkney, following brothers George, (1919), Sidney (1923), Charlie and Edwin (1926). Although playing mostly outwith the Parish Cup era, surely a special award would have been made to the Findlays for 'Finest Football Family'.

Another way of identifying top individual players was to look at teams picked to represent East v West during the mid 1930s. For a few years, this match was a feature at the County Show. As a sample, here are the teams from the 1936 game which ended 3-1 to the East. Unfortunately, Shapinsay players, who would have filled several places in an East Select, were not included.

East: Charlie Fraser (St Ola); Ronald Aitken (Deerness) and Bill Pratt (Holm); Bill Foubister (Tankerness), Davie Eunson (Deerness) and Peter Robertson (Tankerness); Austen Brown (Holm), Colin Cooper (St Ola), Jackie Laughton (Deerness), Mansie Spence (Tankerness) and Ernie Hutchison (St Ola).

West: Benny Norquoy (Birsay); Agmond Flett (Harray) and John Anderson (Stenness); Jim Flett (Harray), Willie Muir (Stenness) and Fraser Anderson (Stenness); James Sinclair (Stromness), Jim Kemp (Stenness), William Anderson (Stenness), Frank Kent (Sandwick) and Jim Ritch (Birsay).

Some illustrious names there to chew over and when we add to these some exceptional talents such as A.J. 'Peem' Skea of Deerness (scorer of nine cup final goals) who was living and working out of Orkney by this time; Jackie Hutchison of Harray, who was only coming to prominence as the decade ended; and 'Bunny' Bruce of Shapinsay who most people felt would have been a county regular had he lived in Kirkwall, then we have some idea of 'who was who' in the 1930s.

But don't ask me to pick any one individual. That would just be asking for trouble!

1946:
Harray retain cup after world war

After the years of disruption and upheaval, normal life slowly began to resume in Orkney. Most servicemen had been demobbed and restrictions which had dictated everyday movements had been lifted. Many young Orcadians had been lost in the conflict and their sacrifice would not be forgotten. But now people and events had to move on and gradually, the activities which added colour and pleasure to life began to resurface.

High on the list of such activities was the game of football.

In the Spring of 1946, Orkney Football Association advertised for entries for the first post war competition, a county league for the Brough Cup. The war time legacy was still evident in the entrants which included Hatston, W.O's and Sergeants and the W.D. Laundry based at Quanterness. Later in the season, teams would enter for the Craigmyle Cup and County Shield and it was heartening also to see the youth council of the education committee taking responsibility for introducing a league for youth clubs and organisations throughout Orkney. A total of nine teams entered for this.

As life was breathed back into our local game, so the Parish Cup awakened from its six years hibernation. A remarkable number of eleven teams entered and a fine tournament was in prospect. However, their poverty of resources was highlighted in the reassurance issued by the O.F.A. that teams who required jerseys, footballs, shorts and boots should contact the secretary at an early date. The spare kit had been acquired from some of the war time teams now being disbanded.

The tournament must have been eagerly anticipated by football supporters countywide and many questions would be asked after such a lapse of time, particularly as regards players. Who would still be playing? Who would have given up? Which young boys would have matured into good players in the interim? Even, sadly, which young men would not be returning to their native parish?

The relative strength of the teams would be affected by all of these factors so let us see which parishes would now hold the ascendancy. The three first round matches produced the following results:

Tankerness	4	Orphir	0
Orphir	3	Tankerness	5
Stenness	2	Sandwick	0
Sandwick	2	Stenness	0

Replay

Stenness	0	Sandwick	4
Shapinsay	5	Deerness	2
Deerness	3	Shapinsay	1

Of the strong pre-war teams, Shapinsay appeared to have retained some momentum but all the games had provided good entertainment. From a letter which appeared in *The Orcadian* of July 25, a visitor from south was most impressed with the fare on offer at one of the games:

"Sir,

As a visitor I derived great enjoyment from the football match on July 10 between Stenness and Sandwick. Good players from both sides did really well on a pitch which was all against the playing of football. I liked the sportsmanship shown by all the players. Hard knocks and robust tackling but never a nasty incident in spite of two penalties, one of which had to be re-taken and never was the referee's decision questioned. Thanks for a really good ninety minutes display of clean, hard, sporting football.

Long may this be a feature of Orcadian sport.

Yours etc.

G.D. Grassick,
Great Western Road,
Aberdeen."

Country footballers would have taken great heart from such comments as the quarter finals now beckoned.

Quarter final Results

Tankerness	1	Sandwick	0
Sandwick	0	Tankerness	2
Harray	6	Shapinsay	0
Shapinsay	2	Harray	1
Birsay	4	Firth	1
Firth	2	Birsay	0
St Mgts Hope	1	Holm	1
Holm	4	St Mgts Hope	1

Both Tankerness and Birsay looked like parishes on the way up while Holm were showing signs of a return to former glories. But it was cup holders, Harray, who were most impressive six years on, disposing of Shapinsay by a wide margin.

They were not to have it all their own way, however, as the closely fought semi finals were to prove. Both ties required three games to find a winner.

Semi final Results

| Birsay | 2 | Holm | 0 |
| Holm | 2 | Birsay | 2 |

Second Leg Replay

Holm	1	Birsay	1
Harray	1	Tankerness	2
Tankerness	0	Harray	1

Replay

| Harray | 3 | Tankerness | 1 |

(after extra time)

Why was the second leg of Holm v Birsay requiring a replay? you may ask. The answer: Birsay had infringed one of the golden rules of the Parish Cup by fielding an ineligible player.

The player in question was Teddy Brown, the Dounby centre forward, who was stationed at Twatt aerodrome as part of the maintenance

Birth, Blood

Teddy Brown

crew retained there. He was a highly rated player who, for a few years, was one of the top goalscorers in Orkney football. But unfortunately for Birsay, he was not resident within the boundaries of their parish so the Holm protest was upheld. Since he did not play in the first game Birsay were not disqualified altogether, and their replayed draw was good enough to see them reach the final for the first time.

The other tie produced three hard competitive games before Harray emerged victorious. On display had been some very fine players. For Harray, Jackie Hutchison, who had missed some of his best and most productive football years during the war, was joined in the team by his brother, Freddie, while outstanding for Tankerness were the Clark brothers, Easton and Archie. In fact, Easton Clark, normally of Hotspur, played outside right in the first Orkney team to face Shetland after the war.

For the first time, then, it was an all West Mainland final and on Saturday, July 27, on a dull but dry evening, a remarkable 3,000 spectators

assembled to enjoy the contest.

Unfortunately, the newspapers did not print the teams so some guesswork is required to reassemble the losing side; the winners were smart (and proud) enough to have their picture taken with the trophy!

Harray: Davie Shearer; Agmond Flett and Tom Aitken; Jim Sinclair, Freddie Hutchison and Davie Flett; Jim Stockan, James Flett (Garth), Jackie Chalmers, Jackie Hutchison and Jim Flett (Nistaben).

Birsay: (probable) Herbert Spence; Arthur Stanger, Billy Brown, Johnny Spence, Frankie Flett, Tommy Spence, Willie Spence, Sandy Smith, John Gaudie, Eddie Mowat, Jim Ritch. Possible: Charlie Hourston, David Taylor.

I've 'probably' given the game away there!

Harray attacked first and inside five minutes, Jackie Hutchison scored with a good shot from close range. They continued to dominate and

Davie Flett struck a magnificent goal from 20yards to make it 2-0 shortly before half time.

Birsay had most of the play in the second half but all they had to show for it was a penalty near the end which had to be retaken after Harray keeper, Shearer, moved. The kicker's name was not given so regrettably his moment of fame will be unrecorded. However his effort made the final score Harray 2 Birsay 1.

Harray had, therefore, performed the remarkable feat of retaining the trophy after six year's inactivity. What they might have achieved in those 'lost' years can only be speculated upon.

The cup was presented to Freddie Hutchison, the youthful captain of Harray, by Mr William Groundwater, president of the O.F.A. amid bursts of hearty cheering as the Harray hordes set off for their 'homeland' to commence celebrations. As they did so, all football followers reflected

Harray, Parish Cup winners in 1946. Back row, left to right, Dave Walker (referee), Agmond Flett, Davie Shearer, Tommy Aitken, Arthur Johnston (linesman). Middle, James ('Tim') Johnston, Jim Sinclair, Freddie Hutchison, Davie Flett, Maurice Johnston. Front, Jim Stockan, James Flett (Garth), Jackie Chalmers, Jackie Hutchison, Jim Flett (Nistaben).

(Picture: Orkney Library)

that Harray's was not the only success of 1946.

The main source of pleasure and satisfaction stemmed from the fact that competition was up and running again with renewed health and vigour and the parishioners of Orkney could look forward with eager anticipation to cheering as their young men who were free once again to fight their battles on the field of sport.

Footnote

Defeat was bad enough, but for Birsay, the ordeal was not yet over. As most readers will appreciate, the parish lies to the north west of Harray and the most common route home for Birsay folk travelling from Kirkwall is via Harray. Now, picture the scene.

The victorious Harray team had made good speed and were already home by the time the Birsay players' bus trundled westward full of silent, downcast, sombre individuals. As they reached the centre of Harray, just opposite the school, they came upon a rejoicing mob, cup in hand, arms in the air, bottles uncorked … an evening of unbridled joy ahead of them.

At the sign of their vanquished opponents, the noise rose to a crescendo, some choice Harray epithets rent the air and a clamour of hands beat a tattoo on the side of the bus.

Inside, the moment of humiliation passed, hackles rose, and murmurs of revenge spread through the passengers.

A Birsay die hard levered himself from his seat, straightened to his full 6'1" and, glaring at his tormentors outside, declared with venom, "Boys, if this ever happens again, … we'll … we'll … we'll cheust hiv' tae mak' sure we go home bae Brodgar!"

1947: Tactics pay off for St Ola team

Now that normal service had been resumed, a keenly contested Parish Cup was anticipated in 1947 and the viewing public would be weighing up the chances of various teams.

Harray would most probably be the side to beat but would face stern opposition from the likes of Holm who now had a team playing regularly in the Brough Cup County League and competing with some success. Some cynics claimed that they were doing this simply to warm up for the Parish Cup. By mid season they were a respectable fifth in the league with John Hepburn the leading Holm scorer with 22 goals.

St Ola, who had entered this year, would also be contenders as they were able to field a team full of regular players, a number of whom were members of Kirkwall 'A' teams. Birsay should be able to consolidate their good progress of last year while Tankerness appeared to have a lot of talent available. Many possibilities, therefore, confronted the parish football supporter.

With crowds at an all time high, it seemed that most people enjoyed the football fare on offer but it didn't satisfy everyone as this letter to *The Orkney Herald* in June, 1947, pointed out:

Modern Orkney Football

Sir, I have been attending a number of football matches in Orkney recently. There is a great change in everybody's attitude to the game since pre war days.

First, the players. In the old days, if my memory serves me, football in Orkney was far more robust and full blooded. Kicks were given and received with the greatest liberality,

and players played on till the final whistle though they were a mass of bruises from head to foot.

Nowadays, for the least little kick sustained by any of the players, the game has to be stopped and the rhythm of the play fatally destroyed, while a host of trainers, linesmen, and other officials rush up to the injured one with thick wads of bandages and pots of ointment.

I conclude that Orkney footballers nowadays can't take it like their fathers. Also the standard of football is much lower nowadays.

Yours, etc., FAN

Now, where have we heard something like that last point before? Of course the standard of football was far better when *we* were young! No argument! Yet in the light of events yet to unfold, maybe FAN had a point.

With the exceptional total of 13 teams entered this year, five first round matches were required.

First round Results

Harray	4	Stenness	1
Stenness	3	Harray	3
Birsay	0	Stromness	1
Stromness	2	Birsay	4
St Mgts Hope	0	Tankerness	2
Tankerness	2	St Mgts Hope	1
Shapinsay	2	Holm	2

Second leg not reported

Holm go through

Deerness	1	Sandwick	2
Sandwick	1	Deerness	2

Replay

Deerness	2	Sandwick	0

Last year's finalists both progressed although Birsay had only one goal to spare. They would now face each other in the next round. Unfortunately there was no evidence from Holm's second leg but they did get through as the quarter finals will show.

Quarter final Results

Orphir	1	Firth	1
Firth	3	Orphir	1
Holm	5	Tankerness	2
Tankerness	1	Holm	5
Harray	3	Birsay	1
Birsay	2	Harray	3
St Ola	2	Deerness	1
Deerness	1	St Ola	2

Harray and Holm were certainly fulfilling pre tournament expectations but they would meet in the semi final while St Ola were slowly getting into their stride and would face Firth who were putting up their best show for many years.

However this was as far as Firth were to get. St Ola now stepped up a gear and fired ten goals past them over the two games. The other semi final was a much more even affair and after falling behind in the first game, Harray rolled their sleeves up and swept their opponents aside in the return.

Semi final Results

St Ola	5	Firth	2
Firth	0	St Ola	5
Holm	3	Harray	1
Harray	4	Holm	0

So Harray would defend their title against St Ola in a classic East v West encounter. A crowd of over 2,000 turned up from all over Orkney on Wednesday evening, August 4, to see the match played for the first time at Pickaquoy Park.

Not only was the venue different; *this game was to be one of the most unusual finals ever played.*

'Cubbie Roo', the legendary sports reporter, had now begun writing for *The Orkney Herald* and he vividly set the scene:

"The police made an excellent job of directing the traffic. Every available parking space off 'The Road to Lord Knows Where' was occupied by cars, buses, motor bikes and push bikes,

85 cars and 6 buses being parked there."

The teams lined up as follows:

St Ola: Jock Russell; Jack Adam and Scottie Harcus; Dave Bews, Cyril Parkes and Charlie Anderson; Douglas Young, Jackie Groundwater, Jerry Groundwater, Jim Bews and Ernie Hutchison.

Harray: Maurice Johnston; Agmond Flett and Jim Stockan; Sammy Flett, Dave Flett and Jim Sinclair; James Johnston, Jackie Chalmers, Jim Flett, Jackie Hutchison and Willie Adamson.

Referee: Edward Simister, England.

Harray fielded most of last year's winning team but a notable absentee was their goalkeeper. Last year, Davie Shearer had played but it had since been 'pointed out' that he in fact lived just to the *other side* of the Harray / Sandwick boundary. This was discovered too late to affect last year's result, but from now on he was, much to Harray's distress, the Sandwick goalkeeper. Meanwhile, left back Jim Stockan still continued

to chance his luck but a similar fate lay in store for him … he was the next door neighbour!

As the crowd waited for kick off, one of the main talking points was an alleged 'secret' meeting held in the community centre on the Monday evening by members of the St Ola team. Apparently they had met to discuss … wait for it … *tactics*!

Now what on earth were they? What ever they were, no good would ever come of it!

The game started with Harray, a very strong physical side, going ahead early on from a penalty scored by 'burly' Dave Flett. Jackie Groundwater levelled for St Ola before Jackie Hutchison escaped his marker to restore Harray's lead. So, 2-1 to Harray at half time and nothing particularly unusual yet.

Be patient!

Shortly after the interval, Jackie Groundwater scored his second to level the scores once again and "then the fun started!"

St Ola were awarded a penalty;

St Ola clinched the trophy in 1947. Back row, left to right, Jim Scott, Teddy Heddle, Jimmy Kemp, Jack Adam, Jock Russell, Charlie Anderson, Bill Moar, Stevie Twatt. Middle, Douglas Young, Jackie Groundwater, Jerry Groundwater, Jim Bews, Scotty Harcus. Front, Davy Bews, Cyril Parkes, Vernon Harcus.
(Picture: Orkney Library)

& Boundaries

Jackie Groundwater drove it against the keeper but followed up to net the rebound, 3-2. Ten minutes later, the same player was going through but was knocked off the ball from behind … *penalty*! (The guest referee was standing no nonsense!) Jackie took the kick and scored, 4-2.

A few minutes later, another Harray infringement … another penalty! The unmistakeable figure came forward, Bang! 5-2.

It was all over now but just to rub it in, Ernie Hutchison scored a beauty with a few minutes left. Even then, there was still time for Harray to score a consolation through Chalmers but it was too late to matter.

Final score: St Ola 6 Harray 3 .

What of the other statistics? *Four* penalty goals in a Parish Cup final; Jackie Groundwater scores *five* in a final including a *hat trick* of penalties. Sounds like a great game. Here's what Cubbie Roo thought:

"The game was the poorest inter parish final I have ever seen. In fact, for most of the 90 minutes, the game never got going properly. The whistle was aye blowing, the best that could have happened, for there has been far too much rough and sometimes dangerous play going on in Orkney football …."

Well, if that was a poor game, I wouldn't have minded seeing it.

The reporter went on to restate his views in a later article by declaring that what Orkney football needed was not a coach but a first class referee (such as Mr Simister) because "many players don't even know the rules. In fact, during the final, the referee had to caution a number of players for deliberately kicking out!"

So that practice was still going on!

Now, what evidence, if any, had there been of 'tactics'? Try to get as many penalties as possible? This was denied, but it was later

revealed that the plan had been to get a regular supply of passes to a pair of very quick wingers and their crosses would create problems for the opposing defence. St Ola were satisfied that orders had been carried out to the letter and were responsible for the victory.

Finally, what would 'FAN' be saying after the game? Granted, there were plenty of stoppages but not for injuries. The 'robust and full blooded' type of play which he so admired was being stamped out by a very efficient referee. I wonder if FAN appreciated the irony?

Footnote:

The last bit of colour in the tale of the 1947 final concerns the post match celebrations. After the cup had been presented to captain Cyril Parkes, the St Ola team travelled by bus to Kirkwall pier, some of the players sitting on the bonnet proudly displaying the trophy. They went there to see Jerry Groundwater off to Shapinsay where he was due to get married the following evening to Miss Moira Scott of 'Livaness'.

I am assured that most of the St Ola team appeared in Shapinsay the next day where both cup and wedding celebrations continued in style. Knowing the Groundwaters (I am also married to one) it was sure to have been a 'no holds barred' occasion!

Finally as a matter of interest and in order to show the rise and rise of Holm, this is the Orkney Senior League, 1947:

	P.	W.	D.	L.	F.	A.	Pts
Thorfinn A	20	17	1	2	101	25	35
Hotspur A	20	17	0	3	69	17	34
Dounby Ath	20	15	2	3	77	41	32
Hatston A	19	14	1	4	69	34	29
Holm	20	9	1	10	57	38	19
Rovers	19	9	0	10	57	49	18
Stromness	20	8	1	11	34	51	17
Hatston B	18	5	1	12	27	75	11
Thorfinn B	19	5	1	13	34	65	11
Hotspur B	19	2	0	17	20	81	4
Thistle	20	2	0	18	24	93	4

1948:
Sheep tie up Crabs' toes

Well, if 'tactics' was the latest buzzword in parish footballing circles, would the 1948 tournament be littered with examples of this 'new fangled' device? Time would tell but as this year's competition neared its climax there was again a clear indication that forward planning and adapting to situations on the field would prove crucial in the winning of the trophy.

Once more there would be a host of good teams in contention, some of them with highly regarded players in their ranks.

Holm, still riding high in the 'A' League could boast three county players, in goalkeeper Jack White and Arthur Dainty (both Englishmen who were employed by the Rockworks company which helped construct and later maintain the Churchill Barriers), as well as left winger Abbie Sutherland.

Harray would benefit with players from the strong Dounby team, the leading light now being Jackie Hutchison, the Orkney inside left.

Tankerness, Firth and Birsay had all shown signs of recent improvement while Orphir would be led by county left back, Jock Cursiter.

Inexplicably, St Ola did not enter a team this year but the bonus for Shapinsay was that both goalkeeper Jock Russell and Jim Bews from last year's winning team would now switch allegiance to their cause.

So many possibilities existed as the games got underway in the middle of June.

First round Results

Holm	5	Tankerness	1
Tankerness	1	Holm	3

Birth, Blood

Orphir	1	Deerness	1
Deerness	0	Orphir	4
Birsay	1	Sandwick	3
Sandwick	2	Birsay	5
Stenness	1	Shapinsay	8
Shapinsay	10	Stenness	1

The 'good old days', which were well in the past as far as Stenness and Deerness were concerned, certainly seemed to be returning to Holm and Shapinsay. The quarter finals would now see the entry of Harray, Firth and St Margaret's Hope along with a Parish Cup debut for newcomers, Stromness.

Quarter final Results

Holm	4	Birsay	1
Birsay	0	Holm	5
Firth	1	Harray	2
Harray	5	Firth	1
St Mgts Hope	6	Stromness	2
Stromness	2	St Mgts Hope	4
Shapinsay	4	Orphir	1
Orphir	2	Shapinsay	5

These matches had all proceeded very smoothly and all results were posted on time to the newspapers. This improvement in efficiency might well have been due to a plea issued in *The Orkney Herald* for the O.F.A. to do something about the chaotic Parish Cup fixture system.

Teams were generally left to fix their own dates for games with the result that nobody outwith the competing parishes knew they were on and were therefore unable to go and spectate. Not only that, games got put off for weddings, hoeing matches and other events without any official sanction. Perhaps the parishes were now taking note.

Three previous winners now lined up in the semi finals, the exception being the boys from St Margaret's Hope. It was felt that they would have little chance against Harray but in fact put up a fine show in two very close games. The outcome was:

St Mgts Hope	2	Harray	2
Harray	2	St Mgts Hope	1

Harray had therefore reached another final but attention now focussed firmly on the other semi final between Shapinsay and Holm. In the first leg in the Bignold Park, Holm recorded a 3-2 victory and were installed as favourites with their home leg in St Mary's to come. Anticipating a great occasion, 'Cubbie Roo' was despatched to cover the game and he began in his inimitable style:

"Four bus loads of fervid football fans from Shapinsay and Kirkwall (and many in private cars) came back from Holm 'croam' but happy, most of them, for the island team had beaten favourites Holm in their second Parish Cup semi final by 3-2 in a whirlwind, neck or nothing, never say die, body charging, free for all! Yet it was a most sporting encounter …!"

More examples of sportsmanship coming up:

" … there were charges from behind, tackling from behind, buttock charging, hands, tripping, shoving, holding, elbows and what have you! There was excitement, thrills, spills, tenseness, drama, sheer speed, strength, energy, endurance, guts and, sandwiched in between, moments of artistry!"

Phew! What a game! … and just the kind of reporting to get folk off their backsides and out to watch a game of football. The goal scorers in a game which 'brought a much needed revival to football in Orkney' were Bill Budge (2) and Jim Bews for Shapinsay; J.R. Budge and Arthur Dainty for Holm.

So a replay was necessary and it was another crowd pleaser, once again producing five goals. First of all Jim Seatter scored for Holm; Bunny Bruce equalised for Shapinsay; Dainty regained the lead for Holm;

John Bews again equalised … before schoolboy left half James Sinclair struck the winner for Shapinsay. This meant that the island team had made it to the final on an 8-7 aggregate after over four and a half hours of hectic action.

Something to note: the replay had taken place in the Bignold Park on County Show night. Naturally, a huge crowd had been present. Now could this possibly give the organisers an idea for next year?

Appetites well whetted, fully 2,000 spectators ringed the Bignold Park ropes on Tuesday evening, August 31, in anticipation of a very competitive final between Shapinsay and Harray. Despite it being an evening of heavy rain, observers noted that it was a bigger crowd than that which had turned out a week earlier to witness Orkney's 4-3 defeat by Caithness in the Archer Shield.

As usual, Shapinsay were heavily supported. A flotilla of craft had left the islands some hours earlier, including the m.v. *Iona* packed to the gunwhales once again, the m.v. *Klydon*, Bob Nicolson's motor boat and the overspill travelling in a dinghy loaned for the occasion by a Mr Tinch, who lived in Balfour village. It is worth pointing out that, with such a big travelling support, the Dennison Shipping Company were always willing to allow the team to travel free of charge.

The Shapinsay voices were supplemented at the park by a large contingent of 'neutral' Kirkwallians, all giving the islanders their backing. At this time, there was intense rivalry between the Kirkwall teams and Dounby in the 'A' League, so these supporters, many of a Thorfinn 'persuasion', would not miss the chance of having a go at some of their 'deadly enemies' playing in the Harray team.

In a vibrant atmosphere, the following teams lined up:

Shapinsay: Jock Russell; Bill Foubister and Tommy Nicolson; Jim Meason, Sammy Bews and Jim Sinclair (Harroldsgarth); Davie Budge, Bunny Bruce, Bill Budge, Jim Bews and John Bews.

Harray: Maurice Johnston; Davie Murray and Agmond Flett; Sammy Flett, Davie Flett and Jim Sinclair (Biggings); James (Tim) Johnston, Bobby Hutchison, Willie Adamson, Jackie Hutchison and Jim Sinclair (Midhouse).

Referee: Dave Walker

It is interesting to note that the inclusion of Jim and Sammy Bews meant that five Bews brothers from 'Strathore' had now played in cup finals for Shapinsay, elder brothers Billy, Davie and Jackie having played during the 1930's. Outside left John Bews was a son of Billy.

The family affair also continued for Harray who had three Flett brothers of 'Furso' on the park, while making his first appearance in the final was Bobby Hutchison, 16 year old brother of Jackie. The third brother, Freddie, would have been playing but had been called up for National Service at the time.

The match got underway and Harray were the first to strike when Bobby Hutchison nodded home a cross from the left by Jim Sinclair (Midhouse). Good football proved difficult on a sodden, slippery pitch but playing downhill was to Shapinsay's advantage.

They soon equalised through the evergreen Bunny Bruce and a few minutes later Jim Bews gave them the lead with a shot from close range. From this point Shapinsay took complete charge and soon Billy Budge, another of their young stars, made it 3-1 with a drive from 15 yards. This was the score at half time.

Things stayed like this until well into the second half and by now the cup

should have been Shapinsay's. But on this occasion they got the tactics wrong. In conditions not suited to fine football they continued to pass the ball when some good old fashioned clearances would have been better. This allowed Harray to force their way back into the game.

Agmond Flett made some spectacular runs down field and from one of these runs and crosses, Jackie Hutchison scored a great goal. Then, with practically the last kick of the match, Bobby Hutchison controlled another Agmond cross, beat his man and coolly banged home the equaliser. 3-3.

With that, the referee blew his whistle and, as it was too dark for extra time, a replay was fixed for Saturday, September 11.

If you can translate the headline above *The Orkney Herald* report of the replay, then you will have worked out the eventual winners:

SHEEP TIE UP CRABS' TOES

If you are unclear, you had better read on.

By contrast to the first match, the replay was blessed with dry weather and only a gentle breeze blew across the Bignold Park. The only team change was that Bob Sinclair replaced Bill Budge at centre forward for Shapinsay.

Playing down the slope Shapinsay took the lead when Agmond Flett, one of the heroes of the previous week, misdirected a clearance past his own keeper. But Harray soon equalised when 'Tim' Johnston cut in from the right and scored with a low drive past Russell. It was now end to end football with either team capable of scoring but it was Shapinsay who took the lead again with a coolly taken goal by Bruce. Half time 2-1.

Remember the reference to 'tactics' at the beginning of the section? Well, now Shapinsay got in on the act!

The victorious Shapinsay team of 1948. Back row, left to right, Bill Foubister, Jock Russell, Tommy Nicolson. Middle, Davie Budge, Joe 'Bunny' Bruce, Bob Sinclair, Jim Bews, Jim Sinclair. Front, Jim Meason, Sammy Bews, John (Jock) Bews. (Picture: Orkney Library)

They decided to reorganise their team to nullify the threat from the Hutchisons, who had scored all the goals in the first match and had greatly impressed the watching Aberdeen F.C. scout with their skill and all round ability.

Jim Sinclair was given the task of marking Bobby … and to do nothing else; Jim Meason was instructed to mark Jackie … and do nothing else; and finally Bunny Bruce, who had been well handled by Dave Flett, was moved from centre to inside right where he would be free to make opportunities for others.

The plan worked a treat! With Harray's danger men 'tied up', Bruce created space and set up Davy Budge to make it 3-1 and finally, to crown it all Jim Sinclair took time off from his marking duties to score a fourth with a 'scorcher' of a shot.

There was no more scoring despite Harray's efforts and Shapinsay had won a memorable final by four goals to one. This was their fourth cup win, equalling Deerness' feat during the 1930's.

Amidst a tumult of noise, Bunny Bruce stepped forward to receive the trophy and after declaring how pleased he was to win he sportingly thanked Harray for a fine game.

'Cubbie Roo' agreed Shapinsay had well deserved their win but he urged them to enjoy their moment! Although Harray had lost this time, he issued a stark warning to other teams for the future:

"They tell me that besides Jackie, Freddie and Bobby, there are two other Hutchison brothers, Ian aged 11, who bids fair to become the pick of the bunch, and Eric, aged six, so that, a few years hence, with five Hutchison boys and three Fletts as the backbone, Harra' will have a parish team second to none."

Maybe so, but this night belonged to Shapinsay. The Armada now set sail from Kirkwall and to keep most of the merrymakers close together on the journey home, the much slower *Klydon* was attached to the *Iona* by tow rope. The crowd on board chugged happily on behind, keeping in touch with the 'carry-on' aboard the bigger boat.

However, half way across the 'String', disaster struck! The *Klydon*'s complement ran out of whisky! But their desperate cries were answered without difficulty. Several hands from the *Iona* simply hauled the smaller vessel alongside, a few 'halfies' were passed down, and the ships sailed merrily on.

Tactics? I tell you, Shapinsay had got them all sussed!

Interesting Facts and Figures

Among his many football related interests, 'Cubbie Roo' kept a record of goal scorers in the Orkney Senior League. Here is part of the list from 1947, which shows the top strikers of the day. Spot the parish players near the top of the list.

	Goals
Jim Donaldson (Thorfinn A) …	44
John Hepburn (Holm) …	32
Teddy Brown (Dounby) …	25
Jacky Hutchison (Dounby) …	23
Jim Bews (Hotspur A) …	16
Jack Clark (Rovers) …	16
Jack Groundwater (Rovers) …	15
Louis Cabrelli (Thorfinn A) …	15
Ogden (Hatston A) …	15
Jocky Sinclair (Thorfinn B) …	14
Johnson (Hatston A) …	14
Norman Robertson (Dounby)	13
David Fox (Thorfinn A) …	13
Russell Croy (Hotspur A) …	12
Jacky Miller (Thorfinn A) …	12
Billy Barnett (Hotspur A) …	11
Yates (Hatston A) …	11
Arthur Dainty (Holm) …	10
John Donaldson (Thorfinn A)	10

1949:
Murder in the Parish Cup final

Shapinsay's cup victory had been achieved in a match brimming over with fast exciting football and exemplary sportsmanship on each side. Credit was due to the players but as always, on a highly charged sporting occasion, a key figure was the referee. Last year the man in charge, Dave Walker, had kept control but allowed the game to flow, and it seemed that, with the quality of refereeing on offer, the days of 'full blooded' football, so beloved of older fans, "where kicks were given and received with great liberality", were now merely a memory.

Think again!

If you want to read about a game where law and order broke down completely, you have now come to the right year … and the 'coorse' game to rival all 'coorse' games occurred on the final stage, itself, on Orkney's night of the year, County Show night!

Yet the football year had proceeded so smoothly and successfully up to this point.

Two high profile guest teams visited Orkney early in the season and their appearance captured the public imagination. Aberdeen F.C. were the guests of Kirkwall Hotspur and showed their class in a 5-0 win. Inverness Caley then travelled north but were hard pushed to overcome an Orkney Select 2-1.

Crowds of 3,000 turned up to the games and, from the country supporter's point of view, it was pleasing to see some parish players taking part in one, or both, of these matches: Easton Clark (Hotspur and Tankerness); Arthur Dainty (Holm), Jackie Hutchison (Dounby and

Harray); Jock Cursiter (Rovers and Orphir).

There was no doubt these games helped our inter county side, because when it came to the matches against Shetland and Caithness, Orkney triumphed 6-1 and 6-0, respectively. The crowd for the Shetland game at the Bignold Park was 4,800. It was a great time to be an Orkney footballer!

Success at this level was reflected elsewhere in local football and a very satisfactory total of twelve teams came forward for Parish Cup duty. Realistically those with the best chance this year were Shapinsay, Holm and Harray who could count a substantial number of 'A' players in their ranks. Those with an outside chance included the improving Tankerness, and Firth who had this year won the 'B' League. St Ola had also got themselves organised again so it would be interesting to see what they had to offer.

First round Results

Stromness	0	Tankerness	5
Tankerness	4	Stromness	0
Harray	6	Stenness	0

Second leg not reported.

Harray go through

Orphir	2	Deerness	2
Deerness	5	Orphir	3
St Ola	1	Birsay	3
Birsay	3	St Ola	3

No real surprises except perhaps, the elimination of St Ola by Birsay. Cup holders Shapinsay now appeared in the quarter finals, where a major shock awaited them.

Quarter final Results

Firth	1	St Mgts Hope	3
St Mgts Hope	2	Firth	1
Tankerness	2	Shapinsay	1
Shapinsay	2	Tankerness	1

Replay:

Tankerness	2	Shapinsay	1
Deerness	0	Holm	6
Holm	1	Deerness	0

Birsay v Harray
No reports. Harray go through.

So Shapinsay were out but Tankerness could now be considered real contenders. Unfortunately, gaps in Press coverage meant no result from Birsay v Harray.

The same problem cropped up with the first semi final between St Margaret's Hope and Holm but it was Holm who moved into the final.

Despite the absence of statistics, the contest was not without incident. One of Orkney's best known footballers, former Scottish junior internationalist Willie Smith, playing for St Margaret's Hope, got into an altercation with referee Simister who was once again holidaying in Orkney. As a result of this difference of opinion, Mr Simister ended up on his back. Willie was sent off and had to be restrained by several spectators.

Following very formal proceedings at O.F.A. headquarters on August 10, the player was suspended 'for an indefinite period.' However, on April 12 the next year, the O.F.A. received a letter from Willie Smith requesting that the suspension be lifted. The happy outcome for the player was that, 'after lengthy discussion, it was agreed the suspension be raised.'

The first leg of the second semi final saw seasoned campaigners Harray take a 2-0 lead at home against Tankerness. But in the return, they were made to fight all the way against their up and coming rivals.

For this game, *The Orkney Herald* reporter was down in Tankerness lapping up the atmosphere and it is worth including the first part of his report to experience the feeling of a big game played on a country ground at this time.

"These twenty two Orkneymen played fast and fearless football, with no quarter asked and none given. Though hard and tough, with plenty of old fashioned shoulder charging,

Those with long memories might argue that this was the best Orkney team of all time. In 1949 they won the Arthur Shield and Milne Cup. Back row, left to right, Bill Sim, Arnold Rendall, Jock Cursiter. Middle, Jim Donaldson, Davo Fox, John Donaldson, Jackie Hutchison, Magnus ('Mugga') Tait. Front, Russell Croy, Freddie Hutchison, Arthur Dainty.

(Picture: Orkney Library)

Birth, Blood

and there was nothing vicious and no dirty play. A treat to watch. Always up with the game, Jimmy Leys had an easy task.

"But it took four footballs to finish the game.

"Two minutes before half time the egg shaped football, surprising how many there are in Orkney, grew suddenly more egg shaped and a light coloured growth sprouted on it when airborne. A loud report and the ball lay burst at the players' feet. Consternation. But someone kicked another ball on to the field. Alas it was a boys' ball (size 4) and referee Leys blew his whistle pointing to the Harray bus. However, neither Tankerness nor Harray wanted to abandon the match and two motor cyclists and a motorist sped eastwards for another ball.

"'Winder whar the nearest ball is?'

"'At the Mull Head,' wise cracked the wag.

"Twelve minutes later the motorist was back but the football he brought was soft. Nevertheless, the game got underway. Then one of the speedway riders appeared, with steam literally rising from his bike. Never mind, he had a football (the fourth in the game) that was both hard and round.

"The bevy of East and West Mainland pin up girls shivered in their summer dresses and bare legs on the touch line, longing for the game to end so that the inevitable following dance could be got going.

"A grand night for football. There was little wind and a heavy dew fell while the sky to the west changed colour every few minutes and the aromatic smell of peat reek delicately scented the evening air.

"Old cars and shining new models (and motor bikes) lined the main Kirk wall to Deerness road and interested spectators from every quarter, including the Holm team, there to study their opponents and plan

accordingly, watched the game … "
After all that, the reporter then told the story of the game!

It was a fine match with Harray winning 3-2. Goals for Tankerness were scored by Easton Clark and Jackie Tait, while Jackie Hutchison (2) and Willie Adamson netted for Harray.

Easton Clark was mentioned as the outstanding Tankerness player but when describing Harray centre half Freddie Hutchison's performance, Cubbie Roo was fulsome in his praise: " … He must have broken the Tankerness forwards' hearts. His positional sense was uncanny, he cleared equally well with either foot, invariably keeping the ball in play, and his heading too was first class. In fact he seemed to read his opponents' minds."

Tankerness had lost this splendid contest but would be a team for the future. For interest, their line up was as follows: Arnold Rendall; Charlie Paterson and Archie Clark; Freddie Shearer, Billy Gorn and Davie Bews; Davie Garrioch, Easton Clark, Jackie

Tait, Robbie Pottinger and Davie Kemp.

One last point to note. The referee was Jimmy Leys, one of Orkney's most respected officials and like all good refs, played his part by keeping a quiet but firm grip of the game. Something to bear in mind in the light of forthcoming events!

The report ended with the author remarking that "Holm and Harray should provide the fans with the most stirring Parish Cup Final for years."

Well, the word 'stirring' does not begin to do justice to the first final held on County Show night, one that will long live in the memory of those present as one of the most infamous matches ever to have been played in Orkney.

This was to be Cubbie Roo's last cup final report, and as a piece of descriptive writing, it takes some beating. Rather than trying to edit or summarise a masterpiece, here now is the unabridged story of the 1949 final in its full glory. Sit back and savour every kick!

HOLM: PARISH CUP WINNERS, 1949

'Everything But Murder'

Roughest, Toughest "Parish Cup" Ever

Holm 2, Harray 0.   By CUBBIE ROO

"Everything but murder," was how one disgusted spectator summed up this Holm-Harray Parish Cup final in the Bignold Park on County Show night. "A disgrace to Orkney" was another's verdict. Never – in my quarter century's experience of Orkney football – have I seen the like.

Early on the game gradually got out of hand and the longer it went the rougher and tougher it became.

It was "dynamite." The teams were twelve minutes late in taking the field – there was no ball – but after what transpired later it would have been just as well if none had been found.

Every man, wife and bairn who could was present to yell their particular team to victory.

IN A NUTSHELL

There was no good football – no sustained, on-the-ground, triangular, up-the-wing, movements – no running into the open space. Instead men were knocked over holus-bolus – were tripped up – the legs clicked from under them – kicked intentionally, when the ball was nowhere near – there was pushing with the hand – scoring a goal with both hands – taking "the poots" – deliberately kicking the ball out of the park – a linesman leaving the field in disgust.

Still I suppose we must be thankful that there were no six-shooters fired – no bowie-knives drawn – no knuckle dusters used – no bottles thrown – nobody killed.

IRONIC

And to think that the collection – £112 16s 6d – at this roughest, toughest football fracas ever was for a footballer accidentally hurt playing the game.

Harray actually had the better team, but defeated themselves. Holm won by two goals to nil – the first scored from a penalty for a most dangerous tackle, the second – just outside the box – from a free-kick, also for most dangerous play.

Dave Flett threw away the game for Harray.

Every man played till the last drop of sweat. For Holm, John Firth has never done better; for Harray Freddy Hutchison stood out, but long before the end of the second half I felt sorry for Freddy – a fine sportsman.

UNBELIEVABLE

Territorially Harray had most of the game, but the prehistoric methods of some of their players had to be seen to be believed. Naturally the Holm boys had to retaliate, and if they had not been big, fast and strong, they must surely have gone under. Arthur Dainty and Davie Moss must be sore yet.

Ask any town or country football fan, "What is the most important match in the Orkney football calendar?" and the answer – without a doubt – will be, "The Parish Cup Final."

True, the inter-county against Shetland is THE MATCH of the year, but for interest, drama, speed, hard-knocks given and taken without a whimper – for excitement, tension and "pulling power," the Parish Cup final has every other game "licked to a frazzle."

But this year's 90-minute thriller – an East versus West fight – the final of all finals – was a disgrace to Orkney, enough to make all Orkney-born folk hide their heads in shame.

If you are a visitor you will never forget this island football "epic." Alas, you will have seen nothing like it in the length and breadth of Scotland. There was precious little football, but for sheer guts, grit, determination, the will-to-win (at all costs), the ability to take hard knocks and carry on – and, unfortunately, for rough play – this game was on a plane by itself.

And to think what it might have been.

Orkney Football Association will have to do something drastic – and that at once – if they are to control football in Orkney.

THE GAME

Englishman Arthur Dainty – Holm's popular, "naturalised Orkneyman" and only "Ferrylouper" of the twenty-two – wins the toss and makes Agmond Flett's boys kick-off against hill and wind.

The East Mainlanders at once carry the ball to Nelson Murray's end and the capacity crowd – happily the entire collection is to go to the injured "Pie" Flett – are on tenter-hooks, certain of "fireworks" for this is the Parish Cup final and anything may happen.

Man goes to man without thought of the circumstances. Players are bowled over like nine-pins, but come up smiling, ready again for the fight. Surprisingly enough, nobody is injured. And except when the ball is out of play, the frenzied pace is kept up continuously.

THE DANGER MEN

With the slope and wind, Holm have the advantage, but Freddy Hutchison is looking after lanky John Hepburn and Arthur Dainty is shadowed by Sam Flett, brother of Agmond and Dave.

The other danger-man on the field is Orkney's inside-left, Jacky Hutchison, but quiet, unobtrusive, "stuggold" Dave Pottinger is in close attendance. Where Jacky goes, Dave is sure to follow – only the Holm half is no lamb.

Finstown's Eric Walter, as is his wont, coaches Harra' from the touchline.

Nelson Murray, the West 'keeper, is getting plenty to do.

From the top-goal comes the once-upon-a-time familiar battle-cry, "Hard lines, hard lines, beastly hard lines." "Desperate Dan" is here again, specially for the occasion.

PENALTY

In the seventeenth minute Arthur Dainty has the legs savagely knocked from under him by Dave Flett, and hits the ground like a meteor. Breathless silence. Will Arthur conquer his weakness to loft over the cross-bar? Straight as an arrow from the spot the ball flies past the petrified Murray – into the back of the net.

And the Holm cheers must have been heard at St Mary's.

Holm 1, Harray 0

HE DIDN'T SEE THIS ONE

Three minutes later – Harray are on the attack – big Jacky Hutchison is held in Holm's penalty area by centre-half David Moss. The big fellow appeals to referee Mears but Jock's whistle must be muted for there isn't a toot.

At the other end John Hepburn races through, but good old Agmond dashes across – from nowhere – and averts danger.

Running like a whippet, "Abbie" Sutherland makes Holm hearts beat faster but his parting shot sails high and wide over the bar.

John Firth in Holm's goal is right on his toes.

Harray fight back – nearly give as good as they get – but the interval arrives with Holm still holding their slender one-goal-to-nil lead.

Will it be enough to stop the bustling West Mainland team after the turn-round?

SECOND HALF

Only four minutes of the second-half have gone when the long-striding John Hepburn is through – but a free-kick is given Harray.

At Firth's end young Willie Sinclair has a great chance, when close in, but sends past.

THIS LOOKS A GOOD GOAL

In the fifty-fourth minute John Bill Garrioch sprints up the right wing with the Harray defence haring after him, but John Bill keeps in front – cuts in for goal – and, from twenty yards, lets rip a "snorter" that travels away from Murray all the time and ends up in the net.

Tremendous cheers. The whistle blows. But what is this? Linesman Dave Walker runs on to the pitch, waving his red flag, danger for Holm. Referee Jock Mears changes his mind and John Bill's goal is wiped-off. Holm supporters howl consternation.

DAVE FLETT'S SECOND BLUNDER

In the sixty-first minute left-back Dave Flett – nothing but a bull-dozer can stop him – again sends Arthur Dainty summersaulting.

Rubbing his hands, Arthur prepares to take the free-kick – from about twenty yards out.

The wind is troublesome – blows the ball downhill, so Arthur gives a dig with his heel and places the ball.

(Linesman Jimmy Leys waves his flag – runs on to the pitch and speaks to the referee).

Midst tense excitement Arthur takes his kick and the ball flies goalwards, Maurice Manson and John Hepburn cottoning-on, Maurice turning it past the 'keeper into the net. The crowd roar.

Holm 2, Harray 0

All this time Leys has been on the field speaking to Mears. Now he flings up his arms in disgust – runs across field – speaks to linesman Dave Walker – again throws up his arms – ducks under the wire and disappears.

PETER RUNS THE LINE

Jock Mears hands the red flag to Orkney Football Association Vice-President Peter Thomson, ex-county player and ex-referee. The game proceeds.

The wind rises. Browned-off, Jacky Hutchison tries to see how far out of the field he can kick the ball. Has another go or two. Agmond goes forward and does his level best to score, but there is always a Holm body, or leg or foot to block the ball. Harray swarm round John Firth, but the white-jerseyed 'keeper is having his best game ever and do what they will – they make the mistake of trying to walk the ball into the net – the Harray boys can't beat him.

DISALLOWED GOAL

In the seventy-seventh minute "Bobbo" Hutchison – who also has tried to see how far he can kick out of field – at last gets the leather past Firth. There is feverish Harray excitement but unfortunately for the West Mainland side, "Bobbo" has pushed the ball over the line with both hands.

It is getting dark. Two Harray corners on end and just on time Jack Hutchison, from close quarters, balloons high and far over the woodwork.

The whistle blows. Holm have won the roughest, toughest, inter-Parish Cup final ever, without having had a goal scored against them in the competition. Strangely, nobody has been killed, and all twenty-two players are actually able to walk off the pitch – all in one piece.

Teams:

Holm – John Firth; Ian Manson and Bob Hepburn; Dave Pottinger, Davie Moss and Ernie Smith; John Bill Garrioch, Maurice Manson, John Hepburn, Arthur Dainty (captain) and "Abbie" Sutherland.

Harray – Nelson Murray; Agmond Flett (captain) and Dave Flett; Sam Flett, Freddy Hutchison and Jim Sinclair; "Tim" Johnstone, "Bobbo" Hutchison, Willie Sinclair, Jacky Hutchison and Willie Adamson.

Referee – Jock Mears; linesmen – Dave Walker, Jimmy Leys and Peter Thomson.

The cup went east in 1949, to Holm. Back row, left to right, Ronnie Aim, Gordon Muir, Ian Manson, John Firth, Bob Hepburn, Roy Bichan. Middle, John Bill Garrioch, Maurice Manson, John Hepburn, Arthur Dainty, Albert Sutherland. Front, Dave Pottinger, Dave Moss, Ernie Smith.
(Picture: Orkney Library)

END PIECE

The crowd collects at the pavillion and in a few minutes big Bill Barrack, O.F.A. honorary treasurer, appears with the magnificent cup, accompanied by Arthur Dainty. In a perfect speech, William hands over the cup. Arthur says he is glad Holm have won. Three cheers are called for Harray – and justly given. But there is not one member of the Harray team present at the ceremony – to call for three cheers for Holm.

Little knots of enthusiasts – fans, four "whistlers" and your reporter – gather outside the pavilion. Loud, long and heated are the arguments until at length, exasperated, Inspector James Cormack "breaks up the crowd" and orders them home.

****

"ARTHUR'S ACT"

In answer to a flood of queries, "Cubbie Roo" states that there is no mention of "digging with the heel" in any of the 17 Laws of football. – Editor.

****

Dounby F.C. 1948. Although the members of this uncompromising looking outfit would be divided between Harray, Birsay and Sandwick for parish duty, a number of them helped form the nucleus of Harray's team in the 1949 epic and "murderous" Parish Cup final. Back row, left to right, Agmond Flett, Jock Spence, Freddie Hutchison, Herbert "Hibby" Spence, Dave Flett, Jim Stockan. Front. Davie Shearer, Willie Spence, Teddy Brown, Jackie Hutchison and Willie Adamson.
(Picture: Orkney Library)

David Horne, alias The Orkney Herald football correspondent 'Cubbie Roo', was a fine player in his own right. In this picture of Kirkwall Butchers' winning Trades Cup team of 1934, he is standing far left on the back row. The full team line up is back row, left to right, David Horne, George Newlands, Tommy Thomson, Fred Copland, Frank Forbes, Sandy Heddle, Jocky Sinclair. Front. Willie Foulis, Billy Jolly, Toddo Borwick, Ian Smith and "Chuffy" Muir.
(Picture: Orkney Library)

The 50s

1950: Showdown No. 2 in final clash

Once you have got your breath back after taking all that in, I will go on to tell how events unravelled the next year. But first a little follow up to the evening of cup final chaos.

When some of the dust had settled, the O.F.A. received a letter from the referee Mr Mears indicating that the linesman, Mr Leys, was guilty of infringing the Rules of Football by leaving his position without the referee's permission.

An extract from the O.F.A. Minutes read as follows:

"After full discussion, the committee decided (Mr Wm. Firth, West Mainland representative dissenting,) that Mr Leys be suspended from acting as referee or linesman for the remainder of the season."

As far as the handling and overall control of the match was concerned, the committee also agreed to put this matter on the agenda for the next A.G.M. However at the meeting the following February no mention was made whatsoever.

It must be assumed therefore, that the only person to receive any form of censure for these events was the linesman who couldn't bear to watch any more.

So that was the official line. What would have been the reaction 'on the street' to happenings on County Show night? No doubt, whenever groups of folk met, whether on street corners, at the mart on Monday, at Harvest Homes … maybe even coming out of the kirk, the topic of conversation would have been 'the game.' Incidents would have been magnified in the telling, characters would have acquired the status of legend and the language would have been found

wanting as folk sought appropriate words to describe the encounter.

But the passing of nine months or so gives people the time to get over traumatic events so when the football season kicked off in April, 1950, all supporters were looking forward to another Parish Cup competition … with maybe extra anticipation at what the draw would produce.

What would be missing this year were eagerly anticipated 'Cubbie Roo' reports. The writer, David Horne, had now emigrated to Australia where he set up home in Frankston, Victoria, and began to work as an estate agent. His home would, in years to come, provide a base for quite a number of emigrating Orcadians to help them get established in the new country.

Although he had only contributed sports reports to *The Orkney Herald* for a matter of three years, they were such as to ensure for their author, everlasting fame in his homeland.

Whether by coincidence or not, the first round cup games went unreported this year apart from the tie between Shapinsay and Orphir.

A shock appeared imminent when Orphir, inspired by Jock Cursiter and 'Tich' Findlay, secured a 4-1 lead at home, the goals coming from Eoin Clouston (2) and Arthur Groundwater (2). Over 100 Orphir fans, hitherto starved of Parish Cup success, travelled to Shapinsay for the return, their hearts filled with optimism. Alas, they were dealt an unkindly blow. Shapinsay, with both Bruce and Measun back in the team after missing the first leg, rallied in style and overturned the deficit, winning 4-0.

They took their place in the quarter final where they would meet Holm who again avoided Harray in the draw.

Quarter final Results

Holm	2	Shapinsay	1
Shapinsay	2	Holm	5
Harray	4	Birsay	1
Birsay	1	Harray	4
Firth	5	Tankerness	1
Tankerness	3	Firth	4
Deerness	0	Sandwick	0

Second leg not reported. Sandwick go through.

The 'big two' were safely through after emphatic wins, as were Firth who had a remarkable win over Tankerness. McDonald Cup holders Deerness could not repeat their 'B' League form and were eliminated.

The draw for the semi finals was awaited with bated breath … Harray and Holm were kept apart! What possibilities existed now!

Holm kept the prospects of a repeat final alive by overcoming Firth but not without an early struggle. After a 2-2 draw, the champions found their top gear and went through after a 4-0 win in the home leg. Now for Harray!

In the opening leg, the Sandwick resistance was finally overpowered and goals by Jackie and Bobby Hutchison and two by new centre forward Tommy Drever who, according to 'Corinthian' in *The Orcadian*, "rumbled them up with his rushing tactics", saw Harray take a 4-1 lead. The second leg was now a formality, Harray winning 5-1.

So there it was again! Surely fate had dealt a hand and brought these adversaries back for renewed hostilities on Orkney's biggest night of the year. But let us pause, and weigh up the chances of a repeat of last year's 'pitched battle'.

If a recent Dounby v Thorfinn match in the 'A' League was anything to go by, the omens were not good. It had been another bruising encounter where Dave Flett of Dounby and Dave Keldie of Thorfinn had been

Birth, Blood

sent off for fighting and the whole situation had been exacerbated by individuals in the crowd trying to incite aggression on the field.

Nothing new in that you might think, but it was enough for concern to be expressed by sports correspondents who believed the O.F.A. was too lenient in dealing with these matters. The only action taken regarding the above match was that referee Jock Mears had been banned from officiating again in Dounby, while the Dounby linesman had been suspended. No action had been taken to sort out feuding players and one letter writer believed that "football was dying on its feet through indiscipline and spectators were voting with their feet."

All this in the days leading up to the return meeting between Harray and Holm, where the bulk of the Harray team would be made up of players from Dounby. The waters were far from calm.

Conditions for the contest were dreadful.

After a lovely County Show day of sunshine and blue skies, the rain simply poured down making the pitch very greasy and the goal areas a sea of mud. Ideal for sliding tackles!

But there was no sign of 'voting with the feet.' Far from it! Despite the weather, a crowd of around 2,000 saw the following teams take the field:

Harray: Maurice Johnston; Agmond Flett and Willie Sinclair; Jim Sinclair, Dave Flett and Willie Adamson; Leslie Flett, Bobby Hutchison, Tommy Drever, Jackie Hutchison and Andrew Adamson.

Holm: Roy Bichan; Dave Pottinger and Bob Hepburn; Mackie Grieve, Davie Moss and Ernie Smith; Maurice Manson, Jim Kirkness, John Hepburn, Arthur Dainty and Abbie Sutherland.

Referee: D.Walker, Kirkwall.

Both teams introduced some new young players, Holm fielding junior inter county goalkeeper Roy Bichan while Harray played, for the first time, Andrew Adamson, and another junior inter county 'cap', Leslie Flett on the right wing.

Holm attacked from kick off and within five minutes had taken the lead when Sutherland's shot from distance skidded off the surface past Johnston into the net.

As the first half went on, Harray's potentially dangerous forwards were being well held by the Holm defence, while Harray defenders found the conditions hard to deal with. They slithered around in the mud conceding corners, and from one of these, Manson crossed for John Hepburn to smash home Holm's second goal.

The rain eased a little after half time. Now playing down the slope, Holm went on the offensive again and John Hepburn ran through to make the score 3-0. Harray did not give up and pressure in the Holm goalmouth resulted in Pottinger putting past his own keeper. 3-1.

A brilliant solo goal by Dainty was then ruled out due to Manson being offside. Despite good efforts at both ends, there was no further scoring, which meant Holm had retained the cup.

Outstanding for the winners were Bob Hepburn, Moss and Grieve in defence with Manson and John Hepburn the top attackers. Dainty had, as usual, been the general and at the heart of all his team's best moves. Harray had never really got going and their skilful players had

The 1950 winners, Holm. Back row, left to right, Dave Pottinger, Roy Bichan, Robert Hepburn. Middle, Maurice Manson, Jim Kirkness, John Hepburn, Arthur Dainty, Albert Sutherland. Front, Mackie Grieve, Dave Moss, Ernie Smith. (Picture: Orkney Library)

found the tight marking and slippery surface difficult to deal with.

Now where, you must be asking, was the controversy?

Well, remarkably, there was none!

"Watchman", who had replaced 'Cubbie Roo' at *The Orkney Herald*, stated that it was one of the *cleanest* finals ever played. There were no incidents and those expecting a 'rough house' were disappointed.

Great credit was bestowed on both teams for forgetting last year's unpleasantness and 'playing in the true spirit of sportsmanship.' There was not a deliberate foul in the match and handshakes were exchanged at the end.

Mr Bill Barrack, treasurer of the O.F.A., handed the cup to Arthur Dainty, captain of Holm, who called for three cheers for the losers. Bobby Hutchison, Harray's captain, in turn congratulated Holm and called for three cheers for the winners.

Atonement was complete!

1951: Harray finally break Holm

Officials of Orkney Football Association had come under fire last year for failing to curb indiscipline and doing little to promote the interests of the game. Maybe they would have restored their tattered image in 1951 if they had followed the example set by Kirkwall's senior clubs who decided that *coaching*, and *high profile coaching* at that, was the way ahead.

In conjunction with the *Daily Record* newspaper, a party of professional footballers was booked to visit Orkney in the middle of May to give demonstrations and hold sessions with both Orkney's established and promising players. Evening shows lasting two and a half hours were fixed for Stromness Town Hall, Garrison Theatre at Hatston, and Harray Hall while, during the daytime, 'hands on' coaching

for senior and junior players was scheduled to take place.

The outlay facing the Kirkwall clubs for this initiative was considerable because the party included three current Scottish internationalists, Jerry Dawson and Willie Thornton of Rangers and George Aitken of East Fife, whose services would not come cheap. However, they gambled on big crowds paying to attend all the evening shows.

To an extent their faith was vindicated. Packed houses were the order of the day in Stromness and twice in Kirkwall but sadly the show in Harray, where, it was expected that the country players would attend, was a flop. There was only a meagre attendance and the dance to follow had to be cancelled.

The explanation? Either it was a fine May evening where farm work took precedence or … some of the country players had already attended the town shows or … the parish players simply couldn't be bothered with any coaching.

Talented Orkney player, Jim 'Dook' Donaldson, centre, receives coaching as some well known local footballing faces look on intently.
(Picture: Orkney Library)

Birth, Blood

However, reluctant learners were not getting off that easily. Anticipating that coaching was the flavour of the times, *The Orkney Herald* capitalised by launching a weekly pictorial series showing famous players of the day demonstrating the skills of football. Entitled simply 'How To Play Football', it was aimed at anyone interested in the art but principally at beginners or those at the lower end of the skill range.

Week 1, for instance, was 'How to play the short pass'; a few frames of illustration, some straight forward instructions and a message at the end: it is much more effective than a lob in the air.

The series continued for the rest of the summer and most of next, so spectators looked forward eagerly to seeing results on the field of play. They must have felt that Orkney's top level players were picking up some tips because the senior inter county side carried on their winning way, defeating both Caithness and Shetland with a bit to spare. But what of football at grass roots level? Would there be a new array of skills on offer in the Parish Cup, for instance?

Well, the big surprise was the small number of entries for this year's competition; only seven compared to twelve last year. No teams were submitted from such staunch parishes as Sandwick, St Margaret's Hope, Birsay, Orphir or Firth.

The first round saw Deerness, who had now plucked up courage and followed Holm's example by entering a team in the 'A' League, come up against Stenness; Tankerness, whose growing strength was shown by their ability to field both a regular 'B' team and junior team, were drawn against Shapinsay; while Harray, still smarting from their fourth cup final defeat in a row, would play Stromness. Champions Holm received a bye.

Quarter final Results

Stenness	0	Deerness	2
Deerness	4	Stromness	1
Tankerness	5	Shapinsay	0
Shapinsay	1	Tankerness	1
Stromness	1	Harray	5
Harray	3	Stromness	0

Now, if Holm and Harray could be kept apart in the semi final, it was just possible that … yes, they were kept apart! A third Harray v Holm final in a row was now a distinct possibility.

Holm set about fulfilling their part of the equation by walloping Deerness 5-0 in the semi final, first leg. The return game was not reported but no matter, Holm were back in the final looking for a hat trick of wins.

Harray had a much harder task on their hands, but were still too strong for Tankerness. Both games were close with Harray emerging 2-1 winners on each occasion.

So there it was. The same teams back for a third consecutive duel on County Show night and this year Harray would be desperate to prevent yet another stumble at the final hurdle. Conscious of the need for improvement, they continued to feed young players in to their team and this year, newcomers at this level were Jim Isbister and Brian Flett, brother of Leslie, who made his debut last year.

Unfortunately Harray were unable to play Freddie Hutchison, described earlier by 'Watchman' in *The Orkney Herald*, as "the best centre half in the North of Scotland" The only parish Freddie could now play for was Shapinsay, where he was born at the home of his maternal grand parents. Now that he had joined the police, and no longer lived in Harray, he was unable to play for the same team as his brothers. Such was the rule at the time.

It was victorious Harray in 1951. Back row, left to right, Cecil Copland, Patty Chalmers, Leslie Johnston, Brian Flett, Sammy Flett. Middle, Jim Isbister, Jim Sinclair, Dave Flett, Willie Adamson, Andrew Adamson. Front, Bobby Hutchison, Leslie Flett, Jackie Hutchison.

(Picture: Orkney Library)

Holm were also able to call on the services of youth and this year, fielded two junior inter county players, Roy Bichan (playing this year at half back rather than goalkeeper) and Ian Allan.

Full teams were as follows:

Harray: Maurice Johnston; Jackie Chalmers and Brian Flett; Jim Sinclair, Dave Flett and Willie Adamson; Jim Isbister, Bobby Hutchison, Leslie Flett, Jackie Hutchison and Andrew Adamson.

Holm: John Firth; Ian Allan and Bob Hepburn; Roy Bichan, Davie Moss and Dave Pottinger; John Bill Garrioch, Jim Kirkness, Maurice Manson, Arthur Dainty and John Hepburn.

Referee: Dave Walker.

Another crowd of 2,000 plus assembled, this year on a fine night for football, and after ten minutes saw Holm take the lead when John Hepburn headed home a cross from the right by Kirkness, Harray retaliated strongly and Jackie Hutchison equalised with a hard low shot. End to end play continued until the interval but no more goals meant the score remained 1-1 at half time.

In the second half, sustained pressure by Harray eventually told and they took the lead when Allan, in attempting to clear, put it past his own goalkeeper. There was no let up and Leslie Flett made it three by sliding home a Bobby Hutchison lob.

According to *The Orcadian*, it had been a typical Parish Cup final with "plenty of hard hitting and plenty of weight being thrown about" but it was played in good spirit without any ill feeling. There were flashes of good football but generally, too little constructive play.

Few benefits of this year's coaching blitz had been in evidence!

For Harray, Jackie Hutchison played a fine game, using the ball intelligently and making effective use of the long pass. Bobby Hutchison, Leslie Flett and Willie Adamson had also caught the eye with good skill and positional play.

Goalkeeper Firth had been best for Holm who were also served by Moss, Bob Hepburn and Allan with Bichan a strong constructive right half. Dainty was orchestrator as usual but after playing *four* games that week seemed rather tired.

After so many cup final defeats, Harray's relief would have been immense and celebrations memorable. Dave Tinch, in his book about his childhood in Kirkwall, *The Shore and Roond Aboot*, recalls sitting on top of the Harray team's bus as they made their way home with the cup, then driving through the parish waving and cheering to people as they passed by. Eventually they stopped at Dunsyre, the home of Willie Firth, where a party was soon underway. I'll bet!

So another competition was over, but where were the missing teams?

Possibly all at home practising and re-practising all the latest coaching techniques before returning with a vengeance next year?

Much more likely they were taking part in the kind of social/sporting occasion described in the Stronsay news. In mid-July a large party crossed over Eday Sound in two Stronsay motor boats crewed by Messrs. Burgess and Messrs. Matches and Stout. No effort was spared to make the passengers comfortable. Canvas shelters and hoods were rigged up "for the health of the excursionists."

The result of the match was Stronsay 2 Eday 1, but that was by the way! Much more important was the evening of "social intercourse" which followed. Dancing in the public hall was enjoyed until early morning before "any thought of returning occurred to the visitors."

That's the answer! More entries from the isles next year with plenty of opportunity for 'social intercourse.' That would be sure to get the teams flooding back!

A happy Stronsay side from the 1950s. Back row, left to right, Rob Stevenson, Bobby Miller, Colin Stevenson, Colin Cooper, Peter Rendall, Sidney Swanney. Front, John Stout, John Reid, Francis Williamson, John Dennison, John Fiddler. *(Picture: Orkney Library)*

1952:
Shapinsay's cradle of despair

There is nothing to beat a game of football for playing havoc with your emotions. It can provide periods of joy and elation when your team is winning but, just as quickly, it can induce feelings of disappointment and despair when you realise the good old days do not last forever.

Such an experience would now be confronting the good people of Holm. Having lived through some wonderful times in the past three years, three cup finals, including two victories, they now began to suspect that the glory days were behind them. Their parish team's success had been founded on a regular 'A' League team, but this year, all of a sudden they were unable to field a team at all, 'A' or 'B'.

The great side had begun to disintegrate.

Several players went south to live and work, while emigration, which was to become a significant factor in the islands and parishes as the decade proceeded, claimed two of the team. Bob Hepburn left for Vancouver in Canada and Jack Seatter went to Australia where, sadly, he was killed in a car crash a short time later. Holm would manage a parish team this year but it would be a shadow of its former self.

But, just as one team descends from its lofty position, so the pendulum swings and another moves upwards to take its place. Showing every sign of being heirs to the throne were near neighbours Tankerness. Here, very significant developments were taking place.

Just as Holm had dropped their league team, so Tankerness entered theirs in the 'A' League … under the new name 'St Andrews'. The old name of Tankerness was absorbed in the all embracing parish name, which also included the district of Toab. Previously, people had been disinclined to use the parish name particularly as their mail tended to be directed to a coastal golfing resort in Fife. But now, at the dawn of a new era, they agreed that it was worth taking the risk.

The evidence that St Andrews would be strong contenders for this year's Parish Cup was provided in their first two league games where, with a team of exclusively home grown players, they drew 1-1 with Rovers and defeated a strong Hotspur team. St Andrews fans were starting to feel the first stirrings of happiness.

An improved entry of ten teams was submitted for this year's competition and as the first round approached it was noticeable that there had been a change in the climate of Orkney football. Gone, appeared to be the days of 'pitch battles' and vendettas between teams. Rough play was scarcely evident and 'Corinthian' in *The Orcadian* was moved to write "Orkney football has taken quite a turn this year. Games are played in a far more friendly atmosphere and teams are accepting defeat in a sporting manner. This is to the benefit of the game. Now, if the remaining player - abusing spectators would cease, or stay away from needle games, there will be even better feeling and better entertainment."

If anyone was thirsting for soccer violence this year, they would have had to resort to reading 'Stenwick Stories' by R.T. Johnston where the 'fictitious' cup-tie between Harray and Stenwick bore an uncanny similarity to recent actual jousts on the field of play. An acrimonious contest came to a climax when Goliath Flett of Harray decided to take revenge on P.C. Timothy Cursiter, a left back of Stenwick, who had previously charged him for cycling with no lights. The 'revenge' had left Cursiter lying on the ground in agony complaining of a broken back. Fearing he may have gone too far, Flett yanked him to his feet, then declared reassuringly, "If thee back wis brocken, thoo wid fall doon again."

Two games were played in this year's first round, one producing a runaway win, the other a tense, thrilling cup tie.

First round Results

St Andrews	9	Deerness	1

Deerness scratched

Shapinsay	4	Harray	3
Harray	4	Shapinsay	3

Replay

Shapinsay	3	Harray	2

The 600 plus spectators who saw the replay witnessed a display of great sportsmanship and at the end winners were heartily congratulated by the losers. Even the referee, Dave Fox, a Thorfinn diehard who had been involved in many a battle with Dounby, was congratulated by the Harray players on the handling of the game. There was certainly a new spirit abroad!

This result meant that the 1952 final would be the first since 1938, not to feature a Harray team.

So, it was on to the quarter finals with both Shapinsay and St Andrews bearing the stamp of 'favourites' although Firth, once again 'B' League winners this year, might provide stiff opposition. Of their players, it was felt that junior inter county goalkeeper Stewart Craigie and brothers, Jim and Billy Wilson, would do well in 'A' League football. A promising youngster Denis Aim, was described in *The Orcadian* as a "veritable box of tricks."

Quarter final Results

St Andrews	8	Evie	0

Evie scratched

Holm	3	Firth	3
Firth	3	Holm	2

Shapinsay	6	Stenness	0
Stenness	0	Shapinsay	4

Birsay	4	St Ola	5
St Ola	6	Birsay	2

There was no doubt that St Andrews were putting the 'scares' into the opposition, Evie being the second team not to appear for a return leg. Meanwhile Shapinsay also looked to be finding top gear. These two strong teams were kept apart by the semi final draw.

Semi final Results

Stronsay	1	St Ola	0
St Ola	3	Shapinsay	4

Firth	0	St Andrews	3
St Andrews	4	Firth	0

A fascinating contest was now in prospect between a team who had last won the cup in 1948 and a 'new' parish appearing in their first ever final. Having a goal scoring ratio of 24:1 in four games, St Andrews were full of confidence; as were Shapinsay, who felt they had their best team in years. As for the supporters? Both sets were brimful of anticipation but as always, one lot were fated to come away with hopes and dreams extinguished.

It was another huge crowd of enthusiasts who arrived on County Show night, hoping for a great game. They, were not to be disappointed although the dismal weather reduced the opportunities for skilful play. A heavy mist hung over the field and rain fell intermittently as the following teams lined up:

Shapinsay: Jim Sinclair; Sammy Bews and Reuben Johnston; Bob Sinclair, Freddie Hutchison and Jim Hepburn; Billy Barnett, Percy Foubister, Billy Mainland, Bunny Bruce and Johnny Bews.

St Andrews: Billy Gorn; Freddie Shearer and Dave Pottinger; Archie Clark, Robbie Pottinger and Jackie Tait; Bryan Clark, Easton Clark, Alton Tait, Zander Bews and Andy Shearer.

Referee: Dave Walker.

St Andrews won the toss and played up the slope with the wind behind and within a minute had taken the lead when Bews shot through a crowd of players into the net. Roars of delight greeted the goal and St Andrews continued to surge forward, their light forward line finding the treacherous underfoot conditions more to their liking. However, the Shapinsay defence with goalkeeper Sinclair, Bews and Hutchison outstanding, gave little away.

Midway through the half, Shapinsay appeared to have equalised when Bunny Bruce, by far the oldest player on the field at 38, went through the middle, beat the keeper, and placed the ball in the net. However, much to Shapinsay's consternation, the goal was chopped off by the linesman, who indicated to the referee that Bruce had handled before scoring. No amount of remonstrating, including Bunny pointing out the guttery mark on his jersey where he had controlled the ball, would alter the ref's mind. So half time arrived with the score 1-0 to St Andrews.

End to end football continued in the second half but no more goals were added until ten minutes before the end when a sweeping move brought the decisive strike from Andy Shearer. That was the end of the scoring and St Andrews, at their first attempt, had lifted the Parish Cup.

Their outstanding team work was praised, together with brilliant performances from brothers, Robbie and Dave Pottinger, the latter now having won the Parish Cup medals with both Holm and St Andrews. Easton Clark and 17 year old junior inter county player Alton Tait, had been the pick of a mobile forward line.

The cup was handed over to Easton Clark, captain of the winning team,

St Andrews F.C., winners of the Parish Cup, 1952. Back row, left to right, Sinclair Groat, John Bews, Freddie Shearer, Billy Gorn, Davie Pottinger, Jim Turner, Sandy Aldie. Middle, Bryan Clark, Easton Clark, Alton Tait, Zander Bews, Andy Shearer. Front, Archie Clark, Robbie Pottinger, Jackie Tait.
(Picture: Orkney Library)

who called for three cheers for the losers. In this year of exemplary sportsmanship, Bunny Bruce returned the compliment and it was heartily endorsed by the large assembled crowd at the Bignold Park pavilion.

Without a doubt, St Andrews' decision to commit to an 'A' team had been responsible for this result. Their comparatively young group of players would surely now look forward to many more successes in years to come.

St Andrews team and supporters would be able to bask in the warm glow of victory but it was a downcast Shapinsay crowd who sailed home that night. So buoyed up had they been, and confident of winning, that a mesh 'cradle' had been constructed in which to hoist the spoils of battle, the Parish Cup, to the mast head of the m.v. *Iona*. Alas, the cradle still hung there, forlorn and empty!

Ah! There's nothing that can take you down to earth quite like a game of football!

Jim Sinclair, Shapinsay's young keeper shown here with the Parish Cup (from another year), had an outstanding game in the 1952 final.

1953:
St Ola goal scoring machine

Happily the Shapinsay folk did not languish in the doldrums for too long and next year bounced back stronger than ever. For the first time the islanders entered a 'B' League team in the hope that regular football would enhance their teamwork. A very sound team it proved to be which led the league from start to finish, only to be pipped at the post on the very last game by Hotspur 'B'. But, they were serious contenders for the Parish Cup this year all right!

So too were St Andrews and Harray, with Firth worth an outside bet. The winners, however, were to emerge from an unexpected source but as the tournament neared its climax, our old friend *controversy* reared his ugly head again.

To begin with everything was very straightforward. Ten teams again came forward and the opening round saw some of the strongest sides in opposition.

First round Results

Shapinsay	2	Harray	3
Harray	2	Shapinsay	1
Firth	1	St Ola	5
St Ola	5	Firth	1

Harray had bounced back strong as ever to end Shapinsay's hopes while St Ola looked well equipped in the goal scoring department as they outclassed Firth. As we shall see, this form continued in the quarter-finals.

Quarter final Results

Orphir	2	Harray	4
Harray	2	Orphir	0
St Ola	8	Stenness	1
Stenness	1	St Ola	5
St Mgts Hope	3	St Andrews	4
St Andrews	1	St Mgts Hope	0
Holm	6	Deerness	1

Deerness scratched

There now appeared to be three teams in real contention for the top prize, although Holm, who had not been tested against Deerness, might yet have something left in the tank. After all, they could still call upon Arthur Dainty. As it happened, both semi finals produced memorable cup ties with only a single goal separating the teams at the end.

Semi final Results

Holm	4	Harray	1
Harray	6	Holm	2
St Andrews	1	St Ola	3
St Ola	4	St Andrews	5

So, it was a repeat of the 1947 final won by St Ola in a high scoring contest. It had been a controversial match distinguished by the number of fouls committed and the awarding of no less than four penalties. Would this game be any different?

The lead up to the final was not promising … or *promising* … depending what you were looking for. In fact, according to 'Watchman' in *The Orkney Herald*, the match was nearly not played at all as Harray threatened to go on strike because their top player, Jackie Hutchison, had been suspended by the O.F.A., having been ordered off along with Arthur Dainty of Holm in a tempestuous semi final second leg in Dounby. Now he would miss the match:

"Harray, resentful of the week's suspension of their star forward Jackie Hutchison, had threatened to scratch and I believe the Association were actually making arrangements for a friendly game as a substitute …"

Not only had there been talk of a boycott, but another 'bone of contention' was being picked over. This was the first real airing of a grievance which was to surface time and again over the years, the issue of the St Ola parish boundary.

Many people, including the football

Press, believed that a new source of players available to St Ola exceeded the bounds of fairness and breached the spirit of the competition. 'Watchman' was unequivocal in his condemnation:

"St Ola are getting no lavish compliments from me as I have difficulty in regarding them as a genuine parish side, though no doubt their qualifications comply with the requirements all right. I rather fancy, however, that if there was no Kirkwall housing shortage, there would be no St Ola team."

Strong stuff! No doubt what was being referred to was the large number of families moving into the former Air Ministry huts at Hatston aerodrome which had been converted into temporary homes in order to ease the housing shortage. At this time, Hatston was outside the Kirkwall town boundary and in the parish of St Ola.

I suspect that this might only have merited a passing comment at best, if no footballers of significance stayed there but, at the time, one of Orkney's finest ever players, Jim 'Dook' Donaldson lived with his family at Hatston. Hence the outcry at the evil and injustice of it all!

So, for one reason or another, there was an 'atmosphere' preceding this match. However, despite the uncertainty as to whether they would actually witness a game, well over 2,000 spectators turned up to see just what would unfold. The 7.30 p.m. kick off time arrived and no Harray team appeared … although they had been seen going into the dressing room! Another ten minutes passed … and still no sign! They were making a point!

Eventually, with the crowd becoming very impatient, they did appear and, well behind schedule, the game was ready for kick off.

The following teams lined up:

St Ola: Jerry Groundwater; Doug Wylie and Dave Wylie; John Moodie, Jack Adam and Sandy Budge; Jackie Groundwater, Jim Donaldson, Russell Groundwater, Jimmy Miller and Jim Robertson.

Harray: Nelson Murray; Dave Flett and Maurice Johnston; Jim Sinclair, Jim Stockan and Brian Flett; Ian Hutchison, Bobby Hutchison, Leslie Flett, Tommy Drever and Willie Adamson.

Referee: Jim Bews

Worth singling out for mention are two players making cup final debuts, one on each side who were to become two of the most highly regarded forwards Orkney ever produced. For Harray, 16 year old Ian Hutchison, Orkney's current junior inter county centre forward had followed his brothers into the team, while St Ola could field 19 year old Russell Groundwater, now well established as Orkney's senior centre forward, and a player capable of plundering goals in any company.

The game got off to a sensational start. With Harray playing down hill, Tommy Drever, Jackie Hutchison's replacement, dashed through a hesitant defence to score. Harray supporters had barely regained their breath when Ian Hutchison crossed from the right, the goalkeeper missed it and Drever was on the spot to score again. The Harray team were quite happy with their sub. now!

It took St Ola a long while to settle but when they did, they slowly began to take the initiative. Harray's lead was cut when Jackie Groundwater crossed from the right for brother, Russell, to bullet a header home. ("Thornton-style" according to Corinthian.)

The equaliser was not long delayed, Robertson the left winger striking home a fine shot. St Ola were now playing with a lot of confidence and just before half time, Jackie Groundwater gave them the lead

St Ola claimed the Parish Cup in 1953. Back row, left to right, James Donaldson Sr, Dougie Wylie, Jerry Groundwater, Davy Wylie, Dave Begley, Dave Keldie. Middle, John Moodie, Jackie Groundwater, Russell Groundwater, Jack Miller, Jim Robertson. Front, Jim Donaldson Jr, Jack Adam, Sandy Budge.
(Picture: Orkney Library)

with a well taken goal from close range. Half-time 3-2 to St Ola.

The second half wasn't a patch on the first for excitement and much of this was down to a frustrating tactic adopted by the St Ola defence (one we have heard before!) of deliberately kicking the ball out of play at every opportunity. The ball was reported to be "more off the field than on it."

Maybe this was an indication of their regard for their opponents but it was a source of irritation to Harray fans and neutrals in the crowd. Then, late on, just to rub salt in their wounds, St Ola scored a fourth, a long range try by Russell Groundwater rolling through Murray's legs.

Due to the late start, the closing stages were played in gathering darkness and thick mist. Although they never gave up trying, Harray were unable to reduce the deficit and St Ola ran out winners by four goals to two.

Bobby Hutchison, Brian Flett and Jim Stockan were praised for their contributions but Harray had lacked the vision, passing ability and shooting power of Jackie Hutchison. For St Ola, Russell and Jackie Groundwater caused a lot of problems up front while the Wylie brothers were very dependable full backs.

So, in a match more memorable for the controversies surrounding it, St Ola emerged winners once again. Despite some negative tactics in the second half they were worthy champions having scored 34 goals during the competition.

Nobody else came close to that!

1954:
An almost dry celebration

A breath of fresh air wafted through the football scene in the lead up to the 1954 Parish Cup competition. A new team had entered, another island team at long last, and speculation was rife as to who might have to make the long journey to play them. Longhope is a peninsula at the very south end of the island of Hoy and their participation had 'Watchman' in *The Orkney Herald* visualising midnight football taking place, rivalling the traditional midnight golf and bowls.

Far from being sacrificial victims, Longhope were expected to provide good opposition. The team was a mixture of local lads and those employed at the Lyness naval base, some of whom were reputed to be fine players. Centre forward Eddie Latchem had already established a reputation throughout Orkney.

Whilst there was delight at seeing Parish Cup 'rookies' appear, there was a degree of sadness at the demise of two former parish 'greats', Holm and Deerness. Neither parish was able to muster a team this year, yet only two years ago, both had sides in the 'A' League competing against the likes of Thorfinn and Dounby. Such is the nature of football in country districts.

Incidentally, it was somewhat ironic given Holm's current plight, that their great general, Arthur Dainty, this year bade farewell to Orkney to return to live in his native Lancashire. How Holm now needed another leader of his calibre.

What were the other key bits of news as the first round approached? To begin with, the fortunes of Shapinsay once again seemed very much in the ascendancy. This year they had succeeded in winning the Corsie

Cup for 'B' teams and now planned to enter some 'A' competitions to test their abilities against top flight opposition.

They would be a team to be feared but the gods did not appear to be shining on Harray. Jackie Hutchison, had his appendix out in April so it was debatable whether he would take part in the Parish Cup at all, while brother, Bobby, had suffered a broken fibula playing for Dounby. The absence of these two would severely hamper Harray's chances.

Finally, it emerged that the enigmatic St Ola had again managed to find a team and intended to defend their trophy.

Well as fate would have it, the only first round tie, from an entry of nine, paired newcomers Longhope with Birsay. With long journeys the order of the day, it was agreed that both games be played on Saturdays. Maybe this would allow players and supporters to make the trip and return home the same day.

In the first leg, played in Dounby, the island team showed that they had much more to offer than enthusiasm. In a 'cracking' cup tie they emerged as 5-4 winners, leaving Birsay an uphill task the following week. Another close game ended 2-2, a result which gave Longhope a very significant victory in their first ever Parish Cup tie.

The adventure now continued when they were drawn against the very strong St Andrews side who could field an entire team playing every week in the 'A' League. This time the hurdle proved too great and Longhope came to grief in their home leg played on a beautiful Saturday evening in Lyness, going down by 5-1. Three goals by Billy Gorn and two by Alton Tait sealed their fate. In the return leg, St Andrews repeated their 5-1 victory and so progressed to the semi finals. However, it was hoped that the

Longhope players would not be down hearted by this experience and would reappear in the competition in the years to come.

The full **quarter final** results were as follows:

Longhope	1	St Andrews	5
St Andrews	5	Longhope	1
Stenness	0	St Ola	7
Stenness scratched			
Harray	4	Orphir	2
Orphir	2	Harray	1
Firth	3	Shapinsay	1
Shapinsay	3	Firth	0

Both Harray and Shapinsay were given quite a fright before winning through to the semi finals by a single goal.

As the survivors now got ready for the semi's, another episode in the remarkable Hutchison football saga was unfolding. Both Jackie and Bobby had unexpectedly recovered full fitness following their 'lay offs' and were raring to go; meanwhile Freddie, who played for Shapinsay, had broken his collar bone playing against Firth and he was now ruled out. How would this affect the fortunes of Harray and Shapinsay?

Semi final Results

St Andrews	0	Harray	2
Harray	3	StAndrews	1
Shapinsay	3	St Ola	0
St Ola	1	Shapinsay	1

The answer: A lot, and not a lot! The Hutchsions were in great form for Harray and scored a goal each in the second leg. However, Sammy Bews proved an able deputy at centre half for Shapinsay, whose strong defence prevented high scoring St Ola from notching more than a single goal.

A great final was now in prospect, the first between the teams since 1948 when Shapinsay had won after a replay. This time, though, Harray were widely regarded as favourites and Shapinsay were certainly not making the mistake of planning for victory again.

On the day of the final, their chances took a 'nose dive' when news filtered through that inter county goalkeeper Jim Sinclair (Ha'quoy), had gone down with an attack of mumps and could not play. What was to be done?

After some deliberation, they decided to take a chance on a young but very promising goalkeeper, 16 year old Jackie Nicolson from Sandwick who, at the time, worked at the farm of Ness in Shapinsay. To play on such an occasion with only a few hours warning should have been a daunting prospect for the inexperienced teenager but Jackie took it all in his stride … so much so that, with less than an hour till kick off, he still hadn't reported to the Bignold Park for team preparations.

Investigations revealed that he had gone to the pictures so a car containing a deputation of frantic Shapinsay officials was despatched to the Phoenix Cinema. Rumour subsequently had it that a notice was flashed across the screen urging Jackie to report for duty immediately but alas, it was only rumour.

The truth was that shortly after the car arrived, Jackie casually made his way to the exit and when he encountered the Shapinsay 'Mafia' jumping up and down, he couldn't understand what all the fuss was about. He was then whisked to the park to take his place in the team.

Incidentally, the film Jackie had gone to see (I thought you would want to know) was called "Five Fingers" starring James Mason and Michael Rennie. Sounds very suitable and full of advice for a young goalkeeper!

Teams were as follows:

Shapinsay: Jackie Nicolson; Dennis Eunson and Jim Hepburn; Bob Sinclair, Sammy Bews and Billy Budge; Gordon Rendall, Dave Drever, Billy Barnett, Bunny Bruce and Johnny Bews.

Harray: Nelson Murray; Dave Flett and Tom Kirkness; Jim Sinclair, Leslie Flett and Brian Flett; Ian Flett, Bobby Hutchison, Ian Hutchison, Jackie Hutchison and Willie Adamson.

Referee: Davie Fox

No, your eyes are not deceiving you! Still well worth his place in the Shapinsay team, 23 years after appearing in his first final, was 40 year old Bunny Bruce. Harray also had a long serving player in uncompromising defender, Davie Flett, now playing in his ninth final, spanning 15 years.

This was to be another memorable match yet for a long time there appeared to be only one team in it and the outcome seemed inevitable.

Harray took the lead in the first half with a penalty by Ian Hutchison after Sammy Bews had handled. Although Shapinsay fought hard, Harray kept control and doubled their lead midway through the second half with a rising shot from winger, Ian Flett.

By now, many of the disconsolate Shapinsay fans, not wishing to be around at the final whistle to witness the last rites, had decided to leave and make their way to the pier. Since there was going to be no cup to celebrate, then at least they would get a decent seat on the boat.

Meanwhile back at the park, there were only ten minutes to go and the cup looked to be heading west. But then, out of nothing, Barnett accepted a pass by Johnny Bews and ran through a suddenly porous Harray defence to score. Now, the whole complexion of the game changed.

Shapinsay stormed into the attack and in one of their raids, Budge equalised with a first time shot. Harray were rattled and hanging on, desperate for the final whistle. But, with only two minutes left, Barnett was there again to side foot home

Birth, Blood

after the ball was missed by the entire Harray defence.

Shortly afterwards the whistle blew and Shapinsay, who had seemed down and out, had snatched a sensational victory from the jaws of defeat.

Harray players and spectators were devastated. The cup had been theirs for the taking but perhaps they became too complacent. However, nobody could dispute Shapinsay's 'never-say-die' spirit and it was a delighted Sammy Bews who collected the cup from Dr. J.B. Gordon, president of the Orkney Football Association.

Meanwhile back at the harbour, the glum passengers were awaiting the arrival of the players and remaining spectators so that they could get home. When some on board spotted a crowd in the distance with the cup, they assumed this was the Harray team down to gloat on their hapless victims. Quite a length to go to … but so what?

But, when it dawned on everyone that the happy smiling faces were those of their fellow islanders and that it was Sammy Bews and Co. with the trophy, they were dumbstruck … then elated … then in agonies of frustration because they had missed all the action.

In fact, so unexpected was this win, a record fifth for Shapinsay, that nobody had even bothered to buy a bottle of whisky to put in the cup.

Unheard of!

However, everything was sorted by Sandy Heddle, owner of the Queen's Hotel, who gifted to his very good customers from across the String, two bottles of the 'hard stuff' to get the celebrations started. … and, recalling their disappointment of two years earlier, it was unanimously agreed that, cradle or no cradle, the cup would be going up to the mast head tonight!

Ah! There's nothing that can uplift your spirits quite like a game of football!

1955:
Cloak and dagger stuff of the cup

"What Is Wrong With Orkney Football?" was a headline which ran for weeks in *The Orkney Herald* during the summer 1955.

"Has Orkney Football Gone Down?" queried Corinthian in *The Orcadian*.

From the heights of only a few years ago it seemed that our local game had now plunged to previously unimagined depths. Both inter county games had been lost last year and the Shetland defeat, after extra time, had been the second in a row. Something must be badly amiss!

Correspondents valiantly tried to resist saying that things were so much better 'in the old days' … but failed. Footballers of 'today', who had only experience of playing against each other, were compared unfavourably with demobbed Orcadians just after the war, who had gained a wide experience playing in all kinds of conditions against all sorts of opposition.

The contribution of 'ferry loupers', now almost non existent in local teams, was also highlighted. These players, by their skill and example had encouraged local players to higher levels but as they had retired or left the islands, so the rot had set in.

As the 'navel-gazing' gained momentum, virtually every aspect of football was found wanting: a lack of training; not enough coaching; poor structure of the local game where there were not enough opportunities for young boys to take part … it was only a matter of time before the critics got to the Parish Cup!

The 'B' League, it was suggested, was simply a training ground for the Parish Cup and totally unsuitable for bringing on younger players:

"With all due respect, to the country

Shapinsay, Parish Cup winners in 1954. Back row, left to right, Jim Meason, Percy Foubister, Denis Eunson, Jackie Nicholson, Jim Hepburn, Jim Sinclair, Freddie Hutchison. Middle, Gordon Rendall, Davie Drever, Billy Barnett, Joe "Bunny" Bruce, Johnny Bews. Front, Bob Sinclair, Sammy Bews, Billy Budge.   *(Picture: Orkney Library)*

teams, the standard of play is not encouraging for the introduction of junior players, unless the promising junior is well endowed physically. 'B' football only encourages a negative approach to the game with a 'get rid of the ball quick' attitude."

Yes, the Parish Cup had a lot to answer for!

After all this steam had been released, the public now wondered what changes, if any, would be made to local football or would the perceived decline in standards be allowed to continue? As for country enthusiasts, the question was, "What bearing would any of this have on the Parish Cup?"

As it happened, the big story of this year's parish tournament did have a lot to do with standards but not the sort we have been referring to on the field of play … more precisely the rules and regulations laid down for this unique competition.

All will be revealed shortly.

To begin with, this year's tournament got off to a stuttering start. Of the three first round games, only one was played, Orphir defeating Stromness 7-1 on aggregate. Both Sandwick and St Ola scratched before their ties with Shapinsay and Birsay could commence. So it was on to the quarter finals where the tie of the round looked to be the one between cup holders Shapinsay and St Andrews. Missing from the line up this year was Longhope who had committed a team to the 'B' League instead. Probably enough travelling involved in that competition.

Quarter final Results

Deerness	1	Harray	8
Deerness scratched			
Orphir	0	Firth	0
Firth	0	Orphir	4
St Mgts Hope	4	Birsay	2
Birsay	1	St Mgts Hope	2
Shapinsay	1	St Andrews	3
St Andrews	2	Shapinsay	1

Shapinsay's hold on the trophy slipped when Archie Clark (2) and Alton Tait scored their side's goals away from home. Not even the splendid hospitality provided by their hosts after the match could weaken their resolve, and they completed the job with a well earned victory at home.

So there would be a new name on the trophy this year again and most experts believed that it would come from the forthcoming 'Battle of the Giants', Harray v St Andrews.

Semi final Results

St Andrews	2	Harray	3
Harray	2	St Andrews	4
Orphir	2	St Mgts Hope	5
St Mgts Hope	3	Orphir	1

It was indeed a contest which lived up to its billing. St Andrews emerged victorious after two thrilling cup ties and would now play St Margaret's Hope in the final. Readers will be delighted to see a new team reach the last stage for the first time … but wait! … all is not as it seems. Hearken to this amazing tale.

After their emphatic away win in Orphir, reaching the final would appear a formality for the 'Hope. The Orphir team should have little chance of overturning such a deficit.

But a spanner was to fall, clanking, into the works!

On the evening of the return leg, the Orphir team bus duly made its way towards the Barriers but en route, stopped in Kirkwall, to give one of the opposition players a lift. The player in question was Maurice Allan, an accomplished left winger, who had represented Orkney versus Shetland three years earlier.

As the bus meandered its way eastwards, the passenger struck up some casual conversation with the Orphir lads and quite innocently remarked, "I don't ken why I am playing for the 'Hope the night, I wasn't even born there." Since he

Maurice Allan

lived in Kirkwall, that would render him ineligible! Oh! it was well seen that Maurice wasn't steeped in the cloak and dagger politics of the Parish Cup.

For Orphir, this was a gift from the Gods. They realised they could get their opponents kicked out of the tournament … if they kept quiet *for now* about the significance of what they had heard. But how to do it effectively?

Fifty years ago, official matters such as protests were handled differently; they could be dealt with by the referee who would make a judgement provided he received the complaint before the match ended.

On the night in question, the Orphir players held their peace until it was established that the aforementioned player was playing, before approaching referee, Jimmy Leys, with their protest at half time. The referee accordingly acted as judge and jury and, after establishing the facts, upheld the protest.

Amidst very little counter protestation from the 'Hope players, it was declared that Orphir would go through to the final. No replay! (Allan had played in both legs) No reprieve!

In an almost surreal atmosphere, the game continued and St Margaret's Hope ran out 3-1 winners on the night, 8-3 winners on aggregate. But they were out.

The moral of the story? Don't accept lifts from strangers! … *or*, you don't mess with the Rules! You might have lived most of your life in a community but *if you were not born there …!*

The final was almost an anti-climax after that drama. It turned out to be "a game that lacked the hurly burly and excitement usually associated with the annual encounter." according to Corinthian in *The Orcadian*. Orphir proved to be a plucky side who made their more experienced opponents work hard for their 2-0 win. Eventually, however, they were worn down.

A goal in each half by Alton Tait sealed Orphir's fate. Outstanding for the losers were Kenny Firth in goal, the experienced Jock Cursiter at full back, while Eoin Clouston "revealed plenty of dash on the right wing." Also praised was centre half Willie Muir, captain of Stenness way back in 1936, who was now representing

the parish of his birth at the age of 40.

For St Andrews, who played well below club form, Billy Gorn, both Pottingers, Bryan Clark and Alton Tait were praised for their consistent performances. But, to use the old cliché it was the result that mattered and St Andrews had recorded their second Parish Cup win. Given that they were now one of Orkney's top 'A' League teams, few would bet against them repeating the feat many more times.

The teams were as follows:

Orphir: Kenny Firth; Billy Stanger and Jock Cursiter; Sandy Flett, Willie Muir and Bob Cunningham; Eoin Clouston, Maurice Clouston, Stanley Thomson, Billy Cursiter and Alan Findlay.

St Andrews: Billy Gorn; Bryan Clark and Dave Pottinger; Maurice Shearer, Robbie Pottinger and Jackie Tait; Tommy Thomson, Zander Bews, Archie Clark, Alton Tait and Wattie Shearer.

Referee: F.G. Mears (Junior)

Now back to the early season controversy about the dire state of the local game. It had been a tame final right enough but there was no shortage of quality on view. Robbie Pottinger was now well established as Orkney's top centre half, Bryan Clark was the widely acclaimed captain of Orkney's junior inter county team while Alton Tait was about to embark on a long career as Orkney's first choice outside left. Orphir's Jock Cursiter had, of course, been a county full back numerous times in the past, while Willie Muir had played against Shetland in 1947.

So the parishes were not bereft of skilful players, but what of the true barometer, the inter county games with Caithness and Shetland? The results were: Archer Shield: Orkney 5 Caithness 4 (on aggregate); Milne Cup: Orkney 3 Shetland 2

"What is wrong with Orkney football?"

"Nothing at all buey! Things cheust couldna' be better!"

St Andrews were the team of the year in 1955. Back row, left to right, Sidney Garrioch, Jackie Mowat, Bryan Clark, Billy Gorn, Davie Pottinger, John Shearer. Middle, Tommy Thomson, Zander Bews, Archie Clark, Alton Tait, Wattie Shearer. Front, Maurice Shearer, Robbie Pottinger, Jackie Tait.
(Picture: Orkney Library)

Page 71

1956: Harray return to winning ways

No doubt about it, the feel good factor was back in Orkney football. The county team had just beaten Highland League Peterhead by 5-4 and … wait for it … had thrashed Shetland 6-1 in Lerwick. Nothing wrong now!

And the Parish Cup?

Just a year ago the competition was being condemned for its physical nature and 'kick and rush' tactics. Now witness what 'Corinthian' had to say in 1956:

"There is something about these Parish Cup ties which is lacking in other cup ties. One sees players who no longer take part in league football, ex-county stars and youngsters, some of them still at school, as well as those who take part in just this one competition, all turning out when the honour of their respective parish is at stake, and play themselves to a standstill. Many hard knocks are given and taken, all in good part, and at the finish of the game, there is the usual tea and something for the inner man, laid on for both teams. Truly the most sporting games that are played during the season."

What a difference a year makes!

But where did this attitude of benevolence to country teams stem from … all of a sudden? Maybe, in part from the remarkable scene at a 'B' League game between Rendall and Longhope:

"Almost a hundred Longhope supporters made the trip to Rendall last week and a stranger would have thought the Scottish Cup was at stake," reported The Orcadian.

"Complete with a miniature pipe band (piper, drummer and kettle drummer) they marched round the pitch with bells, rattles etc. and gave

Longhope F.C. pictured at the Market Green, Stromness in 1955. Back row, left to right, Gordon Robertson, David Gillespie, William Brown, James Baillie, George Tait, Bill Stewart, Basil Groat, Jimmy Inkster. Front, Arnold Grieve, Ian Taylor, Eddie Latchem, Willie Fraser, Patty Wilson. (Picture: Orkney Library)

their team every encouragement throughout the game. After the game, friend and foe alike were given tea, sandwiches and cakes which arrived with the Longhope contingent. The barn at Millbrig was cleared out by the owner for the occasion and Mrs. George Harcus, assisted by a bevy of Rendall beauties had tea ready and everything went with a swing. Longhope duly celebrated their winning of the Corsie Cup in traditional style and as the saying goes, 'a good time was had by all'."

The occasion embodied everything that was good about country football and it was pleasing to see that Longhope, winners of their first ever trophy, would now be taking part in this year's Parish Cup.

The current feeling of optimism had undoubtedly reached the parishes. Twelve teams entered this season's tournament and among these was a new name altogether. After the debacle of last year, St Margaret's Hope had decided on a change of

'label' to see if it would bring better fortune. They would now be known as 'South Ronaldsay', a term more inclusive of the whole island.

Maybe they were reflecting on what happened back in 1952 when Tankerness changed their name?

In fact, South Ronaldsay were expected to do very well. They had benefited greatly from the coaching of Willie Brown, at that time right back for Grimsby Town, whose wife hailed from the parish. Willie had been hired by the Orkney education committee and the O.F.A. for six weeks to train Orkney's young footballers. His good work was shown in the junior inter county game when Orkney outclassed Shetland, recording a 4-1 victory. Two young South Ronaldsay stars, Denis Tait and Andy Sinclair, both played in that match.

When his contract was up, Willie stayed on to holiday in South Ronaldsay and it was then that the local lads enjoyed his undivided attention. Great things were now predicted.

The competition kicked off and the first round went as follows:

South Ron.	5	St Ola	2
St Ola	3	South Ron.	6
Sandwick	0	Harray	8
Harray	5	Sandwick	1
Longhope	6	Holm	1
Holm	3	Longhope	5
St Andrews	4	Firth	0
Firth	3	St Andrews	5

Believe it or not, St Ola lodged a protest against South Ronaldsay, again for playing ineligible players, who lived in or hailed from the neighbouring island of Burray. However, painstaking research proved the islands of South Ronaldsay, Burray and Hunda were always regarded as a single parish so the protest was rejected. But it had been a close thing!

This latest episode prompted a reminder to be posted to committees to make absolutely certain they knew the rules before the competition commenced.

So South Ronaldsay progressed, as did Longhope at the expense of Holm, making their first appearance after a number of years. The next round kept all the big teams apart.

Quarter final Results

Birsay	2	St Andrews	3
St Andrews	3	Birsay	0
Stenness	1	South Ron.	7
Stenness scratched			
Orphir	4	Shapinsay	3
Shapinsay	0	Orphir	3
Longhope	0	Harray	4
Harray	9	Longhope	0

Longhope's dream ended at the hands of a formidable Harray team while Shapinsay seemed to be entering a period of decline. Freddie Hutchison's departure to continue his police career in Paisley would have left a big gap in their defence.

The semi finals now cast the two favourites together again and intriguingly, Orphir and South Ronaldsay in a repeat of last year's fated encounter. I wonder what the policy would be this year on giving, or accepting, lifts from the opposition?

Semi final Results

Harray	3	St Andrews	1
St Andrews	3	Harray	4
South Ron.	2	Orphir	1
Orphir	3	South Ron.	5

Harray had gained revenge for last year's semi final defeat and South Ronaldsay had come through, unscathed by protests, to reach their first ever final. So far, the change of name was working a treat!

The final saw a change of venue this year to the King George VI Memorial Playing field at Pickaquoy due to the muddy and saturated Bignold Park being declared unplayable. A crowd of 2,000 plus again assembled, with the majority hailing from the 'Hope, if the cheers for the emerging teams were anything to go by. Fortunately, the rain, which had fallen for the past 18 hours, stopped just in time and the sun came out to grace the kick off.

Early pressure by South Ronaldsay yielded no goals but in their first attack, Harray took the lead when Jackie Hutchison threaded a ball through to brother, Ian, who scored with a 'fast grounder'.

Midway through the half South Ronaldsay equalised with a long carefully placed lob by right back Denis Tait. Their recovery lasted only a minute before Harray regained the lead when Ian Hutchison converted a cross by Adamson. Both teams came close when first Bobby Smith for South Ronaldsay, and then 14 year old Eric Hutchison, playing his first final for Harray, struck the woodwork. Half-time, 2-1 to Harray.

Harray's cup winning team of 1956. Back row, left to right, Jim Sinclair, Tom Kirkness, Frankie Johnston, Tom Flett, Peter Aim. Middle, Eric Hutchison, Jim Isbister, Ian Hutchison, Jackie Hutchison, Andrew Adamson. Front, Bobby Hutchison, Leslie Flett, Brian Flett.
(Picture: Orkney Library)

The second half saw Harray forcing the pace but Jimmy Doull was outstanding at centre half for South Ronaldsay. However, after ten minutes of the half, Eric Hutchison scored a clever goal from a pass by Ian. Harray now took control of the game but there was no further scoring and they ran out winners by three goals to one.

It had been a quiet game compared to some finals. South Ronaldsay played good football but never succeeded in fully stretching a very experienced Harray team which featured no less than five county players: the three older Hutchison brothers as well as Brian and Leslie Flett of Nistaben.

Teams were as follows:

Harray: Frankie Johnston; Tom Kirkness and Tom Flett; Bobby Hutchison, Leslie Flett and Brian Flett; Eric Hutchison, Jim Isbister, Ian Hutchison, Jackie Hutchison and Andrew Adamson.

South Ronaldsay (Probable): Jim Muir; Denis Tait and Vic Card; Tommy Dearness; Jimmy Doull and Stewart Gray; Jack Walls, Andy Sinclair, Davie Goar, Harold Omand and Bobby Smith.

So, a generally upbeat football season came to a close. Well, 'upbeat' for most. For Longhope, who had contributed so much to the colour and enjoyment in the game in recent years, the story was very different, and it looked as if their glory days would be over when they had merely begun.

News had come through that the Lyness naval base was to close. The Admiralty could no longer afford to maintain the establishment and indeed, could see no further use for the installations.

When so many families depended on the base for employment, this was devastating news. Mr, Isaac Moar, the local councillor, foresaw impoverishment and depopulation on Hoy. One hundred and twenty men, most of them local, would have to look for new jobs and possibly as many as 80 families could be forced to leave.

The prospects for Longhope football did not look good. But let's face it, the loss of a football team would be of secondary consideration compared to the uprooting of families and the dismantling of peoples' lives.

1957:
Ten goal thriller in cup decider

After a couple of years when the Parish Cup final had produced low key, fairly uninspiring fare, the climax to the 1957 tournament delivered a contest liable to remain forever in the minds of those privileged enough to witness it.

A throw back to the great old days of old, you might ask? No, probably better! Yet, the match did not take place without a major hitch beforehand.

Well what do you expect? Everything to be straight forward?

The buoyant mood which pervaded the local game last year continued into the new season. Orkney had again shown they were a good match for Highland League opposition by defeating Peterhead 3-2 and securing a 3-3 draw with Huntly. The Archer Shield was also retained after 6-1 home defeat of Caithness.

With an eye to the future, the services of Willie Brown had again been engaged for coaching the county's young players. No doubt South Ronaldsay would derive some more spin-off benefits if he chose to holiday there again.

Catching the feeling of optimism and not at all put off by the prospective 'Old-Firm' style dominance of Harray and St Andrews, twelve teams again entered for the Parish Cup, eager for the fray. Sadly, as predicted, there was no Longhope but their place had been filled by Stromness.

First round Results

Holm	3	South Ron.	4
South Ron.	3	Holm	3
Orphir	7	Stromness	0
Stromness	4	Orphir	2
Shapinsay	3	Sandwick	0
Sandwick	0	Shapinsay	1

The Orkney team which thrashed Shetland 6 – 1 in 1956 thereby lifting the gloom which hung over the local game. Back row, left to right, (players only) Eddie Craigie (reserve), Leslie Flett, Bobby Hutchison, Murray Macdonald, Zander Donaldson, Jim Merriman, Maurice Wilmott. Front. Jim Donaldson, Dave Fox, Ian Hutchison, Russell Groundwater and Alton Tait.

| Harray | 3 | St Ola | 2 |
| St Ola | 2 | Harray | 3 |

Most significant points to note were the improved showing of Holm and the stern opposition given to Harray by St Ola. The next round saw the cup favourites kept well apart.

Quarter final Results

Stenness	2	Firth	3
Firth	2	Stenness	0
Shapinsay	0	Harray	6
Harray	2	Shapinsay	1
South Ron.	3	Birsay	1
Birsay	3	South Ron.	6
St Andrews	3	Orphir	0
Orphir	1	StAndrews	7

At last! Harray and St Andrews had been kept apart in the semi final draw and if, as expected, both got through, what a final was in prospect. But South Ronaldsay, were laying a strong claim to be third 'super power'. At least their fans thought so. An eye witness recalls trying to get a seat on one of several buses heading for Birsay and ending up having to sit on the step just inside the door of the last bus.

Semi final Results

South Ron.	0	Harray	8
Harray	8	South Ron.	1
Firth	2	St Andrews	4
St Andrews	4	Firth	0

A third power in the land? Not if Harray had anything to do with it. South Ronaldsay were outclassed while Firth were emphatically beaten after putting up a fight at home.

So the favourites were through and the thought of a thrilling encounter prompted 'Corinthian' to wax eloquent:

"Nothing pleases the football fan better than to see a good cup tie and Saturday's one should draw a record crowd. This year the high scoring Harray attack faces the rugged St Andrews defence. Not since the strong going Holm of a few years back met with the Harray team,

which included Dave and Agmond Flett, has so much interest been shown. Don't miss it!"

However, on Saturday evening, everyone did miss it! To explain.

For the second successive year, heavy rain had fallen for most of the day, ruining the County Show as a spectacle, and as there was no sign of any let up by six o'clock, it was felt that the game should be postponed. A decision was taken and the word sent to both teams so that they could halt their transport arrangements, while a loudspeaker van was dispatched around Kirkwall to inform the public.

If you were a supporter at home in the country, preparing to come to town … well, too bad!

But, as fate would have it, as kick off time drew near, the rain stopped and conditions improved greatly; so much so that many felt the game should still go on. Intending spectators cited examples of games which had been played in worse weather. But the decision had been made and it was very disappointed fans who trudged home, heavy with a feeling of anti-climax. The game was rescheduled for the following Friday evening.

Seldom can a more fortuitous decision have been made! In perfect weather conditions, more than 1,800 spectators turned out to see two teams bristling with inter county stars take to the field.

Harray: Nelson Murray; Leslie Flett and Tom Flett; Jim Isbister, Bobby Hutchison and Brian Flett; Eric Hutchison, Frankie Johnston, Ian Hutchison, Jackie Hutchison and Peter Aim.

St Andrews: Arnold Rendall; Colin Tait and Billy Gorn; Bryan Clark, Robbie Pottinger and Jackie Tait; Kenny Ritch, Wattie Shearer, Archie Clark, Alton Tait and Sidney Garrioch.

Referee: Mr J. Leys.

It was as if both teams had been held in harness for a week, straining for release. When the whistle blew, the shackles were off and the players went for each other, hell for leather.

In less than a minute, with his team playing down the slope, Archie Clark raced through the Harray defence to pick his spot in the net. Harray took the ball straight to the other end and were awarded a penalty when Ian Hutchison was impeded. The same player took the kick and scored. 1-1.

Fast, end to end football followed before Archie Clark again burst through to shoot past Murray.

No sooner had play restarted when Bryan Clark scored St Andrews' third, direct from a free kick. Harray were now completely rattled and Alton Tait netted a fourth from close in. Tait then hit the post and Archie Clark almost got his hat trick but struck the bar. It was breathless entertainment!

Harray gradually came more into the picture and scored their second when a shot by Aim eluded goalkeeper Rendall. However, St Andrews restored their three goal lead when Archie Clark notched his third and his team's fifth.

It was 5-2 to St Andrews and still only halftime.

The teams changed right round as fog threatened to close in. Harray pressed strongly and Jackie Hutchison scored the goal of the match when he sent three opponents the wrong way before teeing up the ball and slamming it into the net. Harray piled on the pressure and earned another penalty but this time Ian Hutchison sent it well wide.

It was all Harray now but, as so often happens, the other team breaks away and this time it was Garrioch who put it past Murray. But Harray weren't finished and Ian Hutchison escaped his marker to score their fourth.

1958: Rule change causes high drama

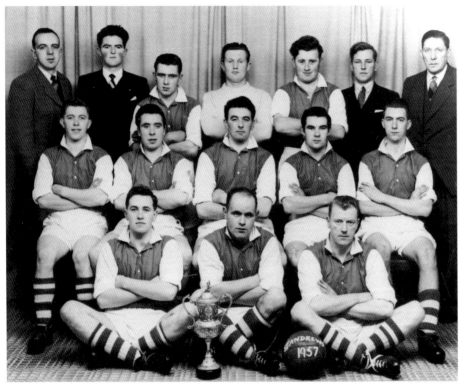

The cup goes East to St Andrews, in 1957. Back row, left to right, Jackie Mowat, Leslie Bichan, Colin Tait, Arnold Rendall, Billy Gorn, Zander Bews, John Shearer. Middle, Kenny Ritch, Andy Shearer, Archie Clark, Alton Tait, Sidney Garrioch. Front, Bryan Clark, Robbie Pottinger, Jackie Tait.
(Picture: Orkney Library)

Some great football was played last year but otherwise, it was an uneventful season. Not a protest in sight! Strange! Word had it, however that the authorities would soon be bombarded by Parish Cup protests unless they held a review of the rules.

The problem was that in the post war period, most children were born, not at home, but in the Balfour Hospital. In a very short time, the 'Born in … ' rule would become redundant leaving Residency as the only relevant qualification.

Ever alert to the signs of impending danger, the O.F.A. sat down to address the issue and came up with a fundamental rule change. Where formerly the rule read:

"Either a player must have been born in, or is resident in, the parish for which he plays."

the amended rule, agreed at the A.G.M. of the association, now went as follows:

"Either a player's mother's usual address, as recorded by the Registrar of Births, shall have been in, or he shall qualify by residence in the Parish for which he plays."

The three month rule of residency still applied. But please note: the 'Born In' clause had been *deleted* in favour of 'Mother's Usual Address'. Surely this would disqualify some who had played before under the old rule?

Both teams seemed to tire towards the end and no wonder! No more goals were scored and St Andrews had won an unforgettable match 6-4. Very few people were criticising the decision to postpone now.

In summing up this epic contest, Corinthian believed that St Andrews deserved their win by having the better all round team. Robbie Pottinger had been outstanding at centre half while Archie Clark was a real opportunist centre forward. Harray's class players, the Hutchison and the Flett brothers, had all caught the eye but had not been given the room to dominate.

In Parish Cup terms, with these two teams we had now truly entered a phase of 'Rangers v Celtic style' supremacy. But if they continued to serve up entertainment of this quality, few people, neutrals included, would complain.

Their respective records now read as follows:

Harray: four wins; St Andrews: three wins. Any odds against either team adding to their total next year?

For the time being everyone seemed happy enough, but just wait until an actual test case cropped up.

With another excellent entry of twelve teams the chances of this happening were quite high. Everyone, it seemed, wanted to play football these days, inspired perhaps by yet more fine displays by the county team. The highlight of the year so far had been a quite astonishing match against Scottish Second Division, Hamilton Accies, which had ended in a 6-6 draw. Definitely one of the finest performances by an Orkney team to date.

This explosive form must have sent shock waves as far as Shetland because, before the Milne Cup encounter, Gilbertson Park in Lerwick was swept with mine detectors. One or two old bits of iron, which had worked their way to the surface were found but no mines. However, all precautions were to no avail as Orkney blew apart the Shetland team 2-0.

Fresh from seeing the legendary Rangers and Scotland centre half, George Young, opening Stromness Shopping Week and later in the week refereeing the East v West football match in the company of fellow Ranger, Jerry Dawson, the parish players got down to their first round games.

First round Results

St Andrews	5	Sandwick	0

Sandwick scratched

Holm	0	Harray	8
Harray	4	Holm	2

South Ron.	4	Birsay	2
Birsay	1	South Ron.	6

Shapinsay	2	Rendall	1
Rendall	1	Shapinsay	5

South Ronaldsay, new winners of the 'B' League, were looking good as were the 'Old Firm'. Rendall, whose first Parish Cup entry this was, fell at the first hurdle.

Quarter final Results

Orphir	1	Stromness	3
Stromness	0	Orphir	2

Replay

Orphir	0	Stromness	3

Harray	v	Stenness	

Stenness scratched

Firth	2	South Ron.	3
South Ron.	3	Firth	3

Shapinsay	0	St Andrews	3
St Andrews	5	Shapinsay	0

The question now was, 'Would Harray and St Andrews be kept apart again in the draw?' The answer: No! They would meet in the semi finals. After last year's ten goal thriller, another dramatic clash was expected and … but wait!

It can't be … Yes it is!

Before the tie could get underway a protest had been lodged by St Andrews. First test for the amended rules.

Here goes…

Freddie Hutchison, now resident in Paisley, was on holiday in Orkney and intended to play for Harray.

Surely not? Ah, but wasn't his mother's *usual address* at the time of his birth in Harray?

It was 'all systems go' at O.F.A. Headquarters.

According to the Minutes, both president and treasurer phoned Shapinsay (where he was born) and ascertained from the registrar there, that it did indeed state on his birth certificate that his parents were domiciled in Harray at the time of his birth. The St Andrews protest was therefore turned down and the five shilling fee forfeited!

So, under the new rule, Freddie was a winner and allowed to play. Of course, should he wish, he could no longer play for Shapinsay … Enough!

Now with Freddie Hutchison in the team playing in their problem

An inspired Orkney performance in 1958 gained a 6-6 draw against Hamilton Accies. Back row, left to right, Geddes Johnston (linesman), Leslie Flett, Bobby Hutchison, Brian Kemp, Findlay Young, Billy Stephen, Jim Merriman, Bill Sim (referee). Middle, Ian Hutchison, Alan Findlay, Jim Donaldson, Russell Groundwater, Alton Tait, Dave Keldie (trainer). Front, (ball boys) Alistair Gordon, Archer Kemp, Dougie Lloyd, Jim Cromarty, Bruce Farquhar, Mervyn Marwick. (Picture: Orkney Library)

position of goalkeeper, Harray dominated the semi final against the holders. They won the first leg at home 6-2 and consolidated their place in the final with a 2-1 victory in St Andrews. A sporting tie but nevertheless, revenge was sweet.

In the other semi final, making far fewer waves, South Ronaldsay eased past an improving Stromness by scores of 4-2 and 2-0. They were back in the final to face Harray in a repeat of the 1956 match. This time their chances should be much better.

Great care was now taken over team selection for the big night. The 'Hope selectors, mindful of the need for secrecy surrounding this important piece of decision making, met one evening in the old stable cum dressing room behind Robertson's shop, to hammer out the final eleven. The door was firmly barred!

After some time, they emerged to make their way to the café, the hub of social activity in the village, to make the formal announcement before an expectant gathering. When they arrived they discovered everybody animatedly discussing the team. It transpired that a well known local youth had been listening, ear to the stable door, and as soon as the last name had been approved, he had sped on his bicycle to the café with the news.

But, most agreed that it was a good selection and several days later, it was a confident crowd who made their way to Kirkwall on cup final night.

Unbeknown to them, however, another drama was being played out in the South Ronaldsay dressing room at the Bignold Park. Yes, it was another protest … this time from Harray.

Picture the scene…

Calvin Slater, a 17 year old South Ronaldsay forward is sitting in the dressing room preparing to get

Calvin Slater

changed for the biggest game of his life, when his team manager Edwin Headley accompanied by referee Bill Sim, come to inform him that Harray have lodged a protest over his eligibility. Although born in South Ronaldsay where his maternal grandparents resided, his *mother's usual address* had been in Kirkwall. Harray had become aware of this situation and the player was now informed that if he played, his team would forfeit the match.

This was a cruel blow since Calvin had played in every round leading to the final. Under the old rule this would have been fine but not now! The protest was upheld. Under the new rule, Calvin lost out!

What effect this had on the morale of his team mates is difficult to gauge. They certainly did not want to forfeit the match and took the field determined to upset the favourites and win the cup for their absent comrade. Calvin's place at inside left was taken by Arthur Dearness.

Harray were along familiar lines but had made one interesting team selection. Not since Jim Johnston of Yeldavale during the 1930s had Harray possessed a goalkeeper

Harray denied South Ronaldsay in 1958. Back row, left to right, Harry Flett, Frankie Johnston, Jackie Hutchison, Tom Flett. Middle, John Newlands, Bobby Hutchison, Ian Hutchison, Eric Hutchison, Peter Aim. Front, Jim Isbister, Leslie Flett, Brian Flett. (Picture: Orkney Library)

Birth, Blood

who played regular football. Davie Shearer had filled the gap for one year but was discovered to be living in Sandwick. Various others had been tried with limited success so this year they went for a drastic solution; play one of Orkney's best forwards, Ian Hutchison, in goal! He might be a safe pair of hands, but doing without his great goal scoring threat? Surely Harray knew what they were doing!

Teams were as follows:

South Ronaldsay: Jim Muir; Jimmy Doull and Steven Dearness; Tommy Dearness, Andy Sinclair and John Dearness; Bruce Esson, Harold Omand, Jack Walls, Arthur Dearness and Alex Rosie.

Harray: Ian Hutchison; Frankie Johnston and Tom Flett; Jim Isbister, Leslie Flett and Brian Flett; Jimmy Newlands, Bobby Hutchison, Jackie Hutchison, Eric Hutchison and Peter Aim.

A big crowd paying record gate receipts saw South Ronaldsay attack from the start. They took the lead after five minutes when a high dropping shot by Jimmy Doull went over the keeper into the net. For the rest of the half they took advantage of wind and slope to pepper the Harray goal with shots but no further scores were added.

At half time Harray made a key tactical switch. Ian Hutchison now gave way in goal to brother, Jackie. This worked instantly! Early in the half, Ian chased a ball down the right wing, crossed, and younger brother, Eric, drove home the equaliser. Harray were on top now and shortly afterwards, Brian Flett slipped the ball through for Eric to run in and score his second.

For the rest of the game, play was mostly in the South Ronaldsay half but there was no addition to the scoring. Harray emerged winners by two goals to one and equal Shapinsay's record of five Parish Cup wins.

Overall it had been a scrappy game, mainly due to the awkward cross wind. South Ronaldsay had displayed a lot of good approach work but lacked shooting power to finish it off. Harray had been below par but always looked capable of raising their game if required.

So, what next year? It was clear that the most important job facing team managers was not training *or* coaching *or* picking the team. It would be to visit the Registrars to find out just exactly where all the mothers were resident when their football playing offspring first saw the light of day.

Freddie Hutchison, for whom the new parish cup eligibility rule worked to advantage, pictured with the Milne Cup after Orkney's 5 – 2 win over Shetland in 1952

1959:
No stopping
St Andrews

Needless to say, the new ruling, which meant this one was allowed to play and that one not, was unsatisfactory. Common sense had to be applied in order to satisfy all possible claimants to a treasured place in a parish team. Therefore, a proposal which had previously been rejected on the grounds that it provided too much choice, was resurrected.

At the 1959 A.G.M. of Orkney Football Association, a motion was put forward by Rendall F.C. in the following terms:

"Either a player must have been born in, or his mother's usual address, as recorded by the Register of Births, must have been in, or he must qualify by residence in, the Parish for which he plays."

The motion was carried. The "*Born In*" clause was back after one year's absence while "*Mother's Usual Address*" was retained. Surely everybody would be happy now!

Details of the 1959 Parish Cup are sketchier than usual due to the printer's dispute which occupied almost seven weeks of the summer. This meant that only a limited news service was available through the provision of weekly News Sheets. While headline grabbing events were covered, more mundane matters such as football were left out, although editors did strive to provide the results. The strike was finally called off in August, in time for the cup final to be reported upon, but if any intrigue or controversy had taken place during the season, a *protest* for example, then it will exist only as a distant memory in the minds of the protagonists.

What we do know is that ten teams entered and the first round ties saw St Andrews defeat Holm while Birsay accounted for Sandwick. By the time the quarter finals came around, the results service had got into gear.

Quarter final Results

Birsay	2	Harray	2
Harray	5	Birsay	1
St Ola	7	Deerness	2
Deerness	0	St Ola	4
St Andrews	2	Stromness	0
Stromness	0	St Andrews	1
South Ron.	3	Shapinsay	0

Second leg was not reported

The results went to form with only Stromness, led by 19 year old county half back Colin Poke, providing stubborn resistance. St Ola, making one of their sporadic appearances in the tournament, looked to have brought their shooting boots. Now what would the semi final draw produce?

For the football purists, hoping to see the top two teams in the final, some disappointment; for the supporter at large, some excitement at the possibility of an outsider winning. Yes, Harray were drawn to face St Andrews.

This year, from the remarkable see-saw rivalry between the teams, it was the turn of St Andrews to emerge victorious. Meanwhile from another high scoring tie it was St Ola who hung on to claim the second cup final place.

Semi final Results

Harray	1	St Andrews	2
St Andrews	3	Harray	2
South Ron.	2	St Ola	4
St Ola	4	South Ron.	4

Despite the absence of Harray, the pundits expected a close game and were looking forward to seeing the high scoring St Ola attack coming up against the rugged St Andrews defence; in particular, how would Robbie Pottinger and Co. cope with the likes of Russell Groundwater and Eric Kemp?

But St Andrews themselves were not short in the attacking department having a forward line which could boast inter county 'cap' Alton Tait and certainly one of the fittest players in Orkney, Wattie Shearer, regular winner and record holder for the Wideford Hill Race.

Not for the first time, it had been a dismal County Show day. Steady, seeping drizzle had fallen all day in Kirkwall although much of Orkney had seen no rain at all. But by evening, skies had cleared and it turned out a very pleasant August evening but the surface of the pitch was left greasy and treacherous after all the rain.

The following teams prepared to do battle before the customary large crowd:

St Andrews: Walter Scott; Ian Rendall and Dave Pottinger; Bryan Clark, Robbie Pottinger and Colin Tait, Eoin Bews, Alton Tait, Archie Clark, Eddie Craigie and Wattie Shearer.

St Ola: Brian Kemp; Gavin Carter and Doug Wylie; Jim Wilson, Dave Wylie and John Byers; Jimmy Miller, Russell Groundwater, Eric Kemp, Geordie Miller and Douglas Corse.

St Andrews won the toss and chose to play up the slope. The early exchanges were fairly even but then Wattie Shearer crossed a high ball beyond the keeper which was missed by the defence and Archie Clark steered it into an empty St Ola net. The same players combined shortly

St Andrews' cup winning team of 1959. Back row, left to right, Ian Rendall, Walter Scott, Davie Pottinger. Middle, Eoin Bews, Alton Tait, Archie Clark, Eddie Craigie, Wattie Shearer. Front, Bryan Clark, Robbie Pottinger, Colin Tait.   *(Picture: Orkney Library)*

Birth, Blood

afterwards for Clark to score his second. One minute later, a mix up in the St Ola box saw the ball roll into the net off a defender.

Three goals nil to St Andrews after half an hour and the St Ola defence were in disarray.

Early in the second half, Bews made it four with a fierce drive. Although St Ola got back into the game briefly through a goal by Groundwater, Alton Tait added a fifth for St Andrews with a powerfully struck free kick.

Final score 5-1 to St Andrews.

The game was something of a disappointment, St Ola coming across as a collection of individuals rather than a team. St Andrews on the other hand earned credit for their teamwork and all round capabilities. A measure of *The Orcadian* correspondent's poor impression of the match was that he regarded the display by Kirkwall City Pipe Band during the interval as one of the highlights of the evening.

But there was no denying St Andrews their success and increasingly impressive record in the competition. Four finals, Four wins! Only one more needed to equal the record of Harray and Shapinsay!

The decade had been dominated by a small number of very good parish teams but several others were not far behind and in another era might well have gone on to greater success. Among them was Firth, who reached the semi final on three occasions. Pictured here are the Firth Corsie Cup winners of 1952, back row, left to right, Victor Clouston, Stewart Craigie, Jim Scott. Middle. Alistair Tulloch, Jim Wilson, Reynold Shearer, Billy Wilson, Robert Miller. Front. Alistair Mackay, Ronnie Flett and Andrew Robertson.

The Swinging 60s

1960: Old Order swings into the 60s

We now hit the decade which was later to be known as "The Swinging Sixties". Everywhere the accent would be on the liberation of youth as they strove to break free from the shackles of the post war years and the dreary days of the 1950s, to express themselves in all sorts of ways.

Two or three years were yet to pass before the Beatles and the Rolling Stones blasted away the crooners and singers of sickly ballads at venues like the Cavern in Liverpool or the Crawdaddy Club in Richmond; before long hair, miniskirts and flower power dominated fashion; before Matt Busby's finest protégé, George Best, hypnotised the nation with a brand of fantasy football never before equalled save by 'Roy of the Rovers.'

Closer to home it was a similar story. The Big Band Sound or Scottish music still dominated the scene at Orkney dances but the Nomads and the Cossacks were only a few years away from wowing the local youth in the Cosmo with their own brand of Pop or Blues; not so many flowers in the hair perhaps, but local fashion would emulate the latest from Carnaby Street, as paraded on Top of the Pops, while no self respecting lad at the mart on Mondays would be without his 'mop-top' hairstyle to go with his bib-and-brace dungarees; and as for football … Orkney had its very own version of Busby and his famous Babes!

Yes, Ben 'Busby' was his name, alias that legendary Parish Cup man, Ben Norquoy, now of Birsay, and he had a team who were likened to Matt's original line up, many of whom had perished in the Munich air disaster.

Scarcely any of Ben's team were beyond their teens or early twenties, the new generation from Birsay

farms whose names originated way back in Norse times: Billy and Barry Tait of 'Ingsay', Gordy Norquoy of 'Mucklequoy', Davy Whitelaw of 'Garthsetter', Jimmy Ritch of 'Langskaill', Billy Wylie of 'Skesquoy', Sandy Meadows of 'Gairsty', Sandy Brown of 'Howally' ….

This team had already won the Corsie Cup for 'B' League teams playing a swash buckling, carefree style of football, and now for the Parish Cup, they could include Stewart and Bertie Spence of 'Norton' and the very experienced Willie Spence, formerly of 'Makerhouse'. Surely this would be the combination to blow away the old order in this season's tournament.

Oh yes, this could be the year for youth all right; there was something in the air!

No fewer than fourteen teams, an all time record, put their names in the hat for this year's draw. Obviously a few fancied their chances.

First round Results

Stromness	1	Harray	5
Harray	6	Stromness	3
Stromness	1	St Ola	4
St Ola	3	Stromness	0
Orphir	4	Holm	0
Holm	5	Orphir	3
Firth	3	Birsay	2
Birsay	4	Firth	3
Replay			
Firth	1	Birsay	3
Deerness	1	Sandwick	4
Sandwick	2	Deerness	0

The young Birsay team gave their legions of supporters an anxious time before seeing off Firth and they would now test themselves against the might of St Andrews.

Quarter final Results

Harray	2	South Ron.	2
South Ron.	1	Harray	5
Shapinsay	1	St Ola	4
St Ola	2	Shapinsay	1

'Ben Busby's Babes', a.k.a. Birsay, winners of the Corsie Cup in 1960. Back row, left to right, Ben Norquoy (senior), Billy Wylie, Jim Hay, Jimmy Ritch, Jim Donaldson (referee). Middle, Benny Norquoy (junior), Barry Tait, Sandy Brown, Eddie Gray, Billy Tait. Front, Bertie Marwick, Gordy Norquoy, Davy Whitelaw.

Birsay   1   St Andrews   3
St Andrews   9   Birsay   3

Sandwick   1   Orphir   3
Orphir   4   Sandwick   0

After all the build up it looked a bit like the 'slaughter of the innocents' Yet by half time in the second leg in St Andrews, the teams were level on aggregate. Then the champions hit Birsay with a second half blitz during which their young defence caved in. Of the eight goals they leaked, Alton Tait and Sidney Garrioch each helped themselves to hat tricks. But maybe Birsay's chance would come again as they gained experience.

For the past two years the 'Old Firm' had met in the semi finals and as fate would have it they were drawn together again. With due respect to St Ola and Orphir, in the minds of the public, the winner of this tie would lift the trophy.

The Harray and St Andrews fans, accustomed to many a bruising battle over the years, were not let down by the latest episode. Desperately close all the way, it took three games to separate them. Orphir, meanwhile, made everyone sit up and take note with an unexpectedly decisive win over St Ola.

In a blistering opening quarter of an hour, Eoin Clouston, the Orphir centre forward, struck four times to leave St Ola reeling. Not only did it ensure victory for his team but it earned the striker £1 from a bet placed by the Orphir bus driver that he wouldn't score three or more in the game. It was plain to see that Eoin had all the makings of a highly successful businessman.

Semi final Results

Harray   2   St Andrews   1
St Andrews   2   Harray   1

Replay

Harray   1   St Andrews   2

Orphir   3   St Ola   3
St Ola   1   Orphir   5

Could Orphir now possibly … just maybe … cause an upset?

The final, alas, played on a perfect evening, proved to be disappointing and one sided. Orphir were outclassed in most areas of the field and once St Andrews got into their stride, goals came at regular intervals. Alton Tait and Eddie Craigie notched a goal each before half time and in the second half, Tait scored again while Craigie added three more to his tally.

Apart from appreciating St Andrews' superiority and goal scoring prowess, there was little to enthuse the large crowd. Only Findlay, Flett, Clouston and goalkeeper Firth earned pass marks for Orphir.

Final score, St Andrews 6 Orphir 0.

As for St Andrews, any number of superlatives could be used. On the night, Robbie Pottinger was again outstanding keeping a tight grip on danger man Eoin Clouston, while Eddie Craigie must have been 'Man of the Match' with his four cup final goals, only the third man to have achieved the feat in the history of the competition. Admittedly St Andrews had merely equalled the record of five Parish Cup wins but, having achieved the feat within a period of nine years, their claim to be the best parish team ever, must now be undisputed.

Teams were as follows:

Orphir: Kenny Firth; Billy Stanger and Douglas Liddle; Sandy Flett, Alan Findlay and Colin Stanger; Arnold Firth, Duncan Currie, Eoin Clouston , Stanley Thomson and Kenny Anderson.

St Andrews: Walter Scott; Ian Rendall and Dave Pottinger; Bryan Clark, Robbie Pottinger and Colin Tait; Eoin Bews, Wattie Shearer, Eddie Craigie, Alton Tait and Sidney Garrioch.

As the sporting year drew to a close, the established performers, who had

been bracing themselves to guard against being swept away by a tide of youthful vigour, were asking what had happened.

Nothing in the air so far! Ah, but maybe the answer lay a couple of years ahead when the current crop of junior footballers came of age? The cream would be on display this year in the match against Shetland.

The outcome had Corinthian reaching into his dictionary to find words suitable to convey his emotions:

"Never in Orkney's football history has such a dismal display ever been witnessed, and never again will such a humiliating defeat be inflicted upon a representative team!"

The score had been Orkney 2, Shetland 11! Admittedly, much of this had been due to a centre forward of genius, Bert Sinclair, who had bagged *eight* goals, but all the same ….

Yes, the 'Old Order' could sleep soundly in their beds for a while yet. It was the 'Sixties' right enough … only, the 'Swinging' bit had yet to arrive!

Eddie Craigie, St Andrews' four goal centre forward in the demolition of Orphir.

1961:
'Hope stumble for third time

Those with memories that go back far enough, may recall a catastrophic event which happened far off in the South Atlantic Ocean but which captured worldwide headlines in 1961. A volcano had erupted on the tiny island of Tristan Da Cunha causing all its inhabitants to be evacuated to escape the lava spill which destroyed homes and habitation.

When new homes were being sought for the evacuees, the local M.P., Jo Grimond, made representations for some of them to be relocated to Orkney; not so much 'offered', as 'pleaded'!

Why the urgency of his request?

The truth was that Orkney's population had plummeted, falling by 11.8 per cent in the previous ten years according to the 1961 census. The reasons for this would have been numerous, smaller size of families for example, but a significant factor now was emigration, as young men, who were no longer required in such numbers on farms, went abroad in search of a new life. The former Colonies encouraged this process by offering assisted passages; £10 would take you as far as Australia!

The falling numbers had an inevitable consequence for parish football teams because it was from the country districts and islands that the greatest drift was to occur.

As an example, Harray had now lost three players from cup winning teams in recent times. Brothers, Willie and Andrew Adamson both emigrated to Canada although Andrew later moved to New Zealand where he still lives. Tom Kirkness of Warth in Sandwick, who had worked on the farm of Northbigging in

Harray, also chose to make a new life for himself in Canada.

Most parish teams would be affected by this process both now and in the future, so when Mr Grimond made his offer to the evacuated islanders, some began to sit up and take note.

Football fan Jo Grimond presents the 1961 Milne Cup to captain Bobby Hutchison after Orkney's 6 – 4 victory over Shetland at the Bignold Park. (Picture: Orkney Library)

Maybe Tristan Da Cunarians could play football?

It was rumoured that Harray had actually inquired if there were any goalkeepers living on the island, such was their 'custodial' crisis. If there were, we shall never know because no evacuees actually came to Orkney but it certainly caused a flutter of excitement at the time.

Now if Harray had secured a new keeper he would have been left twiddling his thumbs this year. Here's what happened.

Harray had been drawn to play Stenness in round one but on the day of the match it had rained steadily and there was no sign of conditions improving as the evening approached. Harray assumed the game had been postponed but the hardy souls of Stenness turned up to play on schedule … as did the referee! The game had not been called off so the outcome

Deerness won the Corsie Cup and McDonald Cup in 1961. The squad comprised, back row, left to right, Bob Foubister, Freddie Wylie, Andy Laird, Denis Laughton, Allan Smith, Jim Wick. Middle, Kenny Ritch, Wilfred Scott, Kenny Eunson, Colin Eunson, Geordie Croy. Front, Leslie Foubister, Jackie Clouston, Ian Rendall. (Picture: Orkney Library)

Birth, Blood

was Harray's elimination from the tournament.

I imagine sympathy would have been in short supply from the other ten entrants who now saw their chances of success greatly enhanced.

Among those fancied to put up a good show was once again Birsay, who had now followed the St Andrews' example of joining the 'A' League in the hope that it would raise the standard sufficiently to capture the Parish Cup. Meanwhile, showing a remarkable return to former glories was Deerness who had swept all before them in 'B' competitions. Maybe they too might make an impact.

First round Results

Sandwick	0	Birsay	3
Birsay	6	Sandwick	2
St Andrews	2	Stromness	1
Stromness	0	St Andrews	4

On then to the quarter finals where the other half of the 'Old Firm' were to suffer an unexpected reversal.

Quarter final Results

| Birsay | 8 | Stenness | 0 |
| Stenness scratched | | | |

| Firth | 0 | South Ron. | 2 |
| South Ron. | 2 | Firth | 2 |

Deerness v Shapinsay
Shapinsay scratched

| St Ola | 3 | St Andrews | 0 |
| St Andrews | 1 | St Ola | 1 |

There you have it! St Ola established their first leg lead with goals by Gavin Carter, Douglas Corse and Russell Groundwater and this was enough to ensure that, for the first time since 1955, there would be a different name on the trophy.

The semi finals now produced two great games with plenty of goals. The outcomes in both were very close until St Ola cut loose in the second leg against Deerness and won with some style. For Birsay, their day had still not dawned.

Semi final Results

Birsay	3	South Ron.	4
South Ron.	4	Birsay	3
Deerness	3	St Ola	4
St Ola	7	Deerness	1

Could South Ronaldsay make it third time lucky and record their first Parish Cup win or could St Ola triumph for the third time? At least this time, there would be no 'niggle' about their 'choice of players'. The boundaries of Kirkwall were extended in April, 1961, to take in both Hatston and Weyland Bay, thus bringing all Town Council housing schemes within the boundary of the Burgh.

The cup final teams were evenly matched with both able to field a liberal sprinkling of 'A' players. St Ola could call on the Kemp brothers (Thorfinn), the Miller brothers (Hotspur), Alistair Muir (Hotspur), Ralph Fotheringhame and Russell Groundwater (Rovers). A strong line up!

South Ronaldsay were bolstered by Andy Sinclair and Bruce Esson (Hotspur) and the reinstated Calvin Slater (Thorfinn).

The following teams took the field on a calm, windless evening before 1,500 spectators:

South Ronaldsay: Jimmy Muir; Robert Mathieson and Billy Norquoy; Harold Omand, Andy Sinclair and John Dearness; Jack Omand, Bruce Esson, Calvin Slater, Alex Rosie and Ron Greenwood.

St Ola: Brian Kemp; Alex Ritchie and Davie Wylie; Jimmy Miller, Eric Kemp and John Byers; Gavin Carter, Russell Groundwater, Ralph Fotheringhame, Douglas Corse and Geordie Miller.

St Ola chose to play up the slope but for most of the half were under pressure. South Ronaldsay were the better team although the closest either side came to a goal was when Carter of St Ola hit a post. At half time, the score sheet was still blank.

Not actually the St Ola winning team of 1961 but a picture taken earlier in that season. Back row, left to right, Eric Kemp, Craigie Fotheringhame, Brian Kemp, Jimmy Miller, Geordie Miller, Davie Wylie. Front, Gavin Carter, Alistair Muir, Russell Groundwater, Bertie Marwick, Ralph Fotheringhame.
(Picture: Orkney Library)

In the second half, St Ola gradually got on top but were also off target. Their opening goal. when it came, was very soft, keeper Muir dropping a cross shot from Carter, which then rolled over the line. St Ola continued to press and scored a second when Groundwater escaped the clutches of Sinclair and ran in to shoot past Muir.

Despite South Ronaldsay's best attempts to draw level, the St Ola defence gave little away and the game finished, St Ola 2, South Ronaldsay 0.

Nobody would grudge St Ola their third Parish Cup success as they were the better team on the night but public sympathy was starting to grow for South Ronaldsay: three finals, three defeats. Their colloquial name 'the 'Hope' was beginning to take on an added degree of significance.

Not helping their cause was the fact that two of their number, Bruce Esson and Ron Greenwood would eventually join the emigration exodus, to Canada and Australia, respectively. To help them secure the top prize they would need reinforcements from somewhere.

Time to get Jo Grimond back on the case!

1962: St Andrews prove unstoppable

The loss of manpower was now having big repercussions for Orkney's football teams. So few were the entries for the 'B' League that the O.F.A. decided the two remaining clubs should join the Reserve teams in their league, but these predominantly Kirkwall based outfits were far from happy at having to travel to the far flung outposts of Deerness and Rendall.

When it came to the Parish Cup, the story was the same. Parishes with proud tradition such as Shapinsay, Sandwick, Orphir, Holm and Firth were unable to muster teams while Stenness, who had originally entered, were forced to withdraw before a ball was kicked. It was a gloomy picture indeed.

Showing no signs of wilting however were the forces of St Andrews or Harray, although Birsay, with their relatively small player pool were beginning to be very stretched, especially if injuries were to occur. Key defender, Gordy Norquoy, for instance, had been forced to stop playing for most of the season.

When the first round kicked off, there were only three games for parish spectators to enjoy:

First round Results

South Ron.	2	Birsay	6
Birsay	4	South Ron.	6
Stromness	1	Harray	1
Harray	5	Stromness	0
St Ola	3	Deerness	4
Deerness	3	St Ola	5
St Andrews	w.o.	Stenness	

Some terrific ties there judging by the score lines with both South Ronaldsay and Deerness unlucky to lose out. When the semi final draw was made, fans were again denied the possibility of a Harray v St Andrews final as these two came out of the hat together. However, the Birsay v St Ola match also promised high quality entertainment.

Semi final Results

Harray	2	St Andrews	1
St Andrews	2	Harray	0
Birsay	2	St Ola	3
St Ola	3	Birsay	3

Although Harray held a first leg advantage, this was cancelled out by Eddie Craigie in the first minute of the return before a Harray player had touched the ball. For the remainder of the match, played in torrential rain, both sides attacked each other relentlessly until with five minutes left, Eoin Bews forced the ball over the line during a goalmouth scramble, to secure St Andrews' place in another final.

Birsay had desperately hard luck in their semi final, playing by far the better football in both legs, but they lacked a finisher of the calibre of Russell Groundwater. With two minutes of the second leg to go the game was all square. Groundwater had scored twice for St Ola but Birsay's three goals by Leslie Flett, Bertie Spence and 16 year old Brian Spence, looked to have earned them a replay at least.

But they reckoned without Groundwater. He got the ball, controlled it in an instant, beat two defenders and slipped the equaliser past Jim Hay. St Ola were through by a 6-5 aggregate, while the Birsay boys were left muttering "Wan o' these days! Wan o' these days!"

1962 must have been a very wet year. The final on County Show night was played in dreadful conditions of strong wind and driving rain which soaked players to the skin and turned the pitch into a quagmire on which it was impossible to play good football. A crowd of only 600 or so braved the elements to see the following teams line up:

St Ola: Brian Kemp; Craigie Fotheringhame and Dave Wylie; Geordie Miller, Eric Kemp and Bertie Marwick; Jimmy Miller, Russell Groundwater, Gavin Carter, Ralph Fotheringhame and Douglas Corse.

St Andrews: Walter Scott; Ian Rendall and Colin Tait; Bryan Clark, Robbie Pottinger and Leslie Tait; Eoin Bews, Alton Tait, Archie Clark, Eddie Craigie and Wattie Shearer.

St Andrews decided to play against the elements in the first half and defended stubbornly throughout. St Ola could not penetrate the powerful opposition defence so there was no scoring at half time.

The teams changed straight over without a break and St Andrews now applied the pressure. They found Brian Kemp the goalkeeper in great form but eventually a defensive misunderstanding allowed Archie Clark to nip in to score.

St Andrews began to dominate the game and it was all over when Eddie Craigie beat two opponents and fired a great shot from the edge of the area into the net. There was no more scoring and St Andrews ran out 2-0 winners.

This final was a landmark win for St Andrews as, with this victory, they had won the coveted trophy more times than any other parish, six in all and moreover, they had a one hundred per cent record: six finals, six wins!

Could they improve on that? Of course they could. This was still a team at the peak of their powers and four of the side, Walter Scott, Bryan Clark, Alton Tait and Eddie Craigie, had been in this year's Orkney team which had beaten Shetland 5-4 in Lerwick.

And not only were they only blessed with an abundance of skill, they could be as hard as nails, as and when required. This is well

illustrated on one occasion when a particularly loud mouthed bystander had been giving a St Andrews' player 'dogs abuse' throughout a game. The victim said nothing but bided his time.

Eventually the ball ran out of play near the source of the irritation.

This was the moment…

The player careered after it at full tilt and ran straight through his antagonist, sending him sprawling in several directions. He then retrieved the ball before approaching the spread-eagled spectator enquiring politely, "Excuse me, is this your cep?"

Unless some of the other parishes could draw up an immigration policy, adopt measures to improve the birth rate, or supply batches of spectators who had a bite to match their bark, it looked like St Andrews would remain at the top of the heap for some time to come.

1963: Footballers go square eyed!

You know what the problem was all along? T.V.! Too many folk were sitting inside watching too much T.V.!

Since television had first arrived in Orkney in 1955 and, more significantly, since the transmitter station at Netherbutton had opened in 1959, the number of people owning sets in the county had increased dramatically. At the dawn of the new decade, there were about 2,000 sets in Orkney and by 1963, that total would almost certainly have doubled.

So now, instead of going out to the football pitch for a kick about of an evening, the local youth would join their elders in catching the latest crime drama on 'Z-Cars'; tremble, trigger fingers twitching at the adventures way out west in 'The Lone Ranger'; or even, perish the thought, 'heuch' along to the weekly tartan tomfoolery in the 'White Heather Club.'

Orcadians were truly smitten. It was said that men coming home for their dinner during the week were frequently arriving late back to work through hanging on for the end of 'Andy Pandy', 'The Flower Pot Men' or 'The Wooden Tops'. As a wide eyed 15 year old at the time, I recall being equally hooked, not so much on 'Andy Pandy' maybe, but more on the likes of 'Grandstand', when, on a Saturday afternoon from one o'clock until five, every last kick, blow or rev. of an engine had to be savoured. It was even better when we got one of these bits of coloured plastic to stick over the screen: blue at the top for the sky; green at the bottom for grass; and pink in the middle for … everything in between! Wow!

What could football organisers do in the face of such widespread addiction to this new drug? So bad had things become that this year, only one, single 'B' team came forward from the country districts; three years earlier there had been *eight!* Unwilling to join the Reserve teams, or play against themselves, the men of Rendall opted to do without football and instead, settled down in their armchairs.

There was some consolation in that Deerness put a team into the 'A' League along with Birsay but, with the exception of Dounby's Harray contingent and St Andrews, as far as country teams playing football was concerned, that was it!

Not a bright prospect for the Parish Cup but surprisingly, nine teams came forward. This meant only one first round game but look at the result!

Harray	2	South Ron.	4
South Ron.	6	Harray	1

Was this the start of Harray's decline as a football force? Certainly their supporters wondered if they were now to go the same road as great champions before them, Shapinsay, Deerness or Holm. As it happened, one of these sides was showing a welcome return to something like former glories.

Quarter final Results

Stromness	v	St Andrews	
Stromness scratched			
Shapinsay	1	Birsay	2
Birsay	3	Shapinsay	0
Deerness	5	South Ron.	2
South Ron.	3	Deerness	2
Sandwick	0	St Ola	4
St Ola	5	Sandwick	1

A great performance by Deerness but instead of celebrating that, the Press chose to concentrate on other issues depicting the poor state of the game at grass roots level, or should I say 'hay roots'! In an article headed "PITCHES LIKE HAYFIELDS", the football correspondent of *The Orcadian* sounded a warning to country teams to improve their habits or face the consequences.

There had been complaints, he said, that grass was allowed to grow so long that in some cases "it trips players up and balls get lost. Sometimes line markings are not visible and corner posts vary from *clothes stretchers to walking sticks!*" Well, they probably got the idea off 'Blue Peter.'

Clubs were further advised that "the referee can call off the game but has not yet done so because of the travel expenses involved for the visiting team. If this were reported to the O.F.A., however, they could order the home team to pay the expenses of the visitors' bus hire."

Tough talking indeed … and there was more! Apparently referees had complained about players not turning up in time for kick off, the official sometimes having to wait up to half an hour until everybody arrived. (Wasn't 'Bronco' or 'Laramie' on just after tea?). Clubs were reminded of the problem of recruiting referees and they would not be attracted if they had to endure more of this sloppy practice.

Oh dear! Morale very low indeed!

On to the semi finals where Birsay were the only West Mainland representatives.

Semi final Results

Deerness	0	St Andrews	2
St Andrews	5	Deerness	0
Birsay	2	St Ola	3
St Ola	1	Birsay	2
Replay			
Birsay	0	St Ola	3

Again Birsay had fallen at the penultimate hurdle. This prompted 'Corinthian' in *The Orcadian* to ask, almost in disbelief: "What is wrong with Birsay? A well balanced team, they should be too good for part time St Ola but never combine as a team. There is too much individual play."

Some supporters believed that breaking up Birsay's league team to include Dounby players in the Parish side was the root of the problem; very good players admittedly but not used to playing with Birsay regulars. Others suggested that team spirit also suffered.

So it was a final between the two 'Saints' and the promise of an excellent game but now, in this year of universal apathy, came another problem.

After thirty years or so of uninterrupted cup final reporting, all of a sudden there is no written report to refer to. Was Corinthian incapacitated in some way; did he go on strike; or was he too super glued to the box? Amidst the usual welter of agricultural show results and horticultural society statistics during the month of August, no cup final information was to be found. Since *The Orkney Herald* had ceased production in January, 1961, there

was no fall back position either.

So what can a body do? Rely on someone's memory? Alas, both these teams were so used to playing cup finals that over a period of 40 years, games tend to blur into each other. I have yet to unearth anyone who can tell me anything other than "It was another poor night." and "Extra time was played." At least the result was recorded:

St Andrews   3   St Ola   2

Seven finals, seven wins. This team had 'greatness' stamped all over it.

Teams were as follows:

St Andrews: Walter Scott; Jockie Rosie and Leslie Tait; Bryan Clark, Robbie Pottinger and Eddie Craigie; Eoin Bews, Wattie Shearer, Archie Clark, Alton Tait and Sidney Garrioch.

St Ola (probable): Brian Kemp; Craigie Fotheringhame and Dave Wylie; Jimmy Miller, Eric Kemp and John Byers; Bertie Marwick,

Gavin Carter, Russell Groundwater, Douglas Corse and Geordie Miller.

In a generally depressing football year, there was one bright note. In addition to the usual teams from Kirkwall and Stromness, juniors from the country districts had begun to emerge again. Teams had come forward from Birsay, Rendall, Deerness and South Ronaldsay and the first named had actually won the Junior League.

This would be the leading edge of the 'baby boomer' generation, those born in the years immediately after the war. Now if they could be kept away from counter attractions, surely 'Opportunity Knocks.' For the very keen and dedicated, 'The Sky's The Limit,' but as to who would have the best prospects, you can 'Take Your Pick.'

Ach! There wis cheust no' gettin' awey fae hid!

It was the second of two consecutive wins for St Andrews in 1963. Back row, left to right, Jackie Tait, Jim Baillie, Bryan Clark, Walter Scott, Eddie Craigie, Billy Gorn, Jackie Mowatt. Middle, Eoin Bews, Alton Tait, Archie Clark, Sidney Garrioch, Jockie Rosie. Front, Leslie Tait, Robbie Pottinger, Wattie Shearer.
(Picture: Orkney Library)

& Boundaries

1964:
Cup goes to the West again

Looking back now, it seems that 1963 marked a low point in terms of interest in football and, for a time, the following year looked like continuing that trend. Coming in for criticism now, however, was not so much the reluctant footballer as the spectating public.

Attendances at games had dropped alarmingly and the first 'Football Feature' of the year in *The Orcadian* contained an appeal for spectators to turn out and support the teams. Whereas only fifteen years earlier, a crowd of close on 5,000 watched the inter county game in the Bignold Park, and figures in excess of 2,000 were common place, now a mere fraction of that number would spectate.

Who or what was getting the blame? Still T.V., of course. Instead of watching the local team, fans could view all the sport they wanted "from the comfort of fireside chairs."

It would remain to be seen whether this call to arms would be successful but, in the meantime, it was not all doom and gloom. If there was hope at all it was to be found in youth. There was still no 'B' League for country teams but there was at least a fairly healthy Junior League. Teams had come forward form K.G.S., Rovers, Hotspur, Thorfinn, Stromness, South Ronaldsay and Rendall. This year it was the turn of Rendall to collect the honours. I tingle yet at the memory. Although their team was drawn from several West Mainland parishes such as Evie, Firth and Sandwick, here could be seen the embryo of future parish teams.

As far as senior football was concerned a remarkable story was unfolding. St Andrews set off at a cracking pace and led the 'A' League from start to finish to finally triumph in the premier competition for the first time in their history. Reward at last for many years of perseverance in the top flight. Now it was felt they would continue to dominate the Parish Cup this year and beyond. But, as 'Corinthian' noted, "Some queer things happen in football." Take note!

Continuing on a slightly more optimistic note, ten teams entered this year and in addition to St Andrews, those thought to be in with a chance were Birsay and St Ola.

First round Results

St Andrews	4	Orphir	0
Orphir	0	St Andrews	2
St Ola	6	Stromness	0
Stromness	0	St Ola	7

St Andrews appeared to be in cruise mode while St Ola's task had been made easier by an injury during the first leg to Stromness' county centre half Colin Poke.

Quarter final Results

Deerness	3	Holm	0
Holm	1	Deerness	7
South Ron.	1	Harray	4
Harray	4	South Ron.	2
St Ola	v	Sandwick	

Sandwick scratched

Birsay	1	St Andrews	2
St Andrews	1	Birsay	0

Harray gained revenge for last year's trouncing by South Ronaldsay but 'Ben Busby's Babes' once again failed to convert their great potential into success. Now to the semi finals where a major surprise awaited.

Semi final Results

Harray	6	Deerness	1
Deerness	1	Harray	4
St Ola	3	St Andrews	1
St Andrews	3	St Ola	3

How about that? St Andrews in their finest hour knocked out of the cup when a hat trick of wins beckoned, while Harray, thought to be down and out judging by recent form, had

Harray's cup winning squad of 1964. Back row, left to right, Mike Drever, Frankie Johnston, Edric Clouston, Stewart Sinclair, John Sinclair. Middle, Stanley Hutchison, Harry Flett, Ian Hutchison, Eric Hutchison, Peter Aim. Front, Bobby Hutchison, Leslie Flett, Robbie Scott.
(Picture: Orkney Library)

reached the final for the first time since 1958 with what looked to be another strong, well balanced team.

Most significantly of all Harray had found a specialist goalkeeper, Edric Clouston, and this had enabled highly effective outfield players such as Ian Hutchison and Frankie Johnston to be used to greater advantage. But a more substantial transition was taking place in the parish as younger players gradually replaced the older generation. Their cup final team now contained a number of players making their first appearance at this level, including the first of a new generation of Hutchisons, Jackie's son, Stanley.

Teams were as follows:

Harray: Edric Clouston; Frankie Johnston and Stewart Sinclair; Bobby Hutchison, Leslie Flett and Robbie Scott; Stanley Hutchison, Harry Flett, Ian Hutchison, Eric Hutchison and Peter Aim.

St Ola (probable): Brian Kemp; Craigie Fotheringhame and Jimmy Miller; Eric Kemp, Alistair Muir and Geordie Miller; Gavin Carter, Ralph Fotheringhame, Bertie Marwick, Russell Groundwater and Douglas Corse.

The clue lies in the word "probable". Whatever the problem was in reporting matches, it was still not resolved. Only a small paragraph appeared in *The Orcadian* as follows:

"Congratulations to Harray on winning the Parish Cup. They were well ahead of St Ola, who only made a fight of it in the second half by which time Harray had made pretty certain the cup would go west."

In fact Harray overpowered St Ola 6-2. They had re-established themselves, not only as champions, but as a team whose long, lean period could well be over.

However, the identity of whoever inflicted the damage on St Ola will have to remain a mystery …

1965:
Titanic struggle in 'hardest' final

We were not out of the woods yet. Although last season had ended on a slightly more positive note, now another crisis loomed on the horizon. There were no referees! Correction … there was *one*! With fifteen teams entered for 'A' and Reserve competitions and the Parish Cup to come on top of that, he would be kept busy. Well, surely they could stagger kick off times or something?

After deliberating on the issue, the O.F.A. decided to set up an instruction class for budding referees and agreed to make a bonus payment to anyone who passed the examination. This would be in addition to the fee paid by the club. So, by increased remuneration, it was hoped not only to obtain more officials but to improve the standard of refereeing.

Well nothing succeeds like a bit of bribery. The bonus was surely a tempting one because no fewer than seventeen candidates came forward for the class. If a proportion of these could pass, Orkney would be better off than it had ever been for 'whistlers.' Peep! Next problem? Well, none for a bit!

Of the fifteen competing teams this year, most interesting newcomers to the 'A' League were Rendall whose side would be built around last season's successful junior team. On the debit side, Deerness, who existed on a small diet of players, were forced to withdraw from all competitions except the Parish Cup. The loss of star forward, Colin Eunson, who had emigrated to Australia, was a severe blow.

The improved number of entries for most competitions this year did not extend to the Parish Cup, where again there was a noticeable

falling off, only eight teams coming forward. Of these, one would withdraw before the action started. The 'baby boomer' generation would be in their late teens by now but they must be pursuing activities other than football.

Peep! Another foul up! There had been problems with match reporting in recent years but now it had extended to the results service. Only sketchy results were published from the first round.

What did happen was as follows:

Shapinsay	0	St Ola	6
St Ola	v	Shapinsay	

(Shapinsay scratched)

St Andrews defeated Stromness

Deerness	0	South Ron.	4

South Ron. defeated Deerness

Birsay	2	Harray	4

Harray defeated Birsay

Although St Andrews were in the semi final it looked as if the great team might just have reached the top of the hill and were beginning the descent. 'A' League champions last year, they had performed poorly this time in comparison and finished well down the order. Were age or injuries taking their toll? In the case of the latter, they had lost key man Eddie Craigie for most of the year with a ligament injury.

Happily, the semi final story was reported in the Press. St Andrews were again drawn with Harray and after the first leg, the headlines referred, not so much to the game itself, as to the Harray team:

"6 HUTCHISONS"

"What must stand as a record in Orkney football happened the other night when the Harray team fielded no less than six Hutchisons in their game against St Andrews in the Parish Cup. And they were all related, three brothers, Bobby, Ian and Eric, and their three nephews, Alan, Stanley and Keith. And the entire forward line read:

S. Hutchison, R. Hutchison, A. Hutchison, E. Hutchison and K. Hutchison. Ian was at centre half. With Harray winning 3-1 and despite some caustic remarks from some of the St Andrews boys, I still think Harray will make the final … "

Now, if Jackie and Fred had still been playing?

Make the final they did as the results show:

Semi final Results

Harray	3	St Andrews	1
St Andrews	1	Harray	2
South Ron.	2	St Ola	3
St Ola	4	South Ron.	3

South Ronaldsay had again come desperately close, the difference between the teams on this occasion being St Ola's Alan Findlay, whose two late goals at Pickaquoy saw his team home.

This should now be an intriguing final between the rejuvenated cup holders and a St Ola team studded with county players. Alan Findlay, Eric Kemp, Alistair Muir, Brian Paterson and Russell Groundwater had all played in this year's matches against Caithness and Shetland. They would take a bit of stopping!

When the line ups were announced for the final, Alan Findlay was missing, injured, for St Ola, his place being taken by Victor Clouston, formerly of Firth. For Harray, the Hutchison front 'five' did not materialise, Emile Flett taking the left wing berth. He must have felt a bit like a gate crasher at a party!

Teams were as follows:

St Ola: Brian Kemp; John Miller and Jimmy Miller; Eric Kemp, Alistair Muir and Brian Paterson; Victor Clouston, Ralph Fotheringhame, Bertie Marwick, Russell Groundwater and Douglas Corse.

Harray: Edric Clouston; Frankie Johnston and Stewart Sinclair; Harry Flett, Bobby Hutchison and

Robbie Scott; Stanley Hutchison, Ian Hutchison, Keith Hutchison, Eric Hutchison and Emile Flett.

Peep! Referee Geddes Johnston got the game going on a cold, windy evening. Harray took the lead when a Flett cross was headed in by Keith Hutchison but Victor Clouston equalised for St Ola before half time.

The second half was a minute old when Marwick put St Ola ahead but Harray again equalised when another Flett cross from the left was turned in off a St Ola defender. No further scoring meant a replay was necessary to find a winner. Final score 2-2.

For the second game, both sides made one change. Peter Aim replaced Emile Flett on Harray's left flank while a barely fit Alan Findlay returned in place of Victor Clouston for St Ola. Another big crowd turned out to witness, according to

'Corinthian' (back on reporting duty for *The Orcadian*), " … the most evenly matched and hardest fought Parish Cup final ever … "

Ah, … canny now!

But, it was a good game, full of excitement right to the end, when it looked as if another replay might be needed.

Harray held the initiative for much of the first half and took the lead inside 15 minutes when Keith Hutchison headed home. Despite plenty of near misses there were no more goals before half time.

Although Findlay was virtually a passenger by now, St Ola came more into the game in the second half and it was not long before Marwick ran through to equalise. Harray regained the advantage when Keith Hutchison again headed in a Ian Hutchison cross. But the lead was short lived as

St Ola, Parish Cup winners, in 1965. Back row, left to right, John Miller, Brian Kemp, Jimmy Miller. Middle, Alan Findlay, Russell Groundwater, Bertie Marwick, Ralph Fotheringhame, Douglas Corse. Front, Alistair Muir, Eric Kemp, Brian Paterson. (Picture: Orkney Library)

Birth, Blood

Fotheringhame hit a low drive past Clouston to make the score 2-2.

At full-time both captains agreed to ten minutes more each way as the fog closed in. The excitement was high and the football frantic as both teams went for the 'kill.' But it looked like another draw when, with only two minutes left, Groundwater gathered the ball in his own penalty area, ran the length of the field, skipped past Johnston and from 22 yards unleashed a left foot shot which flew past Clouston into the roof of the Harray net. As 'Corinthian' remarked " … a shot worthy of winning any match."

Over the past fifteen years, the great striker had scored barrow loads of goals in Orkney football, including 49 in inter counties against Caithness and Shetland but this goal he regarded as his best ever. Now that is saying something!

Overall, St Ola owed their win to their tactic of playing through the middle where their speedy inside trio were capable of outstripping the Harray defence. But Harray would not have been too despondent; with so many young skilful players, the future looked very bright indeed.

I'm sure, like me, you often wonder what goes on at Parish Cup winning celebrations. No doubt, plenty of,

in no particular order, drinking, dancing, drinking, singing, drinking, reminiscing … well, picture this one!

The St Ola party is in full swing at a house in Laverock Road. Davo Fox, ex. county player, *Thorfinn* diehard, and a veteran of many a Thorfinn versus Dounby battle (no fan of Harray, therefore) is present. Russell Groundwater, scorer of the winning goal and for many years a *Rovers* player, arrives late.

Davo calls for silence; their eyes meet across the crowded room.

After a lengthy pause he moves forward. Are these old rivals about to fall a-fighting?

No!

Instead, Davo falls to his knees and reverently plants a kiss on the lethal left foot.

Who says that football is only a game?

Peep! Almost forgot! How many 'referees' passed the exam? Well, not seventeen-*six* to be precise, including well known players or former players Brian Kemp, Arnold Rendall, Freddie Hutchison. For the O.F.A. that was a good number. They would not go bankrupt forking out bonus payments yet still have enough whistlers to allow that one poor soul to have a bit of a rest next season.

1966:
Birsay stumble at final hurdle

With a regiment of new referees on the scene, the 1966 season began with a crackdown on indiscipline on the field and falling standards generally. Warnings were issued through the columns of the local newspaper about players' frequent use of bad or abusive language. Even expressions such as "Open your eyes, ref!" or "Get your specs on!" were to be deemed blasphemous, and could result in a caution or sending off.

As regards actual swearing, there was to be zero tolerance and no excuses would be heard: "Even if a player misses his kick or stubs his toe and responds with unparliamentary language, *not directed at the referee*, he can be sent off." This was going to be a tough season with a lot of unlearning to be done.

As time went on, it was clear the players found the tightening of standards difficult. By the end of May, four 'A' League players had been sent off and a further six cautioned, a lot in those days. Now, another Press release was ordered which, although oozing with empathy, restated the position:

"If you hit your finger with a hammer you will want to give vent to your feelings. But, in a game, one must control one's feelings … and referees must not be questioned about decisions, even by the captain of the team. This will be regarded as dissent."

" … and while we're at it there are some other things needing attended to. The state of some players' boots is bad with nails often protruding from the studs. The ref can stop a player from playing if his boots aren't up to scratch … "

Russell Groundwater, scorer of the "wonder goal", had a phenomenal goal scoring record in the inter counties: 35 goals versus Caithness, 14 versus Shetland. (Remember the Archer Shield contest with Caithness was home and away at this time).

Davo Fox, always an emotional player, couldn't hide his delight at Groundwater's winner against his 'deadly' foes from the West Mainland.

& Boundaries

(should that not be 'if his boots *are* up to scratch?')

" … and what's more, some teams' balls are too soft! Soft balls are dangerous! Footballs must be properly inflated! The home team is responsible and each team must have two balls on hand … "

We can imagine some of the responses to the last command!

Given that parish teams might be prone to the occasional use of agricultural language or possess only one poorly inflated ball, or have players who resurrected fifteen year old boots once a year, perhaps it was no surprise that only seven clubs ventured forth for this year's Parish Cup.

Gone were the days of 13 or 14 teams and folk were beginning to doubt whether this would ever happen again. Only Birsay, Rendall and St Andrews had league teams which meant that many potential players from the parishes were playing no football at all.

But, having said that, when the Parish Cup tournament got underway, it did so with a 'bang'. The first leg between St Ola and St Andrews in the middle of June was widely regarded as the 'game of the year' so far while Birsay's performance led to speculation that, in the seventh year of the decade, this could at last be their year

Quarter final Results

St Ola	2	St Andrews	4
St Andrews	1	St Ola	2
Birsay	7	Orphir	4
Orphir	2	Birsay	4
Sandwick	1	South Ron.	3
South Ron.	1	Sandwick	3

Replay
Sandwick	3	South Ron.	3

South Ron. win second replay

Harray	v	Shapinsay	

Shapinsay scratched

Although the result of the replay

is not known, this was the closest Sandwick had come for a long time to making an impact. Now, it was Harray v St Andrews yet again.

Semi final Results

Harray	1	St Andrews	0
St Andrews	0	Harray	2
South Ron.	3	Birsay	5
Birsay	9	South Ron.	1

Birsay had made the final at long last and having scored 25 goals in four games. They should have a great chance in this all-West Mainland final but it was Harray who had the cup pedigree and would start as favourites.

At a time like this, it would have been useful for Birsay to have had a player of Gordy Norquoy's calibre but he had emigrated to Australia where, word had it, he was playing in the same team as Colin Eunson (ex-Deerness) and Ernie Donaldson (ex-Thorfinn). Even if they considered it,

Birsay funds would hardly stretch to flying him home for the final.

For the match, teams were as follows:

Birsay: Jimmy Norquoy; Jim Rendall and Jimmy Ritch; Stewart Spence, Brian Spence and Bertie Spence; Billy Tait, Harvey Spence, Sandy Brown, Alan Black and Barry Tait.

Harray: Edric Clouston; Mike Drever and Stewart Sinclair; Robbie Scott, Frankie Johnston and Harry Flett; Bobby Hutchison, Ian Hutchison, Keith Hutchison, Eric Hutchison and Emile Flett.

As so often happens when anticipation is high, the reality is a bit of a let down. From a very brief summary of the match in *The Orcadian* it appeared that, in an otherwise even contest, it was the Harray forwards who were able to convert their chances, whereas

England won the World Cup in 1966 but it was Harray in the Parish Cup! Back row, left to right, Mike Drever, Edric Clouston, Stewart Sinclair. Middle, Bobby Hutchison, Ian Hutchison, Keith Hutchison, Eric Hutchison, Emile Flett. Front, Robbie Scott, Frankie Johnston, Harry Flett.
(Picture: Orkney Library)

Birsay missed all of theirs. The score of 4-0 to Harray suggests a one sided game but this did no justice to Birsay's good outfield play. Unfortunately the goal scorers are not recorded and it has proved impossible to find a Harray player who can distinguish this game in his mind from the many other cup finals in which he played.

Gordy Norquoy, another Orkney emigrant, whose loss was keenly felt by Birsay.

Having got there once it was hoped that Birsay could now go on to repeat the feat and finally achieve the success they were undoubtedly capable of. Having said that, Harray looked as if they had years left in the tank.

With Parish Cup interest generally at a fairly low ebb, were there no optimistic signs to be grasped? Well, there was one …

Orkney Youth Clubs Association had been formed under the chairmanship of Marcus Liddle from Orphir. Youth Clubs were formed in many rural districts and soon boasted very healthy memberships. To help them consolidate, and as part of their activities programmes, football and netball leagues were started and soon teams from Harray, Orphir, Rendall, St Andrews, Sandwick, South Ronaldsay, Stenness, Kirkwall and Stromness were playing against each other on a weekly basis.

Now, if this organisation succeeded in drawing more youth into playing a game of football, maybe here would be the breeding ground for future parish teams. In fact, it was looking almost like a Junior Parish Cup already!

1967: Sanday enter the fray

The 'Hippie' philosophy of peace and love might well have been spreading throughout the world during 1967, but, as far as the players in Orkney's youth club teams were concerned, the message had fallen on deaf ears. Having taken part in a number of games in the recently formed Youth Club League, I can testify that the term 'ding-dong' was totally inadequate to describe some of the encounters.

Players had rolled up their sleeves and set to with patriotic fervour. It resembled the Parish Cup in miniature, as the sides representing the parish youth clubs, tussled like dogs defending their territory. At times, play became so primitive it was almost scary, and the volunteer referees were hard pressed to maintain law and order. This football reached the parts that other games failed to reach and boy, did we enjoy it!

But great credit was due to the Youth Clubs organisation because they helped lure many of those who might have slipped through the net, back into playing football. Parish teams of the future would reap the benefit, and already this year, right on cue, there were signs of a resurgence in interest.

Numbers were back up to ten and included, for the first time, a completely new entry from the island of Sanday.

For years it had been felt that Sanday could make a good showing in the tournament. An internal league still

Sanday's Parish Cup team, back row, left to right, James Lennie, David Muir, Andrew Skea, Thomas Garrioch, Hamish Cursiter. Middle, Ian Slater, Eddie Ward, William Muir, Douglas Muir, Roddy Peace. Front, Jim Scott, George Peace, Alistair Muir, William Allan.

(Picture: Orkney Library)

ran between the districts of Cross, Lady and Burness and the island team frequently played matches against Stronsay and Westray. They had almost entered last year but, worried about travel and costs, had asked the O.F.A. if they could skip the earlier rounds and come in at the semi final stage. This bold request was turned down but, bearing in mind the pep-talk given to all teams last year, this proved Sanday need have nothing to fear from the authorities. They had plenty of balls!

This year Sanday had taken the plunge, thanks to schoolteacher John Findlay, who organised the team and convinced the players of their abilities.

When the draw was made, there was great anticipation to see who would draw Sanday. Most teams, apprehensive about the cost of travel, were actually hoping to avoid such a draw but they were assured by 'Corinthian', in *The Orcadian*, that whichever team visited the island would be given "a right royal time, as the hospitality of the 'Gruellie Belkies' is second to none. It will be a night to remember!"

With only two games due in the first round, first out of the hat was … Sanday! … and the 'lucky' team to play them was … St Andrews!

Forty years on, former players remember little of the actual game but details of the hospitality received still linger, secure in the memory bank. On arrival, St Andrews' players were met on the pier by members of the home club and whisked off to many different homes on the island where they were generously fed and watered before later being driven to the field for the match. Offers of home brew were politely rejected. The experience of St Andrews told in a 4-1 victory but Sanday acquitted themselves well and in the return game, showed their gain in confidence, going down by a narrow 2-1 score line.

Their first venture had been short lived but everyone connected with the competition hoped to see them back next year and possibly other North Isles' teams might be inspired to follow their example.

In the other first round tie Stenness went down by 6-0 and 5-0 to Stromness. Their defeat was down to a shortage of experienced players but their return to the tournament was also very much welcomed. Now it was on to the quarter finals.

Quarter final Results

Harray	6	Birsay	1
Birsay	0	Harray	6
Sandwick	7	South Ron.	1
South Ron.	2	Sandwick	3
St Andrews	1	Orphir	1
Orphir	2	St Andrews	8
St Ola	4	Stromness	0
Stromness	0	St Ola	4

Some high-scoring games there. Harray certainly seemed to have Birsay all worked out and looked in ominous form. Of the other semi finalists, maybe Sandwick could prove to be 'dark horses'?

Semi final Results

| Harray | 2 | St Andrews | 2 |
| St Andrews | 1 | Harray | 1 |

Replay: Harray emerged as winners.

| St Ola | 3 | Sandwick | 8 |
| Sandwick | 5 | St Ola | 2 |

The inevitable Harray v St Andrews tie was desperately close but as the play off occurred on the Wednesday evening before the final, the outcome was not published. But now, Harray would meet the free scoring Sandwick in the final.

It would have been tempting fate to play up Sandwick's chances in the way Birsay's had been last year, but

" TWA HOME BREW AFORE THE MATCH, BEUY..? "

Birth, Blood

there was no doubt that this was now a team with prospects. It contained a mix of some very fine players who had just come through the junior ranks and a number of seasoned veterans. Only two, however, had previous cup final experience: Jackie Nicolson, goalkeeper for Shapinsay back in 1954; and recent recruit, Harvey Spence who had played for Birsay last year.

Harray, on the other hand, was laced through with experience at this level, but they did have two first time finalists in their team this year: Alan Flett of Nistaben and Alan Hutchison.

Teams were as follows:

Sandwick: Jackie Nicolson; George Wylie and Robbie Wylie; Jimmy Walls, Norman Couper and Tommy Bain; Harvey Spence, Denis Leonard, Tammo Anderson, John Stockan and Keith Corsie.

Harray: Edric Clouston; Harry Flett and John Sinclair; Robbie Scott, Frankie Johnston and Keith Hutchison; Alan Flett, Ian Hutchison, Alan Hutchison, Eric Hutchison and Peter Aim.

Once again, only a brief report of the match was available but from that, it was clear that Harray's experience was the deciding factor. Sandwick did take the lead through a Harvey Spence penalty but before half time, Harray had gone ahead with goals by Ian and Alan Hutchison. In the second half, Harray remained on top and only some great work by Nicolson in the Sandwick goal prevented further scoring.

The final score was Harray 2 Sandwick 1.

This was a landmark win for Harray, making them the most successful club in the competition's history with eight wins, one ahead of St Andrews. But Sandwick could take heart from their first cup final appearance since 1934 and with their young team,

many felt it would only be a matter of time till they recorded a first victory.

Playing his first Parish Cup final for Sandwick, Harvey Spence gave his team the lead from the spot but ended up on the losing side.

Now, to finish the year off, here's something to shock readers. Remember how, just a few years ago, football officials denounced a new phenomenon which was destroying our local game: the T.V. set! Well, this year a number of games at the Parish Cup quarter final stage were actually *postponed* in order that players could stay at home and watch a football match! And what game was it? Only some trivial affair for some cup or other taking place in Lisbon, or some such remote outpost. I think somebody said the score was Celtic 2 Inter Milan 1.

Honestly, what was the world coming to? Putting that before a Parish Cup match!

1968: Harray remain dominant

I tell you, it went from bad to worse in 1968. Wednesday evening Parish Cup games postponed once more for the sake of football on T.V.!

Oh, all right, it was the European Cup Final again, Manchester United and Benfica this time, but it was ridiculous that …

Hmm, but remember the three United goals in extra time? The one where Best beat three men and slipped the ball into the empty net; and then Charlton, how did he screw the ball in from that angle? and then, Brian Kidd jumping to …

It was high time the O.F.A. were getting their priorities right!

There then followed another concession created by the television age. Cars were to be allowed into the Bignold Park! The reasoning was that armchair fans might be tempted back to showpiece games if they could sit in the warmth and comfort of their own automobiles.

Time would tell.

But if it looked as if football administration was going soft altogether, then think again. First of all the tribal behaviour at some youth club games was to be sorted out by the appointment of fully qualified officials. The likes of Jim Bews, Fred Hutchison and Arnold Rendall were commissioned with restoring civilisation. And as for senior clubs, they still had areas of their own house to put in order.

It was decided that a team failing to produce their own linesman could be fined and lose the points or forfeit the match. In the 'A' League, Rendall tested the system against Stromness. The teams drew 3-3, but Stromness had 'borrowed' a linesman. Rendall protested and were awarded both points. Now, Parish Cup entrants would have to be alert to the latest rule!

The total was back down to nine this year but at least Sanday were still there. As word got round about island hospitality, no longer were teams dreading the long haul trip, they were actually living in hope.

There was only one first round tie but it provided the classic cup situation, the parish on the way up, meets the parish on the way down.

First round Result

| Sandwick | 2 | St Andrews | 1 |
| St Andrews | 2 | Sandwick | 2 |

A narrow victory for the team on the way up, and they now had the good fortune to earn a trip to Sanday in the next round.

Quarter final Results

Deerness	1	Harray	10
Harray	5	Deerness	2
South Ron.	2	Birsay	4
Birsay	4	South Ron.	1
Shapinsay	2	St Ola	12
St Ola	4	Shapinsay	1
Sanday	0	Sandwick	5
Sandwick	8	Sanday	1

After the first legs, both Deerness and Shapinsay were planning to 'scratch' the return game on the grounds of 'a lost cause.' However, they were soon dissuaded from this idea by the O.F.A. who reminded them of the automatic fine of £5 for such a course of action … and once fined, the entire club, individual players and all, would be suspended until the fine was paid. No messing this year!

Sanday's second venture was no more rewarding than their first but Sandwick's visit had been another great occasion.

Post match socialising had gone with a swing and it had all proved too much for one Sandwick supporter who drank well beyond his normal capacity, became violently sick, and

lost his teeth. As the boat had to leave, there was no time to search for them so he returned home toothless.

But Sanday folk never lay claim to what is not rightfully theirs and once the teeth were recovered, they were given a quick swill and returned to their owner on the next day's boat. For a while, every conversation in Sandwick began, "Ye ken about (so-and-so) that geed tae Sanday? Well, he cam home on the boat the wan day, his teeth cam' the next!"

At this point, there was a lull in the Parish Cup while a famous event in the history of Orkney football took place. This was the first visit of an Orkney team to the Faroe Islands to play for the North Atlantic Cup, a triangular tournament also involving Shetland. Fifteen players and six officials made the trip by air and enjoyed a wonderfully hospitable time. It was also a very successful trip, Orkney earning a 2-0 victory and a 1-1 draw, to put themselves in a strong position to secure the trophy.

Although the tournament itself did not develop in the manner intended, the Orkney players involved could 'dine out' on the event for the rest of their lives. Whenever an international side such as Germany or Spain or even the mighty Scotland, struggles desperately on Faroese soil, the Orcadians can proclaim with a casual air, "Oh, we beat the Faroes the last time we were there!"

Now that the Parish Cup players in the Orkney squad, and there were quite a few; Ian, Eric and Keith Hutchison of Harray; Brian and Eric Kemp of St Ola; Brian and Harvey Spence of Sandwick, had all returned home, the semi finals could proceed.

These games saw Harray retain their supremacy over Birsay and Sandwick stage a miraculous come back against St Ola.

An Orkney team lining up to face the Faroes in the North Atlantic Cup series in 1970. Orkney eventually won the tournament, a major achievement. From the left, Eric Kemp, Morgan Harcus, Ian Rendall, Raymond Stanger, Calvin Slater, Jim Davies, Brian Wood, Keith Hutchison, Davy Keldie, Brian Spence, Harry Flett, Brian Kemp, Alistair Muir, Jim Merriman, Ralph Fotheringhame. *(Picture: Orkney Library)*

Semi final Results

Harray	5	Birsay	1
Birsay	3	Harray	6
Sandwick	1	St Ola	4
St Ola	0	Sandwick	5

Apart from the score line, the Sandwick v St Ola second leg was noteworthy in two ways. Tammo Anderson played one of his finest games in a Sandwick shirt and hit a memorable hat trick. It also marked the Parish Cup debut at the age of 15, of one of the finest players of his generation in Orkney, Geordie Leonard. Although he would go on to make his name principally as a forward, Geordie played in goal that night.

The final was now a repeat of last year's and the expectation was that Sandwick would prove a greater threat. Expected to have a major influence on the game was Brian Spence, now a regular in the county team, who had opted to play for Sandwick rather than Birsay this year. Harray were on the usual lines, the only newcomer being Karl Flett, son of the legendary Dave Flett, who had been the scourge of many an opposing forward line in his day.

Teams were as follows:

Harray: Edric Clouston; John Sinclair and Stewart Sinclair; Harry Flett, Frankie Johnston and Ian Hutchison; Karl Flett, Alan Flett, Alan Hutchison, Eric Hutchison and Keith Hutchison. Sub: John Copland.

Sandwick: Geordie Leonard; George Wylie and Robbie Wylie; Tommy Bain, Norman Cooper and Denis Leonard; Harvey Spence, Brian Spence, Tammo Anderson, John Stockan and Keith Corsie.

It proved to be an excellent final, one of the best seen for years, which kept the crowd on their toes until the very last minute. Harray took a 2-0 lead through Alan Hutchison and a George Wylie own goal, but Brian Spence pulled one back for

Sandwick before half time. Early in the second half, Tammo Anderson equalised but almost immediately Eric Hutchison restored Harray's lead. Sandwick fought relentlessly and in the last minute were rewarded when John Stockan swept the ball into the net. Final score 3-3.

The replay took place the following Saturday.

This time Harray fielded Peter Aim on the left wing with John Sinclair dropping out. In another keen but very sporting contest, almost all the players on the park played their regular football for Dounby, Harray emerged as 4-2 winners. Their goal scorers were Harry Flett, Alan Flett and Keith Hutchison (2). For Sandwick Brian Spence and John Stockan each scored once.

So Harray had retained their title making it three wins in a row and consolidated their position as the tournament's most successful parish. They had beaten off repeated challenges from Birsay and were now thwarting Sandwick ambitions.

What could these teams try next? Maybe in the current climate of rule enforcement, nobbling the official Harray linesman would give them as much chance as anything.

Keith Hutchison, whose goals proved decisive for Harray.

1969:

Harray make it four in a row

The decade was ending as it began with one team firmly in control of the cup's destiny. Despite the efforts of Birsay and Sandwick to wrest the crown away, Harray still held sway. But interesting developments were taking place … and, to quote one of the iconic figures of the past ten years, there was something 'Blowin' in the Wind.'

Firstly, Birsay's reserve team had lifted the Reserve trophy at the end of last season indicating that a new wave of Birsay footballers was on the way which would also add strength in depth to the parish squad.

Sandwick's initiative was possibly even more significant. They decided to run their own 'A' League team. They clearly felt they had enough players to make this viable and, with the three Leonard brothers at the helm, nobody would dispute their will to succeed. League success would have been their ultimate goal, but there was no doubt Sandwick had at least one eye on the Parish Cup. Although some of their top parish players continued to play for Dounby, regular, competitive football for other local boys would surely raise the overall standard and improve Sandwick's chances of 'doing a St Andrews.'

Mind you, the formula hadn't yet worked for Birsay!

Interest in football was now on the increase and this was reflected in the number of Parish Cup entrants which had climbed back up to eleven. The names included Holm, after a lapse of several years but Sanday, regrettably, had not entered this time. The three opening matches saw the following outcomes:

Holm	2	South Ron.	5
South Ron.	5	Holm	0
Shapinsay	3	Stromness	1
Stromness	4	Shapinsay	1
Sandwick	7	Orphir	2
Orphir	1	Sandwick	3

No real surprises there but observers would have noted the goal scoring feats of South Ronaldsay and Sandwick.

Quarter final Results

Harray	2	St Andrews	0
St Andrews	0	Harray	2
South Ron.	3	St Ola	2
St Ola	2	South Ron.	3
Deerness	3	Sandwick	3
Sandwick	5	Deerness	0
Birsay	5	Stromness	2
Stromness	2	Birsay	6

The balance of power had clearly shifted to the West Mainland but with a new generation breaking through in South Ronaldsay, the West teams could expect some stern opposition from that quarter … eventually! As the semi finals were to prove, the cup finalists of the past two years were still ahead of the pack.

Semi final Results

Harray	6	Birsay	1
Birsay	4	Harray	2
South Ron.	2	Sandwick	4
Sandwick	6	South Ron.	0

After the first leg matches, 'Corinthian', in *The Orcadian*, had another 'go' at Birsay who he obviously thought should have won the Parish Cup by now.

"What is wrong with Birsay? They are a good all round team on paper. Something is lacking. Can it be team spirit?"

Whatever afflicted Birsay, did not affect Harray. The majority of their players played for Dounby but since there was no Harray league team, the issue of players being displaced for the Parish Cup never arose. Team spirit was taken for granted and may have carried Harray through games

where, on paper, they were not the favourites.

Anyway, perhaps spurred on by Corinthian's rebuke, Birsay tore into their opponents in the second leg and succeeded in ruffling a few Harray feathers. Now, if they could do that next year!

South Ronaldsay's team were not quite ready yet, so it was a Harray v Sandwick final for the third year in a row and this time more than a few fancied Sandwick.

The teams which were announced this year included the name of a *substitute*. In keeping with football nationally, local teams were now allowed to use a substitute, "provided that the player being taken off is genuinely injured." No doubt both teams would have included "feigning an injury when ordered" as part of their cup final preparations.

Teams were as follows:

Sandwick: Charlie Kemp; George Wylie and Brian Leonard; Denis Leonard, Norman Couper, Mervyn Slater; Tommy Bain, Davie Stockan, Tammo Anderson, Geordie Leonard and Keith Corsie. Sub: John Stockan

Harray: Edric Clouston; Mike Drever and Stewart Sinclair; Harry Flett, Alan Flett and John Copland; Jackie Walter; Alan Hutchison; Karl Flett, Eric Hutchison, Jimmy Newlands. Sub: Harvey Johnston

The game did not materialise into the thriller it promised. In fact, it was rather a dull, quiet game, in keeping with the blanket of mist which descended over the Bignold Park, making it difficult to see what was going on.

Harray grabbed the opening goal when a shot by Harry Flett struck the inside of the post and rolled in. They

Harray were rampant in 1969, winning the trophy again to make it four in a row. Back row, left to right, Keith Hutchison, Mike Drever, Edric Clouston, Stewart Sinclair, Peter Aim. Middle, Jackie Walter, Alan Hutchison, Karl Flett, Eric Hutchison, John Newlands. Front, Harry Flett, Alan Flett, John Copland. (Picture: Orkney Library)

increased their lead after Newlands met a punched clearance by Kemp and steered the ball into the net. Alan Hutchison then hit the bar but the ball rebounded into play.

Sandwick, playing down the slope in the second half, were unable to make much impression, and the issue was put beyond doubt when Eric Hutchison got free and slammed in a third goal. Sandwick's efforts were rewarded near the end when, in thickening fog, Tammo Anderson scored with an unsaveable drive. But it was too late and Harray ran out 3-1 winners.

From a statistician's point of view, this result now contributed to some fascinating reading. Harray's tenth Parish Cup win; their fourth win in a row; Sandwick's third consecutive defeat; all to Harray. You couldn't blame Sandwick pessimists for thinking this would go on forever.

But, hang on! Always look on the bright side! This was a young Sandwick team which would only get better; their junior team had just won Orkney's Junior League with essentially local boys; and, looking further down the ranks, the Sandwick South school team had triumphed in the Primary School's Football Cup.

You get the picture of a conveyor belt, don't you? … trundling along, carrying different components, big and small, and delivering them to Skeabrae aerodrome. Some day, in the near future, all these parts might just, if correctly assembled, make the finished article, the shiny, new, smoothly functioning machine.

As the decade of football came to an end, you just had the feeling that, as Bob Dylan might have sung, 'The Times they are a' Changin.'

Well, maybe just a peedie bit!

As the decade ended, the balance of power had finally shifted to the West Mainland. Birsay's was a story of unfulfilled promise, yet still there was hope. With Robbie Norquoy (Ben's son) now at the helm, they ended the 60s as holders of the Corsie Cup. Pictured above, the line up is back row, left to right, Attie Stanger, Brian Wood, Jimmy Norquoy, Jimmy Ritch, Robbie Norquoy. Middle. Jackie Grieve, Colin Richardson, Billy Tait, Raymond Stanger, Barry Tait. Front. Sandy Meadows, Sandy Brown and Lamont Inkster.

But Sandwick were making progress at all levels, right down to primary school. Spot future Parish Cup winners in this picture below of the victorious Sandwick South team of 1969. Back row, left to right, Stevie Slater, Alan Moar, Carl Wood, Kenny Copland, Norman Bain. Front. Colin Davidson, Michael Grieve, Willie Kirkness, Gary Stockan, Brian Brass, Fraser Flett, Willie Hourie.   *(Pictures: Orkney Library)*

The 70s

1970:
Birsay do it ... at last!

Sandwick's next move was to enter both an 'A' and 'B' team as the two tier league system was reintroduced to Orkney football. Birsay, meanwhile, current holders of the Corsie Cup for 'B' teams, pooled all their resources into an 'A' team for the new season.

After years in the doldrums, parish teams were now back in numbers playing league football. Dounby and St Andrews were still in the top division while Shapinsay, Rendall, South Ronaldsay and Deerness helped make up the 'B' League. All this augured well for the Parish Cup and when the entry date closed, there were again eleven names in the frame. Holm had dropped out but were replaced by Firth, making their first appearance for many a year.

The first round ties produced the following results:

St Ola	3	St Andrews	3
St Andrews	1	St Ola	2
Firth	1	South Ron.	7
South Ron.	3	Firth	0
Deerness	v	Stromness	

Stromness scratched

Now the quarter finals beckoned and the draw had thrown up one very interesting clash. Birsay had shown in their semi final last year that Harray could be beaten if a committed approach was taken. Now under the management of Robbie Norquoy, who had taken over from his father, Ben, Birsay appeared to have a new sense of purpose and were looking forward to another joust with their bogey team.

Let's see how they got on.

Quarter final Results

| Birsay | 3 | Harray | 1 |
| Harray | 1 | Birsay | 6 |

South Ron.	1	Sandwick	2
Sandwick	7	South Ron.	2
Shapinsay	2	St Ola	5
St Ola	4	Shapinsay	1
Orphir	1	Deerness	4
Deerness	2	Orphir	2

At the time, that result made the footballing public sit up and shake their heads in disbelief. Harray were trounced by a reinvigorated Birsay and a new era was about to begin.

But who was to lead this new era? Birsay? Just as likely candidates were Sandwick, who under the guiding hand of manager Arthur Herdman, had seen off South Ronaldsay in some style. We did not have to wait long for an answer as these two were drawn to meet in the semi finals.

Semi final Results

Sandwick	0	Birsay	3
Birsay	2	Sandwick	2
St Ola	10	Deerness	2
Deerness	1	St Ola	5

Birsay's newly acquired will to win proved to be the decisive factor and it was they who would fly the West Mainland flag on County Show night, leaving Sandwick frustrated once again.

But in their attempt to win the trophy for the very first time, Birsay would not have things all their own way. They would face a very experienced St Ola line up containing a 'spine' of county players and a few promising newcomers, foremost of whom was future Orkney regular, Fraser Byers.

For their own part, Birsay still contained a goodly number of the original 'Busby Babes' now some ten years older, but also a smattering of strong young players such as Jimmy Norquoy, Eddie Spence, Jackie Grieve and most significantly, Raymond Stanger who represented Orkney for the first time earlier in the year.

The full teams (now written out officially on *team lines* and presented to the referee before the game: the practice of scribbling names on fag packets or bits of toilet paper had been outlawed!) were as follows:

Birsay: Jimmy Norquoy; Sandy Meadows and Jimmy Ritch; Stewart Spence, Brian Spence and Eddie Spence; Jackie Grieve, Raymond Stanger, Sandy Brown, Bertie Spence and Barry Tait. Subs: Billy Wylie and Billy Tait.

St Ola: Brian Kemp; Alistair Muir and Terence Omand; Ralph Fotheringhame, Eric Kemp and Lamont Inkster; Brian Hill, Fraser Byers, Russell Groundwater, Freddie Ward and Brian Stevenson. Subs: Douglas Corse and David Sinclair.

A crowd in excess of that which turned out to see Orkney play their return game with the Faroes, lined the Bignold Park ropes on a dull but dry evening. However, they were to be disappointed by the quality of the match which, although always interesting, rarely lived up to the expected level of excitement.

There were no goals in the first half but Birsay, playing down the slope with a stiff breeze behind, began to take the initiative after the interval. Midway through the half, they secured the opening goal when Brian Kemp and Barry Tait collided and Sandy Brown was able to knock the ball into the empty net. Birsay now took control and near the end were awarded a penalty for handball and Brian Spence made no mistake with the spot kick.

St Ola's strong finish was to no avail and when the whistle blew, Birsay had won the Parish Cup for the first time, by two goals to nil. It was a deserved victory as their team work had been better and they had enjoyed the bulk of the play. St Ola's danger men had been well held, with Brian Spence making a particularly effective job of policing Russell Groundwater.

It is hard to imagine the joyous feeling among Birsay players and supporters that night, as the cherished prize was handed over to captain Brian Spence by Eddie Balfour, president of the O.F.A. Since the tournament's beginnings back in 1929, Birsay had regularly submitted a team, had twice reached the final but only now were they to experience the thrill of victory.

Brian Spence, who had an outstanding game for Birsay.

At times like this, a man can get very sentimental as emotions suppressed over many years strive to break free. Let us picture the Birsay 'faithful' descending upon Robbie and Barrie Norquoy's very hospitable home (another 'perk' of being manager) overlooking the Palace and the Brough of Birsay, for the commencement of celebrations which would continue unabated till the sun came up the following morning.

During the night, groups would spill out for some fresh air and pause to listen to the Atlantic waves crash against Marwick Head or the breakers roll in to Skippigeo … and as they passed the famous cup from mouth to mouth, more than one would be heard to declare, "Buey, Ah'm right prood tae be a Birsay man this night!"

1971:
Birsay see off neighbours

What a difference a few short years make! Not so long ago, the image of Orkney football was fairly rundown. There was a sharp drop in numbers playing the game, far fewer teams, spectators staying away, little enthusiasm.

Then came another piece of bad news. The 1971 Census revealed that Orkney's population had fallen by another 1,500 inhabitants yet the numbers living in Kirkwall and Stromness had gone up.

Conclusion?

The country districts sparser than ever.

In fact, Mainland population had dropped by 1,200 with further depopulation of the islands making up the remainder of the deficit.

For football, this should have spelt *trouble* …but no! Just the opposite was the case. Here is some evidence:

A healthy 'A' and 'B' League set up had been re-established with promotion and relegation operating (Rendall promoted: Stromness and St Andrews relegated.)

A strong Junior League was functioning well (Winners: Sandwick)

The Youth Club League was still a platform for country boys wanting to play football.

A Primary Schools knock-out competition was going from strength to strength.

Finally, an entry of *13* teams for the Parish Cup!

What's more, the crowds were coming back, some even rivalling their forbears for rowdiness. A warning about crowd behaviour among younger fans was issued in *The Orcadian* after the Shetland

The trophy stayed in the west in 1970 but this time in Birsay hands. Back row, left to right, Davy Spence, Alfie Stanger, Sandy Meadows, Jimmy Norquoy, Jimmy Ritch, Robbie Wylie, Billy Tait. Middle, Edwin Harvey, Jackie Grieve, Raymond Stanger, Sandy Brown, Bertie Spence, Barry Tait, Robbie Norquoy (manager). Front, Eddie Spence, Brian Spence, Stuart Spence.
(Picture: Orkney Library)

goalkeeper at the junior inter county had endured a torrid time from spectators clustered around the goal, shouting abuse and generally trying to distract him.

Also frowned upon was the throwing of toilet rolls when penalty kicks were being taken: penalties had now been introduced as the preferred method for deciding matches and throwers were reminded to save them for the purpose intended.

It was a far from drab football scene, therefore, as the latest first round matches got underway.

First round Results

Stromness	4	Sanday	1
Sanday	4	Stromness	3
Stenness	0	Orphir	5
Orphir	7	Stenness	0
Firth	0	Birsay	5
Birsay	1	Firth	1
South Ron.	3	Sandwick	5
Sandwick	2	South Ron.	0
St Ola	1	Harray	8
Harray	7	St Ola	0

The only real surprise was the manner in which Harray had disposed of last year's finalists St Ola. But the story of the round concerned another trip to Sanday – never a dull moment when Sanday are involved. This time the visitors were Stromness. All things considered, they could count themselves lucky to be still here at all, let alone in the next round.

With trips to the Isles still a novelty for Mainland teams, the Stromness party had taken maximum advantage of island hospitality, as had skipper and crew of the hired boat.

After leaving the island much later than planned, the boat was pointed in the general direction of Kirkwall and that seemed to satisfy the merry throng. It was a pleasant evening for a trip and the mood was cheerful but, after what seemed like a long time at sea, none of the familiar landmarks

were coming into view.

As the boat glided by some previously unknown skerries, a few began to realise something was amiss. Comparisons began to be made with the fate of the *Titanic*.

Fortunately the Stromness team contained a member of the *Pole Star* crew who was able to recognise lighthouses. It appeared that the boat was making for Deerness! A bearing was now taken on the Helliar Holm light and the party eventually made it into Kirkwall, very late but mightily relieved.

Well, how would Stromness fare in the quarter final after that scare? Not very well I fear.

Quarter final Results

St Andrews	3	Shapinsay	1
Shapinsay	3	St Andrews	3
Sandwick	9	Stromness	1
Stromness	3	Sandwick	1
Orphir	4	Harray	4
Harray	5	Orphir	1
Birsay	5	Deerness	0
Deerness	5	Birsay	5

Once again the 'big three' from the West Mainland made it through with only St Andrews standing in their way. Not for long!

Semi final Results

St Andrews	0	Birsay	5
Birsay	5	St Andrews	0
Sandwick	4	Harray	0
Harray	3	Sandwick	4

A fascinating final was now in prospect between the neighbouring parishes of Sandwick and Birsay. As can be imagined, the rivalry between the two teams, as in all local 'derbies', was intense and this ran through the players, the supporters, down the age groups.

I am assured by some who played at the time, that when the Birsay and Sandwick teams met in the Primary Schools Cup, the girls formed a guard of honour to greet the opposing boys as they took the field

… and spat on them! I am sure there are plenty of Birsay and Sandwick women, now in their mid 40s, who would deny this but … I have witnesses!

Referees who took charge of those matches would then have their hands full calming down over vociferous parents!

Well, if it was anything like this, the grown-up version had the makings of a final to remember. Just to give an extra edge to proceedings, the game would feature two sets of brothers, *one on each side,* Brian Spence for Birsay, Harvey Spence , Sandwick; George Wylie, as usual for Sandwick, Robbie Wylie, for the parish of his birth, Birsay.

Other notable changes to personnel saw Calvin Poke play his first final for Sandwick while Birsay featured Gordy Norquoy, now back from Australia, and for the first time, Attie Stanger at centre forward. Edwin Harvey from Rendall replaced the absent Jimmy Norquoy in goal.

Full teams were as follows:

Sandwick: George Leonard; Tommy Bain and Ian Copland; Calvin Poke, Norman Couper and Brian Leonard; Tammo Anderson, Harvey Spence, George Wylie, Denis Leonard and Keith Corsie.

Birsay: Edwin Harvey; Eddie Spence and Stewart Spence; Gordy Norquoy, Raymond Stanger and Robbie Wylie; Jackie Grieve, Brian Spence, Attie Stanger, Bertie Spence, Barry Tait.

Sandwick kicked off playing with the wind but fell behind after six minutes when a Bertie Spence corner was driven home by Attie Stanger. This was the signal for a sustained spell of Sandwick pressure with the Birsay defence blocking and clearing as best they could. Harvey performed some heroics in helping to keep a clean sheet for his team until half time.

Playing with the elements, Birsay

now took command and soon Brian Spence ran in to double the lead. With twenty minutes of the half gone, Attie Stanger scored his second with a terrific drive and near the end, he joined the short list of famous names to have scored a hat trick in a Parish Cup final when he hit another great shot into the net from thirty yards. Any further efforts by Sandwick were in vain and Birsay had retained the trophy with an emphatic 4-0 win.

Attie Stanger, hat trick hero in the final.

Apart from Attie with his three goals, the outstanding player had been his brother, Raymond, playing at centre half. He had taken command in the middle and, along with the rest of the defence, had formed an impenetrable barrier to Sandwick who failed to score when they had the elements in their favour.

It had been a good final but the wind had helped minimise the finer arts of football. Competitive, yes, but sportsmanship was well to the fore. And as for the spectators, noisy but pretty well behaved! There was no evidence of toilet rolls being wasted and players were able to make their way to and from the pitch without showers of spittle raining down.

Bit of an anti climax after all that build up!

It was Birsay again in 1971 with this squad. *Back row, left to right, Sandy Meadows, Alfie Stanger, Eddie Spence, Edwin Harvey, Stuart Spence, Sandy Brown, Jimmy Ritch. Middle, Davy Spence, Jackie Grieve, Brian Spence, Attie Stanger, Bertie Spence, Barry Tait, Robbie Norquoy (manager). Front, Gordy Norquoy, Raymond Stanger, Robbie Wylie. (Picture: Orkney Library)*

1972: Hopes dashed by Harray

With two cup wins to their credit, it now looked as if we were in for an extended period of domination by Birsay unless, that is, the Sandwick machine found the correct gear. After putting up only token resistance these past two years, Harray appeared a spent force while out east, despite evidence of some good young players on the scene, no serious challenge really threatened. As for the North Isles, great fun to visit, but as yet, no contenders had emerged.

This year it might just be different!

Another new entry had been submitted, this time from the island of Stronsay. 'High time, too!' some might have said. Football had been played on Stronsay for many years with inter island games taking place between themselves, Westray and Sanday, but not until now had they ventured as far as the Parish Cup.

Transport issues had been a stumbling block but lack of confidence also played a part. Up to this point, the islanders did not feel they could match the Mainland teams and they had needed considerable persuasion for them to believe in their abilities and take the plunge. But now they had made the decision and the Stronsay fishing fleet were in harbour, raring to go!

Since they were newcomers Stronsay officials decided to apply their own interpretation to the Parish Cup rules (Well, nobody had told them otherwise!)

They considered who would be eligible to play by applying the usual criteria, but then deliberated on what actually constituted 'the parish.' Why could it not be a 'parish' as defined by the Church of Scotland? Now, the Stronsay minister also served the island of Eday … in fact, even better, both islands shared the same Orkney Islands Council member. That definition would do just grand!

It just so happened that some fine footballers lived on Eday at the time: John Eccles, head teacher and Dick Low, R.S.P.B. warden, to name but two. So, for Parish Cup duty, the plan was to shoot across from Eday in John's speedboat to join their Stronsay compatriots.

Needless to say, the O.F.A. were blissfully unaware of any of these clandestine activities. Had Stronsay gone on to achieve great success, no doubt someone would have 'twigged' and a protest would have brought the scheme to a halt. However, on this occasion, they were eliminated at the first hurdle by Stromness.

The O.F.A. secretary, Jock Mears, was in hospital at this time and as a result, the reporting of Parish Cup results is somewhat erratic. However, survivors of the encounter believe Stromness won both legs fairly comfortably.

It was a courageous effort by Stronsay but to say the whole operation ran smoothly would be economical with the truth. With numerous sea crossings involved, sometimes at an unearthly hour, the chances of something going wrong were high. Back to the speedboat again!

Early in the morning after the match, followed by the obligatory dance, the Eday contingent, including schoolteacher and bird man, set their compass and timings to take them back to their home island. It was a foggy morning. They set off and all seemed well as they passed the Spurness Holms but, after a time, when no recognisable piece of Eday came into view, they realised they were lost.

They circled round and finally spotted some land … and a fence. Neither had lived on Eday very long so this was probably a part of the island they hadn't seen before. They decided to disembark to check where they were and were fortunate to spot

a postman doing his round. So they hailed him.

"Can you tell us where the nearest phone is?"

"At that farmhoose up the brae!"

"Thank you. By the way, what part of Eday are we actually on?"

The postman gave them a withering glance and asked in a tone of disgust, "Are thoo English?" That said it all! They had landed at Linksness on the north west tip of Stronsay.

Back now to the rest of the Parish Cup first round where events proceeded in a more normal fashion:

First round Results

Sandwick	5	St Andrews	0
St Andrews	2	Sandwick	3
Birsay	1	Harray	2
Harray	2	Birsay	1
Deerness	0	Firth	7
return leg not reported			
St Ola	2	Orphir	2
Orphir	3	St Ola	1

So much for Harray being a 'spent force.' They had bounced back with a remarkable victory but Birsay will claim they were 'hard done by' in the first leg. After dire warnings a few years earlier about players arriving late for matches, this one kicked off on the dot of 7.30, with Birsay only having seven men on the field. Within ten minutes, Harray were two goals up.

The late arrivals were probably due to the fact that it was a "good hay day" up west and some of the players had been working till the last minute … and beyond! To a referee coming all the way from Kirkwall, no excuses were acceptable and the whistle blew on time. Birsay clawed their way back into the match but the damage had effectively been done.

There were no excuses in the second leg and Birsay's three-in-a-row dream was over. Now to the quarter finals.

Stronsay, winners of the Grimond Cup in the mid 1970's. Back row, left to right, Norrie Firth, Jim Miller, Don Peace, Ian Cooper, Rodney Stout, Colin Cooper. Middle, Graham Sinclair, Pat Dennison, Stewart Shearer, Neil Henderson, Victor Reid, Robbie Rendall. Front, Derek Firth, Terry Stout, Martin Williamson.
(Picture: Orkney Library)

Quarter final Results

South Ron.	5	Shapinsay	0
Shapinsay	6	South Ron.	2
Sanday	2	Orphir	3
Orphir	4	Sanday	0
Sandwick	3	Harray	4
Harray	4	Sandwick	2
Firth	6	Stromness	1

Second leg not reported, Firth go through.

Very frustrating not to know the result of the second leg between Harray and Sandwick. Suffice to say, Harray emerged victorious and had now beaten both their main rivals. Could anybody stop them?

Semi final Results

Harray	7	Firth	1
Firth	2	Harray	3
Orphir	1	South Ron.	1
South Ron.	2	Orphir	1

For Harray, the expression 'reports of my death have been somewhat exaggerated', would seem to be appropriate. They looked odds on favourites again. But what were South Ronaldsay's chances in their first final for twelve years?

In 1972, Orkney football was on the crest of a wave. The county team had beaten Shetland twice, once in the North Atlantic Cup, 7-1 and 3-1. They had also won the Archer Shield. Of this fine team, three players could turn out for Harray; Alan Hutchison, Eric Hutchison and Keith Hutchison. Another member of the side, Calvin Slater, played centre half in what was a very fit, young South Ronaldsay team. Despite Harray's experience of the big occasion, the 'Hope would be no pushover.

The teams lined up on a dry evening as follows:

South Ronaldsay: Billy Smith; Bobby Scott; and John Scott; Norrie Drever, Calvin Slater and Mike Barnett; Johnny Bruce, Marcus Wood, Arthur Cromarty, Alex Sinclair and Arthur Barnett.

Harray: Edric Clouston; Harvey Johnston and Stewart Sinclair; Harry Flett, Alan Flett and Keith Hutchison; Billy Tait, John Copland, Alan Hutchison, Emile Flett and Eric Hutchison.

After some good attacking end to end football, South Ronaldsay took the lead midway through the first half when Arthur Cromarty scored with a low drive. At this point, the 'Hope could sense an opportunity to win the cup for the first time but their dream was put 'on hold' when Harray were awarded a penalty which Alan Hutchsion converted.

It was 1-1 at half time and the fast, hard game was keeping the big crowd absorbed.

The second half continued in the same vein with chances at both ends before Emile Flett scored from close in to give Harray the lead. South Ronaldsay piled on the pressure but as often happens, the goal comes at the other end and Harray's third was scored again by Flett, with a great thirty yard shot.

That goal settled it and Harray ran out 3-1 winners. The difference between the teams had been the 'guile and cunning' of the Harray forward line and the fact that they had more experience in their line up than South Ronaldsay.

Two interesting facts now emerged. First of all, a winner's medal for Billy Tait, who had been unable to gain a place in the Birsay team, so played for his parish of residence! For Eric Hutchison, it was the eighth winning team in which he had played, creating an individual record for the competition.

It had been a good final to watch but this was no consolation for South Ronaldsay who had now appeared in four finals without success. However this team was young and they should have more chances. Anything else they could try to end their constant bad luck?

Well, maybe they should try some up to date tactics, pioneered by this season's newcomers. Why not check with their minister, see how big his 'parish' was, and apply that definition?

Who knows … maybe Swona, Stroma or Pentland Skerries were awash with fine players?

Harray, cup winners in 1972. Back row, left to right, Harry Flett, Keith Hutchison, Alan Flett, Edric Clouston, Harvey Johnston, Stewart Sinclair. Front, Billy Tait, John Copland, Alan Hutchison, Eric Hutchison, Emile Flett.
(Picture: Orkney Library)

1973:
Injured hero clinches cup

It is fair to say that Orkney football was now experiencing something of a 'Golden Age' with success being enjoyed on all fronts. The exploits of the inter county side, the usual barometer of fortunes, made for very positive readings. As well as defeating Caithness and Shetland, they secured the North Atlantic Cup in a 2-1 home victory over the Faroes. This cup would now be kept in Orkney while plans were made to begin another three way competition next year.

Spirits were further raised by the visit of two high-profile football names to Orkney. The first was Willie Wallace, a member of the Lisbon Lions, who was invited to conduct coaching sessions by the progressive new club 'Corinthians.'

He also agreed to help coach the junior inter county team while he was here.

He was followed by one of the biggest teams ever to tour the islands and play against local opposition, the first division club, Heart of Midlothian. In the first game, Orkney did remarkably well, only going down 2-0, but in the second, superior fitness told and the visitors ran out 8-2 winners. The tour was a great success and Bobby Seith, Hearts manager, was moved to say. "In all the tours this club has been on, we have never met with such friendliness and hospitality."

Catching the buoyant mood of the times, the parishes totally surpassed themselves, when no fewer than 15 entered this year's tournament. They included two newcomers, Westray and Rendall. Rendall had tried, unsuccessfully, to link up with Evie for Parish Cup purposes but had been turned down. Now they would try it alone.

As fate would have it, Westray's baptism was to be against neighbours Sanday, with whom they had enjoyed many a battle in the past. With the championship of the North Isles often at stake in these matches, no quarter was given to the opposition, and the referee sometimes had his hands full.

A good illustration of this was in a recent match where Sanday's speedy winger had been tormenting the Westray left back with his pace, time and again pushing the ball past him, and sprinting by to collect it. After a while the defender had had enough! Next time the outside right tried it, he was for it!

So he did it again. This time the defender paid no attention to the ball, which was already past him, but shoulder charged the speed merchant, sending him flying over the touchline.

The official, a first class referee from south who was holidaying in Westray at the time, called the full back over and said: "Next time you try that, I'll have to send you off."

"Weel, weel," was the reply, "if I go aff, thoo'll be comin wi' me!"

Mainland referees would now be quaking in their boots at the prospect of handling this fixture.

First round Results

Westray	1	Sanday	5
Sanday	4	Westray	4
Orphir	4	Shapinsay	2
Shapinsay	3	Orphir	1
Replay			
Shapinsay	3	Orphir	2
Sandwick	4	Birsay	4
Birsay	0	Sandwick	2
Firth	1	Harray	6
Harray	6	Firth	2
Stronsay	1	St Ola	1
St Ola	13	Stronsay	0
South Ron.	11	Deerness	0
Deerness	0	South Ron.	4

Although Westray only entered the fray in 1973, football had been alive and kicking in the island for many years. Pictured is a team from 1956. Back row, left to right, Norman Cooper, Henry Rendall (Piggar), Tammy Harcus (Chalmersquoy), Harcus Scott, Alfie Fergus (Newark), Jackie Stout (Kirkbrae), Erland Rendall (Piggar). Front, Billy Rendall (Longhouse), Robbo Rendall (Longhouse), Billy Brown (Noltland), Harry Fergus (Noup), Billy Tulloch (Broughton).
(Picture: Orkney Library).

Stromness   2   Rendall   0
Rendall   2   Stromness   3

Sanday's greater experience told, especially in a competitive, but clean, first leg and it was they who progressed to round two. After a heroic struggle in the first leg, Sandwick edged out Birsay. Would this be their year at last? Harray still looked formidable but South Ronaldsay were also a credible force. Calvin Slater's move from Thorfinn to play for the 'Hope full time, in order to help galvanise them for the Parish Cup, seemed to be paying dividends. The quarter finals were eagerly anticipated.

Quarter final Results

Sandwick	8	St Ola	0
St Ola	0	Sandwick	2
Harray	1	South Ron.	0
South Ron.	6	Harray	3
Stromness	2	St Andrews	6
St Andrews	0	Stromness	2
Shapinsay	4	Sanday	3
Sanday	0	Shapinsay	0

The main talking points were St Ola's thrashing by Sandwick and South Ronaldsay putting six past Harray. These two 'in form' sides were now kept apart in the semi finals.

Semi final Results

Sandwick	5	Shapinsay	1
Shapinsay	1	Sandwick	1
South Ron.	1	St Andrews	0
St Andrews	2	South Ron.	6

As predicted, both favourites again hit goal scoring form to reach the final. What was certain was that a new name would go on the trophy. Coincidentally, both were making their fifth appearance in the final after four previously unsuccessful attempts. There was, therefore, a lot at stake, and over 1,000 spectators turned up on a lovely evening to witness the following teams take the field:

South Ronaldsay: Andy Young; Bobby Scott and John Scott; Marcus Wood, Calvin Slater and Mike Barnett; Norrie Drever, Ian Sinclair, Wilfie Brown, Alex Sinclair and Arthur Barnett. Subs: Billy Smith and Johnny Bruce.

Sandwick: Rae Slater; Calvin Poke and Bob Slater; Tommy Bain, Norman Couper and Brian Leonard; Robbie Oag, Denis Leonard, George Wylie, Harvey Spence and John Stockan. Subs: Mervyn Slater and Geordie Leonard.

South Ronaldsay showed only two changes from last year's beaten finalists, Andy Young taking over in goal and Wilfie Brown, son of ex-professional Willie Brown, playing at centre forward.

Sandwick were a slowly evolving team as more and more young players forced their way in. This would be Rae Slater and Robbie Oag's first final but, while there were two Leonard brothers playing, the youngest, Geordie, was only a substitute. This was the reason why. Earlier in the season Orkney had beaten Caithness 4-0. All four Orkney goals had been scored by the aforementioned George. Quite a feat! Then, playing against Shetland in the week before the Parish Cup final, he sustained a double fracture of the jaw. Needless to say, the jaw had to be wired together and in this fragile state Geordie would miss the vital game … and Sandwick would miss him! He was named as 'substitute' but this was surely only a token gesture?

The game started and the first half was played at a frantic pace with plenty of chances at both ends. It was clear that both sides were very keyed up and desperate to win and this contributed to a shortage of good skilful football. But, it was exciting stuff.

The second half was played in a similar fashion. There were a great number of fouls and several bookings as the tension got the better

Sandwick's cup winning side of 1973. Back row, left to right, Ian Copland, James Poke, Calvin Poke, Rae Slater, Norman Couper, John Stockan, Keith Leonard. Middle, Bob Slater, Robbie Oag, George Wylie, Harvey Spence, Tommy Bain. Front, Mervyn Slater, Brian Leonard, Geordie Leonard.
(Picture: Orkney Library)

of the players. But defences were on top and the game looked to be heading for a replay.

However, on the sidelines another drama was being acted out. Geordie Leonard, he of the broken jaw, was badgering his manager Arthur Herdman to let him have a few minutes action since he had played in all the earlier rounds. He was told that this was very inadvisable. Not only could he risk serious injury but he could forfeit his O.F.A. Insurance money if he took the field, all £3.20 of it! George said he would take the risk so his manager eventually relented, and on he went.

South Ronaldsay, meanwhile, also made a change, Billy Smith coming on for Norrie Drever. The two substitutions were to prove the pivotal point of the match.

In a mix up in the South Ronaldsay penalty area, Billy was forced to handle a net bound shot. He was booked and a penalty was awarded.

Now if you were writing the script, which character would take the penalty? None other! George stepped forward and gave the goalkeeper no chance. And that was it!

South Ronaldsay were unable to find a reply and Sandwick ran out 1-0 winners to claim their first Parish Cup. You could scarcely have made it up!

For South Ronaldsay, the agony continued but for Sandwick the picture was so different. After all their near misses they were now looking like the finished article, not functioning at full capacity yet, but coming close. A glance down that long assembly line revealed an endless supply of young talent ready to replace any old or worn out parts of the team.

Yes, Sandwick would be capable of staying ahead of the field for quite some time.

1974:
Cup stays in the West Mainland

1974 promised to be another 'bumper' Parish Cup year. Fourteen teams made it to the start line but if Stromness and Westray had remembered to submit their entries on time, instead of after the draw had been made, the record total of 16 would have been achieved. Holm and Stenness had ventured forth once again but Deerness had been forced to withdraw through shortage of players.

The four strongest parishes were still Sandwick, Birsay, Harray and South Ronaldsay and it was felt that the winner was bound to emerge from this quartet. Sandwick's win last year was just reward at last for a very go ahead, progressive club. For visiting spectators to their home ground, the signs of their ambition were everywhere apparent.

They had created a first class playing surface on the flat land of Skeabrae aerodrome which was the envy of every team in Orkney and they had put to very practical use as changing rooms, the old control tower, situated at the west end of the pitch. Attention to detail was clearly in evidence, from the neat, low fence which surrounded the field to the line markings which were always fresh and slide rule straight. The grass was cut to perfection and animals were kept well away.

Leaving nothing to chance, the players even knitted their own goal nets after instruction from Johnny Velzian, one of their senior supporters. Yes, the Sandwick boys took a great pride in their club and this permeated through all their players making them now a force to be feared in the 'A' League and, particularly, in the Parish Cup.

As the season progressed and the draw was made, the first round produced the current equivalent of a Rangers v Celtic tie … Sandwick were drawn against Birsay. This match was given added spice by

Sandwick's immaculate Skeabrae pitch, the site of many titanic struggles, with the Control Tower changing 'facility' to the left.
(Picture: Rae Slater)

the fact that, by early June, it was looking as if Birsay could win the 'A' League. They were clearly out in front, although their nearest rivals were not that far behind. They just happened to be Sandwick!

So it was Parish Cup holders v 'A' League leaders … you can bet there wouldn't be much free space round Oxtro Park or Skeabrae on these two nights!

The teams 'lucky' enough to draw Outer Isles opponents this year were Rendall and Harray and they decided to really push the boat out. The boat they pushed was the m.v. *Orcadia* North Isles ferry, which was booked for a joint Saturday trip. So if the football itself did not go to plan, there was sure to be plenty of convivial compensation for the players and anticipated hordes of supporters.

First round Results

Sanday	2	Rendall	0
Rendall	0	Sanday	0
St Andrews	4	South Ron.	1
South Ron.	8	St Andrews	3
Firth	3	Shapinsay	7
Shapinsay	9	Firth	0
Holm	3	St Ola	8
St Ola	4	Holm	1
Stronsay	4	Harray	4
Harray	3	Stronsay	1
Birsay	0	Sandwick	2
Sandwick	1	Birsay	1

Birsay lost the 'battle of the giants' but consolation was at hand as they did indeed go on to capture the 'A' League crown which, with a team almost wholly composed of local lads, was a magnificent achievement. Still, they would have liked the Parish Cup to go along with the Brough Cup.

Stronsay gave Harray a great game at home but ran out of steam on the Mainland. St Andrews also collapsed in their second leg, prompting their district news correspondent to

describe the team as "just like a lot of rookies" in this game. Meanwhile, Sanday progressed from round one for the first time.

The quarter final now pitched Sandwick against South Ronaldsay in a repeat of last year's final. To help prepare them for this encounter, and to stave off relegation from the 'A' League, the 'Hope secured the services of Teddy Scott, the Aberdeen F.C. trainer, who agreed to come north for a week to give of his expertise. In practice, this did not turn out to be very productive as South Ronaldsay teams were involved in matches on three of the evenings and on free occasions, it proved to be difficult to prise players away from vital farm work.

Quarter final Results

Stenness	2	Sanday	7
Sanday	10	Stenness	1
St Ola	4	Shapinsay	0
Shapinsay	3	St Ola	3
Orphir	3	Harray	3
Harray	2	Orphir	1
Sandwick	1	South Ron.	1
South Ron.	1	Sandwick	3

After holding Sandwick at Skeabrae, South Ronaldsay hopes were high for the return. But, playing uphill on the 'Hope's steep pitch against wind and rain, Sandwick snatched two early goals and held on to win.

Apparently, South Ronaldsay had earlier tried to claim this game by default, pointing out that the Sandwick bus was late in arriving. When it eventually appeared over the horizon however, full to overflowing, the protests immediately subsided. The bus, which was going as fast as it could was owned by Mr J.D. Peace and Company of *South Ronaldsay*!

Another significant achievement was that of Sanday, reaching their first semi final. But spare a thought for their expenses!

At this time, no travel grants or awards from community councils

were available to help lower costs. Players had to dig in their own pockets to hire transport, usually in the form of fishing boats–some were even hired from Stronsay–followed by a bus to take the team and supporters to whichever part of the Mainland they were playing.

However, veterans of those days never regretted having to pay and the forfeit of a bit of cash was more than made up for by the post match celebrations and the return journey, when I am told, the main way to pass the time was by singing … whilst in between, lubricating the vocal chords, of course! Sometimes this rendition lasted all the way from Kirkwall to Sanday.

Although 12 was the number officially allowed on board some of the boats, sometimes the choir was greatly in excess of that and a great time was had by all. With a third trip to the Mainland now looming, Sanday pockets would be light and throats would be 'croam.'

Semi final Results

St Ola	0	Sandwick	1
Sandwick	1	St Ola	1
Sanday	1	Harray	4
Harray	4	Sanday	1

The expected Sandwick v Harray final did materialise but not without a great fight by St Ola and a brave show by Sanday who could be justifiably proud of this year's achievement.

The final was a re-run of the encounters of the late 60's when Harray won three times in a row but now that Sandwick had a win under their belts, things might be different.

However, both teams were confident, judging by a pre match, chance meeting in the Smithfield Hotel between players from each team, in to buy whisky to put in the cup.

"Well," said one, "wan o' us is wastin' wir time here the night."

"Aye," replied the other, "I doot jist wan o' us is gan tae enjoy the drink."

The team selections now made interesting reading. Harray's line up was virtually identical to that which appeared in the final two years earlier, the only change being Karl Flett's return to the forward line. Sandwick, meanwhile, continued to introduce new players and this would be the first cup final starts for Michael Grieve, Alan Slater and Keith Leonard.

The teams which ran out on a perfect night for football were as follows:

Harray: Edric Clouston, Harvey Johnston, Stewart Sinclair, Harry Flett, Alan Flett, Keith Hutchison, Karl Flett, John Copland, Alan Hutchison, Emile Flett, Eric Hutchison. Sub: Jimmy Grant.

Sandwick: Bob Slater, Michael Grieve, Calvin Poke, Norman Couper, Brian Leonard, Harvey Spence, Denis Leonard, Alan Slater, Robbie Oag, Geordie Leonard, Keith Leonard.

The match turned out to be an absorbing affair, but the poor playing surface and long grass thwarted attempts to play good, passing football. Sandwick, playing down the slope, took the lead after five minutes when the unpredictable bounce of the ball presented Geordie Leonard with an open goal and he made no mistake. They went two up after fifteen minutes when the ball rebounded off Edric Clouston and Leonard again scored from close range.

Eventually, Harray got back in it and Alan Hutchison reduced the arrears with a shot which went off a post. But Sandwick ensured they took a two goal lead into half time when Robbie Oag's speed took him past the full back yet again and he drove a great shot into the net.

Halftime, 3-1 to Sandwick.

Harray, now playing downhill, laid siege to the Sandwick goal, but by concentrating on attack, they laid themselves open at the back and Oag again broke away, crossed for Keith Leonard, who scored with a powerful shot.

Instead of lying down, Harray fought doggedly and were rewarded by two more goals, both scored by Alan Hutchison, and Sandwick had to pack their defence in the closing stages in order to survive. But survive they did in an exciting finish and they ran out 4-3 winners to gain some long awaited revenge over Harray and retain the cup for a second year.

A measure of a team's self confidence and level of expectation can be seen in the plans made to celebrate a cup winning. In Sandwick's case, this now extended to booking the parish hall and it was to this venue that players, supporters and anyone who could prove they were a supporter by bearing a bulging carrier bag, now proceeded, accompanied by the cherished trophy.

Local musicians would arrive to perform and the cup would do the rounds, the lid with the precariously perched footballer inevitably falling off at some stage with the result that the poor chap would end up once again having to get his broken legs soldered back together. Already his legs were several millimetres shorter than when he was created.

Such memorable nights were a fitting way to mark the achievement but once the euphoria had subsided, it would not have been long before these committed and meticulous club men of Sandwick set about their next task.

It would be time to give the rooms in that old control tower another lick of paint and coat of whitewash. After all, there were now two framed cup-winning team photos to be hung up on display … and there was plenty of bare wall for a few more!

1975:
Sandwick clinch hat trick of wins

The only team to have previously recorded three wins in a row had been Harray. In fact they achieved *four*, from 1966 to 1969, but it now looked as if Sandwick had that target well within their sights. Their young team was strong in every department and few parishes looked capable of knocking them off their perch. Maybe that, in part, explained the reduction in numbers for the 1975 tournament, which were back down to ten.

In the first round, Sandwick continued where they had left off last year.

First round Results

Sandwick	6	Stromness	0
Stromness	1	Sandwick	6
South Ron.	7	Sanday	0
Sanday	2	South Ron.	5

No surprises there but the perennial under achievers from the 'Hope once again looked up for the fight. This was borne out by another impressive performance in the quarter final, where Sandwick were given a very stern examination.

Quarter final Results

St Andrews	5	Shapinsay	0
Shapinsay	2	St Andrews	6
Harray	2	South Ron.	5
South Ron.	3	Harray	1
Sandwick	2	Orphir	1
Orphir	2	Sandwick	1
Replay			
Sandwick win			
Birsay	5	St Ola	4
St Ola	1	Birsay	4

Sandwick were a very well supported club at this time with many ex-players and senior citizens in regular attendance. Often, these veterans would offer advice. Was the second

Birth, Blood

leg game, in Orphir, the occasion when one such individual took over the team talk at half time with Sandwick 2-0 down? He delivered the following inspirational words: "Boys, all ye need tae dae is score three and no' let any more in, and yer bound tae win!"

His team responded sufficiently to earn a replay but frustratingly, the result was not reported; nor has it registered on the memories of any of the participants of over 30 years ago. Sandwick did win the match but Orphir certainly gave them a fright.

They would now face South Ronaldsay, fresh from a fine win over Harray. Birsay had done well to get this far, especially since two of their key players had suffered broken legs in recent weeks: Davy Moar in a league game against Rovers, and Attie Stanger in Dounby. But, Birsay's performance in the semi-final was to make light of their handicap.

Semi final Results

St Andrews	1	Birsay	8
Birsay	5	St Andrews	1
Sandwick	3	South Ron.	1
South Ron.	1	Sandwick	1

Birsay v Sandwick. It should be a great spectacle between the neighbouring parishes, where every player on the field played in the 'A' League. Both teams would include the nucleus of their own 'A' League side supplemented by reinforcements, mainly from Dounby, and when team mates came up against each other in an important game, an extra edge was always guaranteed.

The two changes in the Sandwick team this year were the inclusion of two Dounby players, right back Tommy Bain and forward Stevie Slater, who would play on the left side of the attack. As an indication of the quality in the team: centre half Norman Couper (Corinthians) and

forwards Robbie Oag and Geordie Leonard were well established in Orkney's county side.

Birsay showed a number of changes in personnel from their last final appearance. Newcomers to the side were Alan Flett, Kenny Ross and John Dowell, the last named also from Kirkwall team, Corinthians. Of their line up, Jimmy Norquoy played in goal for Orkney last year, emulating his father, Ben, and Raymond Stanger was always a 'first-pick' in any county team.

After a blisteringly hot County Show day, the evening was perfect for football with hardly a breath of wind.

Over 1,000 shirt sleeved spectators awaited the arrival of the following teams:

Sandwick: Rae Slater; Tommy Bain, Calvin Poke, Norman Couper, Brian Leonard; Keith Leonard, Denis Leonard, Alan Slater; Robbie Oag, Geordie Leonard, Stevie Slater. Subs: Harvey Spence, Michael Grieve.

Birsay: Jimmy Norquoy; Alan Flett, Edwin Harvey, Kenny Ross, Bertie Spence; Eddie Spence, Alfie Stanger, Raymond Stanger; John Dowell, Brian Spence, Stewart Spence. Sub: Jackie Grieve.

In the early part of the game both sets of spectators gave loud vocal encouragement to their respective teams. For one female spectator this had an unexpected outcome. As she opened her mouth to bellow some instructions, her false teeth shot out to land on the grass in front of her. Undaunted, she popped them back in and finished what she had started.

Despite such a rousing introduction, the game settled down into a cagey, 'cat and mouse' affair with the emphasis on defensive football. Only on rare occasions were there any attempts on goal and during one of

Sandwick in the Bignold Park dressing room after the final. Back row, left to right, Keith Leonard, Rae Slater, Denis Leonard. Middle, Calvin Poke, Tommy Bain, Alan Slater, Robbie Oag (cup on head), Geordie Leonard. Front, Stevie Slater, Norman Couper (holding cup), Arthur Herdman (manager).

(Picture: Orkney Library)

the few goalmouth incidents, Robbie Oag rose to head the ball just under the Birsay bar to put Sandwick into the lead.

Robbie Oag, whose header was the only goal of the match.

Maybe the still, balmy evening had something to do with it because the second half was played in a very relaxed manner, with little to enthuse the basking onlookers. Neither goalkeeper was called into serious action and the game eventually petered out in a 1-0 win for Sandwick.

This subdued atmosphere was quite astonishing given the rivalry between the teams. When they chanced to clash at Skeabrae, for instance, the sounds of battle could be heard as far away as Dounby on a still night. It was if removing the combatants from their own territories had deadened hostilities. Now if this final had been played in Show Park on Dounby Show night … that would have been something different altogether!

Still, there was one major talking point from the night, apart from Sandwick's third consecutive cup win that is. As the incident was discussed time and again in the parish over the course of the next week, the standard answer to the most frequently asked question was "My yes! They say hid wis both sets!"

1976: County Show result omen

As preparations were made for the new season, the sad fact emerged that there was to be no Birsay team this year in any of the leagues. A meeting had been held in the Birsay Hall where it was established that there would not be enough players to make a team. The last of 'Ben Busby's Babes' had hung up their boots while the broken limbs sustained last year had added to the loss. So, after sombre deliberation, the decision was taken to disband.

This situation, more than any other, highlighted the precarious nature of parish football. Only two years earlier, Birsay were officially the best team in Orkney, champions of the 'A' League, and the future looked rosy. Now, it was all over! But, while some of the remaining players dispersed to other clubs – Raymond and Alfie Stanger to Rendall, Jackie Grieve to Orphir, for example, there was some consolation in that Birsay still entered a team in the Parish Cup.

As was the case last year, there were a few gaps in the publication of cup results in the Press. Jock Mears, the tireless O.F.A. secretary for 23 years, had now retired from the post as well as the job of football correspondent for *The Orcadian*, where he wrote for many years under the name of 'Corinthian.'

As we shall see, his replacement in the latter role had still to develop Jock's knack of unearthing results from far-flung outposts such as Shapinsay, South Ronaldsay and St Andrews.

First round Results

Sandwick	7	St Ola	4
St Ola	1	Sandwick	3
Orphir	3	Shapinsay	1

Sandwick's powerful cup winning side of 1975. Back row, left to right, Fraser Flett, Stevie Bain, Carl Wood, Bob Slater, Rae Slater, Colin Kirkness, Alan Thomson. Middle, Brian Leonard, Calvin Poke, Alan Slater, Geordie Leonard, Norman Couper, Dennis Leonard, Michael Grieve, Arthur Herdman (manager). Front, Keith Leonard, Stevie Slater, Harvey Spence, Robbie Oag, Tommy Bain.

Birth, Blood

Second leg not reported. Orphir go through.

| Birsay | 1 | South Ron. | 1 |

Second leg not reported. South Ronaldsay go through.

| Harray | 5 | Sanday | 0 |
| Sanday | 3 | Harray | 3 |

The quarter final draw was made and it appeared that Harray's luck was out. After a journey to Sanday in round one, they now drew Westray. To make matters worse, during the trip to the island for the first match, the wind blew up to such an extent that, by the time the game was over, it was impossible to take to sea for the return journey.

But, as you would expect, Westray hospitality came to the rescue and the Harray party was accommodated overnight at different homes throughout the island. The weather improved sufficiently the next day, Sunday, for the trip home to be made.

To show their appreciation, the Harray team once again proceeded to whip their hosts in the return game.

Quarter final Results

Westray	0	Harray	3
Harray	3	Westray	0
Sandwick	6	St Andrews	1

Second leg not reported. Sandwick go through.

Rendall	1	Orphir	1
Orphir	2	Rendall	0
South Ron.	1	Stromness	2
Stromness	2	South Ron.	4

The semi finals were a fascinating prospect. Orphir were building their best team in years and should give travel weary Harray a good run. Meanwhile, would South Ronaldsay again find the psychological barrier presented by Sandwick too high to scale … or was there a renewed will to succeed? Look how close they came:

Semi final Results

| Sandwick | 0 | South Ron. | 1 |
| South Ron. | 2 | Sandwick | 3 |

Replay:

Sandwick	2	South Ron.	0
Harray	3	Orphir	0
Orphir	2	Harray	3

Agonising! Their spirits must have soared after the first leg win in Sandwick. This was their chance … only for their hopes to be dashed again in the replay. Ah well! Back to the drawing board!

Harray had fought off Orphir's challenge to reach yet another final but what chance did they have? On paper, probably not a lot and when the teams were announced there was one very significant omission from their starting line up.

Teams were as follows:

Harray: Edric Clouston; Alan Flett, Agmond Flett, Alan Belford, Keith Hutchison; Harry Flett, Jimmy Grant, John Copland; Alan Hutchison, Emile Flett, Kenny Logie. Subs: Stewart Sinclair, Eric Hutchison.

Sandwick: Rae Slater; Michael Grieve, Calvin Poke, Norman Couper, Brian Leonard; Harvey Spence, Denis Leonard, Alan Slater; Robbie Oag, Geordie Leonard, Stevie Slater. Sub: Keith Leonard.

It was strange to see Eric Hutchison, the last of the original 'Hutchison 5' and record medal winner in the Parish Cup, on the subs bench. After a remarkable career which included 13 'caps' against Shetland, Eric was now a part time footballer, content with an occasional run out in parish games.

Sandwick fielded a virtually unchanged team. As individuals, their status continued to grow and this year, Denis Leonard joined the list of capped players in their ranks.

As kick off approached, more than one spectator was heard to remark that the odds had shifted even further in Sandwick's favour. At the County Show earlier in the day, the overall

1976 winners, Sandwick. Back row, left to right, Brian Leonard, Bob Slater, Rae Slater, Geordie Leonard. Middle, Fraser Flett, Calvin Poke, Alan Slater, Dennis Leonard, Michael Grieve, Arthur Herdman (manager). Front, Keith Leonard, Robbie Oag, Alan Thomson, Harvey Spence.

championship had been won by a bull from the Davidsons of Skaill, *Sandwick*. The runner up was a blue grey cow-in-calf from J.E. Flett, Northbigging, *Harray*. According to the wise ones, the omens were not good for Harray!

Unlike last year's tame anti climax, this year's match was keenly contested and, although not a classic final, had a great deal of honest endeavour from both sides. Playing down the pitch with a breeze behind, Sandwick had the better of the first half but were unable to make their advantage count.

No score at half time but shortly after the interval, Denis Leonard hit the bar with a free kick and Norman Couper, running in, headed into the net. Sandwick went two up shortly after when Geordie Leonard outstripped the Harray defence and slipped the ball past Clouston.

This was a signal for a determined fight back and Alan Hutchison reduced arrears with a free kick. Harray now threw everything into attack, bringing on Eric Hutchison, but in a breakaway raid a penalty was awarded to Sandwick. Although it had to be re-taken, Calvin Poke made no mistake second time.

No more goals were scored and Sandwick ran out 3-1 winners.

The great Sandwick run continued and most galling for Harray, this was the night when Sandwick equalled their record of four straight wins.

Unlike other occasions when teams dominated the competition, there was no sign of the run ending. This side was destined to stay together and were as yet, relatively unaffected by such factors as players moving south to work or missing half the season through being students at college or university.

However, for rivals clutching at straws, there was some hope. Recruitment for jobs at the Flotta oil terminal was now gaining pace and the shift system of employment, due to come into operation in December, would be liable to play havoc with sporting commitments of the successful applicants. Rumour had it that several Sandwick boys had applied. But then, so had boys from South Ronaldsay, St Ola ….

Ah! But just as the season in Orkney drew to a close, another intriguing development took place.

Two Sandwick players, Geordie Leonard and Rae Slater, were invited to play for Brora Rangers in the Highland League, where they were joined by Graham Johnston of Thorfinn. This was a great achievement by Orkney footballers and the possibility existed of these players gaining professional contracts and then … they would be unable to play football in Orkney during the summer!

Now imagine the speculation back home. All footballing people would be hoping the boys succeeded but it's just possible some might have ulterior motives... Although no concrete evidence of such exists, it was said that letters of commendation were winging their way to Brora, bearing Orphir, St Margaret's Hope or Harray postmarks, and all drawing attention to the merits of Calvin Poke, Denis Leonard, Norman Couper, Robbie Oag ….

Geordie Leonard, who went off to seek his fortune in the Highland League.

1977:
Cup finalists break records

A particularly sour note was struck at Orkney Football Association's A.G.M. at the start of the 1977 season, certainly as far as the North Isles were concerned. Perhaps prompted by Harray's experience last year when they drew both Sanday and Westray, O.F.A. club representatives voted to increase the Parish Cup entry fee to £5, a proportion of which would be allocated to the teams who had to travel to the North Isles. It was decided that the North Isles should provide boats for the mainland teams.

The response by Westray and Sanday to this blatant discrimination was to refuse to enter this year's competition but, far from feeling guilty, the O.F.A. correspondent was quoted in the Press as saying that "news of their absence will be received with relief by Mainland clubs."

People in the North Isles were justifiably aggrieved and their feelings were eloquently expressed in a letter to *The Orcadian* by Nora Muir from Sanday who highlighted the unfairness of isles' clubs having to provide boats both home and away ties, while receiving no financial aid themselves.

She went on to say: "The North Isles are part of Orkney and, as such, are entitled to the same conditions of entry as other teams. If the Mainland teams are so lazy that the effort of looking for a boat is too much for them, then perhaps they should withdraw from the competitions."

She concluded by stating that " … the O.F.A. should be disappointed that they have lost entries, and not delighted as their article suggests."

Birth, Blood

Yes, the competition would be all the poorer this year without Sanday and Westray and the situation reflected little credit on the football administrators.

With the absence of all North Isles' teams, only ten entrants lined up for the start of the tournament.

First round Results

Orphir	2	St Ola	2
St Ola	6	Orphir	1
Rendall	2	St Andrews	0
St Andrews	1	Rendall	1

The team of the year in Orkney football was undoubtedly Rendall, who were about to be crowned 'A' League champions for the first time in their history. However, despite progressing through the first round, it was unlikely that this remarkable achievement would be replicated in the Parish Cup.

While the core of the team was from the Parish of Rendall, notably Morgan Harcus, Andy and Stevie Nicolson, Callum Gillon and Ian Fraser, the majority came from the wider catchment of Evie and Firth. Still, Rendall fielded a good competitive Parish team.

Quarter final Results

Birsay	5	St Ola	3
St Ola	3	Birsay	4
Stromness	1	Sandwick	2
Sandwick	3	Stromness	0

Harray	3	Rendall	0
Rendall	1	Harray	0
Shapinsay	3	South Ron.	2
South Ron.	5	Shapinsay	0

Although Birsay still survived, their woeful bad luck continued with another leg break victim. This time it was the turn of Jackie Grieve in a game against Thorfinn in early May.

Sandwick, who were also through, now planned to prepare for the semi finals with a game against Brora Rangers. Building on their connection with the Highland League club, they invited them to Orkney for a short two game tour.

In the first game Brora took on the Sandwick parish team, winning 6-1,

Rendall F.C., 'A' League winners three years in a row with their 1978 line up. Back row, left to right, Robbie Fraser, Alfie Stanger, Alan Miller, Morgan Harcus, Kevin Balfour, Neil Muir, Edgar Balfour, Brian Davies. Middle, Jim Davies, Jimmy Moar, Len Laurenson, Rodney Spence, Jockie Wood, Robin Nicolson, Callum Gillon. Front, Jimmy Stevenson, Ian Fraser, Raymond Stanger, Fraser Balfour, Stevie Nicolson, Andy Nicolson, Stewart Wilkie, Edwin Harvey (manager).

and on the following evening, they played an Orkney select, winning 2-0.

In both games, Geordie Leonard, who had signed a professional contract, played for Brora, but Rae Slater, who had signed on amateur terms, had returned to Orkney at the end of the Highland League season, and was back playing in goal for Sandwick.

Such high level of competition would have done Sandwick nothing but good as the semi finals approached.

Semi final Results

South Ron.	2	Birsay	1
Birsay	0	South Ron.	2
Harray	1	Sandwick	5

Second leg not reported. Sandwick go through.

So here we were again; Sandwick v South Ronaldsay. This was the situation: Sandwick were poised to become the first team in the Parish Cup history to win the trophy five times in a row. South Ronaldsay were now in their sixth final but had lost in their previous five attempts … and crucially, every year since Sandwick began their winning run in 1973, they had eliminated South Ronaldsay at some stage. If a bookmaker had been resident in Kirkwall in 1977, what would have been the odds on a 'Hope victory? Fairly long, I would guess!

But not if it had anything to do with Calvin Slater. There he was, in his late 30's, still striving with every sinew to realise the one sporting triumph to elude him, in the form of a Parish Cup medal. He would once again organise the team from the heart of the defence, a team which retained many names from their last final appearance four years earlier. Newcomers to the side included Brian Cromarty and Albert Burton while Sandwick's latest prodigy was Colin Kirkness, taking the place of

the departed Geordie Leonard.

Full teams were as follows:

Sandwick: Rae Slater; Brian Leonard, Calvin Poke, Norman Couper, Denis Leonard, Alan Slater, Harvey Spence, Colin Kirkness, Robbie Oag, Keith Leonard, Stevie Slater.

South Ronaldsay: Billy Smith; Jim Rosie, Calvin Slater, Marcus Wood, Bobby Scott, Brian Cromarty, John Scott, Albert Burton, Ian Sinclair, Wilfie Brown, Arthur Barnett.

The early part of the game was played at a good tempo with chances at either end but it took half an hour for the first goal to arrive and it went, predictably, to Sandwick. Alan Slater secured possession and from thirty yards, let go a great drive which eluded keeper Smith.

South Ronaldsay fought back hard but the Sandwick defence was well marshalled by Denis Leonard and half time arrived with the score 1-0 to Sandwick.

Alan Slater, scorer of a great winning goal.

Early in the second half, fog descended making it difficult to follow play. South Ronaldsay took on substitutes Billy Scott and Arthur Cromarty and began to dominate. However, they could not break down the opposition defence, and it was Sandwick who came closest to scoring when Stevie Slater hit the bar during a breakaway.

The game ended with the score 1-0 to Sandwick and this meant that two records had been established; Sandwick for the longest winning sequence while South Ronaldsay had recorded most final appearances without a victory.

What was to be done? By this time, self-belief must have been at rock bottom whenever the South Ronaldsay team saw the orange and blue-clad opposition take the field. Maybe their only salvation lay in the realms of sports psychology but it was an art seldom practised in Orkney at that time.

Had such a practitioner been available, he or she might well have scratched around for some familiar analogies to provide motivation for demoralised clients, " … now, just think about the tale of Bruce and the Spider … no! no! not you Johnny! Robert, King of Scotland! Well, during his exile, didn't he shelter in a cave? … and didn't he watch as the spider failed *six* times to scale the cave wall? But, on the *seventh* attempt it finally succeeded!

So inspired was Bruce that he rallied his forces and thrashed the deadly enemy at Bannockburn! … hammered them! … slaughtered them … annihilated them! And remember, according to folklore, it was said that the cave was situated somewhere on the rugged South Ronaldsay coastline! Now just focus on that and …."

All right! All right! It was only a suggestion.

1978: Sandwick reign supreme

Two of the most celebrated figures in the history of the Parish Cup passed away during 1978. The first was one of Orkney's finest ever footballers, Arthur Dainty. In the mid 50s, he had returned to his Lancashire home with his Orcadian wife and family but by then, he had made a considerable mark on local football as a stylish, cultured half back for Holm and Orkney. He had lifted the cup on two occasions and it was significant that his departure from Orkney coincided with the demise of Holm as a footballing force.

The other legendary character from Orkney's past, albeit in a different capacity, was David Horne, alias 'Cubbie Roo'. Although a fine footballer with Thorfinn during the 1920s, his greater claim to fame was as a sportswriter of distinction. His reports on Parish Cup matches and the Kirkwall Ba' were as entertaining as they were perceptive, none more so than the report on the 1949, reproduced earlier in this book. After emigrating, his Australian home had been a welcome base for many young Orcadians who had chosen to go and live in that country.

Given that a place in history could be secured by a telling contribution to the Parish Cup competition, who on the present scene might find their name uttered in tones of reverence, many years hence?

Surely one or more candidates must emerge from the current Sandwick team whose extended run of success showed no sign of coming to an end. A number of their players, such as Norman Couper, Calvin Poke, Denis Leonard, Brian Leonard and Robbie Oag had already played in all five winning teams, with the prospect of many more to come.

But, while unbroken success was a constant source of pride and delight to their supporters, the general football public in Orkney began to ache for a change. As in all periods of prolonged ascendancy such as Celtic's or Rangers' nine-in-row domination of Scottish football, victory for any other team would be preferable.

However, it was with hope rather than expectation, that supporters made their way to the first round matches of this year's competition.

First round Results

Orphir	2	Firth	3
Firth	5	Orphir	1
Stromness	5	St Andrews	3
St Andrews	0	Stromness	6
Birsay	11	Deerness	0
Deerness	1	Birsay	7
South Ron.	4	St Ola	0
St Ola	3	South Ron.	4
Sandwick	5	Harray	1
Harray	1	Sandwick	5

Not much comfort for those pining for change as Sandwick disposed of a Harray team, now entering a period of decline. Of the other sides making progress, perhaps there was a hint of revival in Firth and some stirrings in Stromness, never a finalist in the competition's 50 year history. On to the quarter finals, where Holm appeared to suffer an attack of cold feet!

Quarter final Results

Stromness	4	South Ron.	4
South Ron.	3	Stromness	1
Holm	v	Sandwick	
Holm scratched			
Birsay	7	Shapinsay	4
Shapinsay	3	Birsay	6
Firth	5	Evie	3
Evie	2	Firth	1

Three familiar semi finalists emerged along with relative newcomers, Firth, who would now go on to play Birsay, already the scorers of 31 goals in four games. Meanwhile, down South Ronaldsay way, the semi final draw was received with raptures! With the

A triumphant Sandwick F.C., six in a row winners of the Parish Cup. Back row, left to right, Stewart Wood, Robbie Oag, Alan Slater, Calvin Poke, Rae Slater, Stanley Seator, Michael Grieve, Keith Dunnet, Arthur Herdman (manager). Front row, Derek Chalmers, Harvey Spence, Bob Slater, Dennis Leonard, Colin Kirkness, Stevie Slater.

prospect of their annual meeting with their nemesis looming, what would their tactics be? In the absence of practical help, I suspect a number would have resorted to prayer.

Semi final Results

Birsay	4	Firth	2
Firth	1	Birsay	3
South Ron.	2	Sandwick	2
Sandwick	3	South Ron.	0

Whatever was tried, it brought no better fortune. So once again it was a Birsay v Sandwick final.

Birsay's team continued to evolve and their line up for the final contained three players making their first appearance at this stage, Raymond Flett, Stewart Moar and Steve Foulkes. Attie Stanger had recovered from his broken leg and was back in the team alongside his brothers.

Sandwick showed two changes this year, Bob Slater returning to defence after a few years absence and Fraser Flett, a Sandwick born Stromnessian, playing up front.

While secretly admiring the qualities of the Sandwick side, most neutrals would be hoping for a Birsay win to break the monopoly, and perhaps the need for change was brought home by the disappointing crowd which gathered to see the match, a contest which in the recent past would have drawn a large noisy support.

The following teams lined up:

Sandwick: Rae Slater; Calvin Poke, Norman Couper, Michael Grieve, Denis Leonard, Bob Slater, Keith Leonard, Colin Kirkness, Stevie Slater, Robbie Oag, and Fraser Flett.

Birsay: Jimmy Norquoy; Eddie Spence, Kenny Ross, Raymond Flett, Brian Spence, Stewart Moar, Raymond Stanger, Alfie Stanger, Attie Stanger, Steve Foulkes and Bertie Spence.

Birsay played down the slope and had the better of the first half but were denied an opening goal by a mixture of good goalkeeping and poor finishing.

After the interval, there was a spell of end to end play where both keepers again had to produce fine saves, but as time wore on it looked as if a goalless draw was the likely outcome. However, with only a few minutes left, Robbie Oag worked the ball through to substitute Alan Slater who cracked it home from close range. This was the second year in succession where Slater had popped up with the winning goal and so put paid to Birsay's hopes of ending Sandwick's six year winning sequence.

Sandwick had just deserved their win in a game which never reached the heights hoped for in a Parish Cup final. The shortage of fireworks on the field had been matched by a muted response from the fairly sparse crowd, with even the Sandwick section aspiring to no more than contented applause.

Once again there was no denying the significance of Sandwick's achievement and admiration of their fine team. But next year, something new, exciting or unpredictable was needed to capture the public imagination and breathe new life into the ailing tournament.

A new 'Arthur Dainty' perhaps, who could grab a team by the scruff of the neck and by a mixture of cajoling and will power make it perform: or maybe a new 'Cubbie Roo' who could make even the dullest , scoreless draw sound as exciting as bungee jumping from the Old Man of Hoy, or white-water rafting off Eynhallow.

1979: Sandwick's domination ends

Speaking of 'something new', the 1979 football season began with a spate of new ideas and the ditching of old habits.

At their A.G.M., the O.F.A. decided to affiliate to the Scottish Amateur Football Association so that Orkney teams could enter the newly established Highland Amateur Cup. This competition was intended to cover the entire area from Peterhead in the east to Thurso in the north, but now Orkney would be the first island group to take part. Orkney would be one of the zoned areas with two teams winning through to compete against other zone qualifiers in the quarter final.

This exciting new challenge for Orkney's top teams brought with it, another 'first' for football in the county, playing on a Sunday. This had not been the original intention, but spring and summer of 1979 had been particularly wet, resulting in the cancellation of many games. The only way to keep abreast of fixtures was to play on a Sunday, with the Highland Cup games being the first to break the old taboos.

Once begun, a trend was established which has continued ever since.

Finally, yet another innovation! To players of today, it may seem that the use of red and yellow cards has been with us forever. Not so. This was the season when referees were instructed for the first time to issue the appropriate colour of card for caution or ordering off. But who was the first Orkney footballer to receive a 'yellow' or 'red'?

Come on, somebody out there must know!

With all the change in the air, could this be the year for some unexpected developments in the Parish Cup? Well, there would be little chance in round one where the 'untouchables' had a bye.

First round Results

South Ron.	1	St Andrews	1
St Andrews	0	South Ron.	3
Stromness	10	Firth	2
Firth	4	Stromness	2
Harray	2	Shapinsay	3
Shapinsay	5	Harray	1
Sanday	1	Orphir	2
Orphir	3	Sanday	2

Firth had kicked off with high hopes having re-established themselves as a club side for the first time in nearly twenty years. A new pitch was obtained at Coubister and a great deal of work went into getting it ready. Unfortunately, due to repeated downpours, it was the last day of May before it was playable and the first match there commemorated Firth's exit from the cup at the hands of Stromness.

All footballers would have been glad to see the return of Sanday after two years voluntary exile but they fell to Orphir whose star was definitely in the ascendancy. Now to the quarter finals where some of the 'big guns' joined the fray.

Quarter final Results

Holm	1	Orphir	5
Orphir	5	Holm	1
Sandwick	4	Stromness	2
Stromness	0	Sandwick	7
South Ron.	1	Birsay	0
Birsay	0	South Ron.	4
St Ola	6	Shapinsay	0
Shapinsay	3	St Ola	2

A strong semi final line up now resulted and for once, Sandwick and South Ronaldsay avoided each other. The public now expected these two teams to make their way into the final, followed by the customary outcome on County Show night.

However, events elsewhere should not be ignored as the semi finals approached. The two Orkney teams to qualify from the Orkney zone of the Highland Amateur Cup were Rendall, 'A' League winners for the third year running, and, most unexpectedly, South Ronaldsay! Now, could this achievement provide the tonic needed to lay their Parish Cup hoodoo to rest?

When the results of the first leg semi final ties became known, football fans everywhere were shaken out of their apathetic slumbers. They were:

| Orphir | 3 | Sandwick | 2 |
| South Ron. | 2 | St Ola | 4 |

The question on everybody's lips now was, 'could the unthinkable possibly happen?' The St Ola performance was perhaps less remarkable given that, every few years, they were able to summon quite a formidable team from the environs of Kirkwall. They duly completed their task in the second leg by holding South Ronaldsay to a goalless draw, to reach their first final in almost a decade.

Meanwhile, crowds flocked to Skeabrae to see if Orphir could be the first team to beat Sandwick Parish since 1972. It was one of those beautiful Orkney summer evenings in early August, flat calm, with a glorious sunset in prospect … the kind of setting players can still recall many years on when most others have blurred into one. And the match lived up to the occasion!

For a time, it looked as though Sandwick would once more do enough to go through. They led 3-1 mid-way through the second half before Alan Clouston scored his second of the evening to make it 3-2 and level the tie on aggregate. One more goal would do it for either side and Sandwick pressed for the winner.

But then, Graham Sclater, the Orphir centre, broke clear from the half way line, ran in on goal and steadied himself before slipping the ball past

Alan Clouston, scorer of two of Orphir's goals.

Sandwick keeper, Rae Slater. The noise which greeted the goal was deafening; car horns blasted, Orphir fans cheered, neutrals danced, an elderly lady walking her dog near Swanbister wondered what was happening! This was enough to earn Orphir a 3-3 draw to take them through to the final.

It probably was a splendid sunset, not that Orphir boys noticed as they whooped it up inside the old control tower, but to Sandwick it held a different meaning. The sun had finally set on nearly seven years of supreme achievement. Now it was someone else's turn and that would be good for the competition as a whole.

The result paid immediate dividends as the largest crowd for some years turned up to see if St Ola could win for the first time since 1965 or if Orphir could record their first ever success.

On another perfect evening for football, the following teams took the field:

St Ola: John Foulis; Alan Robertson, Fraser Byers, Eric Kemp, Willie Flett; Ralph Fotheringhame, Andrew Stanger, John Rees; Rab Herbertson, Evan Monkman, Mike Herdman.

Orphir: Ian Moir; Bruce Donaldson, Davie Esslemont, Francis Ballantyne,

Geordie Flett; Jim Frisken, Trevor Anderson, Mervyn Ballantyne; Graham McIntosh, Graham Sclater, Alan Clouston.

Play was fairly even during the early exchanges as both sides strove for the opener but when it came after 25 minutes, it was a disaster for Orphir. A misunderstanding between Ian Moir and Geordie Flett over a pass back resulted in Flett lobbing over the advancing keeper's head into the net, to put St Ola one up.

For the rest of the first half and well into the second, Orphir dominated play but the St Ola defence, with Byers outstanding, could not be breached. But by committing so much to attack in the pursuit of the equaliser, Orphir were left exposed at the back and Herdman broke away on his own to slip the ball past Moir to make it 2-0 to St Ola.

Orphir continued to press and with five minutes left, Sclater reduced the leeway with a drive which beat Foulis at his far post. But it came too late to save the game and St Ola held out for a 2-1 victory.

This win was due in large part to a fine defence where veterans, Kemp and Fotheringhame had used their experience to great effect. For Orphir this must have been an awful anti climax. Their final had been three nights earlier in Sandwick and they simply could not recapture the passion or inspiration of that night. Their defeat meant they were still without a Parish Cup win to their name.

Before the curtain came down on the 1979 season, hearken to this!

A team which could not win a cup in their own county, on September 1, crossed the Pentland Firth and won the most prestigious tournament in which Orkney clubs had ever taken part. South Ronaldsay won the Highland Amateur Cup defeating Halkirk 2-1 in the final.

Now, after arguably the greatest achievement by an Orkney club team, surely the 'Hope would go on to stamp their mark all over domestic football … and top of the agenda? The Parish Cup!

Calvin Slater might even be tempted to play one more year!

South Ronaldsay beat the best of the north in 1979 when they won the Highland Amateur Cup. Back row, left to right, Bobby Scott, Ian Sinclair, Jim Gaddie, Johnny Bruce, Benny Thomson, Marcus Wood, Marty Flett, Arthur Barnett, Glyn Edwards. Front row, Alex Rosie (manager), Calvin Slater, Alan Smith, Jim Seatter, Andy Whyte.
(Picture: Orkney Library)

Birth, Blood

St Ola players enjoy their presentation evening in 1979 in the Lynnfield Hotel. Back row, left to right, Eric Kemp, Evan Monkman, Rab Herbertson, John Foulis, Fraser Byers, Willie Flett. Front. Jim Wilson, Ian Adams, Len Laurenson, Ralph Fotheringhame (standing), Alan Robertson, John Rees, and Dave Wylie.

A very fashionable group of Sandwick players at their presentation dinner in 1975 see captain Brian Leonard accept the third of their six Parish Cups. Also present are a few players who played for their 'A' team but were ineligible for the parish. From left, Arthur Herdman, Geordie Leonard, Fraser Balfour, Stevie Bain, Carl Wood, Rae Slater, Brian Leonard (with cup), Ian Fraser (half hidden), Denis Leonard, Sandy Brown, Mrs Ann Berston (making presentation), Keith Leonard, Michael Grieve, Alan Thomson, George Berston.

The 80s

1980:

Single goal clinches the cup

Although Orphir lost out last year, at least they still retained their membership of a very exclusive club … as did South Ronaldsay, despite their stunning success in the Highland Amateur Cup.

Other members of the club included Evie, Rendall, Sanday, Westray and Stromness, and whenever citizens of these parishes met, especially footballers, there was an immediate bond formed through shared experience and outlook. But in this first year of the new decade there was division in the ranks as one of the members was to resign from the club, never again to qualify for membership.

All will be revealed!

As if taking encouragement from Sandwick's defeat last year, a large entry of 13 teams came forward this time but before any matches could be played, a warning from the newly formed referee's association was directed at parish teams. Some had been taking liberties … for a number of years … rearranging fixtures if some local event such as a wedding or Gala Day coincided with the match date. (Haven't we heard that before?) No games were now to be postponed except for weather conditions and any team not playing on the scheduled day would be fined £10 and banned from playing again until the fine was paid.

Furthermore, anyone red carded in a Parish game, thereby incurring an automatic two match ban, would have to serve their sentence by *missing Parish Cup games*, not less important league games. As if anybody would think like that!

With these warnings ringing in players' ears, the first round got started.

First round Results

South Ron.	2	St Andrews	0
St Andrews	3	South Ron.	5
St Ola	1	Westray	2
Westray	1	St Ola	7
Orphir	4	Stromness	1
Stromness	8	Orphir	1
Firth	2	Sandwick	4

Second leg not reported, Sandwick go through

| Deerness | 0 | Harray | 3 |

Second leg not reported, Harray go through

After upsetting the holders in the first leg, Westray must have fancied their chances, but fell to pieces at home. One of their players, Michael Findlay, sustained a broken leg in their first game.

In an astonishing turnaround, Stromness not only wiped out a three goal deficit to Orphir but went on to score *eight*. A considerable goal scoring threat awaited the next opponents, St Ola.

Quarter final Results

| Birsay | 4 | Rendall | 1 |

Rendall disqualified

Harray	7	Shapinsay	1
Shapinsay	2	Harray	3
South Ron.	2	Sandwick	3
Sandwick	8	South Ron.	1
St Ola	3	Stromness	2
Stromness	1	St Ola	0

Replay

| St Ola | 0 | Stromness | 3 |

Well, a few talking points there!

Rendall, just agonisingly short of having a good Parish Cup team, had played the Balfour brothers from Woodwick Stores, Evie, in the first leg against Birsay. However, they did not yet hold the necessary residential qualification. Outcome? Protest. Disqualified!

As for South Ronaldsay, they might be the best team in the north of Scotland but at the sight of Sandwick … can you picture a towel being thrown on the pitch?

And Stromness … they looked to be real contenders!

The semi finals now pitched together old rivals, Birsay and Sandwick, leaving the upwardly mobile Stromness to face downwardly mobile Harray.

Oh, but revenge was sweet for Birsay after so many defeats throughout the 70s! After a draw in their home leg, played on Dounby's Show Park, Birsay took huge pleasure in crushing their rivals at Skeabrae. Admittedly the 'Flotta Factor' of shift working was affecting Sandwick to a degree, but this was still a great result for Birsay:

| Birsay | 2 | Sandwick | 2 |
| Sandwick | 1 | Birsay | 5 |

In the other semi final, Stromness had a clear edge over Harray. After a narrow win at the Market Green in Stromness, they were roared on to the final by their passionate and vociferous band of supporters whose ranks were swelled in Harray, by the arrival of a group of diehard fans, direct from a day at the Caithness Show.

Harray were on the receiving end at this stage, but any hope of a fight back disappeared as the new arrivals marched up and down the lines like 'extras' from Braveheart, brandishing Shepherd's crooks in a threatening manner, and discouraging Harray wingers from coming anywhere near the touchlines. With this kind of support, Stromness would go far. The scores were:

| Stromness | 2 | Harray | 1 |
| Harray | 1 | Stromness | 5 |

It was most refreshing to see a team in the final which had never competed at that stage before. Of their players, the one exception was Tommy Bain, who had won with

Sandwick before the family moved from Vestrafiold to Quholmslie, near Stromness. Three Bain brothers would now play this year, Tommy, Stevie and Norman.

Birsay also fielded three brothers, not the Stangers this time as only Raymond and Alfie would play, but Alan, Stewart and Eoin Moar from Muce. Two other cup final newcomers in their ranks were Robbie Norquoy, to play in goal for Birsay, the third generation of the Norquoy family to do so, and Robbie Rendall up front.

The following teams took the field before a big crowd in ideal playing conditions:

Birsay: Robbie Norquoy; Eddie Spence, Stewart Moar, Kenny Ross, Raymond Stanger, Raymond Flett, Alfie Stanger, Eoin Moar, Alan Moar, Brian Spence, Robbie Rendall.

Stromness: Alan Tait; Norman Bain, Tommy Bain, Denis Macdonald, Willie Chalmers, Stewart Crichton, Davy Keldie, Dennis Chalmers, Glenn Porter, Norris Chalmers, Stevie Bain.

The Stromness supporters were again out in force, helping to create an atmosphere reminiscent of 'the old days', plenty of noise, cheering and banter, and their team responded by taking the initiative. Playing down the slope, they created numerous chances with Stevie Bain and Glenn Porter both going close to opening the scoring.

A goal was only delayed and it came when Norris Chalmers hooked the ball past Norquoy from eight yards. The vocal section turned up the volume now.

In the second half Stevie Foulkes came on for Brian Spence but it

took Birsay some time to exert any pressure. However, they gradually came into the game and appeared to have equalised when Rendall hit a 20 yard drive into the Stromness net. But the 'goal' was disallowed as another Birsay player was offside.

Birsay were unable to recover from this disappointment and the game finished with the score Stromness 1 Birsay 0.

Stromness had won the cup for the first time in their history (thereby handing in their club membership!) and having played in the competition most years since the war, no one would begrudge them their success. They had deserved their win by being the more aggressive side and the margin of victory could have been greater if they had taken some easy chances.

After all those years of waiting, it

Stromness Parish won the cup in 1980. Back row, left to right, Tommy Bain, Glenn Porter, Stewart Crichton, Alan Tait, Raymond Lyon, Denis Macdonald. Front, Stevie Bain, Willie Chalmers, Norris Chalmers, Denis Chalmers, Davy Keldie, Norman Bain. (Picture: Orkney Library)

was time for some celebration on a grand scale. First stop would be the Braes Hotel, the team's social base, where the kindly host, Denis Tait, a Stromness fan but a South Ronaldsay player in his youth, would fill the cup with his customary generosity.

Then it would be on to the Stromness Hotel, the home of that great supporter, Davie Hutchison, formerly of Arion. Here hospitality would be lavish as Davie held court and regaled the triumphant team with tales of heroic failures of former years.

For those still standing at closing time, the party would continue at one of the dairy farming football strongholds in the parish.

Anyone chancing to drive by on one of the narrow undulating back roads of Stromness on that bright August Sunday morning might have chanced upon a bleary eyed reveller leaning on a gate, speaking to a herd of dairy cows assembled, as if waiting for something. The exchange might have been along the following lines:

Dairy Cow … Whit wey hiv' we no' been milked the day yet?

Reveller … Weel Daisy, ye'll jist hiv' tae had in a bit longer. Ye see, hid's no' every year that Stromness win the Parish Cup!

1981:
Trophy finds familiar home

Perhaps spurred on by the success of Stromness, a team who up to this point had been regarded as outsiders, a stream of entrants poured forth for the 1981 tournament. Fifteen parishes in all were represented, only Stenness and Evie of previous participants being absent.

A big first round was necessary and the only team lucky enough to win a bye was Sanday.

First round Results

Deerness	0	St Ola	10
St Ola	5	Deerness	0
Sandwick	2	Firth	0
Firth	1	Sandwick	3
Birsay	6	Shapinsay	1
Shapinsay	0	Birsay	2
Stromness	5	Westray	1
Westray	1	Stromness	6
Rendall	1	South Ron.	1
South Ron.	3	Rendall	0
Harray	2	Holm	3
Holm	2	Harray	2
St Andrews	1	Orphir	1
Orphir	3	St Andrews	5

The strong teams of the era all progressed although Orphir did not appear to have built on their progress of recent years. Stromness looked to have continued where they left off last year, disposing of Westray.

In the quarter finals all the likely winners managed to avoid each other.

Quarter final Results

Sandwick	3	Sanday	1
Sanday	0	Sandwick	7
St Ola	7	St Andrews	0
St Andrews	0	St Ola	4
Birsay	7	South Ron.	3
South Ron.	2	Birsay	4
Stromness	5	Holm	0
Holm	0	Stromness	3

Four very clear winners emerged and perhaps the most interesting talking point from the round was a pioneering venture by Sanday in terms of Parish Cup travel. With their away leg in Sandwick scheduled for a Wednesday evening many of the players did not fancy arriving home well after midnight by hired boat. So, displaying both initiative and a willingness to part with a substantial amount of cash, they hired a plane instead.

Earlier that year a consortium of local businessmen had launched 'Air Orkney' with Captain Andy Alsop as pilot. This Islander aircraft, capable of carrying nine passengers, was duly hired and flew the bulk of the team direct to Skeabrae, right alongside the football pitch. The players got out, jumped the fence, played the match, jumped back over the fence, climbed back into the plane and were home by 9.30p.m. A pity the result did not match the quality of transport.

The semi finals should now produce much closer ties. On paper, they were four evenly matched teams, each consisting mostly of 'A' team players. The cup winning sides of the past three years were there while regular finalists, Birsay, now had their strongest all round team for some years.

Semi final Results

St Ola	1	Sandwick	3
Sandwick	1	St Ola	1
Stromness	1	Birsay	2
Birsay	3	Stromness	2

So it was old rivals Birsay and Sandwick who emerged from two very even contests. Although Sandwick held a slight advantage over Birsay when the teams had met in previous finals, predicting a winner this time would not be easy.

The teams consisted of very familiar faces but it was Sandwick who introduced some newcomers, including Derek Chalmers, Stanley Seator and Stuart Kirkness.

Also featuring for Sandwick was a mid field player called Davie Sinclair. With such a name, he would seem to be a Sandwick man, born and bred, but in fact he hailed from Alness in Sutherland. He lived at Gerracott in the parish and worked for a time at Skaill. He played for Sandwick's 'A' team, qualified for the parish, and so far had made a considerable impact on Orkney football with his all action style of play.

Full teams were as follows:

Birsay: Robbie Norquoy; Eddie Spence, Stewart Moar, Kenny Ross, Raymond Stanger, Raymond Flett, Alfie Stanger, Eoin Moar, Stevie Foulkes, Brian Spence, Robbie Rendall.

Sandwick: Rae Slater; Michael Grieve, Calvin Poke, Colin Kirkness, Derek Chalmers, Keith Leonard, Davie Sinclair, Stanley Seator, Robbie Oag, Stevie Slater, Stuart Kirkness.

The game started at a frantic pace with Sandwick soon on the attack, but nobody could connect with an Oag cross. Play raced to the other end where Alfie Stanger's shot was saved by Rae Slater. The game then settled down and the quality of play served up by both sides was high, considering the very wet slippery conditions. However, Birsay had the edge and went ahead just before half time with an Alfie Stanger goal.

Sandwick fought for the equaliser in the second half and were rewarded when Davie Sinclair drove home a shot from all of twenty yards. Birsay came back and after a spell of pressure, were awarded a penalty. Raymond Flett took the kick but shot straight at Slater, who held on to the wet ball.

This was the closest either team came to scoring again and the game finished with the score 1-1. So a replay was necessary and it took place the following Saturday, this time in fine, dry conditions.

Again teams were evenly matched with a lot of good football played and both keepers being kept busy. There was no scoring until fifteen minutes into the second half when Sandwick were awarded a free kick just outside the penalty area. Keith Leonard took the kick, laid the ball off to Davie Sinclair and his shot went round the defensive wall to find the net via goalkeeper Norquoy and the post.

This goal proved decisive, Birsay's

attacking efforts going unrewarded, and Sandwick ran out 1-0 winners.

It was maybe premature to suggest that this win would signal the start of another long sequence of Sandwick triumphs, since there were too many good teams around. But what made Sandwick just a little bit different from the rest was that once they reached the final, *they knew how to win* … even if it was only by a single, solitary goal. With the unique ability to grind out results, they would be increasingly hard to beat in years to come.

Glyn Edwards, who became a key figure in the 1982 tournament.

1982: Controversy and more controversy...

Ever since 1949, when organisers grasped the significance of the occasion and the money spinning potential it offered, the Parish Cup final has taken place on County Show night. For hundreds of Orcadians, going to the match had been as automatic as enjoying Christmas dinner or first footing on Hogmanay. Imagine then the sense of loss and feeling of disorientation experienced by many in 1982 when it became known that there would be *NO Parish Cup final on County Show night*!

Curiosity aroused? Right, let's press on!

Once again, there was a big entry for the competition, 16 teams in all, which made for a first round with all teams involved. Everybody wanted to play football these days, it seemed. There were so many entries for the other competitions that the 'B' and Reserve Leagues had to be split once again; a new tournament was introduced for North Isles' teams with a cup presented by the Flotta oil terminal operator, Occidental, and a Primary Schools League was formed to play for a shield presented by Bob Gilmour (Firth) and Eric Kemp (Thorfinn/St Ola).

It was a vibrant time and this was in part due to a significant increase in Orkney's population. The 1981 census revealed an eight per cent increase on the 1971 figure, a total of some 1,400 people, and with increased work opportunities in the county, the majority would be young folk with families. As a result, this was a 'boom time' for sport, in general, and this was reflected in the number of teams now preparing to do Parish Cup battle!

First round Results

Shapinsay	1	Westray	5
Westray	6	Shapinsay	1
Stromness	2	Sandwick	3
Sandwick	5	Stromness	3
St Ola	7	Firth	1

Second leg not reported. St Ola go through.

Birsay	3	Rendall	0
Rendall	3	Birsay	2
Harray	3	Deerness	2
Deerness	2	Harray	2
South Ron.	1	St Andrews	3
St Andrews	1	South Ron.	5
Sanday	5	Evie	1

Second leg not reported. Sanday go through.

| Orphir | 1 | Holm | 4 |
| Holm | 3 | Orphir | 2 |

The progress being made by the North Isles' teams was worth noting. Both Sanday and Westray were becoming a good match for most opponents and could no longer be taken for granted by Mainland sides.

Of those making an early exit, surely the most disappointed would have been Stromness. At this stage the Stromness 'A' team were top of the 'A' League and several members of this team, such as Tommy and Stevie Bain, Norris Chalmers, Raymond Lyon and Denis Macdonald, could play for the parish. But they had the misfortune to draw Sandwick, got caught cold and suffered a first round defeat.

Ironically, the 'A' team simply got better and went on to clinch the Brough Cup 'A' League for the first time since 1939. A superb achievement but small consolation to avid supporters of the parish.

Now to the quarter finals where the isles' teams again caught the eye.

Quarter final Results

| Harray | 4 | Westray | 1 |
| Westray | 5 | Harray | 1 |

Sanday	2	Sandwick	3
Sandwick	1	Sanday	1
St Ola	3	Birsay	1
Birsay	1	St Ola	3
South Ron.	v	Holm	

Game not reported. South Ronaldsay go through.

So Westray reached the semi finals for the first time, following a remarkable home win over Harray. Sanday's narrow defeat to the cup holders hinted at great promise for the future. St Ola gained a notable scalp but lack of information suggested that the 'Hope simply 'ghosted' through.

However, this was not the only occasion when unnatural events affected South Ronaldsay's season. A league match taking place in the 'Hope, when Orphir were the visitors, was abandoned when a thunderstorm, accompanied by severe lightning, forced the referee, players and spectators to dash for cover. The deluge of water rendered the pitch unplayable.

All concerned described it as a terrifying experience, but in some ways, this disturbance was as nothing compared to the footballing storm which was about to engulf the Parish Cup semi finals.

But first, the easy part. Westray gave more evidence of progress in their opening leg against Sandwick but were made to pay for their cheek in the return:

Westray	1	Sandwick	1
Sandwick	10	Westray	0

If only the other semi final had been as easy to report ….

Not for the first time, in the history of the competition, the issue at stake was the residency of a player, in this case, Glyn Edwards, who had been a member of South Ronaldsay's Highland Cup winning team of 1979.

Having an address in the parish, Glyn now played for St Ola, but since he was allegedly 'doing up a house' in another part of Orkney and spending time there, St Ola sought clearance by the O.F.A. to play him in the Parish Cup matches. This permission was given so Edwards proceeded to play.

All went smoothly until the semi final where, in the first leg, St Ola defeated South Ronaldsay 2-0. Now, trouble began to brew! The 'Hope submitted a protest letter to the O.F.A. declaring that Edwards did not reside in the parish of St Ola.

At a heated meeting, evidence for the defence was presented by St Ola in the form of a letter from a 'Mr Thomson' stating that *Mr Edwards paid him rent* for a residential property in St Ola. Contrary word of mouth evidence was brought to the meeting by West Mainland representatives, indicating that the player had lived in Rendall for several weeks.

After more acrimonious debate, two votes were taken.

Firstly, by four votes to three, it was decided that Edwards should play no further part in the competition. But secondly, in a spirit of compromise, it was agreed that the first leg result should stand.

Surely the matter would now be laid to rest.

But not a bit of it!

St Ola were unhappy that Edwards had been banned and issued a formal protest to that effect. As a result, another special meeting was held three days later. More heated argument, more gossip and counter gossip, till, finally, another vote was taken: that the ban be lifted *or* that the ban remain.

Once again, by the narrow margin of four to three, it was concluded that *the ban should remain.*

With just over a week to go until the final on County Show night, the second leg of the semi final still had to be played. It now went ahead without Glyn Edwards and resulted in a 1-0 win for St Ola. Therefore by an aggregate score of 3-0, St Ola were through to meet Sandwick and the match would go ahead on schedule.

Oh no!

From South Ronaldsay's point of view, this outcome reeked of injustice, so another letter was submitted, another protest.

Result?

Another special meeting only, five days before the final.

What happened next was breathtaking in its inconsistency. The O.F.A. voted by five votes to three to *disqualify St Ola for fielding an ineligible player,* leaving South Ronaldsay free to face Sandwick on the Saturday evening.

But, as expected, St Ola did not lie down to this decision.

They argued that the meeting had not been held in accordance with constitution rules in that 'an Associate Club's member' (i.e. a South Ronaldsay player) had attended and furthermore had been allowed to vote.

The events which followed now lifted the Parish Cup competition on to a new level altogether.

St Ola decided that the only course of action open to them was to refer the matter to the Scottish Amateur Football Association (S.A.F.A.). A date for such a hearing could not be set immediately with the result that, unless some agreement could be reached, there was no option but to call off the cup final.

No conciliation was possible so County Show night regulars had to make do with a hastily arranged Heddle Cup semi final between Thorfinn and Sandwick.

On August 30, some two weeks after the County Show, at another tense meeting, it was decided that Freddie Hutchison, president of the O.F.A. and Bobby Leslie, St Ola representative, should attend the S.A.F.A. meeting at Park Gardens, Glasgow, to present the case and seek a solution.

Now the bones of the Parish Cup were sure to be laid bare for national scrutiny.

When they heard how the competition operated, the S.A.F.A. officials were somewhat baffled and bemused. Players were:

- not registered,
- they were not affiliated,
- they had not been officially released from their normal clubs to play in this tournament.

It seemed as if the Parish Cup broke every rule in the book.

However, they recognised its uniqueness and the passions that it generated.

Both representatives got a sympathetic hearing and it was decided that, since the original O.F.A. meeting (prior to the tournament commencing) had considered Glyn Edwards' situation and agreed he could play, then St Ola had done nothing wrong. Accordingly, they stated that St Ola could go ahead and play the final.

Now if the O.F.A. had simply decided to stick by their original ruling, it would have instantly put an end to the matter. Instead it grew into a monumental controversy and, as they say 'left a lot of blood on the carpet.'

Looking back now it all seems a bit of a farce and ex county winger and occasional balladeer Johnny Johnston, probably had the right idea when he got out his satirist's pen and composed the following ode:

The Wrangle of the Parish Cup

In the 'Hope this wrangle of ill will
Began when St Ola won two nil.
Never mind lads said one of the host
There's a protest letter in the post.

The letter from the 'Hope did say
Glyn Edwards is ineligible to play.
St Ola said this is not so
He lives in St Ola now you know.

The O.F.A. they tried their best
To lay this argument to rest.
They played the trump card in their hand
From the second leg big Glyn was banned.

So, everybody accepted this
The second leg Glyn had to miss.
It didn't matter as they say
The 'Hope were beaten anyway.

It happened then again you see
Another protest, another plea,
A special meeting of the O.F.A.
Was called to let them have their say.

At this point without a doubt
The protest should have been thrown out.
Accepting that big Glyn was banned
They hadn't a leg on which to stand.

Another meeting a peculiar pact
St Ola thrown out and that's a fact.
To cries of Gee Whizz, and Good Grief!
St Ola stared in disbelief.

The meeting raged on long and loud
St Ola versus the other crowd.
Amid the bedlam, a voice did say
We'll take it to Glasgow and the S.F.A.

The O.F.A. said if you must, go
But the 'Hope play Sandwick after the Show.
So pen to paper St Ola put
And the County Show final is up the chute.

So the final was off on County Show night
Much to St Ola fans delight.
They played another game instead
A semi-final second leg.

To Glasgow then for a final ruling
The S.F.A. the 'Hope weren't fooling.
They got fair hearing without a doubt
And the ruling was, the 'Hope are out.

So tonight lads is the night for you
Play your best and you'll win through.
It will be a tough game, that we ken
You don't have Graham, Glyn or Len.

But Fraser, Eric and the rest
We know will do their very best
To try to make it all worthwhile
And win the Parish Cup in style.

Whatever happens please don't protest
Just let this poor old final rest.
Justice was done now never fear
And of course there's always another year.

Puts it all in perspective, doesn't it?

Well, after all that, the final was set for Saturday, September 11, one month late. How much appetite anyone had for the football would remain to be seen but one significant decision was taken at the outset; Glyn Edwards, despite being declared eligible, was *not* selected.

The players who did line up were as follows:

Sandwick: Rae Slater; Keith Dunnett, Calvin Poke, Michael Grieve, Colin Kirkness, Derek Chalmers, Keith Leonard, Alex Stanger, Stevie Slater, Robbie Oag, Stuart Kirkness.

St Ola: John Foulis; Alan Robertson, Fraser Byers, Eric Kemp, John Rees, Ian Adams, Davie Miller, George Coltherd, Eoin Learmonth, Andy Sutherland, Andy Stanger.

The six o'clock kick off and the lateness of the season would have contributed to the very poor attendance but just as likely, the public had been turned off by recent events. It was then doubly unfortunate that the game turned out to be a very tame and dull affair. Defences were on top throughout but Foulis was the busier keeper and had an excellent game for St Ola. Eric Kemp, now retired from all other football, and Byers dominated in the St Ola defence while Slater, Poke, Grieve and Kirkness were similarly effective for Sandwick.

The game fizzled out an 0-0 draw which made a replay necessary. Players would soon be playing winter football at this rate.

The question now arose, 'Will St Ola decide to play Glyn Edwards in the replay?', as his height and experience could be a decisive factor. To their credit, they chose not to and fielded a side with only one change, Graham Harcus replacing Andy Sutherland up front. Sandwick also made a change, Stanley Seator taking the place of Keith Dunnett.

Played on a Wednesday evening, the crowd was again well below normal levels. However, those present witnessed a bright, lively game with plenty of goalmouth incident.

The highlight of the first half was a superbly struck 18 yard volley by Stevie Slater which gave Sandwick the lead.

This lead was never relinquished despite a frantic ending when Rees, Learmonth and Harcus all had efforts cleared by the Sandwick defence. Sandwick held out for another 1-0 victory, which they deserved on the run of play. Foulis had another fine game for St Ola.

So the 1982 saga had finally come to an end. The competition would be remembered for the wrong reasons which was rather a shame for Sandwick, who had played no part in the alternative drama. They had won their eighth Parish Cup and another long run appeared likely.

But as for the Parish Cup competition as a whole … would it ever be quite the same again?

Sandwick line up at the Bignold Park before the '82 final. Back row, left to right, Arthur Herdman (manager), Stanley Seator, Calvin Poke, Michael Grieve, Rae Slater, Colin Kirkness, Robbie Oag, Stewart Spence. Front, Alex Stanger, Stewart Kirkness, Keith Leonard, Stevie Slater, Derek Chalmers, Gary Foubister.

1983:
Peace breaks out despite protest

It was clear that some talking had to be done, once passions had cooled and people had time to reflect upon events. Appropriately, a meeting was set up for Parish representatives to have a full and frank discussion and make any recommendations which might help prevent another debacle like last year.

It soon became apparent that common sense had returned. The meeting was both amicable and constructive, where opinions were aired and proposals made. Amongst these was one to increase the residential qualification to *six* months but this was not adopted.

In practice, only one new proposal was carried and that was for away goals to count in the case of teams being level at the end of two games. If level on away goals, penalties would decide the issue. All other rules were considered satisfactory, *as long as they were interpreted and enforced correctly*. This might have seemed a rather low key outcome but at least talking about the issues would have done some good.

There was no evidence that the parishes had been put off by last year's events as once again, 16 teams entered the competition. Now, who would be the first to profit from the new 'away goal/ penalties' rule?

First round Results

Evie	0	Sandwick	1
Sandwick	4	Evie	1
Holm	4	Deerness	1
Deerness	0	Holm	9
Rendall	3	Harray	0
Harray	1	Rendall	5
South Ron.	9	Firth	1
Firth	2	South Ron.	2
Sanday	2	Birsay	1

Birsay	0	Sanday	6
Shapinsay	2	Orphir	2
Orphir	7	Shapinsay	0
Stromness	2	St Ola	2
St Ola	2	Stromness	2

Stromness win on penalties

Westray	4	St Andrews	2
St Andrews	0	Westray	2

The big match between Stromness and St Ola turned out to be the one where the new rule was enacted, and Stromness achieved immortal fame by being the first team to win a penalty shoot out in the Parish Cup.

Observers will also have noted the continuing rise of Sanday and Westray. Both again defeated ex winners of the cup. Sanday's result in Dounby was quite remarkable and it was going to be interesting to see which island would be first to reach a final.

Quarter final Results

Sandwick	2	Rendall	2
Rendall	0	Sandwick	2
Holm	3	Orphir	6
Orphir	5	Holm	2
South Ron.	3	Westray	2
Westray	0	South Ron.	1
Stromness	2	Sanday	2
Sanday	0	Stromness	1

In anticipation of a closely fought second leg match, a large crowd of Stromness supporters travelled by boat to Sanday, but were most surprised to notice that some of their staunchest comrades were not on board. "Where is Davie?"; "What's happened to Sinclair?" "Fancy them missing a trip to the isles!"

However, as the boat neared Sanday, a light aircraft flew low overhead, several grinning figures gesturing from the windows. Davie Hutchison of the Stromness Hotel had networked one of his many contacts and, emulating the Sanday pioneers of two years earlier, had secured a much more congenial mode of transport. Given the outcome of the game, I'm sure the aviators would have regarded it as money well spent.

The semi finals took shape minus all the isles teams and included two sides who had never won the trophy. But, speaking of 'trophy', the grand old cup, which had been played for since 1929, was now giving out strong intimations of mortality and had been sent to the jewellers to see if its life might be extended for a few more years. If not, there would have to be a new cup.

The semi finals now took place but be prepared for another sensational turn of events.

Semi final Results

South Ron.	0	Orphir	2
Orphir	2	South Ron.	2
Sandwick	3	Stromness	1
Stromness	1	Sandwick	2

No sooner had the finalists been decided when a familiar rumour swept through Orkney. "The Parish Cup Final is off again!" A fantasy? A figment of somebody's imagination? Don't you believe it!

A letter had been submitted to the O.F.A. from Stromness Parish to the effect that Geordie Leonard, back playing for Sandwick, was still a semi professional footballer and therefore not eligible to take part in the Parish Cup.

The constitution did have a rule banning professionals from local football which had been introduced back in the days when South Ronaldsay tried to field Willie Brown, a professional with Grimsby Town, when he was 'home' on holiday. But was George still a semi pro'?

Well apparently he was! Although he possessed a 'Release Document' from Brora Rangers, this did not in itself clear him to play in amateur football. He still had to be officially reinstated to the amateur code by the S.F.A.

Birth, Blood

There was no alternative but to convene another special meeting to consider the case, and to that extent, the rumour was correct and the final was in doubt again.

However, the committee decided that, since it was a genuine mistake on the player's part, no further action would be taken except to ban him from the club's remaining fixtures. They were probably aided in their decision by the fact that the Stromness letter had arrived outwith the deadline of 48 hours after the match had been played, but, looking back, it seems a sensible decision anyway.

Mercifully, the findings were accepted without complaint, but to formally acknowledge the breach of rules by Sandwick, the club was fined £10 at a subsequent O.F.A. meeting. But how close we had come to history repeating itself.

Amidst all the furore, Orphir had slipped very quietly past South Ronaldsay into the final. Although he did not go on to play in the final, Billy Brown from Stromness was Orphir's goalkeeper in the semi final and he recalls an amusing coincidence relating to that tie.

It just so happened that he was doing some electrical work in a South Ronaldsay mansion on the day of the second leg match, when the conversation with the housekeeper turned to football. It went along the following lines:

Billy: Who do you think's gan tae win the night?

Housekeeper: Oh, South Ronaldsay I should think. They say Orphir have an old goalkeeper who is very small and can't jump for high balls.

Billy: Oh aye?

Housekeeper: Yes. I believe Orphir were very lucky in the first game.

Billy: Hmm.

Housekeeper: Do you play football?

Billy: Oh I try.

Housekeeper: For what team?

Billy: Weel, ah'm the peedie owld keeper that'll be in goals for Orphir the night.

Orphir won the Corsie Cup and Oxy Cup in 1983 but couldn't topple Sandwick in the Parish Cup. Back row, left to right, Kenny Firth, Frankie Tait, Billy Stanger, Dave Esslemont, Edric Clouston, Davie Mainland, Eoin Clouston. Middle, Brian Flett, Jim Frisken, Mervyn Ballantyne, Alan Clouston, Jake Craigie. Front, Geordie Flett, Bruce Donaldson, Francis Ballantyne. (Picture: Orkney Library)

Judging by the result, he didn't do too badly either!

So on to County Show night and the final.

Sandwick were once again looking for a hat trick of wins while Orphir were hoping to make it fifth time lucky. Arguably, Orphir had a stronger team than in their last appearance in 1979 and had made three changes, bringing in young players who would make a major impact on Orkney football in years to come: Ian Findlay, Bob Clouston and Brian Firth.

Sandwick continued to evolve and making their first final appearance were Stewart Spence, Alex Stanger, Stewart Kirkness and Stevie Linklater.

Full teams were as follows:

Sandwick: Rae Slater, Stewart Spence, Colin Kirkness, Michael Grieve, Alex Stanger, Derek Chalmers, Keith Leonard, Calvin Poke, Robbie Oag, Stuart Kirkness, Stevie Slater. Subs: Stanley Seator, Stevie Linklater.

Orphir: Ian Moir, Ian Findlay, Geordie Flett, Bob Clouston, Bruce Donaldson, Davie Esslemont, Trevor Anderson, Francis Ballantyne, Alan Clouston, Brian Firth, Mervyn Ballantyne. Subs: Billy Brown, John Stockan.

The crowd was back up to cup final standards with the most prominent spectator being none other than Geordie Leonard, who had booked himself the best seat in the house, in the fully extended bucket of a Heddle Construction digger which was still remaining from the County Show. From his vantage point overlooking the centre line, he gave full vent to his support for his first footballing love, Sandwick F.C.

Sandwick responded by having the best of the early action, twice hitting the woodwork, once with a lob by Stewart Kirkness and then when

Freddie Hutchison, past president of the O.F.A., presents the coveted trophy to Sandwick's Rae Slater on the balcony of the Bignold Park pavilion.

Moir pushed a Keith Leonard drive on to the bar. Orphir had good efforts from Francis Ballantyne and Alan Clouston but half time arrived with the score 0-0.

Soon after the interval Sandwick breached the Orphir defence, Oag heading home a corner from the left. Shortly afterwards it was 2-0 when a long clearance from the goalkeeper was picked up by Stevie Slater and he cut in from the left to beat Moir with a low drive. Sandwick now looked comfortable and brought on both substitutes. It paid off right away when a lob by Stanley Seator was headed past his own keeper by an Orphir defender.

Orphir were seldom in the picture and in fading light, the final whistle came with the score Sandwick 3 Orphir 0. On the whole it was a relatively easy win for the holders. Their play showed the benefits of competing in the 'A' League while Orphir, despite having won their league, had competed against 'B' teams all year.

Having recorded their ninth victory, Sandwick now had Harray's record of 11 wins well within their sights. But speaking of records, two of their players, Calvin Poke and Robbie Oag, had played in all the triumphs and, although they may not have known it at the time, they now shared the record for most appearances in a winning team, having just passed Eric Hutchison of Harray's total of eight.

If there happened to be an enterprising craftsman starting up in business out Sandwick way, there was a real opening in the market … for trophy cabinets. I am sure Parish Cup medals would never be consigned, as so many others, to shoe boxes in the attic and the way things were going, many more medals would soon be filling up the ever decreasing spaces on Sandwick mantelpieces.

1984:
Classic East v West tussle

Those with a superstitious nature would now approach the new Parish Cup season anticipating trouble. "Bad news comes in threes. Hid's jist a metter o' time afore we hear o' anither protest! Jist wait!"

Administrators desperately hoped to avoid any crises in this, a landmark year for the Parish Cup. This was to be the fiftieth year of competition since its beginning back in 1929 (war years excepted) and officials hoped to celebrate a trouble free anniversary.

Despite Sandwick's continuing monopoly of events, there was again no shortage of challengers as virtually every parish submitted a team. Only one bye was required in round one and to everyone else's dismay, it went to Sandwick.

First round Results

Sanday	7	Evie	1
Evie	1	Sanday	3
Shapinsay	0	Birsay	3
Birsay	13	Shapinsay	0
Holm	3	Stromness	2
Stromness	2	Holm	2
Westray	1	Rendall	2
Rendall	3	Westray	2
Firth	4	Harray	0
Harray	0	Firth	7
St Ola	8	St Andrews	0
St Andrews	1	St Ola	8
Orphir	3	South Ron.	2
South Ron.	4	Orphir	1

Of special note in these results was a defeat of a strong Stromness team by a resurgent Holm, who would later go on to win this year's 'B' League. Last year's 'B' League winners, Orphir, had been promoted but were defeated by South Ronaldsay who, ironically, had been relegated from the 'A' League.

The thrashing of Harray by Firth, a result which would have been unthinkable only a few years ago, gave notice of things to come in that part of the world. Football had been quietly developing in the parish for some time and, among younger boys, a lot had been achieved. The primary school team had won their cup on several occasions and the club were able to field competitive juvenile and junior teams. Shortly, it would seem, the parish would begin to benefit as some of these youngsters came of age but surprisingly Firth did not have to wait that long before scaling previously undreamt of heights.

This came about, not in the Parish Cup, but competing for another trophy which has not been referred to for many years, the Thornley Binders Challenge Cup. This magnificent trophy had been played for intermittently, until 1938 when the winners were Harray, but on the outbreak of war, all local football had been suspended.

After the war, various inquiries had been launched to determine the whereabouts of the cup but the trail had always gone cold. A number of theories were put forward: it had been lost; whoever had it in their possession had forgotten of its existence; somebody was holding on to it for sentimental reasons: and some even thought they knew where it was!

However, as time passed, the question receded into the backs of peoples' minds and the cup was barely remembered … until the passing of Harray resident, ex-councillor Willie Firth of Dunsyre. As his property and possessions were being sorted, a wooden box was discovered in a cupboard under the stairs and when opened, it revealed the solid silver beauty of the Thornley Binders Cup.

To anyone remotely knowledgeable about local football, this was the equivalent of glimpsing for the first time, the treasures in the tomb of Tutankamun or a long lost Leonardo Da Vinci painting. Scarcely anyone under the age of 50 had ever seen

Firth, Thornley Binders Cup winners in 1984 and the first side to have won the trophy since 1939. Back row, left to right, Eddie Seator, James Clouston, Steven Herbertson, Bob Gilmour, Graham Shearer, Brian Clouston, Martin Aim, Raymond Hourston, Jim Davies. Front, Agmond Flett, Andy Newlands, Jimmy Taylor, Leslie Merriman, Ronald Thomson, David McPherson.
(Picture: Harold Esson)

the trophy before although many had heard it spoken about by veterans of the 20s and 30s. Myth had now become reality and everyone wanted a look. The question was, "What to do with it?" It was a magnificent trophy, more valuable by far than any other in local football, and surely it must be brought back into competition.

To cut a long story short, a meeting was held among West Mainland club representatives and it was decided to reintroduce the trophy for competition between those for whom it was originally intended, the West Mainland parishes and a team from Stromness. It would *not* be used, as had been suggested, as a replacement for either the ageing Parish Cup or the Brough Cup. The draw was made, the tournament started, and by the middle of June, the two finalists had emerged, and they were Sandwick and Firth.

The final was a showpiece occasion and several pre war players joined the Sandwick and Firth players before kick off at the Stromness Market Green. A strong connection was made with the last final back in 1938, in that the son of Agmond Flett, Harray's right back that day, lined up at right back for Firth. His name? Why, none other than Agmond Flett! Could this be a good omen for Firth?

Maybe so, because the overwhelming favourites, Sandwick, were beaten 2-1 by a determined Firth side. I would like to have seen the Firth captain, Leslie Merriman receive his club's first trophy since 1959 but, unfortunately, a bad knee injury sustained near the end meant that I had to hear the news from a hospital bed. The consequence was no more football for me, but at least it had been a grand occasion to go out on.

Now, back to the main business of the Parish Cup. Could Firth carry this form into the main tournament?

Quarter final Results

South Ron.	2	Sanday	4
Sanday	1	South Ron.	5
Firth	1	Holm	3
Holm	4	Firth	1
Sandwick	3	St Ola	3
St Ola	1	Sandwick	0
Rendall	0	Birsay	1
Birsay	5	Rendall	0

Much to comment upon there. Of greatest significance was the elimination of Sandwick by St Ola. After a six goal thriller in the first leg, a large crowd turned out at Picky to see a closely fought encounter settled by a George Coltherd goal, 15 minutes from time. So, there would be new winners in this anniversary year.

The next talking point was the remarkable change in fortune for South Ronaldsay and their five goals in Sanday, including a hat trick from Andy Whyte. Meanwhile, Holm ensured that there would be no parish 'double' for Firth.

Semi final Results

South Ron.	1	St Ola	4
St Ola	3	South Ron.	1
Birsay	5	Holm	0
Holm	1	Birsay	7

St Ola made their way into the final

having more or less settled the tie in the first leg with goals by Graham Harcus (2), Davie Miller and Gordon Wilson. Birsay made short work of Holm and Attie Stanger was back among the goals with a hat trick in the second leg.

So a classic East v West final was set between two teams who last met at this stage in 1970. On that occasion Birsay won their first Parish Cup. Since then, both teams had undergone almost complete evolution yet three players who had graced the 1970 game ran out again 14 years later. They were Eric Kemp and Fraser Byers for St Ola and the Birsay captain Raymond Stanger.

Full teams were as follows:

Birsay: Robbie Norquoy; Martin Oag, Stewart Moar, Raymond Flett, Raymond Stanger, Kenny Ross, Stuart Flett, Eoin Moar, Robbie Rendall, Alfie Stanger, Attie Stanger

St Ola: Evan Monkman; Ian Wilson, John Rees, Fraser Byers, Eric Kemp, Eoin Learmonth, Ian Adams, George Coltherd, Davie Miller, Gordon Wilson, Graham Harcus.

Once again, the biggest crowd of the year gathered in the Bignold Park. Birsay elected to play up the slope with the wind behind and quickly took control of the game. They

1984, the year of George Orwell and Birsay! Back row, left to right, Steve Foulkes, Keith Johnston, Raymond Flett, Martin Oag, Robbie Norquoy, Raymond Stanger, Alfie Stanger, Stuart Flett, Martin Johnston. Front, Michael Mowat, Kenny Ross, Robbie Rendall, Alfie Stanger, Stewart Moar, Eoin Moar, Colin Ross. (Picture: Orkney Photographic)

Birth, Blood

launched a series of attacks with Robbie Rendall and Alfie Stanger stretching the St Ola defence. Continuous pressure resulted in a free kick being awarded just outside the penalty box and it was taken by Stuart Flett, who sent a powerful drive round the edge of the 'wall' into the roof of the net.

More attacking play by Birsay brought another free kick in an almost identical position and this time, Stuart Flett curled the ball over the wall into the opposite corner past Monkman. Another great goal and at half time, the score was 2-0 to Birsay.

The second half was more evenly contested but the closest either team came to another score was when a Kenny Ross 'goal' was chalked off for an infringement.

So the game finished with Birsay two nil winners. It had been an absorbing if not outstanding game and Birsay deserved victory after a determined and committed display. It was now appropriate that Alton Tait, a previous winner on many occasions with St Andrews, should be asked to present the fiftieth Parish Cup to Raymond Stanger of Birsay.

As the Birsay legions headed westward to begin celebrations, maybe the O.F.A. officials would have afforded themselves the luxury of a small dram or two. No protests this year, no emergency meetings, no threats to postpone the final ….

Running Orkney football? It was just a dawdle!

1985:
Classy Sandwick win new trophy

Having finally reached the top after many 'near misses', Birsay's hopes of retaining the Parish Cup were dealt a severe blow when their captain and main driving force, Raymond Stanger, moved house from Birsay to Schoolha' in Costa. Since he had been born in Sandwick, Raymond was no longer eligible to represent his 'home' parish. He now chose to play for his adopted parish, so what was Birsay's loss would now be Evie's significant gain.

The move bore fruit almost immediately. Evie, who could field a nucleus of the Rendall 'A' team in their parish line up, reached the final of the Thornley Binder's Cup, knocking out holders, Firth, on the way. In the final they lost 2-0, to a far from 'rudderless' Birsay team, but this was the closest Evie had ever come to winning anything. The downside to their adventure was that they had lost influential full back, Marcus Spence, with a broken leg.

Parish Cup fans would now be watching Evie's progress with interest and their performance in round one would have set more tongues wagging.

First round Results

Sandwick	5	Holm	1
Holm	3	Sandwick	3
Harray	4	Evie	12

Harray scratched

Sanday	4	Deerness	1
Deerness	2	Sanday	1
Westray	0	Birsay	1
Birsay	6	Westray	1

South Ron. w.o. Shapinsay

| St Ola | 8 | St Andrews | 2 |
| St Andrews | 1 | St Ola | 6 |

Orphir	2	Firth	1
Firth	1	Orphir	2
Rendall	0	Stromness	3
Stromness	3	Rendall	1

Some high scoring performances there with Evie's defeat of Harray producing a score line more commonly associated with rugby. Much closer games were expected in the quarter finals.

Quarter final Results

Birsay	3	Sanday	2
Sanday	1	Birsay	1
St Ola	0	Orphir	0
Orphir	0	St Ola	1
Stromness	1	Sandwick	2
Sandwick	3	Stromness	1
South Ron.	1	Evie	0
Evie	7	South Ron.	1

No doubt about the highlight of that round. Evie's goal scoring form continued at the expense of renowned cup fighters South Ronaldsay. In one of these curious twists, Evie were able to call on the services of Jim Seatter from South Ronaldsay for Parish Cup duty to do battle against the 'Hope and his parish neighbours.

Evie now found themselves among distinguished company in the semi finals.

Semi final Results

Birsay	3	Evie	0
Evie	3	Birsay	7
St Ola	4	Sandwick	3
Sandwick	4	St Ola	2

Even with Raymond Stanger playing for the opposition, Birsay were too good for Evie but it had been a brave effort by the outsiders. In the other semi final Sandwick's experience and fighting spirit saw them through with a late goal, securing victory in the second leg. Once again the big neighbouring parishes would contest the final.

The County Show celebrated its Centenary in 1985 and it turned out to be a beautiful day befitting the occasion. The guest of honour was the Queen Mother and she spent the day touring the rings and displays accompanied by the show president, Davie Kirkpatrick of Newhall, Stromness. How he must have wished that his beloved parish team had made the final to round off a memorable day.

Robbie Stanger (above) who made his debut for Sandwick and would in time become a Parish Cup legend. Gary Foubister (below) also made his debut and created the third and decisive goal.

Regrettably, Her Majesty flew back to Wick in the late afternoon and missed what turned out to be a very attractive game of football. The Royals could really do with some better advisors at times!

The teams were on the usual lines but Sandwick had one notable change. Geordie Leonard, a great all rounder on the football field, was selected as goalkeeper, allowing Rae Slater, no mean outfield player himself, to play his first final out of goal. They also had two players making their cup final debuts, Robbie Stanger and Gary Foubister.

Birsay, for their part, had to find a replacement for Raymond Stanger and were fortunate to be able to call on Rovers 'A' player Stuart Leslie.

Teams were as follows:

Sandwick: Geordie Leonard, Robbie Stanger, Calvin Poke, Michael Grieve, Alex Stanger, Colin Kirkness, Keith Leonard, Gary Foubister, Stuart Kirkness, Rae Slater, Stevie Slater.

Birsay: Robbie Norquoy, Martin Oag, Stewart Moar, Raymond Flett, Kenny Ross, Stuart Flett, Stuart Leslie, Eoin Moar, Robbie Rendall, Alfie Stanger, Steve Foulkes.

Another big crowd turned out on a clear night, although a cold wind blew down the slope in Sandwick's favour in the first half. After a scrappy opening spell, Birsay took the lead when Steve Foulkes forced an Alfie Stanger cross past Leonard in the Sandwick goal.

Birsay were the better side and should have gone further ahead but just before half time Sandwick equalised when an attempted clearance fell to Rae Slater and he scored from six yards.

In the second half, Birsay still had the upper hand but Sandwick's ability to play the game tight kept them at bay. Then the pattern began to change. First a Rae Slater header

hit the bar and then Stevie Slater placed a lob over the advancing keeper to give Sandwick the lead.

Birsay fought furiously to keep their title and had several close efforts but were caught on the break as Gary Foubister held off three defenders for Stuart Kirkness to turn in a third goal. Final desperate Birsay efforts went unrewarded and Sandwick ran out winners by three goals to one.

This great cup side had now won their tenth final in 13 years and having taken their chances, probably just deserved to win it. It was fitting that the inscription *Sandwick 1985* should be the first to appear on the brand new Parish Cup. After 50 years valiant service, the original trophy had now been withdrawn into a well-earned retirement.

As football people reflected on the achievements of one fine team, a very sad piece of news now brought to mind another great side of the recent past. The death was announced of the legendary St Andrews centre half Robbie Pottinger at the early age of 52.

Robbie had been the rock round which the St Andrews side had been built from the early 50's until the mid 60's and had played in all seven Parish Cup winning teams. He had represented Orkney on several occasions and had continued his interest in the game by serving on the O.F.A. committee and becoming a county selector … and of course, as a passionate supporter of his home parish.

There was no doubt that whenever all time 'greats' in the Parish Cup became a topic of conversation, the name of Robbie Pottinger would be fairly near the top of most folks' lists.

Birth, Blood

1986:
Stromness claim second victory

When the entries were submitted for this year's competition, there was one notable absentee. For the first time in over 50 years, there was to be no team from Harray. One of the outstanding names in Parish Cup history, they had quite simply run out of manpower. The wells which had produced a seemingly endless supply of Fletts or Hutchisons had finally run dry.

But, by way of consolation, their fall from grace is by no means unique in the world of sport. The history of football, national, regional, local, is littered with the corpses or faintly breathing relics of once great teams: Nottingham Forest- twice European Cup winners; Aberdeen F.C.- European Cup Winner's Cup holders in 1983; Dundee F.C., European Cup semi finalists, 1963; Clydebank, once a Premier League team and the first and last club of that fine Scottish player, the late Davie Cooper, now languishing in the Scottish junior ranks; Third Lanark (now there's a name to conjure with) a great Scottish club until 1967, but now defunct.

Closer to home, think of some Parish Cup 'greats' of yesteryear, now struggling to go through the motions: Deerness, Shapinsay, St Andrews … Stenness, where are they? No, the ability to conquer and dominate does not last forever and come time, once formidable champions may find themselves well down the pecking order … or out of business altogether.

So Harray were not alone in their plight but nobody expected them to fall quite so far. In their absence, the following first round matches took place:

South Ron.	1	Birsay	3
Birsay	4	South Ron.	1
St Andrews	1	Holm	3
Holm	7	St Andrews	1
Shapinsay	0	Rendall	4

Second leg not reported. Rendall go through.

Firth	1	Sanday	1
Sanday	0	Firth	1
Westray	3	Orphir	4
Orphir	3	Westray	0
Sandwick	8	Evie	0

Second leg not reported. Sandwick go through.

| Stromness | 3 | Deerness | 0 |
| Deerness | 0 | Stromness | 0 |

There were no major surprises there but pundits were giving Firth an outside chance after this win and their recapture of the Thornley Binder's Cup, where they had beaten Birsay 2-1 in the final. They were now drawn against Birsay again in the quarter final, a Birsay team without a Stanger in their ranks for the first time in many years. Alfie had suffered a broken leg in the Thornley Binders' tie with Sandwick and complications from this injury were to result in him being unable to play football again. The newly resurrected competition was claiming a victim every year!

Quarter final Results

| Orphir | 1 | Stromness | 3 |
| Stromness | 2 | Orphir | 4 |

Sandwick	4	Holm	1
Holm	1	Sandwick	3
St Ola	5	Rendall	0
Rendall	3	St Ola	6
Firth	1	Birsay	3
Birsay	2	Firth	0

Firth were unable to raise their game over two legs and the semi finals now took on a very familiar look. The three big teams of the period were there again but Birsay and Sandwick were kept apart in the draw and it was assumed that they would come through to another final.

After Sandwick beat St Ola 2-0 at Picky with goals by Stuart Kirkness and Stewart Spence, the first part of the prediction looked like coming true. But in a remarkable turnaround in Sandwick, two goals by George Coltherd and one by Eoin Learmonth were enough to see the champions eliminated on their own ground.

After this shock, surely Birsay would prove too good for Stromness. However, on the Dounby pitch, four goals by Glenn Porter for Stromness proved too much for Birsay, who could only manage two in reply by Allan Spence. In the return game at the Market Green, a 1-1 draw was sufficient to ensure that both underdogs had won to set up a Stromness v St Ola final.

To recap, the **semi final results** were:

| Birsay | 2 | Stromness | 4 |
| Stromness | 1 | Birsay | 1 |

"WHAR IS EVERYWAN THIS YEAR…?"

| St Ola | 0 | Sandwick | 2 |
| Sandwick | 0 | St Ola | 3 |

Anticipating a good game, a large crowd turned out on a perfect evening for football. St Ola, last in the final two years ago, showed a few changes in personnel. Both Alan and Keith Hutchison were available since Harray had no team and Alan was to play in goal. Another notable inclusion was Arthur Barnett after many years service on South Ronaldsay's left flank. Ironically, Norman Bain, a Stromness winner in 1980, was substitute for St Ola and could yet line up against his brothers.

Stromness fielded a remarkably similar line up compared to their team of six years earlier, the only newcomers being Brian Chalmers, Ronald Ritch and Raymond Lyon.

Full teams were as follows:

St Ola: Alan Hutchison; Ian Wilson, Ian Hutcheon, Fraser Byers, John Rees, Mike Stout, Eoin Learmonth, Keith Hutchison, George Coltherd, Davie Miller, Arthur Barnett.

Stromness: Alan Tait; Brian Chalmers, Tommy Bain, Denis Macdonald, Ronald Ritch, Dennis Chalmers, Raymond Lyon, Willie Chalmers, Norris Chalmers, Stevie Bain, Glenn Porter.

The match turned out to be hard and competitive but no goals were scored. The nearest St Ola came to scoring was when a George Coltherd penalty was saved by Alan Tait in the first half while Stromness' best effort was a Porter shot, which came back off the bar late on.

So a replay was necessary. This arrangement was becoming frustrating for spectators, now more accustomed to seeing games settled on the night by extra time and penalties. It would mean an earlier start but it would be preferable to the feeling of anti climax at the end of 90 inconclusive minutes.

Unlike some finals which have taken place in a very tame atmosphere, this one had generated quite a degree of heat … so much so, that

Gordon Rorie, O.F.A. secretary, had to issue a reminder to fans about "swearing on the sidelines and behaviour towards the referee." He went on to say "I hope the replay will be regarded as a game with sportsmanship on and off the field the main feature."

It was to be hoped that Stromness fans who had brought much needed colour and atmosphere to games would not be silenced altogether.

A second perfect evening greeted the teams a week later and St Ola tore into their opponents from the start. However, Stromness weathered the storm and in an amazing ten minute spell turned the game right round.

First, Stevie Bain got on the end of a Macdonald pass to give them the lead and minutes later, Porter sent a long range header into the St Ola net. St Ola had barely recovered when Rees handled a shot in the penalty box and Dennis Chalmers converted to put Stromness 3-0 up.

There were more chances at both

The cup found a home in Stromness Parish in 1986. Back row, left to right, Kevin Groundwater, Brian Chalmers, Glenn Porter, Alan Tait, Raymond Lyon, Gareth Crichton, Norris Chalmers, Stevie Bain, James Kirkpatrick (manager). Front, Tommy Bain, Willie Chalmers, Denis Macdonald, Ronald Ritch, Dennis Chalmers, Keith Groundwater.

(Picture: Orkney Photographic)

ends, including a Keith Hutchison effort which hit a post, but there was no further scoring in the match. This meant that Stromness had deservedly won their second Parish Cup and the coveted trophy was presented to Denis Macdonald by O.F.A. president Morgan Harcus .

The crowd, although cheerfully boisterous, had been on their best behaviour and the Stromness contingent, by far the majority in another big attendance, would now be welcomed home by 'Mine Host' of the Stromness Hotel, the parish sponsor, Davie Hutchison. Here, liberal toasts would be drunk to the lads who had once again made Stromness the champion parish of Orkney.

'Enjoy it while it lests!' somebody might have said as he raised the gleaming, virtually new cup to his lips. 'And on a night when wir enjoyin' wirsels like this, mebbe we should spare a thowt fir eens less fortunate, the likes o' Clydebank … and Third Lanark … and Harray! Here's tae absent freends!'

Aye that'll be right!

1987:
Player dismissed on sex grounds

In these days of equal opportunities and the disappearance of discrimination on the basis of gender, readers will be wondering why no ladies have ever been mentioned in connection with the Parish Cup. It was certainly not the case that women were discouraged from playing football.

For the past two years, a ladies football league had been in existence and the current champions of Orkney were Dounby Ladies, who won the Alton Tait Cup beating Kirkwall Ladies in the final. Seven teams had taken part, which indicated plenty of interest, but the sport had not yet taken off at parish level. Maybe a future development though?

In primary schools, participation in football by girls was now becoming quite common place. A picture in *The Orcadian* had proclaimed that Katie Hancock, a key member of the Glaitness Primary seven a side team was the only girl playing in the Primary League but this was refuted by Jim Anderson, an itinerant teacher of P.E., who explained in a letter that girls had been selected *on merit* for various teams in recent years.

Primary schools were clearly

pursuing an equal opportunities agenda but how long would it be before the concept was put to the test in senior football? The answer was, 'Not long at all! In fact, *now*!'

For the first time in the history of the island, Rousay had entered a team in the Parish Cup … and they wanted to field a woman! The player concerned was Ellen Grieve. She was a very accomplished footballer who had gained wide experience playing in the Scottish Ladies League and was now married and living on the island.

To quote a team mate, "She is a better player than 99.9 per cent of the others in Rousay." Incidentally, she was also a key member of the all conquering Dounby Ladies team.

Ellen had suspected there might be a problem and had checked with the O.F.A. as to her eligibility, only to be given the rather vague reply that under S.F.A. rules, she was probably not allowed to play in competitive matches, but if nobody objected, "then it would likely be O.K."

Worth a try then!

Certainly Rousay's first round opponents, Sandwick, had no objection but it was left to the referee to apply strict ruling and Ellen was refused permission to play. She was effectively sent off before the game began. In a strong show of solidarity, the Rousay team then went on strike and withdrew from the competition

Only at your specialists
39 Albert Street, Kirkwall
Phone Kirkwall 3140

ESTABLISHED 1854   KIRKWALL, THURSDAY, JUNE 11, 1987   TWENTY-THREE PENCE

Footballer Ellen calls 'foul' as she's banned from team

The footballing hopes of the island of Rousay have been kicked into touch in a row which seems set to enter the Orkney soccer record books.

For spectators at the Parish Cup game between Rousay and Sandwick last week were astonished when the Rousay captain was sent back to the touchline — before the kick-off.

The reason was that the captain of the team was a woman — Mrs Ellen Grieve.

She was told that under Scottish Football Association rules, women are not allowed to play in such competitive matches.

Because of the ban, her Rousay team mates decided to withdraw from the competition, rather than play without her.

Mrs Grieve, of Pier Houses, Rousay explained: "The first I knew of it was when the referee came up to me on the field. I was really disappointed.

"They should have told us before. I'd telephoned the secretary of the Orkney Amateur Football Association, Gordon Rorie, to check if women could play and he said it would be all right, but didn't know where we'd stand if there were any objections on the day."

Later Mr Rorie said: "I told her it would be perfectly all right to start with, but then we had our monthly meeting and it came out that women couldn't play in league matches or competitions so I rang her up after the meeting to warn her.

"I told her it was up to her to come to the match and that they might overlook the rule, and let her play."

However, despite the confusion over the ruling, the men were all behind her. She said: "The Sandwick team had no objection to me playing, and the Rousay men refused to play because of the ruling. They thought it was awfully unfair. It was the first time in 40 years for Rousay to enter the Parish Cup."

The two teams eventually decided to play a friendly match and Rousay were thrashed 22-1, their one goal being scored by Mrs Grieve's husband, Atholl.

Rousay team-mate Adrian Davidson said: "It wasn't fair. She's one of the best players on the island, better than 99.9 per cent of the men."

Mrs Grieve said: "I love playing. I played in the Scottish Ladies League in Motherwell. It's a shame, as I started up the Rousay team and got them training.

"I'll be writing to the Scottish Amateur Football Association to say it's unfair that on a local level women are discriminated against. The boys treat me just like one of them, and I get just as many bruises!"

Secretary of the Scottish Amateur Football Association, Mr Ian McTweed said later: "We have to apply the ruling laid down by the Scottish Football Association that women cannot play in these matches."

Rousay team captain Ellen Grieve — left on the touchline by a Football Association ban — with her male team mates.
(Picture: Orkney Photographic)

rather than play without her.

Instead of having no game at all, the teams agreed to a 'friendly' match, for which, ironically, Ellen was eligible. The outcome, Sandwick 22 Rousay 1, does not suggest that Rousay would have been serious contenders for the cup, but their pluck in entering and challenging existing conventions was to be warmly applauded.

As a point of interest, Rousay's goal, noisily acclaimed by local fans, was scored by Ellen's husband, Athole.

In contrast to the front page headlines generated by this controversy, the rest of the first round now seemed rather tame.

First round Results

| Westray | 1 | South Ron. | 2 |
| South Ron. | 1 | Westray | 3 |

(after extra time)

Deerness	2	Sanday	3
Sanday	4	Deerness	2
Stromness	2	Orphir	2
Orphir	2	Stromness	3
Holm	1	Rendall	1
Rendall	4	Holm	4

Holm win on away goals.

Shapinsay	0	Evie	3
Evie	11	Shapinsay	0
Firth	1	Birsay	3
Birsay	3	Firth	1

Sandwick w.o. Rousay

| St Ola | 11 | St Andrews | 1 |

St Andrews scratched.

An intriguing development in Orkney at the end of last year had seen permission granted by Sheriff A.A. Macdonald to Rails Bookmakers to establish the first betting shop in Orkney. This shop was now in business with the start of the flat racing season and no doubt some local punters were keen to place bets on the Parish Cup.

What odds might have been given on likely winners?

Predictably, fairly short prices would

have been placed on the likes of Sandwick, Stromness, Birsay and St Ola but Rails would have been careful not to risk a big pay out by making either Sanday or Westray rank outsiders. Both teams were continuing to mature.

Quarter final Results

St Ola	2	Stromness	4
Stromness	2	St Ola	3
Holm	3	Birsay	3
Birsay	3	Holm	0
Evie	1	Sanday	3

Evie scratched.

| Westray | 0 | Sandwick | 4 |
| Sandwick | 10 | Westray | 3 |

Parish football in the West Mainland remained on a 'high' with three teams in the semi finals and they were joined by Sanday, who had reached this stage for the first time. Could they now clear the penultimate hurdle?

Semi final Results

Sanday	1	Birsay	1
Birsay	3	Sanday	0
Stromness	2	Sandwick	1
Sandwick	5	Stromness	1

After the first leg matches, any outcome was possible but the return

games removed any doubts. Goals by Stuart Flett, Keith Johnston and Robbie Rendall put paid to Sanday's hopes of a first final, while Stevie Linklater (3), Michael Grieve and Stuart Kirkness were the scorers in a crushing display by Sandwick to put out the cup holders.

So, two very familiar opponents again lined up to face each other on County Show night. Perhaps because of the predictability of the finalists, and the absence of a genuine underdog, a smaller than usual crowd turned up to watch the game. The only players making their debut in a final were Donald Foubister of Sandwick and Keith Johnston of Birsay.

Teams were selected as follows:

Sandwick: Rae Slater; Robbie Stanger; Michael Grieve, Calvin Poke, Donald Foubister, Gary Foubister, Geordie Leonard, Colin Kirkness, Keith Leonard, Stuart Kirkness, Stevie Slater.

Birsay: Robbie Norquoy, Martin Oag, Stewart Moar, Kenny Ross, Raymond Flett, Stuart Leslie, Stuart Flett, Keith Johnston, Eoin Moar, Steve Foulkes, Robbie Rendall.

Sandwick played down the slope into

Sandwick overcame neighbours Birsay in 1987 to win. Back row, left to right, Alex Stanger, Stevie Linklater, Robbie Stanger, Gary Foubister, Rae Slater, Michael Grieve, Stewart Kirkness, Jimmy Moar, Alan Slater. Front, Stevie Slater, Stewart Spence, Donald Foubister, Calvin Poke, Geordie Leonard, Keith Leonard, Colin Kirkness, Robin Crichton.

(Picture: Orkney Photographic)

a cold northerly breeze and looked the more dangerous side during a first half, which failed to enliven the very subdued crowd. No goals were scored but shortly after the interval Birsay broke the deadlock when Eoin Moar met a cross at the far post and drove the ball past Rae Slater.

Ten minutes later Sandwick equalised with a similar goal and this time Stevie Slater was in the right spot to slam the ball home. The game now seemed to be heading for a replay when, with only seven minutes left, a mix up in the Birsay penalty box allowed substitute Stevie Linklater to score from close range. This made the final score Sandwick 2 Birsay 1.

Time once again for the statisticians to get busy. They would have noted that Calvin Poke had featured in all 11 of Sandwick's victories making him the all time leader in the 'winners medals' table. Sandwick as a club had gone eleven finals unbeaten and had equalled Harray's record of eleven cup wins in total.

Rails Bookmakers would now be badgered by punters wanting to bet on which of these teams would be first to twelve. Somehow, on current prospects, they would probably be unwise to offer any odds at all.

And finally, how were the ladies doing at the end of the season? Sadly, Orkney ladies league had collapsed, so that put an end to speculation about an alternative Parish Cup. But as for Ellen Grieve, she was far from finished!

She had attended referees classes *which she passed* and, to prove that women could hold their own in this particular 'man's world', she now prepared to embark on her career as the first female referee in Orkney.

If it ever … even for a fleeting moment … flitted through her mind that this could be a chance to settle old scores, Sandwick had better look out!

1988:
Tragedy follows final debut

Something which had been forecast for a number of years finally came to pass in 1988 and when it did, it gave the Parish Cup competition a much needed shot in the arm.

For over twenty years, teams from Sanday had run up colossal mileages by land and sea in order to test their mettle against Mainland parishes without ever reaching the final stage. But many had felt that, sooner or later, it must happen and on a gloriously sunny afternoon in the heart of Sandwick, the reality took a tantalising step nearer.

When Sandwick drew Sanday in round one, the holders knew they had a fight on their hands. The challenge then increased in scale when the islanders won their home leg 2-0, so Sanday now travelled to Skeabrae with genuine hopes of victory.

A large crowd came from the island and they were supplemented by many neutral supporters from all over Orkney, desperate to see 'David slay Goliath.'

Calvin Poke scored first for the champions and it looked as if Sandwick would come back but a penalty for Sanday was converted by George A'Hara and that was enough to ensure a different name on the cup this year.

The crowd left in a happy frame of mind hopeful that, if their own team didn't win, then Sanday would lift the cup.

First round Results

Sanday	2	Sandwick	0
Sandwick	1	Sanday	1
Stromness	2	Westray	0
Westray	2	Stromness	4
Deerness	0	Rendall	2
Rendall	6	Deerness	1

St Andrews	1	St Ola	8
St Ola	15	St Andrews	5
Holm	0	South Ron.	3
South Ron.	2	Holm	2
Birsay	0	Firth	0
Firth	2	Birsay	1
Longhope	0	Orphir	10
Orphir	10	Longhope	0

A team on the way up was Firth, while heading in the same direction as Harray was their once feared opponents, St Andrews. They too were finding that fortune goes in cycles.

With Sandwick and Birsay out, St Ola and Stromness would seem to be the strongest teams left but when the draw for the quarter finals was published, one tie read, Rendall v *Westray*.

How come?

Weren't they knocked out?

Indeed, Stromness had beaten Westray twice but an irregularity had been spotted by cross border patrols who noted that Sandwick people now had Stromness player, Glenn Porter, living in their midst. Well not 'in their midst' exactly, but just across the boundary on the Sandwick side, near Voy. 'Unsuspecting' Stromness had continued to play him but once maps had been examined, it was found that they had acted in error.

Westray were tipped off, the protest submitted, and the only judgement which could await Stromness at the hands of the O.F.A. was *disqualification*.

Stromness retaliated with a counter protest claiming that, since Porter had played the first leg with no complaint, he should be allowed to continue for the remainder of Stromness' involvement in the tournament. However this was thrown out, and Westray could hardly believe their luck and they were through to the next round.

& Boundaries

So with Sanday and Westray having no difficulty deciding on their boundaries, the quarter finals went ahead.

Quarter final Results

Sanday	1	Orphir	2
Orphir	1	Sanday	3
(after extra time)			
Firth	4	South Ron.	1
South Ron.	2	Firth	5
Evie	3	St Ola	4
St Ola	7	Evie	1
Westray	4	Rendall	2
Rendall	2	Westray	3

North Isles' pulses now began to quicken. Both teams had made it through to the semi finals, Sanday after a nail biting encounter in Orphir where Mellie Grieve scored the decisive goal in extra time.

As fate would have it, Westray and Sanday were drawn to play each other in the next round so, for the first time since Shapinsay won in 1954, an island team would contest the final.

Their opponents would be the emerging Firth team or the very powerful St Ola. In the event, St Ola were too good for Firth and won with plenty to spare. The scores were:

| St Ola | 5 | Firth | 0 |
| Firth | 1 | St Ola | 4 |

Attention now focussed on the inter island battle with the big prize at stake. Contests between the islands had always been highly competitive affairs and the formula was always the same: greet your opponents 'warmly' at the pier; escort them to the pitch; kick the living daylights out of them for ninety minutes; head to the pub with them for a good drink and a laugh when it was all over.

On this occasion it was no different but in a footballing sense, Sanday had the edge. In the first game in Westray, they established a 3-1 lead with goals by Mellie Grieve, Billy Harcus and an own goal by a

Westray defender.

In the return, Sanday consolidated their advantage recording a 4-2 win with their scorers this time being Kevin and Andrew Skea and George A'Hara (2). Although disappointed to lose, Westray were glad it was to their near neighbours and they now gave them their full support for the big occasion on County Show night.

Now, what do teams do when they travel long distances for an important match? They book into a hotel of course … and that is just what the Sanday players did. Instead of traipsing round the show yard using up valuable energy, the team was granted the use of the Ayre Hotel by Roy and Moira Dennison, a couple with strong North Isles sympathies, so that they could relax and prepare properly.

Any perk like this would be vital as Sanday were clearly the underdogs. But they were a very fit team and had highly rated players such as Billy Harcus, the Thorfinn striker, and

George A'Hara and Mellie Grieve, who would grace any 'A' team's midfield. They were also totally committed and this was illustrated perfectly by John Dearness, who broke off his honeymoon to come home for the game.

Contrary to some rumours, Sanday did not intend to field David Harvey, the ex Leeds United and Scotland goalkeeper, who had recently moved to the island with his family. (Now that would have sent the experts scurrying for rule books and constitutions!)

But no matter who Sanday fielded, St Ola presented a huge challenge. Many of their team played for Thorfinn, who had just become the second Orkney club to lift the Highland Amateur Cup, while Fraser Byers, George Coltherd and Colin Kirkpatrick were members of the Orkney team which had beaten Shetland and Caithness earlier in the season. They would be formidable opponents.

On a fine evening in front of a large crowd including, it seemed, most of the island of Sanday, the following teams lined up:

Sanday: Ivan Leslie, Alan Gray, Ian Brown, Dave Drever, Raymond Muir, Mellie Grieve, George A'Hara, John Dearness, Billy Harcus, Andrew Skea, Billy Drever. Subs: Kevin Skea, Bruce Thomson.

St Ola: Davie Miller, Norman Bain, Ian Wilson, Eoin Learmonth, John Rees, Allan Norquoy, Fraser Byers, Colin Kirkpatrick, Ian Stout, Gordon Wilson, George Coltherd. Subs: Kevin Hancock, Lester Sutherland.

Any notion that the occasion might be too big for Sanday was soon dispelled as they attacked their opponents from the kick off. They forced a series of corners and the St Ola goal endured some heavy pressure. But after weathering the storm, St Ola took the lead when a dangerous cross by Kirkpatrick was deflected into his own net by Ivan Leslie. At half time it was 1-0 to St Ola.

Sanday again took the initiative in the second half with Grieve and A'Hara controlling much of the play, but they could not get men into danger areas. Billy Harcus was being well held by Fraser Byers.

Then, St Ola struck twice. First, Coltherd showed a great piece of skill, beat two players, and drove the ball into the net. Byers made it three after a 50 yard run to turn in a cross at the near post.

The final whistle arrived with the score, St Ola 3 Sanday 0.

St Ola probably deserved their win against a side who gave a great account of themselves. The extra fitness and sharpness from playing every week helped give them the edge.

Vice convener of Orkney Islands Council and former St Andrews player, Jackie Tait now handed over the cup to Eoin Learmonth of St Ola but Sanday had some consolation

The defeated Sanday squad of 1988 who were struck by tragedy barely weeks later. Back row, left to right, John Dearness, Alan Gray, Billy Harcus, Ivan Leslie, Bruce Thomson, Davie Drever, Billy Drever. Front, Raymond Muir, Ian Brown, Kevin Skea, George A'Hara, Mellie Grieve, Andrew Skea. (Picture: Orkney Photographic)

Jubilant St Ola after clinching victory. Back row, left to right, Alistair Firth, Alan Hutchison, Fraser Byers, Norman Bain, Davy Miller, Colin Kirkpatrick, Allan Norquoy, Eoin Learmonth, Bobby Leslie, Ian Adams, George Coltherd, Stevie Twatt (with cup), John Rees, Andy Sutherland, Eric Kemp. Front, Kevin Hancock, Ian Stout, Gordon Wilson, Ian Wilson, Lester Sutherland. (Picture: Orkney Photographic)

when left back Raymond Muir was named Man of the Match.

Were Sanday downhearted? Probably a bit but they didn't let it show too badly. Their hosts at the Ayre Hotel laid on a 'celebration' meal where players were joined by family, friends and supporters. All had enjoyed the occasion and having savoured it once, they believed that there was no reason why they should not do so again. By the time the boat left for Sanday, everybody was looking forward to next year.

Mellie Grieve, Sanday's skilful and inspirational midfield player, had declared more than once that if his team reached the final, win or lose, that would be his last game. Team mates did not take him too seriously and when the time came to get the boots out again, they were confident he would be there.

What nobody could have anticipated was how chillingly prophetic Mellie's words would be. In the last week of August, barely two weeks after the cup final, he was out in his 13 foot boat shooting creels off Tressness in Sanday. When he failed to return at the appointed time a search was launched involving Sanday coast rescue company and a coastguard helicopter from Sumburgh. Eventually, after an exhaustive inspection of the coastline, the wreckage of his boat was spotted, but of its occupant there was no trace.

This tragic event, involving the loss of one of Sanday's favourite sons, cast a heavy gloom over the island. As family, friends and fellow islanders struggled to come to terms with the tragedy, any lingering thoughts of football were banished far into the remote distance.

1989: Sandwick in twelfth heaven

Time moved on and the new season came round once more. As if to reward their prodigious efforts of last year and as a mark of sympathy for their tragic loss, the only team to receive a 'bye' into the Parish Cup quarter final draw was Sanday. Under normal circumstances, an Isles team would have preferred to play, given that they have fewer opportunities to compete, but maybe just this once, the players would be grateful for the extra time to regroup.

In Sanday's absence, **first round results** were as follows:

Holm	2	Rendall	2
Rendall	1	Holm	2
Birsay	5	Evie	0
Evie	3	Birsay	4
St Ola	11	South Ron.	0

South Ronaldsay scratched

St Andrews	2	Firth	7
Firth	10	St Andrews	1
Deerness	1	Stromness	1
Stromness	1	Deerness	0
Sandwick	1	Orphir	0
Orphir	2	Sandwick	1

(Sandwick win on away goals)

| Stronsay | 1 | Westray | 3 |
| Westray | 6 | Stronsay | 0 |

Clearly South Ronaldsay had hit the bottom of the trough and would have to wait for a new wave of players to revive their fortunes. In fact, very little was stirring out in the East Mainland. The league teams of Holm, Deerness and St Andrews had all withered and died but a new 'hybrid' was formed to accommodate any survivors who wished to play competitively. The team was called Eastonians and would play in the 'A' League. Cynics would mutter, "Drappin' the owld parish names!

Hid'll never lest!" But it would be worth a try, and might even help to keep their Parish Cup teams in existence.

Meanwhile, cursing their luck were Orphir who came within an ace of upsetting Sandwick.

Quarter final Results

St Ola	2	Sanday	0
Sanday	0	St Ola	0
Stromness	0	Firth	6
Firth	4	Stromness	0
Birsay	1	Westray	1
Westray	1	Birsay	2
Sandwick	8	Holm	0
Holm	2	Sandwick	4

The Stromness v Firth tie saw the meeting of two teams at the crossroads. Heading in a downward direction were Stromness, and rapidly so. Had Glenn Porter been so influential? He had been a key player but the fact was that the successful Stromness team which had played together virtually unchanged through the 80s, was now breaking up. Tommy and Stevie Bain had stopped playing; Willie Chalmers moved away; Raymond Lyon retired …. Relying on the same players for so long, there simply weren't any ready made replacements.

Firth, on the other hand, were on the way up. So far they had accumulated 27 goals in four games but more importantly, in the background, the foundations for success were being laid. Already this year, Firth had won both the 'B' League and the Oxy Cup; had claimed the Thornley Binders' Cup for the third time; and their junior team, containing mostly home grown players, had picked up the Dr Gordon Cup. "Future cup winners," some were predicting.

The semi finals now brought Firth and St Ola face to face for the second year running while old rivals Birsay and Sandwick crossed swords in the West Mainland.

Birth, Blood

Semi final Results

Firth	4	St Ola	4
St Ola	0	Firth	0
Birsay	0	Sandwick	0
Sandwick	1	Birsay	0

Both matches could have gone either way. Firth showed how much they had closed the gap in a thrilling tie in Finstown. Leslie Merriman, Brian Clouston and Alistair Wood (2) gave the home fans four reasons to celebrate but St Ola replied in equal measure.

Firth took a large crowd to Picky, full of optimism for a first final appearance since 1932 but, in a heart stopping encounter, where they went close on numerous occasions, they could not create the vital breakthrough. But, another year maybe!

Birsay and Sandwick, meanwhile, fought a dour battle and a single goal by Stewart Kirkness was enough to see Sandwick secure their place in the final yet again to play cup holders, St Ola.

The squads, which bore remarkable similarity to previous line ups, were as follows:

Sandwick: Rae Slater; Calvin Poke, Michael Grieve, Alex Stanger, Stuart Kirkness, Geordie Leonard, Keith Leonard, Donald Foubister, Glenn Porter, Stevie Slater, Stevie Linklater, Jimmy Sinclair, Stewart Spence.

St Ola: Alistair Firth; Allan Norquoy, Fraser Byers, Ian Wilson, Eoin Learmonth, Colin Kirkpatrick, Alex Banks, George Coltherd, Paul Kirkpatrick, Ian Stout, Lester Sutherland, Johnny Russell, Kevin Hancock.

Anyone expecting a defensive struggle with possibly a 1-0 score line at best, were soon in for a brusque awakening. Sandwick scored early through Alex Stanger and before half time got a second when Donald Foubister forced the ball over the line in a goalmouth scramble.

Foubister scored again shortly after the interval, with a low hard drive, and it was effectively 'game over.' Glenn Porter, Sandwick's new recruit, was having a storming game and he got into the act by scoring from close in. Although Colin Kirkpatrick converted a penalty to make it 4-1, back came Sandwick

and with only ten minutes left, Porter scored his second and Sandwick's fifth with a well taken shot.

The game ended with the score 5-1 to Sandwick. This their twelfth Parish Cup win had seen them produce one of their best displays. They were fast and sharp up front and the forwards were ably supported by a strong running midfield. St Ola's highly rated team never got going and all their best work was stifled by a side who were really 'up for the occasion.'

Sandwick's cause had been done no harm by one of Orkney's fastest and most dangerous forwards moving across the parish boundary from Stromness. You can be sure Customs officials would be on the look out for any more infiltrators, but if they were of Porter's calibre, a Sandwick passport would be made up and issued immediately!

Sandwick's Calvin Poke is presented with the Parish Cup by Roy Davidson of the Bank of Scotland, the tournament sponsors.
(Picture: Rae Slater)

Sandwick cruised to victory in the '89 final. Back row, left to right, Rae Slater, Michael Grieve, Stuart Kirkness, Glenn Porter, Jimmy Sinclair, Ian Linklater, Alan Slater, Stewart Spence, Kevin Dick. Front, Kenny Chalmers, Stevie Slater, Alex Stanger, Keith Leonard, Calvin Poke, Donald Foubister, Stevie Linklater, Geordie Leonard.
(Picture: Rae Slater)

The 90s

1990: Experience prevails over youth

During the winter and spring of 1989/90, it was easy to identify the favourite topic of conversation in the village of Finstown. Whether it be in Esson's Garage, Post Office, Baikie's shop or pub, Pottinger's shop or the Pomona Inn, discussions about the weather, the latest 'seek bug' doing the rounds or the plummeting prices of baests at the mart, were quickly rounded off as attention turned to a much more pressing subject, 'Firth's chances in the Parish Cup this year.'

The talk was of a young team, average age not much more than 20, the peedie boys who used to win the Primary School's Cup had grown up a bit, with only a few, such as Graham Shearer, Brian Clouston or Kenny Garriock who could properly be described as 'experienced.'

The merits of the respective players were chewed over, and the conclusion was that the local lads could be a match this time for Sandwick or their 'bogey' team, St Ola; " … and jist luk' at hoo close we cam' last year!"

Given a favourable draw, village hopes were high.

The first round draw did indeed keep apart the main contenders, while Firth and St Ola did not play at all as their intended opponents, Stenness and Deerness, both 'scratched' before a ball was kicked.

First round Results

Rendall	0	Stromness	1
Stromness	1	Rendall	0
Sandwick	6	Holm	1
Holm	1	Sandwick	5
Stenness	v	St Ola	

Stenness scratched

Orphir	2	Evie	3
Evie	7	Orphir	1
Westray	5	South Ron.	1
South Ron.	3	Westray	4
Birsay	3	Sanday	0
Sanday	1	Birsay	0
Firth	v	Deerness	

Deerness scratched

Westray now appeared to be the strongest side in the North Isles as Sanday did not look capable, at the present moment, of scaling the heights of two years earlier.

It is worth noting at this point, that travel to and from the North Isles was becoming much easier. Two new 'roll on, roll off' vehicle ferries, m.v.s *Earl Thorfinn* and *Earl Sigurd* were introduced in 1990 and new terminals were being constructed at places such as Rapness on Westray, and Loth on Sanday. Although Rapness was not completed until 1992, the Loth pier now appeared to be ready and the locals were very keen to test it out.

One evening, after a five-a-side tournament in Eday, followed by the usual 'pleasantries', the Sanday skipper hired for the occasion decided that his passengers should be the first to use the new facilities. In darkness, they were all duly deposited on the pier.

As he was pulling away, the skipper became vaguely aware of some shouts and yells behind him so he turned back to the source of the noise. It was his passengers … in an agitated state! They discovered that, although this part of the pier was indeed finished, it had still to be attached to the land. They had come within an ace of being stranded on an island of concrete all night!

There would be no further chance for the players to use the new facilities this year for footballing purposes because Sanday were now out of the cup.

Quarter final Results

Firth	3	Evie	2
Evie	1	Firth	6
Stromness	0	Sandwick	2
Sandwick	4	Stromness	0
St Ola	10	St Andrews	0

St Andrews scratched

| Birsay | 4 | Westray | 3 |
| Westray | 1 | Birsay | 1 |

Firth and Sandwick were comfortable winners but Westray's brave attempt foundered at home where just one goal would have been enough. St Ola meanwhile, were scaring the life out of their opponents, St Andrews being the second team to withdraw rather than face a drubbing.

Two fine semi finals were now in prospect and this year Firth and St Ola were kept apart.

Semi final Results

St Ola	3	Birsay	1
Birsay	0	St Ola	2
Sandwick	0	Firth	2
Firth	2	Sandwick	3

Needless to say, joy was unconfined in Finstown! The boys had done it! They had played magnificently in Sandwick and urged on by the inheritors of the title, 'Most Noisy Partisan Crowd in Orkney', had held out at home and qualified for the parish's first final in sixty years.

But it was a close run thing! With only minutes remaining and the score 3-1 to Sandwick, which would have put them through on the away goal rule, Andrew Corsie struck a magnificent shot from almost 40 yards, which soared into the roof of the net over Rae Slater's head. Such was the rejoicing that it seemed as if the cup itself had been won.

In the other semi final, amidst much less clamour, St Ola efficiently overcame Birsay and took their place in the final for the third year in a row.

Now for the final itself and as preparations began in earnest, Firth

Birth, Blood

suffered one or two major set backs. First, regular keeper Graham Shearer had injured his shoulder playing against Sandwick and this would keep him out of the final. This was a great disappointment for Graham but he had an able deputy in James Linklater, who had already played in the second Sandwick game.

So this hurdle was surmounted but then, during a mid week practice session, Bob Gilmour Jnr. collided

Bob Gilmour of Firth is bloodied but unbowed in the final. Paddy Kirkpatrick of St Ola looks on.

(Picture: Orkney Photographic)

with a goalpost which resulted in a trip to the Balfour Hospital where stitches were inserted in a head wound. However, this did not deter him from playing and he got ready to appear on Saturday evening, head bandaged like an extra from 'Holby City.'

So, cup final day dawned and most folk from the parish of Firth planned to be in the Bignold Park that evening. Players were advised to stay away from the County Show to rest and avoid the temptations of the beer tent.

For Manager, Bob Gilmour Snr, the day was to be agonisingly long. However, a solution was at hand. A morning's silent contemplation on the beach was followed by an afternoon's sojourn in the hills, where he was able to commune with nature, calm his frayed nerves and rediscover his soul, all at the same time. Come the evening, Bob was spiritually refreshed and ready for the fray.

St Ola approached the final with the usual quiet confidence borne of a side which had been relatively unchanged for a number of years. The only notable addition this year was Billy Harcus who had been in Sanday's forward line two years ago. His pace and power should be significant.

Set against St Ola's experience Firth believed their best chance lay in the fact that their cup final team was the same as their 'A' League team. Maybe familiarity with each other would see them through.

Team squads were as follows:

St Ola: Alistair Firth, Allan Norquoy, Eoin Learmonth, Fraser Byers, Ian Wilson, Kevin Hancock, Johnny Russell, Alex Banks, Billy Johnstone, Colin Kirkpatrick, Ian Stout, George Coltherd, Billy Harcus.

Firth: James Linklater, Agmond Flett, Leonard Merriman, Kenny

Regular finalists, St Ola, tasted victory again in 1990. Back row, left to right, Paul Kirkpatrick, Billy Harcus, Fraser Byers, Alistair Firth, Kevin Hancock, Alan Norquoy, Eoin Learmonth, Johnny Russell, Angus Fotheringhame. Front, Billy Johnstone, Ian Wilson, George Coltherd, Ian Stout, Colin (Paddy) Kirkpatrick, Alex Banks.

(Picture: Orkney Photographic)

Garriock, Brian Clouston, Bob Gilmour Jnr, Colin Wood, Andrew Corsie, David Tait, Keith Moar, Alistair Wood, Brian Davis, David Gilmour.

After the keenly fought cup ties between the sides in recent years, a great game was anticipated but in the first half the occasion seemed to get to the players and the result was a lot of hurried, scrappy play from both teams. Half time arrived with no goals scored.

The deadlock was broken 15 minutes into the second half when Ian Stout was brought down in the penalty area and George Coltherd gave St Ola the lead from the spot. They now took control and shortly afterwards Colin Kirkpatrick crashed home a Coltherd pass.

Try as they might, Firth could not get back in the game and St Ola ran out 2-0 winners. Overall it was a dour, uninspiring game and a bit of an anti climax for the big crowd. St Ola deserved their win, being the more composed team on the night, whereas the Firth players were unable to find their form of earlier rounds.

But, after losing to St Ola twice at the semi final stage and now in the final, most spectators agreed that Firth would learn from their experiences and were convinced that they would soon reappear on County Show night.

No, we, the Firth fans, were not too downhearted. The privations of the day were soon made up in the local hostelries, where the talk turned to tactics for next year. More practice, more training, more meditation on shore and hill … while during the winter and spring of 1990/91, discussions in the village of Finstown about the weather, the latest 'seek bug', or the plummeting price of baests were quickly rounded off as attention turned to a much more pressing subject …!

1991: Isles team reach final

"And now for something completely different," was a frequently uttered catch phrase on that memorable T.V. series 'Monty Python's Flying Circus.' Such was the popularity of the long running show that the expression gradually entered common usage, and recalling events occurring in Orkney in 1991 somehow brings it right back to mind.

If the Orkney population was asked to choose an event from that year which fits the 'completely different' description, there is quite a range to choose from. A large number would select the glorious midsummer evening when the band, Runrig, played an open air 'gig' at Picky which came to a climax as the sun set over Wideford Hill with 5,000 voices chorusing "The Bonnie Bonnie Banks of Loch Lomond" at full volume.

Absolutely unforgettable!

Others may recall different happenings each in their own way well out of the ordinary: the Rotary Club's mercy mission to Romania, for example; the near riot in Kirkwall by a mob protesting about curbs on the licensing laws; the 'Childcare Case' in South Ronaldsay, which put Orkney in the national spotlight for all the wrong reasons.

But, as you would expect, none of these is the subject of this chapter. You will be expecting the chosen event to come from the world of football and you would of course be correct. But, you will have to wait a little while yet , before all is revealed.

To begin with, everything proceeded as normal. Fourteen teams entered for the Parish Cup including Harray,

after an absence of seven years. Their team would represent quite an age span and consist of veterans, Alan and Keith Hutchison and Harvey Johnston accompanied by a band of raw, young recruits. But it was a start.

Firth and Sanday were the teams with byes in this year's first round.

First round Results

Rendall	3	Evie	0
Evie	1	Rendall	0
Westray	7	South Ron.	0
South Ron.	0	Westray	1
Sanday	9	Holm	0
Holm	0	Sanday	5
Orphir	3	Stromness	2
Stromness	0	Orphir	3
Sandwick	2	St Andrews	0
St Andrews	0	Sandwick	6
St Ola	1	Birsay	1
Birsay	4	St Ola	2

It was obvious from these score lines that no teams now welcomed a trip to the isles. While most results raised few eyebrows, there was considerable surprise at the elimination of habitual finalists, St Ola. A few teams would breathe easier as the quarter finals approached.

Quarter final Results

Sandwick	1	Firth	0
Firth	2	Sandwick	1

Sandwick win on the away goal

Westray	5	Harray	0
Harray	0	Westray	6
Sanday	1	Birsay	1
Birsay	2	Sanday	1
Rendall	0	Orphir	3
Orphir	3	Rendall	1

Both Sanday and Firth could count themselves unlucky to lose out by narrow margins but no such problem for Westray: four games played, 19 goals for: and none against. The form team so far.

However, with Birsay and Sandwick kept apart in the semi finals, most people predicted yet another final between the old foes. But, and this is one of the great joys of the game, forecasts can sometimes be well wide of the mark.

First of all, Orphir v Sandwick. In their home leg Orphir did well, with a Brian Firth goal being enough to earn them a 1-1 draw. Then, against all odds, Orphir scored first in the return leg through Bob Clouston, and hung on to this slender lead to run out 1-0 winners.

Orphir must now have felt that their time had arrived at last. But were they aware of the 'curse' hanging over them? Not since the early 70s had any team eliminating Sandwick gone on to win the Parish Cup.

Now to Westray v Birsay. These teams had met for the past two years and on each occasion, Birsay had won by the odd goal. Was this the year for the Westray men's revenge?

The first leg in Westray opened up that possibility, when goals by Colin Kirkness and Raymond Rendall gave them a two goal advantage. However James Gaudie notched a priceless away goal to reduce Westray's advantage to 2-1.

The return leg, played in Dounby on the Monday evening of County Show week, provided an evening of high drama. This time, a big crowd saw Birsay lead 2-1 after 90 minutes, with goals by Raymond Flett and Steve Foulkes. Raymond Rendall's

penalty kept Westray alive so the tie went into extra time.

Mid way through the extra period, Geordie Rendall got on the end of a cross to give Westray the lead, leaving Birsay needing two goals to win. This proved too much for them and Westray ran out winners to book their place in the final for the first time in their history.

What a shot in the arm this result gave the competition as a whole and the forthcoming final in particular. Interest had been tailing off as the tournament became monopolised by a few teams, but here were two finalists who had never won the cup. There had to be a new name on the trophy.

The usual big crowd attends the presentation at the Bignold Park.

(Picture: Orkney Photographic)

With only five days to go until the final, there would now be a sense of build up to the game and a 'bumper' attendance was guaranteed. How would the island team, in particular, approach the final and deal with what was bound to be a nerve wracking time?

Well, their build-up was deliberately low key. A practice out in Westray on the Wednesday evening; the announcement of the squad; players allowed to make their own way to Kirkwall, and those lucky enough to be on holiday would go a day or two early.

On match day itself, still a very 'laid back' approach! Players could spend some time at the County Show if they wished before a team gathering at Geordie Rendall's house in Willow Road to discuss ideas and tactics.

Geordie Rendall was one of Westray's three Mainland based players, the others being cousin Raymond Rendall and Robbie Stanger, who was already the holder of a winner's medal with Sandwick. Since he no longer lived there, he was now representing the island of his birth.

The role of 'Mainland' players in Westray's history is worth commenting on. Prior to 1987, Westray refused to field anyone in their parish team who did not live on the island. The team always did well in the North Isles' Cup competitions so the players felt that taking in 'outsiders' would prove unsettling. But the decision was always taken democratically. Each year, a vote would be held: *"Outsiders" in?* or *"Outsiders" out?* It was always the same result: *out* won the day.

However, success in the Parish Cup did not come with this policy and several Westray people, foremost of whom was manager Jim Rendall, were convinced that the inclusion of non residents would help the team and could even lead to a cup win

itself. This prospect was initially scoffed at but after much lobbying and cajoling, the vote was taken in 1987 and the result: *"outsiders" in*!

Westray's fortunes had improved ever since and now here they were with three 'Mainlanders' in their starting eleven and standing on the threshold of history.

Immortality also beckoned for Orphir, whose last final appearance had been eight years ago. Could it be sixth time lucky? At least they could say they had more cup final experience than their opponents and their team had changed little over the years. Seven of their squad had been on the losing side in 1983.

The teams which ran out before a crowd well in excess of 1,500 were as follows:

Westray: Robbie Peace; Keith Rendall, Robbie Stanger, Robbie Rendall, Denis Fergus, Jack Rendall, Colin Kirkness. Jim Brown, Geordie Rendall, Raymond Rendall, Alan Stevenson. Subs: Martin Tulloch, Jimmy Thomson.

Orphir: Davie Hay, Ian Findlay, Mervyn Ballantyne, Francis Ballantyne, Bob Clouston, Kenny Flett, Lorne Craigie, Keith Desmond, Colin Liddle, Brian Firth, Alan Clouston. Subs: Ian Moir, David Smith.

After a tentative start by both teams, Orphir were presented with the ideal chance to settle early nerves when they were awarded a penalty for hand ball. Brian Firth took the kick but put it past the outside of the keeper's left hand post.

Westray took heart from the 'let off' and began to settle into the game and the longer the half went on, the better they played. But, despite there being good attempts at both ends, no goals were scored before half time.

The big crowd, many of whom were now sheltering under umbrellas, did not have to wait long after the interval for the first goal to arrive. In a Westray counter attack, Geordie Rendall broke through, controlled the ball and slipped it past the Orphir keeper.

In 1991 the cup went to the outer North Isles for the first time when Westray achieved victory. Back row, left to right, Jim Rendall (manager), Dennis Fergus, Keith Rendall, Jack Rendall, Robbie Peace, Raymond Rendall, Martin Tulloch, Robbie Stanger. Front, Robbie Rendall, Jimmy Thomson, Geordie Rendall, Colin Kirkness, Jim Brown, Allan Stevenson.

(Picture: Orkney Photographic)

Birth, Blood

Westray now seemed to find an extra gear as their early apprehension disappeared and with Raymond Rendall pulling the strings in midfield, they went two ahead when Alan Stevenson outstripped the Orphir defence to score. Ian Moir now came off the bench to play in the Orphir goal while Davie Hay came outfield, but before this change had a chance to work, Westray scored a third, again through Geordie Rendall.

It was now impossible for Orphir and Jimmy Thomson headed an excellent fourth goal for Westray. The final whistle blew and finally it had happened … a team from the outer North Isles had won the coveted Parish Cup.

And now for something completely different!

Witnessed by virtually the entire crowd who had stayed behind, the cup was handed over on the Bignold Park balcony by Jack Walls of the Bank of Scotland to Jack Rendall, captain of Westray. The ceremony was accompanied by prolonged cheering. Some of this was reserved for a sporting Orphir team who must, by now, have been heartily sick of the 'good losers' tag.

Now you'll be anxious to know what happened next?

Well, all very down to earth and civilised … to begin with. First of all, a meal at the Ayre Hotel, a few drinks, the cup passed round. But then, the town beckoned!

The boat was not going back to Westray until Sunday evening so that would leave plenty of time. Any Westray exiles resident in Kirkwall … or indeed, any known Westray sympathisers, had better not bother locking their door or retiring to bed. Visitations were certain, and batches of the famous island home brew would be made ready to toast victory after almost twenty years of trying.

This heady concoction, combined with more than a dash of euphoria, would ensure that many would be doing the 'Westray One Step' to blissful oblivion!

1992:
Victory ends unfulfilled years

Snap! … Too late! You are caught off guard by a member of the paparazzi in that 'candid camera' moment. It is now too late to undo the damage and, not wanting to create a scene by grabbing his camera and smashing it to smithereens, you just have to hope that he does not use it to make you a figure of ridicule. (Of course, you may have been so 'Out of your skull' that you were not aware of his actions anyway!)

Many of us will have endured such a fate but at least the result will have been kept secure for family and friends to enjoy. I'm afraid the example opposite was published for the amusement of *The Orcadian* newspaper's 11,000 plus readership.

To find out more about its origin, you will have to read on.

Westray's victory last year had given renewed hope to underdogs everywhere and once again a substantial entry of 14 teams came forward. Those receiving byes were Holm and Westray, but the champions would probably have preferred an easy first round game to get themselves warmed up for the defence of their crown.

First round Results

St Ola	0	Sandwick	2
Sandwick	2	St Ola	4
South Ron.	3	Stromness	4
Stromness	1	South Ron.	3
Orphir	2	Evie	0
Evie	1	Orphir	0
Birsay	1	Harray	0
Harray	1	Birsay	3
St Andrews	1	Firth	4
Firth	3	St Andrews	1
Rendall	0	Sanday	2

Rendall Scratched

Westray captain Jack Rendall receives the cup from Jack Walls, Bank of Scotland, tournament sponsors.
(Picture: Orkney Photographic)

Some remarkable 'away' results with both St Ola and South Ronaldsay managing to turn their ties right round in the return legs. But Rendall did not have a good 'away' result and came in for censure from the O.F.A. for not fulfilling their fixture in Sanday, thereby denying the islanders much needed match practice. Teams were officially reminded of their duty to fulfil such fixtures.

Quarter final Results

Sanday	2	Holm	2
Holm	1	Sanday	3
Westray	1	St Ola	4
St Ola	2	Westray	2
Birsay	1	South Ron.	0
South Ron.	5	Birsay	2
Orphir	0	Firth	5
Firth	4	Orphir	0

Performance of the round belonged to South Ronaldsay who scored all their goals in the last 45 minutes of their tie; but Westray's lack of practice saw them 'caught cold' by St Ola and they were effectively out after the first leg. However, Sanday were still alive to represent the North Isles, whilst making scarcely noticed progress were Firth who had easily accounted for St Andrews and Orphir. Hearts were now beating a little faster in Finstown breasts.

Sanday began their semi final with a remarkable performance in the Bignold Park against St Ola. A fine Sunday afternoon brought out a big crowd to witness the island team secure a 3-0 victory with goals by Eric Walls (2) and Billy Harcus. Surely this unexpected win would be enough to take them through to their second final?

However, events were to take a drastic turn in the return leg in Sanday. It was scheduled for the evening of the Sanday Show, and while a 'showcase' match might provide a fitting climax to the show, it was hardly the ideal time for men who had been working with animals in the yard all day. Attempts to change the time of the fixture failed and the game went ahead.

Within the first few minutes, St Ola had scored twice and suddenly the contest was alive again. Sanday desperately tried to defend their single goal lead but were unable to assert any control on the game. St Ola went on to score three more to a single consolation goal for the home team. The dream of a return visit to the Bignold Park was shattered.

In the other semi final, there were no

Undiluted joy in the crowd as Firth get their hands on the trophy at last. The author is on the right, arms aloft. (Picture: Orkney Photographic)

Birth, Blood

unpredictable twists and Firth ran out emphatic winners against the 'Hope.

Semi final Results

St Ola	0	Sanday	3
Sanday	1	St Ola	5
South Ron.	0	Firth	2
Firth	6	South Ron.	2

Once again the tide of optimism began to flow and carry most of the inhabitants of Finstown along with it. Could this finally be their year? They would probably have preferred Sanday as opponents as they had a dread of St Ola, who had beaten them regularly in recent years, including the final two years ago. However, in the days leading up to the big night, no negative thoughts were allowed to prevail and manager Keith Corsie prepared the team in a low key manner in order to avoid the risk of injury to any of his players.

Both Firth and St Ola were to field quite a number of new young players since that 1990 match but perhaps the most surprising inclusion was

goalkeeper Alistair Firth of St Ola.

In the very first league game of the season, playing for Orphir against Rendall, he had broken his neck! Part of the rehabilitation process was to wear a neck brace for a considerable time and it was obvious to everyone that he would play no more football this season … obvious to everyone, that is, except Aly Firth!

By the time the semi final came along, he had flung off the brace and declared himself fit. Suffering no ill effects from that match, here he was once again claiming his rightful place between the St Ola posts. Now, that takes some neck!

The full squads for the final were as follows:

Firth: Graham Shearer; Alistair Watson, Kevin Clouston, Leonard Merriman, Bob Gilmour, Kenny Garriock, Colin Wood, Brian Clouston, Andrew Corsie, Gareth Davies, Steven Wood, Steven Russell, Keith Moar.

St Ola: Alistair Firth; Ian Wilson, Fraser Byers, Eoin Learmonth, Erlend Hutchison, Kevin Hancock, Keith Oddie, Colin Kirkpatrick, Neil Stevenson, Kevin Tait, Billy Johnstone, Stewart Fotheringhame, Karl King.

The evening was cool but dry and good for football. It was clear that Firth supporters greatly outnumbered St Ola fans and they positioned themselves in large groups at strategic points around the pitch. From the outset, they certainly made themselves heard.

Firth, playing uphill, held the advantage early on as their fast forwards caused the St Ola defence many problems. But they had to wait until ten minutes before interval for the breakthrough and it happened when a Colin Wood through ball found Andrew Corsie and his famous left foot did the rest.

St Ola seemed revived after half time and now it was their turn to

It was Firth's year in 1992. Back row, left to right, Keith Corsie (manager), Kevin Clouston, Colin Wood, Andrew Corsie, Graham Shearer, Leonard Merriman, Brian Clouston, Kenny Garriock. Front, Bob Gilmour, Gareth Davies, Steven Russell, Keith Moar, Steven Wood, Al Watson.
(Picture: Orkney Photographic)

dominate. Firth were forced back and eventually conceded a penalty for hand ball. Colin Kirkpatrick slotted home the equaliser.

The game could now go either way but joy! oh joy! (Sorry! Supposed to be unbiased!) it went in favour of Firth. With only five minutes left, a great Brian Clouston pass found Keith Moar and he drove a shot over the diving keeper into the net. This goal had come against the run of play but that made no difference to Firth players and supporters. They were consumed with delight!

And now, to *that* photograph I mentioned at the start of this chapter. Ken Amer of Orkney Photographic, always on the look out for a picture that tells a story, turned round at that instant and I was captured in a state of delirious abandon with some other Firth fans, including my airborne wife, dancing round about.

Realising he was on to a good thing, Ken snapped again five minutes later at full time and he got a similar shot. Mrs Wood had still not touched ground!

Now what story did these snapshots tell? Crazy fools getting worked up about something as trivial as football?

Maybe!

I like to think that they illustrate 60 empty, barren, unfulfilled years finally coming to an end. This generation had managed what their fathers had attempted many times and failed; what the fine Firth team of the 1950s could not do; and what the pre war generation, most of whom had now passed on, had achieved but once, in 1931. The cheers which could almost be heard in Finstown were for now, for the joy of the moment, but for many, they were for much, much more than that.

We now knew what Birsay people must have felt in 1971; Sandwick supporters in 1973; Stromness in 1980; Westray last year … and why not England fans in 1966, Scottish supporters when Scotland beat England at Wembley in 1967? Difference in scale does not diminish the passion. The pride stems from not simply victory for your team but for the place you call *home*. It touches something very deep within your being!

Well, the rest of that night is a joyous blur. The cup had been received by captain Brian Clouston whose grandfather Jimmo Clouston of Cruan had been a member of the last winning Firth team 60 years earlier, and the rejoicing multitude headed for Finstown.

The Pomona Inn, one of the oldest hostelries in Orkney, had seen few occasions like it as folk who rarely cross its threshold now blended into a sea of recognisable faces. Veterans of former Firth teams recounted their tales of glorious victory or heroic failure and toasted tonight's heroes, who would in time become legends whenever local football was discussed.

Mothers of the players were accorded reverence as never before … "my, yer peedie boy played right weel the night!" … and they revelled in their unaccustomed role. Footballers' wives and girlfriends enjoyed their new celebrity status while bairns took advantage of all this bonhomie to indulge themselves to the limit.

In the early hours of the morning, as the merry throng headed towards Brian Clouston's large garage on the western outskirts of Finstown, converted for the night into a spectacular party venue, a few of us paused and sat on a dyke to draw breath. I vaguely recall snatches of that conversation.

"Weel, … we'll be able tae had wur heads up noo for a whole year!"

"A whole year! Buey, this is only the stert! Wur gan tae win this thing every year.

We'll be like Sandwick and … "

"Dinna be so sure! We should enjoy hid jist noo becis ye never ken, this might never happen again!"

(long pause)

"Ach! Spaek sense, min!"

We got up unsteadily and staggered onward towards the sound of music and laughter.

Firth skipper Brian Clouston receives the cup from Raymond Smith representing sponsors Bank of Scotland.   *(Picture: Orkney Photographic)*

Birth, Blood

1993:
Unique family affair in final

The following nine months were a time when Finstown citizens walked with a more upright posture, an unaccustomed lightness in the step, and met the gaze of fellow Orcadians 'full on.' Although hard to define – there were no actual recorded incidents of bowing, saluting or laying down of cloaks in puddles – it did feel as if a greater degree of reverence was accorded to anyone with a Firth connection.

Opinions on any subject ranging from global warming to the state of the economy, carried more weight with the public at large and Orkney's most famous visitor of the year, Space Shuttle Commander John Young, who had walked on the moon, is alleged to have paid the village the ultimate compliment when speaking at the Science Festival.

"Even though I've never set foot on Orkney before, I've flown over it," he said, while displaying a set of photographs taken from orbit.

"There you can see Scotland, and if you look closely, you can just make out Orkney … and see that small dot there … well, that is Finstown!" he is reputed to have said.

Alas, this reign could not go unchallenged for ever and soon it was time to defend the crown. Once again the month of May came round and fourteen 'hopefuls' prepared to do battle. After a hesitant start, the cup holders were soon on their way.

First round Results

St Andrews	0	Firth	0
Firth	3	St Andrews	1
South Ron.	2	Harray	0
Harray	0	South Ron.	3
Stromness	4	Evie	2
Evie	1	Stromness	1

Birsay	4	Orphir	0
Orphir	1	Birsay	2
St Ola	5	Sanday	0
Sanday	1	St Ola	3
Rendall	1	Holm	0
Holm	2	Rendall	0

A predictable round with only the margin of St Ola's win over Sanday causing surprise. Barely noticed at the bottom of the results was Rendall's defeat by Holm, and it would indeed be unremarkable but for the fact that, for the first time in 30 years, there was no Morgan Harcus in the Rendall goal.

A 'one club' man most of his life, he had scaled the heights in local football representing Orkney against Shetland no fewer than 18 times. But coming from a parish with limited resources he had never paraded his talent at the final stages of Orkney's premier cup competition. However, the story of the Parish Cup would not be complete without reference to such an outstanding career which ended last year with his club lifting the Oxy Cup.

Now to the quarter finals, where some big games were scheduled to take place.

Quarter final Results

Stromness	2	South Ron.	4
South Ron.	2	Stromness	1
Sandwick	5	Birsay	0
Birsay	0	Sandwick	5
Holm	1	St Ola	3
St Ola	4	Holm	0
Westray	2	Firth	1
Firth	0	Westray	0

There was much weeping, wailing and gnashing of the teeth in Finstown. Like Westray the previous year, they found defending the title to be too daunting a task. Ranks of supporters with slumped shoulders leaving the school pitch signified that the good times were over … for now!

Sandwick's demolition of Birsay came as something of a surprise. Many had predicted the demise of Sandwick as a Parish Cup force following their decision to end their league team after more than 20 years.

In fact, football in that part of Orkney was now in a very fragile state compared to former years. Where, not so long ago, there were three very strong West Mainland 'A' League teams: Birsay, Sandwick and Dounby, now there was only Dounby and they were not doing very well. Their 'A' team ended up second bottom of the league with a meagre four points, while the 'B' team were bottom of their division with two. Included in their 111 'goals against' tally was a 30-0 defeat by Thorfinn!

Well, you wouldn't expect either of these teams to show the other mercy!

So things were at a low ebb up west but the Parish Cup never fails to bring out something extra in players and Sandwick once again looked up for the fight.

Semi final Results

St Ola	2	Westray	2
Westray	1	St Ola	1
Sandwick	1	South Ron.	0
South Ron.	1	Sandwick	2

After Westray clawed their way back into the first leg tie with two late goals, the return in Westray was played on an evening of incessant rain. Robert Walker gave St Ola the lead but Westray replied through Robbie Rendall and managed to hold out to reach their second final.

Sandwick had the edge in both their games and their place in the final was sealed by goals from Jimmy Sinclair and Steven Poke in the away leg.

The reappearance of Westray in the final once again captured the public imagination and the anticipated large crowd filed into the Bignold Park on Saturday evening (but the glorious weather of earlier in the day had now given way to cloud and rain). As spectators scrutinised team selections in their programmes, a number of talking points emerged.

The Westray squad contained no fewer than six Rendalls but absent were stalwarts of two years ago, Robbie Stanger, who was suspended, and Alan 'Bu' Stevenson, who had a broken leg. Both these players would be badly missed.

Sandwick, meanwhile, had changed significantly from their last final appearance in 1989. No longer there were established Parish Cup 'greats' like Rae Slater, Keith Leonard or Geordie Leonard, but a continuous stream of younger players had emerged to take their place. Still present, however, at the heart of their defence were Mike Grieve and Calvin Poke and, in what must be an almost unique situation in cup history, Calvin was joined in the starting line up by both sons, Erlend and Steven.

Full line ups were as follows:

Sandwick: Erlend Poke; Ian Linklater, Martin Oag, Michael Grieve, Calvin Poke, Jimmy Moar, Allan Spence, Jimmy Sinclair, Stevie Linklater, Steven Poke, Stevie Slater. Subs: Michael Mowat, Glenn Porter.

Westray: Robbie Peace; Denis Fergus, Billy Drever, Martin Tulloch, Geordie Rendall, Colin Kirkness, Jim Brown, Raymond Rendall, Jack Rendall, Jimmy Thomson, Stewart Rendall. Subs: Ivor Rendall, Mark Rendall.

Sandwick played uphill in the first half and did not take long to assert themselves in the greasy conditions. Their strong defence snuffed out any Westray attacks while both Spence and Poke were creating problems up front. Robbie Stanger's influence was being badly missed in Westray's midfield.

After half an hour, Sandwick scored twice in quick succession. First Jimmy Sinclair netted from Allan Spence's pass and almost immediately Steven Poke headed a second.

Shortly after half time Westray got back in contention when Jimmy Thomson scored from 25 yards range but the two goal lead was restored when Stevie Linklater was on hand to slot the ball home after the Westray keeper had parried an earlier shot.

During the last 20 minutes, there were chances at both ends but the closest to another goal came when Poke hit a post. The final whistle sounded with the score Sandwick 3 Westray 1.

At the end of the match, the cup was handed to Stevie Slater by Bob Kellett, Manager of the Bank of Scotland. It was Sandwick's thirteenth cup victory.

The game was not a classic but had been full of endeavour by both sides. Sandwick's cup final experience had once more been to their advantage while Westray, who had been ably led by Raymond Rendall, had badly missed their absent colleagues.

Although there would continue to be strong opposition from the likes of Westray, Firth and St Ola, there was more than just an inkling around that Sandwick had rediscovered their winning habit … and the pleasure to be derived from strutting around all year with heads in the air!

Sandwick returned to winning ways in 1993. Back row, left to right, Michael Mowat, Glenn Porter, Ian Linklater, Jimmy Sinclair, Erlend Poke, Jimmy Moar, Michael Grieve, Martin Oag, Alex Stanger, Bobby Hazlehurst. Front, Erlend Grieve, Calvin Poke, Stevie Linklater, Stevie Slater, Allan Spence, Steven Poke, Kenny Chalmers.
(Picture: Orkney Photographic)

1994:
Isles celebrate cup glory again

All this talk of self government and devolution which had been gaining momentum throughout Scotland during the 1990's, finally got to the good people of Burray. Always fiercely proud of their own identity, (just look at the determination to keep their own school) for example, the footballers decided to sever their links with their "mother parish", South Ronaldsay, and set up their own parish football team.

Up to this point, Burray and South Ronaldsay players had played together as a united parish but always under the name "St Margaret's Hope" or "South Ronaldsay." Since the 1930s the name "Burray" had disappeared off the football map … but now the urge to restore it was irresistible.

It came about, not with a revolt, but in a fairly conventional way. The population of Burray was on the increase, a lot of young lads were living there and very few were getting a game for South Ronaldsay. Then, most crucial of all, a pitch became available.

The O.I.C. had acquired the land of Westermill and they agreed to lease a field to the Burray hall committee who in turn made it available to the footballers. A team was put together by Douglas Montgomery and a few others, initially to play friendly games, but now in 1994, they felt well enough established to compete seriously.

So, for the first time, the free and independent 'state' of Burray would feature in the Parish Cup.

First round Results

Burray	1	Birsay	6
Birsay	9	Burray	0
South Ron.	4	Stenness	0
Stenness	0	South Ron.	7

Holm v St Ola
Holm scratched.

Firth	2	Sanday	1
Sanday	1	Firth	2
Sandwick	1	Westray	3
Westray	2	Sandwick	1
Stromness	3	Evie	2
Evie	2	Stromness	3
St Andrews	0	Orphir	1
Orphir	2	St Andrews	2

Well, Burray weren't 'world beaters' yet but at least they were having a go! The player who would go down in history as the scorer of their first Parish Cup goal was Gary Drever. South Ronaldsay did not seem badly affected by player loss and easily saw off Stenness, also making a first appearance for many years.

The performance of the round belonged to Westray who avenged last season's cup final defeat in emphatic style. A stirring performance in Dounby with goals by Brian Sandison (2) and Jimmy Thomson, saw them establish a lead they were not going to relinquish. They would now face South Ronaldsay.

Quarter final Results

Westray	3	South Ron.	2
South Ron.	1	Westray	1
Firth	4	St Ola	1
St Ola	5	Firth	2
(after extra time)			
Stromness	2	Birsay	1
Birsay	1	Stromness	1
Orphir	0	Harray	0
Harray	1	Orphir	2

Four very close ties served notice that this was to be one of the most open competitions for years. But this time it was the Firth v St Ola match which had fans talking.

After a convincing home win, the second leg looked like a formality for Firth. But before a large crowd at Picky on a Sunday afternoon, (77 cars were counted), the result was in doubt until the very last kick. In fact, Firth were 4-0 down after 89 minutes and only a scrambled goal in the last minute by Bob Gilmour took the game into extra time. Then Nicky Barnett put St Ola ahead again only for Leonard Merriman to get a vital second away goal for Firth. They now hung on grimly and the noise made by horns at the final whistle suggested that few of the car drivers hailed from the Kirkwall region.

Minus Sandwick and St Ola, the semi finals now bore an unaccustomed look.

Semi final Results

Stromness	1	Orphir	1
Orphir	0	Stromness	1
Firth	0	Westray	1
Westray	4	Firth	3

So Stromness, showing great signs of revival, were once again in the final and in the year of the Stromness Athletic centenary celebrations, it was very fitting to see one of their teams in the position to carry home the most prized trophy of all.

But first they would have to overcome Westray, who left it late before overcoming Firth at home. Two late goals were required to secure their place in another final.

This time Westray were probably the favourites having had recent County Show night experience whereas this young Stromness team had never been there before. Only Dennis Chalmers and Ronald Ritch remained of the victorious 1986 side … but they did hold one advantage. Westray had beaten Sandwick and no team that put Sandwick out had ever gone on to …

Hmm!

On a cool, dry evening, against a background of fairground music and flashing lights, the following squads took the field:

Westray: Leslie Drever, Keith Rendall, Mark Rendall, Raymond

Rendall, Robbie Stanger, Jack Rendall, Martin Tulloch, Alan Stevenson, Colin Kirkness, Jimmy Thomson, Denis Fergus, Steven Tulloch, Ralph Stevenson.

Stromness: Colin McLeod, Karl Adamson, Barry Johnston, John Scott, Dennis Chalmers, Ronald Ritch, Michael Ritch, John Young, Alan Scott, Bill Innes, David Kirkpatrick, Paul Sinclair, Keith Chalmers.

In a tentative first half there was only one goal when Jimmy Thomson scored from the penalty spot for Westray after 35 minutes. A second 'goal' was ruled out for offside.

In the second half, Westray took the initiative immediately and soon increased their lead when Alan Stevenson ran through the Stromness defence to place the ball past Colin McLeod. Westray never relaxed their hold on the game and it was to Stromness' credit that they kept the

score down, even after McLeod was sent off in the closing minutes for taking down Mark Rendall.

The final whistle went and by a score of 2-0, Westray had claimed their second Parish Cup.

Amidst loud celebration from Westray fans, it was a proud Denis Fergus who received the cup from Bob Kellett of the Bank of Scotland.

Taking nothing from a plucky Stromness team, this was a well

Westray manager Jim Rendall and Mark Rendall (sub) celebrate the opening goal.
(Picture: Orkney Photographic)

deserved Westray victory and it is worth considering just how much of an achievement it was. Here were a group of lads who had relatively few opportunities to play competitive football, getting their skill and fitness levels up to a high standard before bringing in a few 'outsiders' and working the whole into a cohesive blend, good enough to beat all comers. True, they were blessed at this time with some very talented players such as Raymond Rendall, Steven Tulloch and Alan Stevenson but nevertheless, this was a triumph of teamwork and togetherness.

But this had not happened over night. It had taken some 20 years for the islanders of Westray to reach this consistently high level of performance. We can just picture the latest entrants from the island of Burray making their way home that night.

"Noo, boys, in 2014 …."

Westray went one better in 1994 than the previous year to take the cup home. Back row, left to right, Keith Rendall, Mark Rendall, Raymond Rendall, Robbie Stanger, Jack Rendall, Leslie Drever, Martin Tulloch, Jim Rendall (manager). Front, Alan Stevenson, Colin Kirkness, Jimmy Thomson, Dennis Fergus, Steven Tulloch, Ralph Stevenson.
(Picture: Orkney Photographic)

Birth, Blood

1995:
Decisive triumph for talented side

Westray's achievements, and to an extent, those of Firth, had helped retain the public's high level of interest in the Parish Cup. These teams had succeeded in unseating on a few occasions, the perennial favourites, Sandwick and St Ola, and thereby prevented the tournament from being completely monopolised … or more accurately, *duopolised*.

But for football fans always on the look out for a new challenger or another sleeping giant showing signs of stirring, the evidence was fairly slim. No country team, 'A' or 'B', showed much aptitude for competing with Kirkwall teams in the leagues while, of the parishes, only Stromness offered evidence of revival.

However, at both junior and juvenile level there were some rays of hope. Teams from South Ronaldsay and Holm were actually heading the leagues in the secondary school 1 and 2 age groups so there must be some promising players among the 12 and 13 year olds in these parishes. Maybe a few years down the line?

When the draw for this year's tournament was announced there was no sign of last year's newcomers, Burray, but a ripple of excitement was created by the first appearance in many years of Stronsay. Those hoping for a Stronsay trip would have to wait, though, as they, along with Sanday, received a first round bye.

First round Results

| Harray | 1 | Stromness | 4 |
| Stromness | 1 | Harray | 1 |

Shapinsay	0	St Andrews	3
St Andrews	2	Shapinsay	2
Birsay	2	South Ron.	3
South Ron.	2	Birsay	0
Westray	2	Orphir	0
Orphir	1	Westray	2
Firth	1	Sandwick	3
Sandwick	2	Firth	1
Holm	1	St Ola	4
St Ola	6	Holm	0

The familiar names continued to advance, Westray, Sandwick, St Ola …. The tournament was taking on an accustomed look. But, much interest in the next round would focus on the North Isles 'derby' and the performance of Stronsay against Stromness.

Quarter final Results

Sanday	2	Westray	3
Westray	3	Sanday	1
Stromness	4	Stronsay	1
Stronsay	1	Stromness	0

The Orcadian, Thursday, August 17, 1995   35

la capture the Parish Cup

Sandwick again made an upfield sortie, this time with S. Poke and S. Linklater linking on the right as they put pressure on St Ola as the first half moved into its closing stages. A through pass to A. Spence gave him a chance on goal but it was gathered by the St Ola keeper.

As Sandwick continued to push for something before half time a pass from S. Slater attempting to link with S. Linklater on the wing was cut out, and in the ensuing attack St Ola played into the Sandwick box and went 3-0 up through a well-placed shot from N. Stevenson.

Into the second half and Sandwick kicked off bidding to get back into the game as soon as possible, but it was the veteran combination of C. Kirkpatrick and F. Byers that looked most authoritative, moving up the left for St Ola, though M. Grieve and S. Linklater, working back for Sandwick, kept things solid at the back. Sandwick did threaten, but a looping header off target from substitute Marcus Wood was the nearest thing in the early minutes of the second half.

Then a St Ola attack switching from left to right followed by a cross, brought a corner but it came to nothing.

A Sandwick corner minutes

The victorious St Ola team celebrate with the cup after their 3-0 win over Sandwick in Saturday evening's Parish Cup Final. Back row, from left: Eoin Learmonth, Fraser Byers, Martin Sutherland, Neil Stockan, Gary Farquhar, Ronnie Peterson, Neil Stevenson, Graham Johnston. Front row, from left: Keith Oddie, Colin Kirkpatrick, Ian Wilson, Billy Johnstone, Kevin Groundwater.

(Picture: Orkney Photographic)

St Ola	11	St Andrews	0

St Andrews scratched.

Sandwick	2	South Ron.	0
South Ron.	1	Sandwick	1

Stronsay gave a very good account of themselves, especially in their home leg, where the crowd, mainly housed in more than 70 vehicles around the pitch, saw a great display by 'keeper Davie Cooper and the winning goal scored by John Miller. However, Stronsay were out.

Semi final Results

Sandwick	1	Westray	0
Westray	1	Sandwick	1
St Ola	4	Stromness	1
Stromness	0	St Ola	4

So the final brought together two of the strongest sides of recent years and in normal circumstances, you would expect the team who had been unbeaten in 13 finals to be the favourites. But this St Ola squad, containing a good blend of youth and experience, would take some beating.

Team squads were as follows:

St Ola: Neil Stockan, Eoin Learmonth, Fraser Byers, Martin Sutherland , Gary Farquhar, Ronnie Paterson, Neil Stevenson, Graham Johnston, Keith Oddie, Colin Kirkpatrick, Ian Wilson, Billy Johnstone, Kevin Groundwater.

Sandwick: Erlend Poke, Michael Grieve, Ian Linklater, Calvin Poke, Jimmy Moar, Jimmy Sinclair, Michael Mowat, Martin Oag, Stevie Linklater, Allan Spence, Stevie Slater, Marcus Wood, Bobby Hazlehurst.

After a fairly even opening spell, St Ola took the lead after half an hour when Keith Oddie drove home from outside the box and minutes later Colin Kirkpatrick picked up a slack clearance to calmly slip the ball past Poke.

Sandwick were dealt a further blow just before half time when Neil Stevenson scored St Ola's third with a well placed shot.

A 3-0 deficit proved too much for Sandwick in the second half. A fine, open end to end game continued under ever darkening skies but no further goals were scored at either end. The better chances fell to St Ola who could have increased their tally but a 3-0 result was enough to see their captain Billy Johnstone, lead his team up the pavilion steps to receive the trophy from Frank McGinn, senior manager of the Bank of Scotland.

This was a decisive win for a fine St Ola side, which contained a generous sprinkling of county players. But, more intriguingly, did this match finally spell the end of Sandwick's invincibility? Had they at last exposed their soft underbelly?

Well, they could now be described as vulnerable in two senses. Last year, Westray had proved that a team who had beaten Sandwick could go on to lift the Parish Cup. Now, Sandwick had actually *lost* in a final!

Ah yes! Other teams could take heart! Sandwick's grip was surely weakening at last!

Neil Stevenson, whose goal for St Ola put the tie outwith Sandwick's reach.

1996: Trophy back in familiar hands

St Ola's dominance of last year's tournament was perhaps, not surprising. All of their players were members of Kirkwall clubs and a stark reminder of the gulf between the likes of Thorfinn, Rovers, Hotspur and the rest came this year in the list of players invited to inter county training. All 26 players came from these three clubs with not a single 'country' player making it to first base.

Admittedly, the Poke brothers from Dounby were included in the final squads for the inter county matches but the overall impression was, nevertheless, a gloomy one for the standard of football outwith the Capital.

Now, if the Kirkwall teams' supremacy was extended into the Parish Cup, then St Ola should be unbeatable.

Well this theory would be put to the test immediately when the draw for this year's competition was announced. St Ola would play Sandwick, a Sandwick maybe showing some cracks, in a repeat of last season's final.

First round Results

St Ola	1	Sandwick	0
Sandwick	1	St Ola	0

(Sandwick won 3-1 on penalties a.e.t.)

Firth	4	Birsay	1
Birsay	1	Firth	7
Orphir	6	Shapinsay	0
Shapinsay	1	Orphir	2
Stromness	3	Rendall	2
Rendall	3	Stromness	4
Stronsay	2	Harray	1
Harray	0	Stronsay	0

If there were cracks, they were wafer-thin! Sandwick gained

revenge, albeit narrowly, but they were on the march again. Also worth noting was the fine achievement by Stronsay who claimed a famous 'scalp.' Westray and Sanday now joined the quarter finalists.

Quarter final Results

Stronsay	0	Stromness	3
Stromness	4	Stronsay	0
Orphir	1	Firth	0
Firth	10	Orphir	0
Sandwick	1	South Ron.	0
South Ron.	1	Sandwick	5
Westray	1	Sanday	3
Sanday	0	Westray	1

Sanday for once, gained the upper hand over their old rivals. The first game in this tie was marred by the leg break sustained by 17 year old Sanday player, Raymond Brown. An air ambulance was summoned from Kirkwall to take the player to the Balfour Hospital but since the plane was involved in another emergency at the time, Raymond had to wait four hours in considerable pain before the aircraft was able to transfer him to hospital.

Despite having his leg in plaster for all of 20 weeks, Raymond went on to make a full recovery from his injury and is still playing football, currently the captain of Sanday's Parish Cup team. But the incident certainly illustrated why island communities fear any dilution of their medical services.

Sanday would now face a rejuvenated, high scoring Firth in the semi finals.

Semi final Results

Sandwick	3	Stromness	1
Stromness	1	Sandwick	0
Firth	3	Sanday	1
Sanday	2	Firth	1

Anyone who had dared suggest that Sandwick were showing signs of weakness would be eating their words now as their battle hardened, cup fighting mentality took them into yet another final. Their opponents would be Firth, who had to cling on desperately in Sanday.

In fact Sanday's was rather a hard luck story. They had controlled much of the first leg after taking the lead through Ivan Leslie before second half goals by Steven Wood and Kenny Garriock (2) gave Firth a 'cushion' which was just enough to see them back at the Bignold Park for the first time since their victory in 1992.

These two teams had never met in the final before and on paper it looked like a fairly even contest. Firth had enjoyed a good season winning the Thomson, Oxy and Thornley Binders cups while most of Sandwick's team represented Dounby, who had also done well this year, finishing a very creditable runner up to Thorfinn in the 'A' League.

The constant trickle of newcomers continued to filter into both teams and it appeared that Sandwick had had a real stroke of luck. They had unearthed a talented young Hotspur player, Gary Dowell, whose parents had lived in the Sandwick portion of Dounby when he was born. We can just hear Sandwick player manager Calvin Poke, purring with pleasure at this unexpected discovery.

The following team squads took the field in dull, overcast conditions:

Firth: Graham Shearer, Kevin Clouston, Bob Gilmour, Leonard Merriman, Andrew Corsie, Brian Clouston, Kenny Garriock, Eoin

Stevie Linklater of Sandwick (left) and Firth's Kenny Garriock both make uncompromising challenges for the ball.
(Picture: Orkney Photographic)

Dennison, Steven Wood, Gareth Davies, Kevan Harvey, Brian Davis, James Clouston, Andrew Dickey.

Sandwick: Erlend Poke, Steven Wylie, Ian Linklater, Jimmy Sinclair, Michael Grieve, Erlend Grieve, Steven Poke, Gary Dowell, Michael Mowat, Calvin Poke, Derek Chalmers, Stevie Linklater, Allan Spence, Stevie Slater.

The first half produced a goalless stalemate with little to enthuse the crowd. The best moment had been a powerful Andrew Corsie drive which brought a tremendous save by Erlend Poke, but for the most part, according to *The Orcadian* correspondent Robert Leslie, "the ball spent as much time in the air as the fairground rides in the afternoon."

The second half however, told a different story. Both teams started more brightly and there were chances at either end before Gareth Davies opened the scoring for Firth with a shot from the edge of the box. The pace of the game now stepped up considerably. Sandwick equalised after one of their newcomers, Erlend Grieve, lobbed the ball over Graham Shearer into the net.

Rattled by this goal, Firth went behind five minutes later when Allan Spence scored with a header at the far post. 2-1 remained the score right up to the closing moments of injury time when, with Firth throwing everyone forward, Steven Poke broke away and his pass was slotted home by Spence for his second and Sandwick's third goal.

Seconds after the restart, the final whistle went to proclaim Sandwick winners of the Parish Cup. It was fitting that goal scoring hero, Allan Spence should now receive the cup from Frank McGinn representing the Bank of Scotland.

So Sandwick were deserving winners yet again, reaffirming their status as the finest parish side ever. While their win may have had an air of repetitiveness, it went a long way to proving several things. First, Sandwick as a footballing force were far from finished; secondly, that football out 'in the sticks' was in robust good health; and finally, it served as a reminder to future Orkney selectors that decent players could still be found just a few miles out of Kirkwall.

Sandwick's relentless desire for success continued in 1996. Back row, left to right, Kevin Dick, Steven Wylie, Ian Linklater, Jimmy Sinclair, Michael Grieve, Erlend Grieve, Steven Poke, Gary Dowell, Michael Mowat, Rae Slater. Front, Graham Poke, Calvin Poke, Derek Chalmers, Stevie Linklater, Allan Spence, Stevie Slater, Erlend Poke. (Picture: Orkney Photographic)

1997:
Sandwick make it triumph No. 15

Any downtrodden football supporter would have been inspired by the publication in the 1990s of Ron Ferguson's history of his beloved club, Cowdenbeath F.C., entitled 'Black Diamonds and the Blue Brazil.' In this delightful volume, Ron not only gives an entertaining account of his club's roots and origin, but also explains the source of his devotion to the team through thick and thin, principally thin.

Supporters of smaller clubs everywhere would identify with the emotions involved, from the fleeting moments of joy to the more regular periods of despair. In Orkney, where Ron was at that time minister at St Magnus Cathedral, the book struck a particularly resonant chord. Here too were many sufferers in the cause, wearied by decades of mediocrity.

Especially heartened would have been the lifelong fans of parish teams who had never scaled the 'victory steps', and also those whose glory days were several generations ago. Yet every year, undaunted by constant adversity, these teams and their supporters turned out, filled with hope at the dawning of a new campaign, clinging to the belief that this year it just might be their turn.

Once again, an impressive total of 15 made ready.

First round Results

St Ola	3	South Ron.	0
South Ron.	1	St Ola	3
Harray	2	Orphir	3
Orphir	5	Harray	0
Stronsay	1	Sanday	3
Sanday	4	Stronsay	1
Rendall	1	Shapinsay	1
Shapinsay	0	Rendall	5
Sandwick	2	Westray	3

Westray	0	Sandwick	3
Firth	2	Holm	0
Holm	2	Firth	2
Birsay	0	Stromness	4
Stromness	1	Birsay	1

Seven parishes had their hopes dashed again with the Westray folk counting themselves as most unfortunate. It just went to prove that Sandwick could never be written off.

Quarter final Results

Stromness	0	St Ola	5
St Ola	7	Stromness	1
Sandwick	3	St Andrews	0
St Andrews	0	Sandwick	3
Firth	1	Rendall	2
Rendall	1	Firth	4
Orphir	2	Sanday	0
anday	1	Orphir	0

The 'big two', Sandwick and St Ola, progressed with something to spare but Firth received a fright from Rendall before hitting form in the return leg. Perhaps the biggest surprise was the defeat of Sanday, semi finalists last year, by Orphir. The draw now made a repeat of last year's final a distinct possibility but Sandwick would have to be at the top of their game to dispose of St Ola.

Semi final Results

Sandwick	0	St Ola	0
St Ola	0	Sandwick	1
Orphir	1	Firth	5
Firth	6	Orphir	1

A repeat of last year's final it was. Orphir fans, whose hands had never touched the Parish Cup, had to trudge home resignedly once again. Ah well, they could seek some comfort from their fellow parishioner's book.

There was no doubt that Sandwick held the psychological advantage going into this year's game. Not only had they beaten the same opponents twelve months earlier but into the bargain had acquired one of Firth's best players. Kenny Garriock, a powerful midfield player, had sold

his house in the smart, residential suburbs of Finstown and moved with his family to a fine traditional house overlooking Skaill Loch. A winner with Firth in 1992 he would now seek to become one of a rare breed who had won the cup with different parishes.

However, good fortune was not all one way. Firth for their part were able to field an ex Sandwick player who had played in their winning team of 1983, Stewart Spence. Another hard running, strong tackling player, maybe they would cancel each other out.

Full team squads were as follows:

Sandwick: Erlend Poke, Steven Wylie, Michael Grieve, Calvin Poke, Kenny Garriock, Gary Dowell, Stevie Linklater, Marcus Wood, Erlend Grieve, Steven Poke, Ian Linklater, Michael Mowat, Jamie Peppitt, Bobby Hazlehurst.

Firth: Graham Shearer, Andrew Dickey, Kevin Clouston, Leonard Merriman, Andrew Corsie, Stewart Spence, Brian Clouston, Kevan Harvey, Gareth Davies, Ronald Thomson, Eoin Dennison, David Gilmour, Christopher Seator, Brian Davis.

The match got off to a flying start and within 15 minutes, Sandwick were two ahead. The scoring was opened by none other than Kenny Garriock and Steven Wylie made it two with a well placed shot.

Two nil was the score at half time but immediately after the interval Firth pressure led to a Sandwick defender putting into his own net and now the game sparked back into life. Steven Poke put Sandwick 3-1 ahead but Brian Clouston put Firth back into the game with a well timed header.

For a time Firth looked the stronger team but a break away by Gary Dowell led to Erlend Grieve notching Sandwick's fourth. Firth hopes were finally dashed when Kevin Clouston was sent off for a late tackle on the tireless Garriock. With only a few minutes remaining, Grieve made another swift break down the wing and crossed for Kenny Garriock, who else, to score his second and Sandwick's fifth. This made the final score Sandwick 5 Firth 2.

Nobody could dispute the fact that Sandwick deserved this victory given the emphatic score line. Firth might feel hard done by to lose by so wide a margin but goals are what count and on this occasion, the 'Garriock factor' was significant. Kenny was further proof that playing against ex team mates often brings out that something extra.

As the Sandwick crowd headed west to celebrate their fifteenth Parish Cup win, the Firth faithful were once again left to drown their sorrows and reflect ruefully on what might have

been. As the evening wore on a few began to make worrying references to a late night conversation conducted sitting on a dyke some five years ago … "I tellt ye! I tellt ye!" … while others contented themselves with the occasional grumble … "It would be somewhat unwise for 'a certain ex Firth player' to honour us with his presence tonight!" (or words to that effect!)

Ah well, not to worry! With a bit of luck the Firth goalkeeper, Graham Shearer would have cleared out his garage for a party and soon all would be well with the world again. As Ron Ferguson said at the end of his book, "In the beginning was the Dream. And the dream was of a new season …"

Of course Ron was referring to much more than football, but tonight … that would have to do for us!

A delighted Ian Linklater of Sandwick receives the trophy from Brian Lanni of the Bank of Scotland, the sponsors. (Picture: Orkney Photographic)

1998: Unstoppable Sandwick

That the Parish Cup was central to the Orkney way of life was brought home most strikingly in the obituaries of two very well known local figures who passed away during 1998. Both had gone on to make their name in other ways in later life, but it was as footballers in their home parish that they established their early reputations.

The first was Willie Muir, who had been centre half and captain of the only Stenness team to have won the trophy back in 1936. Willie had been a very accomplished player who had also represented Stromness, Hotspur, Orkney and on occasion, Orphir, the parish of his birth.

A playing colleague of his, Fraser Anderson, who still lives at Voan in Stenness, recalls him as being the driving force behind football in the parish and someone who was very keen on physical fitness. In addition to playing football most evenings, the boys were encouraged by Willie to run or cycle to Stromness, up Howe Brae and home by Deepdale. This was usually a Sunday evening treat after Bible Class. Such fitness obviously stood him in good stead as Willie was able to continue playing to a high standard well into his 40s.

Later in the year, another famous name in Parish Cup history passed away at the age of 86. Joe 'Bunny' Bruce from Shapinsay truly deserved the term 'legend.' He had played in all five of Shapinsay's cup wins spanning the years 1933, when he would have been 21, to 1954, when he was 42.

Kenny Meason's eloquent tribute in *The Orcadian* refers to his "superb balance, lightning reactions, acceleration and unique ability to shoot with either foot." In fact,

Birth, Blood

Matt Busby, with whom Bunny was stationed on Flotta during the war, suggested he try to become professional but this did not appeal. Bunny was content to work on the farm and spent the rest of his life on Shapinsay where he was a highly respected pillar of the community.

Both of these great pioneers from the early days of the Parish Cup had now passed on but it was fitting to see their contributions so highlighted.

What they would have made of the current state of the game in their respective parishes is hard to say but they would probably have appreciated the cyclical nature of parish football. Stenness and Shapinsay were now at the lowest point in the revolution while virtually stationary at the top were Sandwick, who were now in pursuit of another three-in-a-row winning sequence as the competition got underway again.

First round Results

Westray	1	Rendall	3
Rendall	0	Westray	6
Shapinsay	0	St Ola	6
St Ola	7	Shapinsay	1
South Ron.	2	Stromness	1
Stromness	3	South Ron.	1
Stronsay	0	Birsay	5

Stronsay scratched

St Andrews	5	Harray	0
Harray	2	St Andrews	2
Sandwick	2	Sanday	1
Sanday	0	Sandwick	4
Holm	1	Firth	1
Firth	5	Holm	2

The only hint of a surprise came in Rendall's first leg showing in Westray but apart from that, it was generally, 'business as usual.'

Quarter final Results

Sandwick	1	Westray	0
Westray	0	Sandwick	2
St Andrews	0	Stromness	1
Stromness	3	St Andrews	2

St Ola	6	Orphir	1
Orphir	2	St Ola	1
Birsay	2	Firth	1
Firth	3	Birsay	0

The semi finals took on a very familiar look but the prospect of a third successive Firth v Sandwick final was avoided when they were drawn together at this stage.

Semi final Results

Firth	0	Sandwick	3
Sandwick	3	Firth	1
St Ola	0	Stromness	2
Stromness	5	St Ola	3

Stromness fully justified their growing reputation with an excellent win. In the second leg, two goals by Keith Chalmers, two from Simon Penn and a fifth by Wayne Porter (son of Glenn) showed that they had enough firepower to test Sandwick's defence in the final.

Firth, psychologically beaten from the start, capitulated rather tamely in the other semi final so now it would be the turn of the young Stromness team to see if they had the ability and the nerve to upset this remarkable Sandwick side.

It was a fine evening in the Bignold Park when the following squads took the field.

Sandwick: Erlend Poke, Ian Linklater, Steven Wylie, Michael Grieve, Calvin Poke, Stevie Slater, Steven Poke, Kenny Garriock, Erlend Grieve, Stevie Linklater, Gary Dowell, Martin Oag, Marcus Wood, Jimmy Sinclair.

Stromness: Trevor Lee, Alan Gordon, Simon Penn, Dennis Chalmers, Ronald Ritch, Gareth Crichton, Barry Johnston, Andrew Groundwater, Wayne Porter, Karl Adamson, Keith Chalmers, David Kirkpatrick, Andrew Rendall, Michael Ritch.

The first half, although goalless, saw plenty of incidents at either end with the closest to a score coming from a 30 yard free kick by Steven Poke, which goalkeeper Lee managed to push on to a post and away to safety.

It was Poke who opened the scoring in the second half with another long range free kick which dipped at the last moment into the Stromness net, leaving the keeper stranded. They added a second in 56 minutes, when

Sandwick, cup winners in 1998. Back row, left to right, Stevie Linklater, Gareth Wood, Michael Grieve, Jimmy Sinclair, Erlend Poke, Steven Wylie, Gary Dowell, Ian Linklater, Calvin Poke, Mark Seator. Front, Marcus Wood, Steven Poke, Kenny Garriock, Stevie Slater, Erlend Grieve, Martin Oag. (Picture Orkney Photographic)

Kenny Garriock, who was popping up all over the pitch, latched on to a loose ball and made no mistake from close range.

Much of the last half hour was played out in the Sandwick half but the defence, in which Steven Wylie was outstanding, gave nothing away. So a fast, sporting, keenly contested game ended with the final score, Sandwick 2 Stromness 0.

What can be said that has not been said many times already?

For the viewing public it was a touch mind numbing to have witnessed yet another Sandwick win but nobody could deny the worth of a team which could do this, year on year; a real Parish Cup superpower!

Since we began this section reflecting on Parish Cup 'legends', we should end it by referring to a 'legend' in the making. Calvin Poke had now collected his sixteenth cup winner's medal stretching right back to 1973, a span of 25 years! A remarkable achievement and he was showing no signs of retiring yet.

Ah, but just a reminder that this game does not allow its heroes to get too carried away; in fact it can take them down to earth with a bump! As a footnote to *The Orcadian*'s cup final report, an appeal was published by the aforementioned Calvin Poke for the return of one of Sandwick's footballs. Apparently their best ball, worth about £50, disappeared during the presentation ceremony and hadn't been seen since.

Player/manager Calvin was co-ordinating the search. It was unclear whether this was a souvenir hunter at work or someone with a sense of malice. Perhaps it was even a genuine football tactic; if the Sandwick players cannot be overcome on the field of play, then try pinching their balls.

Maybe we would see more of these desperate measures in years to come?

1999: New home for Parish Cup final

Picture the scene of frantic activity as another County Show draws to a close. For exhibitors and spectators alike, there is little chance to have a leisurely seat on the corner of a pen or to lean on a railing, sipping a last glass of beer and reflecting on the ups and downs of a busy day. Instead, from late afternoon onwards, everyone, officials of Orkney Agricultural Society, employees of the council's Direct Labour Organisation, the Bignold Park grounds man and representatives of the O.F.A., is busily engaged in clearing the show field in preparation for the next event, the Parish Cup final.

Those not wishing to offer their services hurriedly make themselves scarce.

Rings and pens have to be dismantled, repairs made to gouged up turf, animal deposits removed. The pitch will have to be relined, fences reinstalled, goalposts and nets erected. On a day when the weather has been kind, this represents a lot of work: on a day when the show has been blighted by rain, it is an onerous task indeed, requiring many hands … and sometimes these hands are not forthcoming!

On one occasion, the O.F.A. president at the time, Jim Moar of Crook in Rendall, had sought assurance at a meeting that every club would send a representative to help with preparing the pitch. As the Minute records, "All clubs readily agreed." At the next meeting, after

Michael Scott of South Ronaldsay powers in a header against Westray.

(Picture: Orkney Photographic).

Birth, Blood

the final had taken place, Mr Moar thanked *one* club rep., the secretary and himself for doing the work.

However, by 7 p.m., the field must be ready for kick off and it had been like this for most of 70 years. But now, in the final year of the century, all was to change, and the great annual football showpiece was to be moved to a brand new location at the sports complex at Pickaquoy.

How would this work? What would be the reaction of the players, the supporters bound by traditional ways, the foot soldiers at the Bignold Park? Let us find out ….

Fifteen teams set out on the trail and this included the reappearance of Burray, who had also gone as far as to submit a 'B' League team this year. Stronsay had regrettably dropped out.

First round Results

Westray	2	Harray	0
Harray	0	Westray	6
Sandwick	3	Holm	0
Holm	0	Sandwick	7
Sanday	4	Firth	0
Firth	4	Sanday	1
South Ron.	6	Burray	0
Burray	1	South Ron.	10
Orphir	0	Stromness	0
Stromness	2	Orphir	0
Rendall	5	Shapinsay	1
Shapinsay	1	Rendall	4
St Ola	1	St Andrews	1
St Andrews	1	St Ola	2

Sandwick soon got into gear, an Ian Linklater hat trick setting them on their way against Holm; Firth were eliminated by Sanday, despite Andrew Corsie scoring four in the second leg; St Ola were pushed hard by a slowly improving St Andrews.

Quarter final Results

Sanday	0	South Ron.	2
South Ron.	2	Sanday	1
Westray	4	St Ola	1
St Ola	1	Westray	1

Birsay	9	Rendall	0

Rendall scratched

Orphir	0	Sandwick	0
Sandwick	0	Orphir	0

Orphir win on penalties.

The footballing public jumped up, wide awake after these results! Sandwick had been beaten, albeit on penalties, after two dour struggles with Orphir, while Westray had got rid of St Ola. Whatever happened now, there would be an air of freshness surrounding the rest of the tournament. With both Orphir and South Ronaldsay remaining, some even dared to ask, "Could there be a first time winner to see out the century?"

Semi final Results

Birsay	1	South Ron.	1
South Ron.	4	Birsay	1
Orphir	0	Westray	4
Westray	8	Orphir	0

It was not to be Orphir, thrashed by a Westray side firing on all cylinders. However, it could be South Ronaldsay, through to their first final since 1977 but, having had their dreams dashed so often in the past, they were intent on keeping predictions well under wraps.

So, on Saturday August 14, fans of both sides and neutrals from all parts of Orkney descended upon the Pickaquoy Centre to see the very first final to be staged on the new pitch, surrounded by the 400 metre running track. It was a fine evening and many in the 700 plus crowd were able to sit on the elevated embankment on the west side and get a clear view of the action. The following groups of players then took the field on this historic occasion.

Westray: Leslie Drever, Stewart Rendall, Keith Rendall, Jack Rendall, Steven Tulloch, Mark Rendall, Ian Tulloch, Robbie Stanger, Alan Stevenson, Ralph Stevenson, Brian Sandison, Colin Kirkness, James Thomson, Chris Findlay.

South Ronaldsay: Steve Cogle, Hugh Mackenzie, Glen Thomson, Kenny Scott, Michael Scott, Andrew Cromarty, George Cogle, Finlay Wood, Kevin Walls, James Wishart, Richie Whiting, Craig Rosie, Nicky Thomson, Brian Lydon.

In a rousing first half which contained spirited play from both sides, only one goal was scored. This came from Westray's captain, Colin Kirkness, who netted in 35 minutes, sending his team into a half time lead. The crowd seemed to be enjoying the new surroundings and gave the players plenty of vocal support.

As the game progressed, South Ronaldsay applied a great deal of pressure, forcing Westray into a series of wild clearances. But, as often happens, the goal did not come from the expected source. A free kick for Westray was played into the path of Robbie Stanger, who sent it into the net to put Westray 2-0 ahead.

With only 15 minutes left, South Ronaldsay were rewarded when Michael Scott met a cross at the far post and sent a fine volley past Leslie Drever. The last few minutes were hectic for Westray but they managed to hold out and by a score of 2-1. became the first team to win on the new pitch.

Not only a new pitch, a new balcony! The Westray players climbed the Picky Centre vantage point where

Westray's Colin Kirkness claims victory in the '99 final.   (Picture: Orkney Photographic)

captain Colin Kirkness was presented with the trophy by David Henderson of the Bank of Scotland.

On the basis of their tenacious display and defensive strength, Westray probably just deserved their victory, but South Ronaldsay, who had shown a higher level of skill, would have felt hard done by to lose yet again.

It was a small measure of consolation when Michael Scott was chosen by Calvin Slater as Man of the Match.

Well, what of the new stadium? Certainly the level pitch compared favourably with the Bignold Park slope, while the grass bank helped create the effect of terracing where, in bonny weather like this, the crowd could sit and still get an unbroken view of the spectacle.

But despite some advantages, the main criticism was a loss of atmosphere. The crowd were kept back from the edge of the pitch, made to stand outside the running track, and many felt that this was too far away from the action. And if you didn't sit on the bank … and let's face it, there were plenty of evenings when that would be impossible … there were no barriers or fences to lean on. But, whenever an age old tradition is replaced there will be misgivings. As for a conclusive verdict on the new facilities, the jury was still out!

Meanwhile, up at the Bignold Park,

activity was proceeding at a very leisurely pace. No panic now! Those not dashing to the County Show dinner would have plenty of time for a yarn and a celebratory dram after the rigours of the day … then a few would make a casual inspection of the old pitch and, no matter how many hoof marks to repair or barrow loads of dung to remove, would crack open another can and agree, "Monday'll be seun enough tae mak' a stert on hid."

The triumphant Westray squad. Back row, left to right, Stewart Rendall, Keith Rendall, Jack Rendall, Leslie Drever, Steven Tulloch, Mark Rendall, Ian Tulloch, Robbie Stanger, Jim Rendall (manager). Front, Alan Stevenson, Ralph Stevenson, Brian Sandison, Colin Kirkness, Jimmy Thomson, Chris Findlay.

(Picture: Orkney Photographic)

Birth, Blood

Action photographs progress from black and white to the era of colour.
Throughout the 80s and 90s Ken Amer of Orkney Photographic strove to catch the best of the action during Parish Cup finals. Here is a selection of images.

Sandwick goalkeeper Rae Slater (now a fine photographer himself) gathers the ball in the 1989 final despite the close attentions of Paddy Kirkpatrick (St Ola). Alex Stanger and Geordie Leonard look on.

Alistair Wood (Firth) and Fraser Byers (St Ola) get to grips with each other during the 1990 final.

Kevan Harvey of Firth, left, and Ian Linklater of Sandwick clash near the centre circle during the 1997 final.

Nicky Thomson of South Ronaldsay, left, is about to be tackled by Ralph Stevenson (Westray) as George Cogle (on knees) awaits the outcome during the first final at Pickaquoy in 1999.

A New Millennium

2000: The Millennium Final

The new millennium had arrived and along with communities throughout the world, Orkney had celebrated the event in rousing fashion. Parishes had found their own ways to mark the occasion with entertainments and festivities in local halls while some had even gone as far as create their own tangible, lasting reminders. As a permanent commemoration for Orkney as a whole, the county had adopted as its principal Millennium Project, the 'Picky Centre' which was already operational and playing host to top sporting events such as the inter county football and hockey matches, junior inter county sports and of course, the Parish Cup final.

Generally, comments on the facilities had been favourable but like all new establishments, there would be teething troubles. The inquest into last year's Parish Cup final highlighted, for example, the dearth of toilet facilities: only a single toilet had been available on the night, resulting in long queues forming. But this year, undertakings were given that the full toilet facilities at the centre would be open to spectators.

What a relief! (Mind you, I don't recall the toilet facilities at the Bignold Park being particularly generous either!)

But of greater concern had been the fact that sharp eyed punters had been able to get into last year's match *for free*, by avoiding the main entrances and slipping in via the side of the building. Shock! Horror! This year there would be better stewarding to ensure that the enjoyment of watching Orkney's top parish teams in action would be paid for.

There was plenty of interest among the parishes to see who could be the first winners of the new millennium and thereby acquire the added status that would go with it. Who knows, maybe the Parish Cup would still be going a thousand years from now and historians then will look back with special interest at the name of this year's champions?

The number of entrants reached the 'magical' sixteen ensuring first round action for all teams. The team coming back this year was Stronsay and, as a special reward for their courage they were drawn against Sandwick.

First round Results

Stromness	2	Holm	4
Holm	3	Stromness	4
Orphir	2	Harray	6
Harray	3	Orphir	2
Sanday	0	St Andrews	0
St Andrews	2	Sanday	0
St Ola	0	Westray	1
Westray	2	St Ola	0
Burray	2	Shapinsay	1
Shapinsay	1	Burray	2
Sandwick	3	Stronsay	1
Stronsay	1	Sandwick	4
South Ron.	v	Rendall	

Rendall scratched

Worth noting was the fact that the once distinguished parishes of Holm, St Andrews and Harray were all capable of winning games again. But special mention should be made of Burray, who recorded their first ever Parish Cup win by defeating Shapinsay. Goals by Danny Wards and Paul Hourston set them on their way to this historic victory.

Quarter final Results

Harray	0	South Ron.	6
South Ron.	2	Harray	2
Sandwick	6	St Andrews	0
St Andrews	2	Sandwick	5
Holm	0	Birsay	3
Birsay	2	Holm	3
Burray	0	Westray	7
Westray	6	Burray	2

Mostly very clear winners in that round although Holm gave yet more strong hints of future promise. Birsay, who had not featured much of late would now face Sandwick while South Ronaldsay would try to avenge last year's final defeat by Westray.

Semi final Results

Sandwick	1	Birsay	1
Birsay	1	Sandwick	4
South Ron.	0	Westray	0
Westray	5	South Ron.	1

Birsay and the 'Hope put up stubborn resistance in the first legs but by the second game, both Sandwick and Westray had the measure of their opponents and ran out convincing winners. So the scene was set for a Millennium Final between two strong sides, cup holders versus habitual winners. It should be a close one to call!

Picky was blessed with another beautiful County Show evening and a large crowd of 1,200 plus *paid* their way through the gates. Both teams were along familiar lines. Westray were delighted to have back one of their top men, Raymond Rendall, who had not been available last year while Sandwick were still able to put out a very well balanced squad ranging from seasoned veterans, who had played close on 20 finals, to a clutch of players right in their prime.

Teams were as follows:

Westray: Leslie Drever, Stewart Rendall, Jack Rendall, Steven Tulloch, Mark Rendall, Ian Tulloch, Robbie Stanger, Alan Stevenson, Keith Rendall, Raymond Rendall, Bryan Sandison, Colin Kirkness, Jimmy Thomson, Chris Findlay.

Sandwick: Erlend Poke, Ian Linklater, Steven Wylie, Michael Grieve, Kenny Garriock, Erlend Grieve, Stevie Linklater, Gary Dowell, Marcus Wood, Allan Spence, Steven Poke, Gareth Wood, Mark Seator, Stevie Slater.

Birth, Blood

The message in the Sandwick dressing room must have been, "Hit 'em early and hit 'em hard!" The crowd were still filing in when Allan Spence put them ahead with a well hit shot and, while still trying to recover from that shock, Westray were stunned again when the same player put Sandwick two up in seven minutes.

Westray recovered after this and got to half time without losing any more goals and they should have got back in the game after the interval when they were awarded a penalty for hand ball. Unfortunately for them, Alan Stevenson's shot was saved. Then, on 60 minutes Mark Rendall put the ball into his own net while attempting a clearance. 3-0 to Sandwick.

Westray now threw all their resources into attack but this left them exposed at the back and further Sandwick goals were added by Gary Dowell and Allan Spence, who completed a fine hat trick.

This left Sandwick as 5-0 winners and it was captain Marcus Wood who led his team on to the balcony to receive the cup from David Henderson of the Bank of Scotland.

Well before the end, some neutrals in the crowd had begun to drift away … and it wasn't to make use of the ample toilet facilities on offer. Rather, they were disenchanted at the prospect of yet another Sandwick victory. However, they could not deny that the better team had won, although Westray were unlucky to lose by so wide a margin. Their feelings of disgust were summed up in a comment overheard from one of their dejected players. "I might as weel hiv bidden heem and baled hey!"

Although those yearning for a change would disagree, it was fitting that Sandwick had won the first cup of the new century. They had been beyond question, the best side in the last one and now they were setting the bench mark again. It would be up to the others to end this domination and establish their own dynasty … and it must be possible soon! Surely Calvin Poke, Michael Grieve, Stevie Slater, Kenny Garriock, etc.. couldn't go on forever?

Well, certainly not to the next millennium … or could they?

Now, there's a thought!

2001: Finalists fight the elements

Long before the 2001 County Show night 'grand finale' was due to take place, members of the public knew that things would not be quite the same as normal. The reason? *The County Show had been cancelled!* Not only that, so also was the Dounby Show, the East Mainland Show, the Sanday Show … because, for the first time since 1960, parts of the country had been ravaged by Foot and Mouth Disease.

As yet, the plague had not made its way into Orkney but memories of that previous outbreak were still raw and precautions against its return could be seen everywhere. To hold agricultural shows, with the usual large influx of visitors, in such a climate of fear would have been foolish in the extreme.

However, rather than have nothing at all on the traditional County Show day, some diehard souls got together to plan an 'Alternative County Show' in the Bignold Park, which would include a Horse Show followed by Show Jumping, a Dog Show and a Vintage Display. Down at Pickaquoy, Orkney Athletics Club planned an afternoon of 'It's a Knockout' style games with emphasis firmly on fun!

All was not lost therefore, and of course, from a football enthusiast's point of view, there were no plans to cancel the Parish Cup so happily, it would be *Business as usual* on the Saturday evening.

By the middle of May, the first round got underway. The only change to the line up this year was the withdrawal of Rendall.

First round Results

Birsay	4	Stromness	0
Stromness	4	Birsay	1

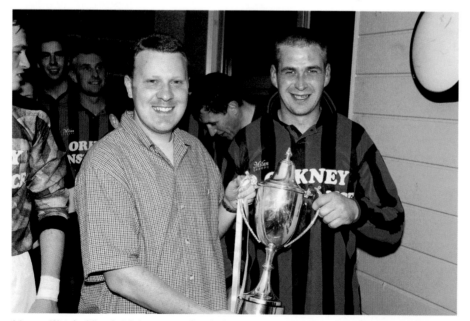

Marcus Wood of Sandwick is presented with the Parish Cup by the sponsor's representative, David Henderson of the Bank of Scotland. (Picture: Orkney Photographic).

Burray	1	Holm	2
Holm	2	Burray	1
Shapinsay	1	Firth	9
Firth	4	Shapinsay	0
Harray	0	South Ron.	4
South Ron.	4	Harray	0
St Ola	1	Sanday	0
Sanday	1	St Ola	3
Sandwick	9	Stronsay	0
Stronsay	1	Sandwick	5
Orphir	1	St Andrews	10
St Andrews	2	Orphir	1

It was the last result which created most interest. Just as in Holm, the new crop of youngsters emerging in St Andrews were giving hope to a parish which had been 'asleep' for some time … and to develop their abilities that bit more, the club had entered a good competitive team in the 'B' League.

Quarter final Results

Sandwick	6	South Ron.	2
South Ron.	1	Sandwick	0
Firth	3	Birsay	2
Birsay	2	Firth	3
St Andrews	2	St Ola	3
St Ola	4	St Andrews	1
Westray	3	Holm	1
Holm	3	Westray	6

Although it was the usual crop of well established teams which got through, the losers had all provided decent opposition with both St Andrews and Holm continuing to show promise. The semi finals now saw a repeat of last year's final when Westray were overwhelmed by Sandwick.

Semi final Results

St Ola	3	Firth	0
Firth	2	St Ola	2
Sandwick	6	Westray	0
Westray	0	Sandwick	0

The finalists were virtually decided after the first leg games. For Firth, St Ola's lead proved insurmountable while Sandwick's devastating burst of scoring killed off Westray. A hat trick by Marcus Wood and further goals by Kenny Garriock, Jimmy Sinclair and Stevie Linklater ensured that the perennial winners would once again be there to defend the trophy.

'Not the County Show Day' dawned dry but with a particularly cold, biting wind for the time of year. Activities planned for the day got going and for a while, all seemed well. But as the morning progressed, cloud layers steadily built up until by dinner time, the skies opened. The deluge was such that the afternoon programme of Show Jumping was abandoned on the grounds of safety, although down at Pickaquoy, the games went on in the pouring rain.

Organisers concluded that this year's Show was jinxed in every way.

Any prospect that the weather would clear for the evening soon disappeared as the wind began to pick up. By kick off time, sheeting rain was being driven across the pitch by a ferocious wind.

But the game went on … before a crowd estimated at little over *50*, the smallest ever to witness a Parish Cup final.

The players who had probably never ventured out of doors, let alone play football, in worse conditions were as follows:

St Ola: Davy Leonard, Eoin Learmonth, Keith Leonard, Wayne Monkman, Roy Foubister, Kevin Groundwater, Kevin Hancock, Fraser Byers, Paul Kemp, Eoin Anderson, Rodney Spence, Ivan Johnston, Paul Kirkpatrick.

Sandwick: Erlend Poke, Michael Grieve, Steven Wylie, Ian Linklater, Gary Dowell, Stevie Linklater, Marcus Wood, Steven Poke, Stevie Slater, Kenny Garriock, Erlend Grieve, Mark Seator, Jimmy Sinclair, Calvin Poke.

Sandwick played with the driving wind and rain behind them in the first half but St Ola gave as good as they got with a few decent strikes on goal. Inevitably, though, it was Sandwick

The rugby's club's marquee for the traditional county show dance was literally blown away in the gales.
(Picture: Rae Slater)

Birth, Blood

who scored first, when Gary Dowell hit a shot past Leonard from the edge of the box after 15 minutes. Shortly afterwards, Steven Poke put Sandwick two up with a well taken goal.

But by holding the score to 2-0, St Ola felt they still had a chance with the elements behind them. And, boy, were they behind them! So strong had the wind now become that a marquee erected by the rugby club for the annual dance was blown down. But still the warriors battled gamely on!

St Ola attacked relentlessly without reward until, with 20 minutes left, Kevin Groundwater connected perfectly and the ball flew into the bottom corner of the Sandwick net.

The floodlights now came on to illuminate the heroic struggle and simply add to the surreal atmosphere.

As St Ola strained for the equaliser which would have taken the game into extra time, imagine 30 more minutes in this tempest, further punishment was avoided when Steven Poke broke away to score Sandwick's third, and decisive goal. The sighs of relief could almost be heard above the howling of the wind!

So ended one of the strangest cup finals ever. Another Sandwick win was complete when Steven Poke received the trophy from David Henderson of the Bank of Scotland, but the ceremony was witnessed by scarcely any spectators. They had staggered, numbed and dripping, to the sanctuary of their homes.

So, another cup for Sandwick and great credit was due for their unwavering winning mentality, no matter what the circumstances. But all things considered, the Orkney public looked forward to brighter things next year: an end to the threat of Foot and Mouth disease; the return of the County Show, complete with better weather; and, on the football front, maybe something just a little bit different.

The smallest crowd ever for a Parish Cup final take shelter behind the Picky Centre from driving winds and lashing rain..
(Picture: Rae Slater)

It was win number 18 for Sandwick in 2001. Back row, left to right, Calvin Poke, Gareth Wood, Kenny Garriock, Erlend Poke, Michael Grieve, Steven Wylie, Gary Dowell, Mark Seator, Alan Spence, Ian Linklater, Graham Poke. Front, Chris Wood, Erlend Grieve, Stevie Linklater, Jimmy Sinclair, Steven Poke, Marcus Wood, Stevie Slater.
(Picture: Rae Slater)

2002:
Sandwick see off familiar rivals

And it came to pass that the wise men cast their eyes to the east … and there appeared unto them a star. And lo, the star which they saw in the east went before them, till it stood over the land whence the new messiah would come. And they sayeth unto one another, "Behold, the light is too faint … "

Did it stand over South Ronaldsay, the land of eternal 'Hope'? Here were to be found young men bearing the names of a past generation of great sportsmen: Cromarty, Anderton, Whyte …. If they could form a blend with the Scotts, the Cogles, the Thomsons … alas, this land had promised so much for so long ….

Had the star stopped above St Andrews, a land steeped in tradition and triumphs of old, now the kingdom of Baillies, Eunsons, Rendall, Kirkpatrick, … and Robbie Norquoy, he of impeccable parish pedigree? Had their time come again?

Or, had it hovered over Holm? More youthful promise here: Aim, Dearness, Flett, Horne … and others taking up residence within its bounds. Young ladies have been tempting footballers into matrimony and bringing them home to stay!

And there was Marty Flett!

And one sayeth unto the other, "Methinks the light shineth brightest here!"

Sixteen teams once again set out on the quest for glory.

First round Results

St Andrews	6	Harray	1
Harray	1	St Andrews	3
Holm	0	Sandwick	2
Sandwick	2	Holm	0
South Ron.	1	Stronsay	1
Stronsay	2	South Ron.	1
Westray	0	Stromness	2
Stromness	3	Westray	3
Shapinsay	1	St Ola	2
St Ola	4	Shapinsay	0
Sanday	5	Orphir	0
Orphir	0	Sanday	4

Firth v Burray

Result not recorded. Firth go through.

Birsay v Rendall

Result not recorded. Birsay go through.

Ah well! So much for 'Eastern Promise.' Only one of the three 'hopefuls' left. Holm had run Sandwick reasonably close, losing late goals in both games but surely the performance of the round belonged to Stronsay, who produced their finest display in the Parish Cup. St Andrews, having decided to emulate their forebears exactly 50 years ago by entering a team in the 'A' League, looked well equipped to make an impact this year.

Quarter final Results

Birsay	1	St Ola	2
St Ola	4	Birsay	1
Stronsay	5	Stromness	1
Stromness	2	Stronsay	0
Firth	0	Sandwick	2
Sandwick	2	Firth	1
St Andrews	2	Sanday	0
Sanday	0	St Andrews	3

St Ola and Sandwick were back in the semi finals along with St Andrews but what about the fourth member of the group? "Stronsay!" you utter in wonderment. They were here on merit all right but the question being asked was, "How did this come about?"

Well, a favourable set of circumstances really. The island had a fairly limited pool of players and these ranged from Paul Miller, manager, coach and general organiser, still playing well into his 40s, to a number of promising juniors. However, this year some of the young players had been gaining valuable experience playing for league teams: Damien Stout and Gary Dennison (Thorfinn); Graham Miller (South Ronaldsay); John Miller and Trevor Shearer (Shapinsay) and they were all available to Stronsay for Parish Cup duty.

Add to that the fact that, for once, the Stronsay pitch had been dry in the early part of the season and the players had been able to get together for training and practice games. So, instead of arriving at the tournament cold, they were well warmed up and the results now spoke for themselves.

Now if they could go one step further … Stronsay v St Andrews in the final, wouldn't that be the answer to countless prayers?

Semi final Results

Stronsay	1	St Ola	4
St Ola	3	Stronsay	3
Sandwick	1	St Andrews	1
St Andrews	1	Sandwick	4

But it was not to be! Yet there were signs that the miracle could have happened. Stronsay had abandoned their normal 'defend and counter attack' game in the first leg and attempted to match St Ola's more skilful approach … with disastrous results. The return to Plan A in the return showed what might have been possible. But it had been a memorable campaign.

St Andrews gave their legion of fans hope of a first final in 40 years during their home leg but again Sandwick's overall strength propelled them to a meeting with their old rivals on County Show night.

No problems this year. Foot and Mouth disease had been eradicated, the weather was fine and rather more than 50 spectators turned up.

The teams were along familiar lines although a few younger players, Erik Bews, Eoin Anderson and Steven

Budge for example, were now establishing themselves in the St Ola squad. But alongside them, keeping control of their youthful exuberance, was Fraser Byers, still competitive as ever at the age of 51!

Teams were as follows:

St Ola: John Thomson, Fraser Byers, John Stephen, Kevin Groundwater, Erik Bews, Wayne Monkman, Eoin Anderson, Kevin Hancock, Paul Kemp, Roy Foubister, Steven Tulloch, Steven Budge, Paul Kirkpatrick, James Linklater.

Sandwick: Erlend Poke, Mark Seator, Calvin Poke, Kenny Garrioch, Steven Wylie, Gary Dowell, Erlend Grieve, Allan Spence, Marcus Wood, Gareth Wood, Stevie Linklater, Jimmy Sinclair, Jonathan Spence, Steven Poke.

In the early stages Sandwick were on the receiving end as St Ola mounted a number of attacks but the closest they came to scoring was when Paul Kirkpatrick's shot came back off the post. Sandwick gradually settled and took the lead after 15 minutes when Gary Dowell made a long run from his own penalty area and hit a 30 yard drive past Thomson.

This fine goal proved to be the only score of the half, despite

numerous very good efforts by St Ola. Erlend Poke in the Sandwick goal was having a splendid match. The second half was hotly contested but many chances were missed and St Ola's frustration came to a head shortly before the end when Wayne Monkman, who had been at the heart of all his team's best moves, was sent off for retaliation.

This signalled the end for St Ola and once again they had to join in the polite applause as the Parish Cup was awarded to Sandwick for the sixth time in seven years.

Final score, Sandwick 1 St Ola 0.

No change at the top then but still the optimists clung to any vestige of hope. News filtered through of further developments in the matrimonial and property markets down Holm way. And moving in to this new expanding commuter belt were not just any old Tom, Dick or Harry but a very precious commodity indeed! Footballers!

And the wise men turned to the East and lo, the star shone brightly! When they saw the star, they rejoiced with exceeding great joy!

2003:
Eastern star delivers promise

Before the start of this momentous season, Holm possessed a solid Parish Cup team with moderate prospects. Martin Flett and some of the young brigade have been mentioned but to them could be added the experience of Stuart Flett (previous winner with Birsay), Bruce Moar, Alan Scott and goalkeeper Robbie Thomson. Colin Risbridger, an inter county 'cap' for both Caithness and Orkney had then moved into the parish last year and helped to raise the level a further notch. But the team was still short of a few quality players to enable them to compete with the best.

Then, as if at a given signal, fate (or Cupid!) decided to lend a hand. Robbie Stanger, a previous winner with both Sandwick and Westray, now owned a farm in Holm and decided to commit himself to his adopted parish. Kevin Hancock, a previous winner with St Ola, had married a local girl and bought a house in the parish. After a little persuasion, he decided to follow suit and play for Holm.

Alan 'Bu' Stevenson, a former winner with Westray, also married a Holm girl and bought a house there. He made his commitment to 'all things in Holm.' The irresistible qualities of these Holm girls, well, one in particular, then brought Neil Ewing, a former player with Dundee Timex in the Midlands Amateur League, to live in the parish!

All of a sudden, a team of once average potential was being regarded as a red hot tip for the big prize itself. And with John Copland, several times winner with Harray in the 60s and 70s at the managerial helm, they would not be allowed to waver too far off course.

The serious approach to this campaign was underlined by the decision to create a pitch in the parish. Not having a league team in recent years, Holm had been content to play their parish fixtures in Burray. But this would no longer do!

So, after scouring the length and breadth of the domain, it was decided that a field at Wilderness, on Robbie Stanger's land, would be most suitable. Robbie's coos would have to graze elsewhere for the summer. The pitch was then carefully measured and laid out. Finally, everyone was ready, eagerly awaiting the draw for this year's tournament. Fifteen entries meant one team would get a bye.

That team? Holm!

Ah well patience required.

First round Results

Sandwick	4	Shapinsay	0
Shapinsay	0	Sandwick	6
Rendall	0	St Andrews	12
St Andrews	8	Rendall	1
Harray	v	Birsay	
Harray scratched			
Sanday	1	St Ola	0
St Ola	5	Sanday	3
Westray	4	Orphir	2
Orphir	2	Westray	2

Firth	1	Stromness	2
Stromness	3	Firth	7
South Ron.	1	Stronsay	1
Stronsay	4	South Ron.	2

Stronsay proved last year's performance was no fluke by accounting for South Ronaldsay again. Meanwhile Sandwick and St Ola both advanced, although the latter were given a severe fright by Sanday. Now to the quarter finals, where Firth were the first visitors to Wilderness Park.

Quarter final Results

Birsay	5	Stronsay	0
Stronsay	1	Birsay	2
St Andrews	1	St Ola	0
St Ola	2	St Andrews	0
Westray	0	Sandwick	5
Sandwick	9	Westray	3
Holm	1	Firth	0
Firth	0	Holm	2

The backers of St Andrews would have to wait for another year as their improving team fell just short again. Sandwick were again in ominous form and Birsay gave hints of progress. Holm, meanwhile, proceeded to the semi finals for the first time since 1984. Next, they had to face the might of Sandwick.

Semi final Results

Birsay	1	St Ola	4
St Ola	3	Birsay	1
Holm	3	Sandwick	1
Sandwick	0	Holm	0

Holm had done it and reached their first final in over 50 years! The contest had been a bruising encounter, especially in the first leg. Here a player from each side had been sent off, Paterson of Holm and Dowell of Sandwick, but two goals by the veteran Stuart Flett had proved the difference between the teams.

Hardly able to comprehend their misfortune at being defeated on what felt like a very small playing area, Sandwick had the dimensions of

the Wilderness pitch checked, but everything complied with the rules.

The 0-0 score line belied a fiercely fought but sporting second leg and Holm emerged the winners, much to the delight of their multitude of vocal and highly colourful fans. Even, the pantomime horse did a dance of delight!

The other tie was tame and predictable by comparison with this carnival as St Ola reached their third consecutive final with a fairly easy win over Birsay.

So the stage was set for a cup final which had the Orkney public buzzing with anticipation. The prospect of a new team with a realistic chance of winning saw the biggest crowd for many years swarm into Picky and fittingly, it was a pleasant sunny evening. Many of the neutrals sprawled comfortably on the grass banks while Holm hordes made their boisterous presence felt along the touchlines, as the following teams lined up:

Holm: Robbie Thomson, Bruce Moar, Martin Flett, Robbie Stanger, Graeme Horne, Neil Ewing, Kevin Hancock, Colin Risbridger, Alan Aim, John Dearness, Stuart Flett, Alan Scott, Magnus Flett, Alan Stevenson.

St Ola: Davy Leonard, Fraser Byers, Roy Foubister, Kevin Groundwater, Francis Learmonth, Erlend Hutchison, Paul Kemp, Wayne Monkman, Scott Tulloch, Steven Tulloch, Erik Bews, Eoin Anderson, Steven Budge, Duncan Gray.

Well, the game did not disappoint. Both sides played with great commitment and energy and in the early stages a host of chances went begging at either end. It took a penalty converted in 35 minutes by Paul Kemp of St Ola to break the deadlock but after this setback, Holm simply redoubled their efforts.

They got back on level terms five

Birth, Blood

minutes later when John Dearness, who had been harassing the opposing defence constantly with his strong running, forced his way past three defenders to fire the ball into the corner of the net. The Holm supporters celebrated wildly and turned up the volume.

The second half started and Dearness continued to menace the opposition. One of his shots bounced back off a St Ola post, and then Scott Tulloch was booked trying to stop him forcing his way through again.

In a pulsating period of play chances fell to both teams but, with only 15 minutes to go, the crowd were beginning to wonder if they were going to get an extra half hour of this unrelenting action. Very soon they were to get their answer.

Alan Stevenson, who had been taken on as a sub., raced on to a through ball and hit a powerful drive underneath the keeper to give Holm the lead. St Ola now threw everyone forward but their last chance disappeared when Scott Tulloch was sent off for tripping … you've guessed, John Dearness!

The final whistle was the signal for the release of sheer ecstatic joy among Holm players and supporters. Not since 1950 had citizens of that parish been able to relish such a moment. The entire crowd, many leaping, dancing and hugging each other now made their way to the presentation, where captain Marty Flett accepted the trophy on behalf of his team.

After paying tribute to his players

and supporters, he dedicated the cup win to the late Bertie Thomson, father of Holm's goalkeeper Robbie, who had worked tirelessly to keep the parish team alive during many very lean years for Holm football.

All lovers of football and this competition in particular now offered their congratulations to the winners. A breath of fresh air had been badly needed and the whole 'Holm thing' had provided just that. A new team, a new crowd of ultra enthusiastic fans, new champions!

It felt as if a whole new chapter in Parish Cup history was just about to unfold.

Victorious Holm in 2003. Back row, left to right, Neil Cormack, Neil Ewing, Kevin Hancock, Robbie Stanger, Alan Scott, Colin Risbridger, Marty Flett, Stuart Flett, Alan Stevenson. Front, Craig Horne, Magnus Flett, Robbie Thomson, John Dearness, Graeme Horne, Bruce Moar and his children, Alan Aim.

2004:
Extra time in classic climax

As other parishes had experienced in the past, particularly when it is not a regular occurrence, the winning of this trophy gives a major boost to the community spirit. So it was the case in Holm. There was a positive, confident air about the place and talk now turned to building on this success and maintaining momentum.

The first important decision was that Holm would field a regular team in the 'B' League next season. Most of the Parish Cup players were only too happy to play although a few decided not to renounce their loyalty to their regular club. However, with plenty of youngsters coming through, it should be a very respectable team which wore Holm colours.

Next, where would the team play? Robbie Stanger was needing his field back but local farmer and contractor Erlend Flett, granted them the use of a field at Hurtiso, opposite the Holm kirk. On a bit of a slope certainly, but a flat, even surface and this would do splendidly until plans took shape for a more permanent home.

Now what about new signings?

Winning the Parish Cup again was the main goal so the emphasis must be on fielding local footballers. In this regard, at least one newcomer was available. Another Holm girl had woven her magic spell and now a very accomplished Shetland footballer, James Henry, ex Lerwick Thistle, was resident in the parish and ready to fight for the cause.

Finally, just to prove that this was a very modern, go ahead enterprise, the club launched its own official website, 'Holm Rulz', under the diligent stewardship of loyal supporter Hazel Berston. Soon this was to provide a veritable trove of information on Holm teams of the past and updates of all the current on goings, news, fixtures, pictures, profiles of local heroes.

It was 'all systems go' then as the Parish Cup season 2004 came around but Holm would not have it all their own way. Sandwick would be festering for revenge and the return of their rightful crown; St Ola would be thoroughly disgruntled at losing three finals in a row; St Andrews, meanwhile, still promised much. Last year, the St Andrews 'A' team, minus a couple of key parish players, had won the Challenge Shield trophy beating the mighty Thorfinn in the final. Now, if they could only replicate that form in this year's Parish Cup.

Popular as ever, this year a record *17* parishes entered so a preliminary round was necessary.

Preliminary Round

| St Andrews | 3 | Westray | 1 |
| Westray | 0 | St Andrews | 7 |

An astonishing score line, especially in the leg in Westray, which should serve notice that St Andrews meant business this year.

First round Results

Evie	1	Birsay	0
Birsay	2	Evie	4
Orphir	3	Stromness	1
Stromness	4	Orphir	0
St Andrews	2	Harray	2
Harray	1	St Andrews	5
Firth	1	Sanday	2
Sanday	1	Firth	1
Shapinsay	0	Stronsay	1
Stronsay	2	Shapinsay	3

Shapinsay win on away goals.

Holm	4	Rendall	3
Rendall	0	Holm	2
Burray	1	St Ola	8
St Ola	13	Burray	1
South Ron.	0	Sandwick	6
Sandwick	5	South Ron.	3

There were notable performances from both Evie and Rendall,

reflecting the gradual resurgence of Rendall as a 'B' League force. There were a number of very promising young players 'oot north' but as ever, when it came to parish duty, the riches were divided. It took goals by Stuart Flett and Neil Cormack in the away leg to see Holm finally overcome Rendall. Now a mouth watering prospect awaited with another tie against Sandwick. If it was anything like last year's encounter, it would not be for the faint hearted!

Quarter final Results

Sanday	2	Shapinsay	1
Shapinsay	0	Sanday	3
Evie	0	St Andrews	4
St Andrews	6	Evie	2
St Ola	8	Stromness	2
Stromness	2	St Ola	7
Holm	1	Sandwick	1
Sandwick	2	Holm	2

Holm win on away goals.

Three of the semi finalists qualified fairly easily but bare statistics do not come close to telling the drama of the fourth tie. After a closely contested draw in Holm, it looked as if home advantage might be good enough for Sandwick, and once Steven Poke had netted twice in the return leg, predictions appeared to be coming true.

John Dearness pulled one back but time was running out. Towards the end of injury time, Sandwick carelessly conceded a corner and from the resultant kick, Colin Risbridger met the ball with his head and it ended up in the back of the net off a defender. With the last kick of the game, Holm had not only survived but proceeded to the semi final on the away goals rule.

With Sandwick out of the way, next on the menu was another contest to savour, an East Mainland derby against St Andrews. St Ola, who had scored 36 goals in four games, would face Sanday.

Birth, Blood

Semi final Results

St Andrews	0	Holm	3
Holm	2	St Andrews	1
Sanday	1	St Ola	2
St Ola	3	Sanday	1

The St Andrews v Holm tie was much closer than the score suggests. In the first leg, Holm simply took their chances better with a late Graeme Horne penalty adding to earlier strikes by Stuart Flett and David Tait. But the crowd which turned out for the return indicated clearly that the outcome was not taken for granted.

I recall arriving, early for once, at the Hurtiso ground at 7.05p.m. for a 7.30p.m. kick off, only to find not a single space in the first rank of cars which entirely surrounded the pitch. In addition the St Andrews fans lined up along one touch line facing their Holm counterparts along the other.

In a lively atmosphere, Thorfinn Eunson gave St Andrews hope before John Dearness equalised and then sealed victory from the penalty spot. This sent Holm into the final again where their opponents were once more St Ola, who overcame stout resistance by Sanday.

If a repeat of the same final implies a degree of tedium, forget it! This was a game to remember, played on another glorious summer's evening in front of a huge crowd, reminiscent of cup final attendances of years gone by.

Holm lined up with only two changes from last year. James Henry replaced Bruce Moar, while Magnus Flett swapped places with Stewart Flett, the latter dropping to the bench. St Ola contained mostly familiar faces, although they were minus the services of the influential Paul Kemp.

Teams were as follows:

Holm: Robbie Thomson, Martin Flett, Robbie Stanger, Alan Aim, Colin Risbridger, Kevin Hancock, James Henry, Neil Ewing, Graeme Horne, John Dearness, Magnus Flett. Subs: Stuart Flett, Craig Horne, Neil MacIntosh, Alan Stevenson, David Tait.

St Ola: Davy Leonard, Francis Learmonth, Erik Bews, Kevin Groundwater, Roy Foubister, Erlend Hutchison, Wayne Monkman, Eoin Anderson, Steven Tulloch, Steven Budge, Ivan Johnston. Subs: James Linklater. Richard Kemp, Ryan Craigie, Scott Tulloch, James V. G. Linklater.

Spectators were still coming in or browsing the magnificent programme produced by the new sponsors of the competition, *The Orcadian* newspaper, when Steven Budge sent a beautiful pass to Roy Foubister, who slipped the ball past Thomson in the Holm

St Ola's Eoin Anderson blasts the ball past Thomson to give his side the lead in extra time.
(Picture: Rae Slater)

& Boundaries

goal. This was a severe setback and it took some time for the cup holders to settle but their anxieties were calmed after 30 minutes when dependable goal scorer, John Dearness, was on the spot to tap in a cross which was missed by the St Ola defence.

Holm played more composed football now and took the lead just before half-time when Neil Ewing found Dearness with a pass and his shot went across Leonard into the far corner of the net. Holm clung on to this lead thanks to some great work by Robbie Thomson in goal and as time passed, their army of fans began to prepare for another great night of celebration.

Stoppage time arrived and even keeper Leonard joined in St Ola attacks but it seemed as if Holm would hold out. Then, with only seconds remaining, Wayne Monkman gained possession, showed great control and composure, and floated a perfectly placed shot into the top corner of the net, 2-2 … and the final whistle blew!

This last gasp equaliser had a devastating effect on Holm. Psychologically, they were crushed!

St Ola on the other hand, were buoyed up and drove into the attack as extra time commenced. Soon Eoin Anderson put them ahead with a powerful drive. Holm shuffled their team in a bid to salvage the game, but to no avail.

With only six minutes to go, Steven Tulloch put the result beyond doubt by slipping home the rebound after Ryan Craigie's shot had been saved. Shortly afterwards, referee Melvin Johnston called 'time up' and St Ola had emerged victors of a dramatic final by four goals to two.

The Holm contingent would have found this moment hard to bear. After being on the crest of a wave for over a year they came crashing down in a matter of seconds with an almighty splash! But given the character of the people concerned, depression would not last too long. They would become philosophical; after all, Holm had only survived by the last kick in the semi final, and by the time the cup had been handed over to St Ola by Christine Miller, wife of *The Orcadian* owner, James Miller, some would have concluded that Holm would emerge next year all the stronger for the experience.

For St Ola, who had last won the trophy back in 1995, it was just reward at last for a team showing bags of 'never say die' spirit.

As for the general viewing public? They would have felt a lot of sympathy for the losers but as they left the ground, more than one found consolation in the remark, "Ah weel, hid's fine tae see things gan roond!"

Roy Foubister, the triumphant St Ola skipper, is congratulated by Christine Miller representing the tournament's new sponsors, The Orcadian. (Picture: Rae Slater)

Jubilant St Ola celebrate under the Picky floodlights. Back row, left to right, Scott Tulloch, Erik Bews, Erlend Hutchison, Eoin Anderson, Davy Leonard, Ryan Craigie, Duncan Gray, Steven Tulloch, Richard Kemp. Front, James Linklater, Steven Budge, Francis Learmonth, Roy Foubister, Wayne Monkman, Kevin Groundwater, Ivan Johnston. (Picture: Rae Slater)

2005: Sandwick notch up 20 victories

Once more in the second week of May, there were clear signs that summer was nearly with us. A gale force north westerly wind drove frequent hail showers across a grey, bleak landscape. Dark shadows darted across the Bay of Firth while a lone 'scarfie', the only creature sufficiently motivated to brave the elements, struggled to keep himself upright at the water's edge.

Being a Sunday, no one but an 'extreme sports' enthusiast or a fool would venture out, but that day every accessible vantage point surrounding Firth football pitch was crammed with cars, the occupants securely ensconced within. Any latecomers had to be turned away, unable to squeeze by the barricade of vehicles strung across the entrance to the park.

Between further bursts of lancing sleet, reluctant footballers, many clad in gloves and woollen hats, were pushed from the safety of the changing rooms but dashed back inside as another salvo threatened. However, outside they had to go because the photographers were demanding pictures to help launch this year's Press coverage of what continued to be one of the most significant events in the Orkney Sporting calendar, the Parish Cup.

The resultant photographs of fourteen grimacing individuals leaning into the teeth of the wind, graced the pages of next week's paper, along with a report telling a very unlikely story.

Holm, many people's favourites to do well again this year had been beaten 2-0 by Firth. Admittedly they had been missing a few key players, Colin Risbridger's departure to live in Westray had been a big blow, but Firth had adapted better to the conditions and deserved their win. Still, Holm would surely reverse this in the return leg.

But it was not to be. Again they were not at full strength and despite scoring twice to draw level, Firth's away goal was good enough to take them through. For Holm what a difference two years make! A score check reads:

Preliminary round

| Firth | 2 | Holm | 0 |
| Holm | 2 | Firth | 1 |

The first round proper now got underway with 16 teams left in the competition.

First round Results

Westray	3	Sanday	1
Sanday	1	Westray	1
Shapinsay	0	St Andrews	2
St Andrews	3	Shapinsay	1
Firth	0	St Ola	3
St Ola	3	Firth	2
South Ron.	1	Birsay	1
Birsay	2	South Ron.	3
Evie	2	Sandwick	7
Sandwick	12	Evie	0
Harray	6	Stronsay	1
Stronsay	0	Harray	2
Stromness	0	Rendall	3
Rendall	4	Stromness	1
Burray	3	Orphir	3
Orphir	5	Burray	3

The most dramatic moment of the round took place in Dounby in the return leg of Birsay v South Ronaldsay. The home side were leading 2-1 into injury time when two very late strikes from Andrew Cromarty and Martin Whyte sent the 'Hope into the next round. The mini pitch invasion which followed indicated no lack of passion for this success starved side.

Quarter final Results

| Rendall | 0 | St Ola | 1 |
| St Ola | 7 | Rendall | 0 |

Westray	1	South Ron.	2
South Ron.	1	Westray	4
Orphir	0	St Andrews	4
St Andrews	2	Orphir	1
Harray	0	Sandwick	3
Sandwick	4	Harray	1

Again the team catching most attention was South Ronaldsay. After a fine away win in Westray they approached the return with too much complacency; a number of their players failed to observe an eve of match curfew and they were soundly beaten by a spirited Westray team. As far as the semi finals were concerned, the ties now took on a familiar appearance.

Semi final Results

St Andrews	1	Sandwick	2
Sandwick	1	St Andrews	0
Westray	2	St Ola	0
St Ola	3	Westray	1

Westray win on away goal.

After a break in domestic football for the island games in Shetland, to which Orkney sent a side, the semi finals were played. St Andrews worked hard in the home leg, taking the lead through Erlend Eunson but two second half goals by Stevie Linklater and Steven Poke gave Sandwick a valuable away lead which they consolidated in a narrow home victory.

Westray's win over St Ola was full of drama. Early in the second leg, St Ola had wiped out Westray's lead. Two goals by Wayne Monkman and a penalty by Eoin Anderson seemed to have set them on the road to the final.

But Westray scored early in the second half through Nicky Watson, then clung on in a backs to wall display to reach the final for the first time since 1999, on the away goal rule.

County Show night had come round again. A thick, clinging mist enveloped Kirkwall and the rain which had been threatening since late afternoon began in earnest. Despite the prospect of yet another miserable evening, in a generally miserable summer, a big crowd turned out.

Westray's supporters were clearly visible, noisy and colourful, carrying banners and wearing T-shirts bearing the slogan *I Love Westray!* Sandwick's, accustomed to success, were more restrained by comparison, but exuded a well practised air of confidence, as the two teams to contest the final of Orkney's premier football competition marched proudly together on to the pitch at Pickaquoy.

Both teams had undergone some changes since their last final appearances. For Sandwick, their most significant gain was Paul Kirkpatrick, formerly of St Ola, who had taken up residence in the parish, while Westray were blessed with the arrival of Colin Risbridger, a vital member of Holm's two cup final teams.

Readers will note the absence of two rather familiar names from the Sandwick ranks.

For the first time in over *30 years*, the names of Calvin Poke and Michael Grieve were missing. With grand totals of 19 and 18 cup winner's medals, respectively, they had established individual records which would possibly never be surpassed, but far from deserting the cause now, they continued to share management duties. Westray could be assured therefore, that the Sandwick will to win was still alive and kicking!

Full teams were as follows:

Sandwick: Erlend Poke, Paul Kirkpatrick, Mark Garson, Gareth Wood, Ian Linklater, Steven Wylie, Cameron Garson, Erlend Grieve, Marcus Wood, Steven Poke, Stevie Linklater. Subs: Kevan Harvey, Dale Slater, Jamie Peppitt.

Westray: Stewart Rendall, Trevor Rendall, Raymond Rendall snr., Colin Risbridger, Calvin Rendall, Steven Tulloch, Johnny Drever, Colin Kirkness, Raymond Rendall jnr., Nicky Watson, Alan Thomson. Subs: Raymond Moodie, George Thomson, Mark Rendall.

The first half, which was played in increasingly wet and gloomy conditions, was mostly dictated by Westray. Colin Risbridger and Raymond Rendall snr, controlled the middle of the field, while the speedy Watson and Thomson caused problems down the left. It was fitting that, just before half time Thomson's pass sent Watson clear and his powerful left foot shot gave Erlend Poke no chance. 1-0 to Westray.

For the early part of the second half, exchanges were fairly even but then two situations conspired to change the course of the game. First, Westray forward Colin Kirkness twisted his ankle and had to come off and then Westray chose to move Risbridger up front. This weakened their central grip and Sandwick began to dominate.

Rivalry in the Parish Cup is intense. Left to right, Nicky Watson, Raymond Rendall and Steven Poke. (Picture: Rae Slater).

Westray's Raymond Rendall, left, is challenged by Steven Wylie. (Picture: Rae Slater).

Birth, Blood

Stewart Rendall gathers the ball despite the close attention of Steven Wylie for Sandwick. (Picture: Rae Slater).

After a sequence of well taken corner kicks, another fine in swinger from Marcus Wood went directly into the Westray net for the equaliser. Wood continued to harass the Westray defence and from one of his excellent crosses, Erlend Grieve got in front of his marker to slip the ball home.

Despite Westray's efforts in the time remaining, the match ended 2-1 in Sandwick's favour.

As Robbie Norquoy, president of the O.F.A. said at the trophy presentation by Lesley Mainland, general manager of sponsors *The Orcadian*, if the game had lasted 65 minutes, there would have been green and yellow rather than orange and black ribbons fastened to the cup. However, the youngsters in the Sandwick team had learned the lesson well at their 'Masters' knees' … "Boys, ye jist don't ever give up!"

As a result, it was they who left Pickaquoy, heading West, holding aloft an unprecedented *20th Parish Cup!*

2006:
It's coming Home!

It is a great comfort in these days of constant change and innovation to find people clinging to their age old customs and traditions. Perhaps they are trying to hold on to meaning in a world being propelled forward at frightening speed by technological advances and incessant directives by various governments to alter the way we live and work. At times it seems, nothing ever stays the same.

In Orkney, interest in long established pursuits is at an all time high. Attendance at and participation in the Ba' games at Christmas and New Year for example, is such that it is difficult to see how many more people can be shoe-horned into the streets of Kirkwall. Scrums and crowds of some 30 or 40 years ago are paltry by comparison.

So too with our favourite football competition, the Parish Cup. Over the course of its eighty year history there have been times when no more than a third of possible contenders have submitted an entry. Now everybody wants to take part and swarms of both new and long dormant spectators turn out to watch.

This year every community in Orkney with a viable sporting population entered a team and 18 names, an all time record, were forwarded. For a few it appeared that reality did not quite match ambition as injuries and work commitments stretched fragile resources to breaking point. As a result Harray and Burray were forced to scratch before a ball was kicked while Stronsay, Evie and Stromness were unable to fulfil the second leg of their fixtures. However the intentions were honourable and the withdrawals did not detract from an eagerly anticipated tournament.

Undisguised joy in the Sandwick dressing room. Back row, left to right, Steven Poke, Ian Linklater, Gareth Wood, Steven Wylie, Marcus Wood, Paul Kirkpatrick, Jamie Peppitt. Front, Mark Garson, Dale Slater, Kevan Harvey, Erlend Poke, Erlend Grieve (with cup), Stevie Linklater, Cameron Garson.
(Picture: Rae Slater)

&Boundaries

This was partly explained by the draw. Cup holders Sandwick and regular finalists St Ola were paired with the winners to face last years finalists Westray. Some big names were therefore due to tumble in the early stages and fringe teams felt their chances to be already much brighter. There was to be no dimming of hopes after the first round ties were resolved.

First round Results

Sandwick	0	St Ola	4
St Ola	4	Sandwick	0
Birsay	8	Stromness	0

Stromness scratched

Sandwick, although having mostly the same players, were but a shadow of the team who won the cup last year and crashed at the first hurdle. But to be fair, St Ola who could field county players, Davy Leonard, Erik Bews, Kevin Groundwater and Wayne Monkman, were very good indeed. They were now the team to fear.

Their next opponents Westray were, for the first time, getting used to regular football in Orkneys new 3-tier league set up. Despite being in Division 3, it was felt that their teamwork would be improved and this would supplement their unquestioned individual talent.

As the second round got underway this was the fixture which captured most attention.

Second round Results

St Ola	1	Westray	0
Westray	3	St Ola	1
Rendall	2	Deerness	0
Deerness	1	Rendall	3
Evie	3	South Ron.	7

Evie scratched

| Stronsay | 2 | Birsay | 2 |

Stronsay scratched

Sanday	4	Firth	1
Firth	2	Sanday	2
Shapinsay	0	Holm	7
Holm	6	Shapinsay	0

| St Andrews | v | Burray |

(Burray scratched)

| Harray | v | Orphir |

(Harray scratched)

Now St Ola had fallen. A great fight back by Westray culminating in a last minute winner had eliminated the new favourites, but in a sense St Ola had contributed to their own downfall by failing to persuade their strongest team to travel to Westray. For a few young Kirkwall boys the traditions of the Parish Cup do not run deep.

That can hardly be said of Deerness. For the first time in 15 years they had managed to enter a team and their effort evoked powerful comparison with the great Deerness teams of old. Remember the four times winners from the 30s? That team always contained three Skea brothers from Aikerskaill, two of whom had to return from their studies or work in the south in order to play.

This year the similarity was uncanny. Both Andrew and Alan Skea made a special journey home to join their brother Robert in the Deerness line up. To complete the family picture, father Ernie came north from Stonehaven to help organise team affairs.

And this tale of remarkable commitment did not stop there. Graeme Eunson, who had played in the last Deerness team, travelled from Tain to resume goalkeeping duties where he had left off in 1991.

Unfortunately, the combined effort of the Deerness exiles was in vain this time but at least they had helped to rouse a sleeping giant from its slumbers.

With two heavy weights knocked out, the competition took on new meaning and it was felt that a number of teams now had a realistic chance. Once again the Parish Cup became a hot topic of conversation throughout Orkney.

Quarter final Results

Westray	6	South Ron.	2
South Ron.	3	Westray	1
Birsay	1	St Andrews	3
St Andrews	1	Birsay	0
Holm	2	Rendall	3
Rendall	2	Holm	2
Sanday	5	Orphir	0
Orphir	1	Sanday	0

The four semi finalists now comprised Westray, with their eyes fixed on another final; St Andrews, in the last four for the fourth time in five years; and two teams who had never won the cup, Rendall and Sanday.

But the round had not been without controversy as the call of the Parish Cup got in the way of the authorities trying to organise representative matches.

There is a long standing rule that players who have been selected for the junior inter county game with Shetland must not play any competitive football within seven days of the match. However, three young players, Edrian Skea of Sanday and James Tait and Luke Savage of Orphir, played in the tie between the two parishes and as a result were dropped from the Orkney squad.

They argued that their parish might not have been able to field a team had they not played but this plea cut no ice with the county management and the ban stood. A robust exchange of views followed in the Press. Probably the best solution would have been a formal request by either parish to change the date of the fixture.

The semi finals now promised close games and it was just possible to envisage the two non-winners getting through.

Semi final Results

| Sanday | 0 | St Andrews | 3 |
| St Andrews | 6 | Sanday | 0 |

Birth, Blood

| Westray | 2 | Rendall | 1 |
| Rendall | 1 | Westray | 1 |

It was not to be. St Andrews progressed to their first final since 1963 with something to spare. Long before the second leg was completed, local hero, player/manager Paddy Kirkpatrick, was being lauded in song 'We're on the march with Paddy's army.' He certainly deserved the honour for his work in shaping St Andrews into such a competitive force again but whether the rendition was a good omen, time would tell.

Rendall's young team put up a very spirited challenge before a huge second leg crowd at the Firth pitch but came up just short. Westray were back in the final on merit but Rendall gave strong hints of being a threat in years to come.

So to the final, the most eagerly anticipated for years. In scenes reminiscent of a bygone age, droves of spectators began to file into Picky well before the 6.45pm kick off. Supporters of both teams were there in force decked out in hats, wigs, painted faces, balloons on baby buggies and T-shirts proclaiming undying love for 'the Aaks' or 'the Reds'. It was also evident that many neutrals had recovered their thirst for local football although their time keeping left something to be desired.

Although almost 1,000 fans were assembled to welcome the teams as many had still to enter the ground. As the game kicked off queues could be seen snaking back for 50 metres or more. Never can latecomers have so rued misreading the starting time. After less than 20 minutes, with hundreds still outside, four goals had been scored.

But first the respective squads for what turned out to be a momentous occasion:

St Andrews: Robbie Norquoy, Ronnie Baillie, Neil Robertson, Ross Groundwater, Ivan Rendall, Graeme Bain, James Baillie, Graham Reid, Neil Macdonald, Colin Kirkpatrick, Balfour Baillie, Thorfinn Eunson, Shane Scott, Sinclair Craigie, Fraser Laird, Derek Manson.

Westray: Stewart Rendall, Erland Drever, Ramond Moodie, Steven Tulloch, Calvin Rendall, Chris. Findlay, Alan Thomson, Colin Kirkness, Johnny Drever, Nicky Watson, Andrew Seatter, Mark Rendall, Liam Drever, Kieran Muir.

A first glance at the teams lining up provided several talking points. Yes, St Andrews were fielding Neil Macdonald, Thorfinn and Orkney's speedy skilful forward who had recently taken up resident in the parish. Although he had not played in any of the earlier rounds, no team would turn down the chance to draft

Erlend Drever handles the ball to prevent a goal and was then sent off. Left to right, Nicky Watson (Westray), Stewart Rendall, the Westray goalkeeper, and Paddy Kirkpatrick, who struck the shot. (Picture: Rae Slater).

Paddy Kirkpatrick slots home the penalty for St Andrews. Left to right, Chris Findlay (Westray), Neil MacDonald (St Andrews), Paddy taking kick, Ronald Baillie, Alan Thomson, Colin Kirkness, Colin Risbridger. (Picture: Rae Slater).

A grim chase for possession. Left to right, Calvin Rendall (Westray), Steven Tulloch (Westray), Neil Robertson (St Andrews), Neil MacDonald, Johnny Drever. *(Picture: Rae Slater).*

in a young player with an Inverness Caley Thistle pedigree. Also spotted was fullback Neil Robertson who had cut short his honeymoon to come home and play. Some things are just too important!

Westray meanwhile did not have the services of Raymond Rendall, their great servant over the years, who had retired, but where was his tall younger namesake? Injured apparently, during a practice session earlier in the week, so his athletic presence would be a considerable loss.

The game began in sensational fashion. St Andrews took the lead after eight minutes when James Baillie's volley from 35 yards left the Westray goalkeeper stranded. With the 'Red' masses still celebrating this magnificent strike, Westray equalised

The current cup holders, St Andrews. Back row, left to right, Ross Groundwater, Ronald Baillie, Neil MacDonald, Graeme Bain, Graham Reid, Michael Kemp, Derek Manson, Balfour Baillie, Fraser Laird, Neil Robertson, Erlend Eunson, Ivan Rendall. Front, Paddy Kirkpatrick, Sinclair Craigie, Robbie Norquoy, Thorfinn Eunson, James Baillie, Shane Scott, Graham Rendall. *(Picture: Rae Slater).*

with Johnny Drever's low shot eluding Robbie Norquoy.

The queues at the gate were straining to catch a glimpse of the breathtaking action when another deafening cheer increased their agony. Colin Kirkpatrick crossed a precision ball into the Westray goal mouth and it was met by Graham Reid whose header put his side back into the lead. Could things get any more exciting?

Not half! With still only 16 minutes played Kirkpatrick cut through a fragile Westray defence only to see his net bound shot palmed away by full back Erland Drever. The red card was rightly produced by referee Mike Cursiter and Kirkpatrick's cleanly hit penalty made the score, incredibly, St Andrews 3 Westray 1.

The dismissal brought a slowing down in the frantic pace. Westray were forced to regroup and for a while did so effectively but before half time Balfour Baillie killed off their chances by slotting home a fourth St Andrews goal.

The second half, while always absorbing, had a degree of inevitability about it. Westray, inspired by Colin Risbridger and Steven Tulloch, made a real game of it but in driving forward, left the defence exposed. Two further St Andrews goals were scored by Macdonald and near the end by substitute Shane Scott. This made the final score St Andrews 6 Westray 1.

The large galleries now made their way to the Picky Centre balcony to see the cup being presented to St Andrews captain Ronnie Baillie by Christine Miller, representing sponsors *The Orcadian*. He paid tribute to Westray and sympathised with their misfortune of the sending off. Of his own players he singled out for praise their team spirit and the work of player/coaches Robbie Norquoy and Paddy Kirkpatrick; both incidentally, former Parish Cup winners with other teams, Paddy with St Ola in 1990 and 95 and Robbie with Birsay way back in 1984.

Looking round at all the expressions of joy on the faces of the crowd it was clear how much this victory meant to a community which had not tasted success for so long. The message on the backs of many red T. shirts seemed to sum it all up perfectly: After 43 years of hurt, *It's coming home!*

Indeed it was, for the eighth time in eight attempts, and it would be accompanied on its journey to the Quoyburray Inn by the good citizens of St Andrews including veterans of those celebrations many years ago.

There, we can be assured, the age old customs and traditions would be re-enacted in splendid style!

The Last Kick . . .

That now takes us right up to date and the story of the Parish Cup, so far, is told. A rich and varied tale it is, full of conflict and intrigue, pride and courage, heroes and villains, glorious triumph and ignominious defeat, joy and despair.

I read somewhere that sport could be described as the 'moral equivalent of war' or 'the image of war without the guilt.' The implication is that a bit of sporting rivalry can act as a substitute for more violent conflict but at the same time, it is able to engage the emotions, encourage displays of bravery or self sacrifice and inspire patriotic feeling.

Some might think that this is going a bit far. A game is just a game after all! Personally, I regard this definition as quite accurate and it sums up very neatly just what the Parish Cup is about.

There is no doubt that it engages the emotions and I hope the preceding pages have given ample proof of how much passion the Orkney footballer or supporter feels for his or her parish. On the field of play it is accepted that every player will give 'his all' in the contest, but in this competition, that often amounts to a greater degree of effort than he will contribute in any other.

To illustrate this fact, I recall the story I was told of two young men who worked on the same farm but who played for different, neighbouring parishes. This night, they found themselves in opposition and they were, as expected, kicking lumps out of one another. When they tackled, no prisoners were taken!

The farmer's wife, who was a spectator, was appalled and remarked in horror to her companion, "My jist luk at that! An' tae think that they aet their dinner at the sam teeble!"

Such examples are common place but happily, once hostilities are over, friendships are restored and everyone lives peacefully together as before.

In fact, off the pitch, the feeling of goodwill often runs deeper and a special bond of fellowship is formed between rivals that can last a life time.

But just imagine how things might be in Orkney if we did not have this safety valve of the Parish Cup. Gangs of young men from various parishes making forays across boundaries engaging in punch ups with rival youths; farmers making night time raids setting fire to fields of barley, spraying weed killer on crops of tatties, cutting fences; women snipping the heads off a rival Branch's blooms at the annual W.R.I. bulb show; children bombarding their cross border neighbours with hate filled text messages.

We could be back living in the Dark Ages!

But instead, we all live in peace and harmony because of our annual 'blood letting' on the football field.

Consider also, the effect that sporting success has on peoples' state of mind. Victory for your team introduces a feel good factor into daily life. When it happens on a national scale, witness, England's winning of the Ashes or Scotland's medal successes at the recent Commonwealth Games, it lightens the country's mood. When success happens locally, the inhabitants of that area tend also to go around with cheerier dispositions and there is a greater feeling of solidarity about the place.

It would be interesting to find out how many new cars are bought, how many house alterations are done, or how many parishioners attend the harvest home in a year when the local team has won the Parish Cup. Probably *more* in every case! Of course, Sandwick folk will only be able to afford so many new cars or extensions, and by the same token, there ought to be an awful lot of old 'bangers' in Sanday, Orphir or South Ronaldsay!

To the outsider Orkney can often seem like an idyllic place to live. It has wonderful landscapes, great sense of history and culture, friendly and welcoming people, a vibrant community life. Woven into the very fabric of that life is this rather unique football tournament and many years from now, I have no doubt that the young men of the parishes, urged on by older 'warriors' and loyal armies of supporters, will be engaged in their own particular brand of warfare … without any feelings of guilt whatsoever.

And everybody will be the better for it!

Parish Cup Winners

1929	**Holm 3**	Deerness 2
1930	**Deerness 4**	Firth 3
1931	**Firth 3**	Shapinsay 1
1932	**Deerness 5**	Firth 2
1933	**Shapinsay 1**	Holm 1
(Shapinsay won on corners)		
1934	**Deerness 6**	Sandwick 2
1935	**Deerness 3**	Shapinsay 0
1936	**Stenness 4**	Deerness 1
1937	**Shapinsay 3**	Stenness 2
1938	**Shapinsay 4**	Deerness 3
1939	**Harray 4**	Orphir 3
(World War Two)		
1946	**Harray 2**	Birsay 1
1947	**St Ola 6**	Harray 3
1948	**Shapinsay 4**	Harray 1 (after replay)
1949	**Holm 2**	Harray 0
1950	**Holm 3**	Harray 1
1951	**Harray 3**	Holm 2
1952	**St Andrews 2**	Shapinsay 0
1953	**St Ola 4**	Harray 2
1954	**Shapinsay 3**	Harray 2
1955	**St Andrews 2**	Orphir 0
1956	**Harray 3**	South Ronaldsay 1
1957	**St Andrews 6**	Harray 4
1958	**Harray 2**	South Ronaldsay 1
1959	**St Andrews 5**	St Ola 1
1960	**St Andrews 6**	Orphir 0
1961	**St Ola 2**	South Ronaldsay 0
1962	**St Andrews 2**	St Ola 0
1963	**St Andrews 3**	St Ola 2
1964	**Harray 6**	St Ola 2
1965	**St Ola 3**	Harray 2 (after replay)
1966	**Harray 4**	Birsay 0
1967	**Harray 2**	Sandwick 1
1968	**Harray 4**	Sandwick 2 (after replay)
1969	**Harray 3**	Sandwick 1
1970	**Birsay 2**	St Ola 0
1971	**Birsay 4**	Sandwick 0
1972	**Harray 3**	South Ronaldsay 1
1973	**Sandwick 1**	South Ronaldsay 0
1974	**Sandwick 4**	Harray 3
1975	**Sandwick 1**	Birsay 0

1976	**Sandwick 3**	Harray 1
1977	**Sandwick 1**	South Ronaldsay 0
1978	**Sandwick 1**	Birsay 0
1979	**St Ola 2**	Orphir 1
1980	**Stromness 1**	Birsay 0
1981	**Sandwick 1**	Birsay 0 (after replay)
1982	**Sandwick 1**	St Ola 0
1983	**Sandwick 3**	Orphir 0
1984	**Birsay 2**	St Ola 0
1985	**Sandwick 3**	Birsay 1
1986	**Stromness 3**	St Ola 0 (after replay)
1987	**Sandwick 2**	Birsay 1
1988	**St Ola 3**	Sanday 0
1989	**Sandwick 5**	St Ola 1
1990	**St Ola 2**	Firth 0
1991	**Westray 4**	Orphir 0
1992	**Firth 2**	St Ola 1
1993	**Sandwick 3**	Westray 1
1994	**Westray 2**	Stromness 0
1995	**St Ola 3**	Sandwick 0
1996	**Sandwick 3**	Firth 1
1997	**Sandwick 5**	Firth 2
1998	**Sandwick 2**	Stromness 0
1999	**Westray 2**	South Ronaldsay 1
2000	**Sandwick 5**	Westray 0
2001	**Sandwick 3**	St Ola 1
2002	**Sandwick 1**	St Ola 0
2003	**Holm 2**	St Ola 1
2004	**St Ola 4**	Holm 2 (after extra time)
2005	**Sandwick 2**	Westray 1
2006	**St Andrews 6**	Westray 1

	Won	App		Won	App
Sandwick	20	26	Birsay	3	11
Harray	11	21	Stromness	2	4
St Ola	9	22	Firth	2	7
St Andrews	8	8	Stenness	1	2
Shapinsay	5	8	Sanday	0	1
Deerness	4	7	Orphir	0	6
Holm	4	7	South Ronaldsay	0	7
Westray	3	7			

And not forgetting

Two communities which have never taken part in the Parish Cup are North Ronaldsay and Rousay (although the latter almost did in 1987). But, just as in all other parts of Orkney, organised football was a feature of social life particularly in the earlier decades of the twentieth century when the population was so much greater.

A publication which has sought to be as representative as possible would not be complete without a glimpse of some of the exponents of the game in these islands.

North Ronaldsay used to have two teams during the 20s and 30s and as well as playing each other would engage in some lusty encounters with neighbouring Sanday. Right is a team from the 1930's.

Rousay, being closer to the Mainland would often entertain visiting teams and in addition played inter-district tournaments within the island itself. Pictured below, right is a team from the Wasbister district during the 1920s. Can you spot any ancestors or do the names jog any memories?

North Ronaldsay footballers pose for a picture in the early 1930s. Back row, left to right, Roy Scott (North Manse), Alan Tulloch (Upper Linnay), William Swanney (Cott). Middle, William Tulloch (Cruesbreck), Ritchie Tulloch (Greenwall), Thomas Thomson (Quoybanks). Front, Donald Mathieson (Lighthouse), Thomas Tulloch (Garso), Robert Munro (U.F. Kirk Manse), Hugh Scott (North Manse), George Mackenzie (Lighthouse). (Picture: Orkney Library).

An early picture from the 1920s of a Rousay team from the Wasbister district. Back row, left to right, James Craigie (Fioldquoy), James Marwick (Innister), Bill Flaws (Hammerfield). Middle, Mackie Hourie (Braehead), Armit Sinclair (Sketquoy), Fred Kirkness (Quoyostry), George Craigie (Fioldquoy), Spencer Dexter (Cubbidie), Bill Moar (Saviskaill). Front, James Moar (Saviskaill), Hugh Robertson (Langskaill), James Craigie (Furse). (Picture: Orkney Library)

Birth, Blood

The Author

The author is an Orcadian and has lived most of his life in Orkney. He has always had a keen interest in sport, particularly football.

He played the game primarily with Firth and Rendall, winning league honours with the latter, but glory in the Parish Cup proved elusive as Firth never got further than the semi-finals in those days.

He recently retired as Depute Rector of Stromness Academy, where he taught English.

The author lives in his home village of Finstown with his wife, Fiona, whose own family, Groundwater, feature prominently in local football folklore.

The couple have three grown-up sons who have all managed to go one better than their father and appeared in Parish Cup finals.

The author has a number of hobbies but his passion is gardening.